Theorizing Self in Samoa

Theorizing Self in Samoa
Emotions, Genders, and Sexualities

Jeannette Marie Mageo

Ann Arbor
THE UNIVERSITY OF MICHIGAN PRESS

Copyright © by the University of Michigan 1998
All rights reserved
Published in the United States of America by
The University of Michigan Press
Manufactured in the United States of America
⊚ Printed on acid-free paper

2001   2000   1999   1998   4   3   2   1

No part of this publication may be reproduced, stored in a retrieval system, or transmitted in any form or by any means, electronic, mechanical, or otherwise, without the written permission of the publisher.

A CIP catalog record for this book is available from the British Library.

Library of Congress Cataloging-in-Publication Data

Mageo, Jeannette Marie.
    Theorizing self in Samoa : emotions, genders, and sexualities / Jeannette Marie Mageo.
      p. cm.
    Includes bibliographical references and index.
    ISBN 0-472-10920-0 (cloth : acid-free paper)
    ISBN 0-472-08518-2 (pbk. : acid-free paper)
    1. Ethnology—Samoan Islands.   2. Samoans—Psychology.   3. Self.   4. Personality and culture—Samoan Islands.   5. Samoans—Socialization.   6. Samoan Islands—Social life and customs.   I. Title.
GN671.S2 M24   1998
305.8'009961'3—dc21
                                                                      98-9016
                                                                         CIP

*To Sanele, for it is not love that alters
when it alternation finds.*

*May we always be the stars to one
another's wandering barks.*

Contents

Preface and Acknowledgments   ix

INTRODUCTION

1. A Theory of Cultural Selves   3

SELF SYSTEMS AND DEVELOPMENT

2. Ontological Lexicons: Essentializing and Eliding   37
3. Moral Lexicons: Negatives and Double Negatives   52
4. Moral Discourse: Classification or Narration   69
5. Contextual Discourses and the Tropics of Childhood   81
6. Strategic Discourses and Cultural Antinomies   102

SELVES IN CULTURE HISTORY

7. Bodies, Selves, and Sexualities in Pre-Christian Samoa   119
8. Foreign Incursions on Samoan Discourses of Self   141
9. Possession and Reconfiguring Moral Discourse   164
10. Entertainment and Reconfiguring Informal Discourse   191
11. Lives and Reconfiguring Strategic Discourse   218

Notes   241
Glossary   263
References   265
Index   283

Preface and Acknowledgments

When Samoans attend an event of note, they introduce themselves by explaining the pathway, road, ʻauala, by which they came. Their path is their genealogy or, at any rate, that part of it relevant to the event. This opening seems to me both logical and gracious, and so it will be my opening as well. My path is not one of actual genealogy but is composed of a series of contingencies and relationships that began when I moved to American Samoa in 1981.

When I initially set off for the South Pacific, I intended to spend some years as an ethnographic vagabond. I would begin by teaching in Samoa, where friends of friends provided me with an introduction and, subsequently, a job at the community college. From there I intended to move on to various small colleges and universities around the South Pacific and possibly Southeast Asia. By the end of my first two-year contract in American Samoa I had secured a job offer from the University of the South Pacific in Fiji. I realized, however, my understanding of the local culture was still impressionistic and that my original plan precluded doing significant work, for which I needed to stay in one place for a lengthy period of time.

I had also fallen in love with a Samoan, whom I subsequently married. My marriage was fortunate for my work, as my husband's paternal uncle was the chief of an immense family in American Samoa, one whose name is included on the original deed of cession to the United States. His maternal uncle was chief of another historically significant family in a remote village in Western Samoa. These contacts provided me interviews with people ranging from chiefs to children as well as opportunities to collect folklore, songs, spirit lore, and accounts of possession.

Several of the Samoan women at the college where I taught were full of sage advice and helpful information. I offered classes in both anthropology and psychology and for five years ran dream groups. Here my students shed light upon their anxieties and concerns in a manner not possible in ordinary con-

Meet Sanele, Savai'i, circa 1984. Photo by the author.

texts. I also helped to found a Samoan-Pacific Studies Program. Under the auspices of this program I worked with students conducting interviews in the villages. Sometimes we conducted psychological surveys, sometimes collected spirit lore or investigated moral discourse, depending upon the focus of class discussion during the period when our excursions to the villages took place. Occasionally, we would go on *malaga*, "formal traveling parties," to Western Samoa. The hosting village would receive us in ceremony, after which we would interview villagers.

Apart from family connections, congenial colleagues, and student partners, I also explored the culture on my own, interviewing, attending public events from funerals to festivities, investigating court records in American Samoa on topics relevant to my research, and reading the excellent Pacific collection at the college where I taught. Much of my material came not from formal interviews nor from conscious attempts to study Samoan culture but simply from being friends with many Samoans for many years. Particularly during my last few years in Samoa, when I was clearer about the specific topics I wanted to pursue ethnographically, someone would casually mention a story or a memory and I would cast about for a scrap of paper on which to take notes.

In other respects as well I was no typical ethnographer, conducting fieldwork for the limited duration of a grant. I made my living like any other member of the local economy. In order to hold a job I learned to participate in the politics intrinsic to Samoan social existence. Although I had the advantage of graduate education, I was disadvantaged by not being Samoan. Samoans act as delegates for their extended families. This representative status is protective in the interpersonal maneuvering unavoidable in everyday Samoan life. In this maneuvering my work benefited from my vulnerability and from my innate lack of tact and adaptability: I often failed to catch on and was then made painfully aware of the rules of the game.

Having come to Samoa as an employee of the local college rather than in what is for Samoans the mythologized status of an "anthropologist," I was a small person, relatively anonymous and left to construct the culture as I would. I had many opportunities to witness how deftly Samoans managed outsiders who were classed as important personages. Like chiefs, they were showered with *alofa* (love, hospitality, feasts), allowed to do little for themselves, chauffeured and shepherded about, their visits becoming a succession of formal and subtly continued informal performances. I pitied members of the U.S. Department of the Interior, the government agency responsible for American Samoa. Their representatives would leave with trinkets presented in ceremonial style, appreciative smiles, and not very well regulated government coffers.

When I finally returned to a postdoctoral position in the anthropology department at University of California at San Diego in 1989, my perspective on Samoa gradually began to take on a historical dimension, and I pursued my ethnographic questions in expedition reports from UCSD's Hill Collection, later in the wide-ranging sources of Pacific Collection at the University of Hawai'i, and finally in the London Missionary Society archives in London. The London Missionary Society (LMS) was responsible for converting Samoans to Christianity and left an invaluable historical record of Samoa's transition from relatively undisturbed life ways to the circumstances of modernity.

Because the second half of the study is historical, a word or two about historical records on Samoa is in order. Samoa is not featured in eighteenth-century accounts of Pacific explorers. When LaPerouse visited Samoa in 1787, several members of his crew were killed. Because of LaPersouse's report, Samoa acquired a reputation for savagery and inhospitality and was left in relative peace until the missionaries began arriving in the early nineteenth century (Linnekin 1991a). The missionary sources are, therefore, the best available data on precontact Samoan society, and the most important accounts date from observations made during the first few decades after contact.[1] After the initial wave of missionary depictions one finds a series of ethnographic works by various government functionaries, military and civilian, who represented or were in the employ of European powers. These accounts date from the late 1830s through, and a bit into, the second decade of the twentieth century.[2] My last series of sources are anthropological and date from the 1920s to the present day.[3]

These sources have an assortment of biases. Missionaries were concerned with convincing contributors at home of the need for christianizing the heathen. Thus, the first resident missionary in Samoa, George Turner, published an account of his Polynesian missionary labors shortly after his return to England ([1861] 1986). The text is at least in part addressed to friends of the mission, as it describes mission progress in detail and comments upon how little the Samoan mission costs relative to its profit in converts. Twenty years later, however, Turner again published his ethnographic material in separate form, believing that these data had independent interest ([1884] 1984). The Rev. John Stair published his accounts over fifty years after his residence in Samoa from extensive ethnographic notes, supplemented by Samoan friends who had resided with him in England. This publication came long after he had severed his connection to the LMS. In Stair's case his purpose in collection and writing was consciously ethnographic. "Yet, from the very first," Stair remarks, "I felt great interest in Samoa and the Samoans, and endeavored on every occasion to collect data and memoranda bearing upon their past history and customs, as well as conditions of life, knowing full well that such facts might soon be difficult to obtain" (1897:13).[4]

Mission accounts were tinged by mission morals and agenda and by the cultural biases that limit all travelers' tales. Nonetheless, it is unlikely that missionary authors lied about factual details such as nudity, being Christian men and not given to slander for whatever purpose. Further, on the whole the missionaries who visited Samoa had respect for Samoan culture, and, if they imposed their views, they also showed a susceptibility to local beliefs.[5] Thus, Stair tells tales of Samoan spirits who were wont to bowl with oranges all night in the hallways of his Samoan house (1897:261–65). His guests, none of whom he ever forewarned about these hauntings, would complain about the ceaseless noise made at night by his "servants." Stair patiently explained that his servants returned to the village at night, and he finally gave up the house because the hauntings were overtaxing the nerves of his wife! Nor was Stair the only missionary who became acquainted with local spirits (259).[6]

One might suspect accounts of those nineteenth- and early-twentieth-century sojourners who worked in the employ of colonial powers of colonialist bias. A book written by British consul, Churchward, had an explicit purpose of convincing Britains that there was cause to annex Samoa (1887). On the whole, however, these accounts do not portray Samoans as childlike or uncivilized and therefore in need of looking after. Rather, the authors seemed genuinely to delight in Samoan culture. At worst one suspects them of a degree of romanticism. For example, the German medic Krämer comments:

> I spent too many happy days among those friendly people ever to forget them. . . . I went fishing with them, joined their malagas, traveling from village to village, in order to learn to think and feel with them. He who has once been ensnared by the magic of Samoa, will not easily break the bonds. ([1923] 1949:iii)

Anthropologists, too, have their intellectual biases. They are biased by the style of ethnographic research and writing of their time and in favor of proving the author's personal theory. In Samoa anthropological accounts are less mutually congruent than those of their predecessors, the most dramatic instance of this incongruence being Mead and Freeman. I have discussed their disagreement elsewhere (1988). For now let me say only that Mead attempted a synchronic portrait of Samoa in the 1920s. This type of ethnography was standard during the period when she wrote but was to a degree distorting because, while Samoa may have given an impression of historical stasis, it was anything but static at the time. With less excuse, however, Freeman gives an equally static picture of Samoa in regards to sexual mores.[7] The moral history that follows casts light upon the shortcomings of both of these positions.

There are already two excellent histories of the period from contact to Western Samoa's mid-twentieth-century independence (Gilson 1970, Davidson 1967), but these works mainly concern political events and changes in governmental institutions and economy, while I seek a history of experience and of the discourses that shape it and are shaped by it. My intent is to silhouette the discursive/psychological elements of Samoan history and to trace their continuity and transformation. This intent is, however, nested in another: to offer a theory on self that has proved useful in one ethnographic location and, I believe, may have usefulness elsewhere.

We have long known how different cultures are from one another, and postmodernism has acquainted us with how we inscribe cultural biases in the very terms of our theories. This realization, I believe, calls not for a retreat from theorizing about our human commonalties but for a certain tentativeness, a middle ground, an offering of concepts that aspire to more than local knowledge but also invite further participation, like Barthes's idea of the text as an open field for play (1977). I offer a set of "intermediate" concepts, positioned between the transcultural claims of Western science and the shifting sites and histories of ethnography.[8] *Theorizing Self* will show how discourses on self are culturally reproduced in Samoa and how these discourses have been situated in historically shifting relations of power. But it also aims to generate a provocative and general portrait of how discourses of personhood, and the meanings attendant upon them, are formed and how, like the people who practice them, they respond to historical change and cultural interchange.

As ambitious as this project is, there is much it will not do, and these omissions are best admitted at the outset. Inasmuch as this book concerns discourses on self, it employs a language model, but not in any narrow sense. The discourses I examine are replete with images and are performative as well as verbal. I also believe that images have their own logic, differing from that of language (Mageo 1992b); however, the scope of the present book is very large already, and I must defer what would necessarily be a lengthy exploration of the self and images to future work.

Much of what I say about Samoa can be applied more broadly, albeit with variation, to other Pacific locales. The first half of this volume is about socialization, and there are a number of excellent studies of growing up in Polynesia, to which my analysis of Samoa is pertinent—neighboring Tonga being the most salient example.[9] The second half is a culture history of self, gender, and sexuality and offers reconfigured spirit possession practices among girls and a rise of transvestism among boys as telling indices of this history. In the case of possession parallel changes have been documented in Western Polynesia and Micronesia (Mageo and Howard 1996). Little work has been done on transvestism and Pacific culture history, although here again Tonga offers the closest parallel (Besnier 1994, James 1994). Unfortunately, drawing out comparisons of socialization and history would also distract from the theoretical project at hand, which requires the clarity that only a relatively simple and singular ethnographic focus can provide. I must also, therefore, defer tracing areal implications, although some implications will be mentioned in the notes.

The text refers to a location in the world, and a brief word about this location will help to orient the reader. Samoa is located in the southeasterly sector of the Polynesian triangle, 14 degrees beneath the Equator and approximately 8 degrees east of the international dateline. It is warm and rainy even by tropical standards. Like most cultural entities in the Pacific, Samoa is composed of a number of islands. At the turn of the century these islands were divided into Western Samoa and American Samoa by the colonial powers, who ceded the western islands to Germany and the eastern islands to the United States. At the opening of World War II, New Zealand occupied Western Samoa, which became a New Zealand protectorate under the League of Nations after the war. Later it became a United Nations Trust Territory under New Zealand, finally gaining independence in the early 1960s. American Samoa, too, gained progressive degrees of independence as the century wore on, finally electing its own governor in 1977.

Western Samoa has two major islands, 'Upolu and Savai'i, and a number of lesser islands. Apia is the capital of Western Samoa and is on the island of 'Upolu. Relatively speaking, 'Upolu is more accessible and urban, Savai'i more remote and rural. American Samoa is composed of the Manu'an Islands and Tutuila as well as several smaller islands. Tutuila is famous for Pago Pago Harbor, an excellent natural harbor that has hosted whalers, naval ships, and cruise vessels since contact. Today the villages around the harbor form the hub of American Samoa.

Some may ask who precisely this book is about—urbanites or villagers, educated or not, American Samoans or Western Samoans, and so forth—to which I answer all of these. Further, these distinctions do not hold up as well among Samoans as they do among ourselves: the culture has a permeability that mediates them. Long before contact, traveling between villages was a favorite pastime. Embroidering on these historical proclivities, contemporary Samoans frequently travel to visit their often widely dispersed families, socializing and exchanging ideas. My Samoan mother-in-law, for example, a wonderful, funny, ancient tigress who spent half her time in each of the Samoas, could not speak English but spent many afternoons with her Western-educated teenage niece (whom she had adopted as a daughter) watching "Days of Our Lives" in English and arguing about the plot in Samoan. There are more urban areas, villages situated at harbors, but these villages often maintain many traditional structures. Thus, although the *aualuma,* the pre-Christian women's association, has virtually died out in Western Samoa (which is generally thought of as more traditional and includes quite remote rural areas), the village of Pago Pago—the most urban of the American Samoan villages—still has an *aualuma.*

Samoans live in extended families called *'āiga.* Depending on its size, an *'āiga* may have a number of closely situated dwellings in a village and a number of plantation sites outside it. But people trace their ancestry back through grandparents and great-grandparents to a number of different *'āiga,* usually situated in different villages. Postmarital residence is opportunistic: a couple will live where their chances of obtaining desirable land and titles are greatest. For this reason members of an *'āiga* are concentrated in one or several villages and scattered as well; their dispersion mutes the political dividing line between American and Western Samoa.[10]

As deeply rooted as I hope the text is in the Samoan people and their families and their ancestry, because it presents a theory with hopes of going beyond a specific place, my initial presentation is unavoidably abstract. Theory, however, will help us return to a way of life, to a local history, to the ethnographic controversies that Samoa has generated and even to my personal contingencies, richer and more able to interpret them.

I thank the National Endowment for the Humanities and University College London for support that helped to make the writing of this book possible. I also thank the Institute of Intercultural Studies and the Hawai'i Branch of the American Association of University Women for small grants for writing and research with which I began the work. Some of this material draws upon previous articles of mine in *Ethos, American Ethnologist, American Anthropologist, Man, Pacific Studies,* and *Oceania* (Mageo 1989a, 1991a,b,c, 1992a, 1994, 1995, 1996a,c). The project was so lengthy and my contacts at various stages so numerous, it is impossible to thank everyone, and so I mention only a few people whose ready support throughout made carrying on and then concluding both emotionally and intellectually possible. I thank Roy D'Andrade, Alan Howard, Melford Spiro, Gananath Obeyesekere, Nicholas Thomas, Claudia Strauss, Allen Johnson, and Anne Allison for their support and comments. I also thank Nia Laulu, Pili Mageo, Loia Fiaui, and all my Samoan relatives, students, as well as my Samoan and American friends, for their unfailing assistance. I am indebted particularly to Karen Wheat and also to the Rautenstrauch-Joset-Museum of Ethnology for the historical photographs.[11] Susan Love Brown and Linda Stone gave generous editorial help. Gregory Graber helped with formatting. Most of all I thank my former husband and beloved friend, Sanele Mageo, for his many and invaluable contributions.

Introduction

Repressed contents are the very ones that have the best chance of survival.
                    Carl Jung, "On the Psychology of the Trickster"

1

A Theory of Cultural Selves

My initial experiences in Samoa were hard to reconcile. Samoans told me with great unanimity that respect, *fa'aaloalo,* was the signature of the *Fa'aSāmoa,* "the Samoan way of life." A song, "Samoan Custom" (Le Aganu'u Sāmoa), counsels listeners to "stand on Samoan custom . . . the best custom of all countries" and proclaims that this "beautiful custom" is to give "respect to people" because "everything is made from mutual support."[1] One should extend respect to everyone, my first Samoan language teacher explained to me, greeting them as "Lord this" and "Lady that" and by speaking "T-language," the Samoan respect dialect. Concurrently, I had been reading Robert Louis Stevenson's account of late-nineteenth-century Samoa. "Terms of ceremony fly as thick as oaths upon a ship," Stevenson remarks, "commoners 'my-lord' one another as they meet—and urchins as they play marbles" (1892:2). Later, when I married a Samoan and spent time with him and his relatives, I noticed that my husband often addressed even his younger brother as *ali'i,* "noble sir."

Yet, when I rented a car and drove through a sea-bordered back village in Western Samoa, a horde of children surrounded and playfully attacked my car, shouting words that I later discovered to be obscene. As I was driving down a narrow, winding dirt road through an out-of-the-way banana plantation, a preadolescent exposed himself to me with somewhat the same mischievous and daunting glee I had noted in the children. Later I read that "Eat shit" is the first thing Samoan babies learn to say (Ochs 1982), a belief seconded by my husband. While respect, *fa'aaloalo,* was preached, *tautalaitiiti,* "cheekiness" was often practiced. Indeed, *tautalaitiiti* was the most common reproach made to children, and the ordinariness of the reproach was a constant reminder to me that the behavior was more than a little widespread. So, on the one hand, there was the proper scheme of things, showing respect; on the other, there seemed to be adamant resistance to showing respect.

As time went by, I learned that in Samoa respect amounted to appropriate role playing. Samoan society is hierarchical; villages and families are ranked according to the titles they hold. Within the family the younger members respect and serve those who are older. Counsels, therefore, come from those above in the age-grade hierarchy and are aimed at those below, never the reverse. But there is one dictum that is so fundamental a guide for conduct that it can be made even to someone older, "Stand at your post" (Tū i lou tūlaga). Here *tūlaga* refers both to a position and to a role. "Stand at your post" is a spacial metaphor for performing a role in the group that accords with one's status and rank, which to Samoans is tantamount to behaving respectfully.

In a novel by a Samoan, *Pouliuli* (*Dark Night*), the protagonist is a bitter, wry, old chief, Faleasa, who feigns spirit possession (Wendt 1977). Prior to his "possession," his were the most enviable roles in Samoan society: Faleasa was a deacon, a lay preacher, the village's highest-ranking chief, owner of a large plantation, a nationally respected orator, and so forth. In seeming madness Faleasa vomits at and wildly derides family and village in order to escape the confinement of these roles.

> Deepening his voice to make it sound like his mother's who had died years before, he said, "I am inhabiting my son's body. . . . Faleasa laughed his mother's laugh as though he was completely mad. . . . He tried his best to keep on looking possessed, his eyes glazed with madness, his body stiffly frozen in that defiant posture which was beginning to exact a painful toll on his old muscles, back, and backside. (1977:5–6)

While trying to escape his post, Wendt's chief is still role playing; indeed, he skillfully manipulates his audience, making the village pastor tremble, punishing his family by giving away their best clothes when they send a local healer to return him to normality, calculating that the irate village council will not fine him because it would be unchristian to fine a person afflicted by a demon.

As beyond the norm as Faleasa seems, the wily chief who manipulates an audience for purposes very much his own is a social archetype in Samoa and holds a normative place. Samoan orators, also called talking chiefs, "are described (although never formally or publicly) as . . . *kulukū* (from the English 'crooked'). . . . By 'crooked' is meant . . . skillfully manipulative," and, just like Faleasa, often they are so "with an eye to . . . self interest" (Shore 1977:437). Watching cheeky children and wily chiefs, I came to believe that a conception of persons as role players in Samoa generated a series of reversals and accommodations that bore tellingly on current debates in anthropology.

From its outset the ethnography of persons as psychological actors has been fraught with an order of complexity that seems virtually irreducible to scholarly discourse. Again and again a convincing anthropological account is contradicted by another that demonstrates the first account left out depth and nuance but which itself often errs by underplaying those aspects of personhood depicted by its predecessor.[2] The problem, I believe, is a vision of culture that is not architecturally sufficient to the work it has to do. Despite postmodern critiques, too often ethnographies offer a monolithic view, presenting culture as a fixed repertoire of schemas and discursive habits. This architectural insufficiency is conspicuous in anthropological attempts to account for the self.

When theorizing about the self, anthropologists typically distinguish between two types of selves—namely, egocentric selves and sociocentric selves—that are cultivated by two types of cultures. Geertz's famous characterizations of these selves remain the most eloquent.[3] The egocentric self is a

> bounded, unique, more or less integrated motivational and cognitive universe, a dynamic center of awareness, emotion, judgment, and action organized into a distinctive whole and set contrastingly both against other wholes and against a social and natural background. ([1974] 1984:126)

While the sociocentric self is a persona:

> it is the dramatis personae, not actors, that endure; indeed that in a proper sense really exist . . . the masks they wear, the stage they occupy, the parts they play, and . . . the spectacle they mount remain and constitute not the facade but the substance of things, not least the self. (128–29)

This last portrait is actually of the Balinese, and not all versions of sociocentrism are quite this theatrical. Bali represents an extreme case, but sociocentrism generally brings with it a tacit assumption, or "premise," that people are in essence role players within a larger group, that people take both their nature and raison d'être from role playing. Egocentrism entails the premise that the essential self is inner, or subjective. I call such essentializing premises "ontological," because they are, *au fond,* premises about what it means to *be* a person: they presume to describe the essence of being a person. Ontological premises, however, are productive of ambiguity.

Samoan selves seem sociocentric. One could not find a better example of a sociocentric ethic than the dictum that one should, above all else, stand at one's post, yet the cheeky children who so gleefully attacked my car and Wendt's "mad" chief disputed as much as exemplified this sociocentric orientation. For them sociocentrism was a point of departure rather than a final definition, the beginning of a story rather than its summation. The problem is that experience, in the phenomenological sense of the word, has both subjective and social aspects; ontological premises tend to be unequally weighted; therefore, these premises are likely to produce views of people that are frequently belied by the experience of people.

Once, when teaching *Coming of Age in Samoa* at the community college in American Samoa, I argued against the placid emotions Mead ascribed to Samoans: "When a man commits adultery, his wife and her sisters (or sometimes her husband's sisters) may pursue the girl, and beat her, and cut off an ear! Surely this is not evidence of even emotions," I said. "Oh no," one of my older male students interjected, "it is not that the wife is jealous, but, if she does not punish the girl, the girl will show off the affair, and it is a disgrace to the wife's family."

My student was offering me a sociocentric premise about the wife's behavior. She acted not from jealousy but from a rational assessment of her family's interest. But is it plausible that the violence of betrayed wives is entirely bereft of personal sentiment?[4] Extending this sociocentric premise about the behavior of wives yet further, Chief Tuiteleleapaga tells us that in old Samoa wives lauded their husband's infidelities for the sake of family honor.

> When a village set out for a *malaga* (trip or visit . . .), it is the custom of the young men—married or unmarried—to elope with as many girls as possible in the villages visited. Their wives, who followed them, would laugh and congratulate their men for gallantry and popularity . . . well knowing it was just . . . a means to add prestige . . . to their families and village. . . . The elopements and the act itself were, and still are, called *ai o malaga* (scores of the . . . trip). (1980:63)

But Chief Tuiteleleapaga admits that

> there were always cases of some young wife who was unable to contain her jealousy and went right to the family of the vixen or vixens who had eloped with her husband and . . . made a speech within the hearing of family and other spectators. . . . "Hark ye, you villagers, I have a sow that I would like to be given to you to eat, provided you like the meat, because she is tough and skinny." [Or] "I have a horse that I am willing to lend to anyone who would like to ride . . ." [Or] "I have a latrine with one big opening. . . ." (63–64)

So, Samoans appear to themselves to be role players, and yet there are always cases that confound their sociocentric explanations for behavior.

Such contradictions are by no means confined to the Samoan case. While Geertz paints the Balinese as sociocentric, Wikan paints them as at least equally preoccupied with the effort to manage their inner life (1990). She tells a tale of an informant, Suriati, who cries herself to sleep nightly over her recently deceased fiancé but is sparkling and gay during the day. Suriati is, furthermore, so fearful of the personal malevolence of others, performed in witchcraft, that she dare not travel to other villages. These tendencies to hide the personal self and to fear the personal side of others are, I believe, interlinked and are the logical underside of Geertz's portrait.

Geertz is right that the Balinese see people as actors upon a stage. Because everyone continually acts a part, unambiguous information about others' personal thoughts and feelings is sparse; therefore, Balinese fall into suspicious musing upon these sentiments, imagining others to be engaged in witchcraft. These musings make for "turbulent hearts." So it would seem that in Bali, as in

Samoa, a sociocentric orientation generates an intense and even obsessive relation to inner life that is as much a part of everyday talk about persons as the sociocentric pageantry that Geertz so well captures.

I use the terms *sociocentrism* and *egocentrism* to characterize ontological premises not in any absolute sense but as one might refer to hair as fair or dark: they are ends of a continuum along which there may be infinitely many shadings, different initial weighting of sociality and subjectivity. Whatever their shade, however, ontological premises about the nature of persons are inherently selective, privileging relevant features of experience above others. Invalidating experiences are apt to be downplayed. One can imagine these invalidating experiences are for a first moment unsaid in some hypothetical epiphany of a conceptual system, but I hope to show that the unsaid becomes the obsession of the system that at first neglects it. To the degree that social experience is initially relegated to the status of an epiphenomenon, it comes to be featured in later discursive practices. To the degree that subjective experience is understood to be the epiphenomenon, it comes to be featured. I am not positing a realm of experience uncolored by cultural categories, but, however deeply tinged, experience retains a refractory character, intimating things beyond the categories through which we constitute it. Further, people are more preoccupied by these intimations than we, as anthropologists, usually recognize. The result, I believe, is an ever-repeated attempt to encompass stray experiences of self within a premise-discourse series.[5]

The Premise-Discourse Series

In his work on Foucault, White says, "in any given effort to capture the order of things in language, we condemn a certain aspect of that order to obscurity" (1978:239). We will see that sociocentric or egocentric premises are coded in cultural lexicons of personhood, consisting of referential terms for the nature of people. These lexicons are efforts to capture the self in language, which condemn an alternative aspect to obscurity. But this initial obscurity is not a fait accompli; it is the sand that makes the pearl, for experiences of self initially consigned to silence beleaguer the self system through which this consignment is made with entreaties to be noticed and to be taken more fairly into account.[6]

When people cannot but notice that some experience does not wholly correspond to their culture's ontological premise, their first response is moralistic. They attempt to suppress behavior incongruent with this premise through a moral lexicon and a moral discourse. Moral lexicons consist of catalogs of virtues and vices and make possible moral discourses, those discourses people employ to evaluate and adjudicate one another's behavior, such as sermonizing and gossiping. Moral lexicons valorize behavior consistent with the ontological premise and demonize incongruent behavior. Moral discourses are obsessed with discovering this incongruent, demonized experience and thereby inadvertently reveal it to be an unerasable part of people.

People respond by trying to bound this experience, codifying its expression in stylized performances and localizing these performances in informal contexts associated with camaraderie, play, and popular entertainment. Meanwhile, a formal discourse arises that codes the values lauded in moral discourse as types of performance that people are expected to practice only within the more limited parameters of situations judged to be formal. These informal and formal discourses together I call contextual because they revolve around judgments about social context. Last, people recognize that the binary division of contexts into formal and informal is insufficient to the real variety of cultural life and, therefore, adapt discourses strategically to fit real situations. These strategic discourses evince a crafted blending of other discourse types and are evident in the complex approaches people take to the aleatory flow of ongoing events and relationships.

Thus, the premise-discourse series moves from a focus on ontology to morality to contextuality to praxis, coming ever closer to a characterization of experience in a phenomenological sense of the word. We will see that these discourses become progressively more self-conscious and reflective: moral discourse implicitly contradicts and comments upon the initial premise, while contextual and strategic discourses contradict and comment upon the preceding discourse type. When I call these "discourses on self," I do not mean that in content they are always about the topic of self. Rather, these discourses find their telos in realizing a part of the self as it is culturally construed and, therefore, are integral to a self system.

I readily admit that actual instances of talk are a potpourri of discourses; the categories I depict are ideal types in the Weberian sense, heuristic devices that serve as reference points. But I hope to show that they are reference points for natives too. Generally, people recognize that their culture has a concept of what it means to be a person, although they tend to essentialize this concept, taking it to be the same as "human nature." People also recognize that some talk is moral, that one form of talk is apt to be assumed when people mean to be formal and another when informality is judged appropriate and that at times people play upon discursive conventions to further an aim, be it their own advantage and that of affiliated others or one more altruistic in character. Anthropologists, for example Comaroff (1975:150), have discussed one or another of these discourse types before, but my theory attempts a more comprehensive catalog and lays out a dynamic sequence in which the relationship between an initial premise and later discourses creates a play of possible self-representations that people shuffle and combine in developing a workable identity.

While I describe this premise-discourse series as having a temporal progression, here temporality is merely a trope for a logical process; the complete series is ever present in culture. If contradictory ways of talking about the self are an ineluctable feature of self systems, it makes sense that cultural subjects are sites for shifting and potentially conflicting meanings, as Strauss

(1990), Ewing (1990), and Kondo (1990) contend.[7] People lack a consistent outlook, but I propose that this conceptual disjointedness is systematic in its cultural character.

I present this theory in the ethnographic mode, through a deep study of one culture, because of my belief that culture can only be fully understood from within a local context and in a manner that resonates with the native's viewpoint. Because of this approach, my claims for the general applicability of this theory must be modest: I hope to provide a plausible account of the self in Samoa and to suggest certain larger relationships. Proof about whether or not this theory generalizes must be left to others. Their is a further problem with the ethnographic mode of presentation: as a sociocentric culture, Samoa represents only one end of the sociocentric/egocentric continuum; to set forth the theory fully one would explore an example of each end and perhaps several intermediate cases as well. This book, therefore, must be considered only as an introduction to the theory. In order to present the theory in somewhat fuller terms, however, in the next few pages I cursorily cite American culture as an illustration of the egocentric case. A cautionary note must be appended to this illustration. "The West and the rest," to use Sahlins's felicitous phrase, have been geographical metaphors for egocentric and sociocentric orientations. The idea that two such orientations exist is a good one; the idea that these orientations are geographically sorted is a reification that reflects no useful or consistent distinction between the vast array of Western cultures and the vaster array of cultures elsewhere.[8] Further, any case historically considered probably never remains securely tethered to either sociocentrism or egocentrism. While it so happens that precontact Samoa is close to the sociocentric pole, through the process of missionization, colonization, and modernization Samoa became a hybrid, drifting from the pole near which it was once more securely moored. All this said, let us rehearse the series in somewhat more depth.

Ontological Premises

Ontological premises can be found in the local lexicon of personhood, specifically in those terms people use to denote "human nature"—not in the Hobbesian sense of what is violent and untamed but in the sense of essential attributes and activities.[9] Thus, in egocentric America the word *self*—as it is found in constructions like "I'm not myself today"—has connotations of an inner self, constitutive of personhood. This inner self is understood as transcendent of fluctuating social contingencies and is seen as synonymous with the individual's true nature. Thus, in American myth the Self-Made Man begins in the humblest circumstances: Lincoln teaches himself to read before an evening fire, for example, in Eastman Johnson's famous 1868 painting *The Boyhood of Lincoln*. In relation to this perduring "nature" socioeconomic and even biological factors are pictured as circumstantial.

In sociocentric Samoa "the substance of things, not least the self" is indexed by the term *aga*. *Aga* translates as "nature" in the sense of essential character (Freeman 1984:249); however, it also means "persona"—that is, a social mask, face, or role. Thus, Samoan language implies that the person's roles are constitutive of their nature. As in Geertz's Bali, in Samoa it is the "dramatis personae . . . that in a proper sense really exist."[10]

Humans generally tend to believe that the part of themselves that "really exists" transcends the body; therefore, ontological premises—that is, premises about the beingness of persons—are also detectable in words used for the part of the person that survives the body's death. In Western metaphysics it is the inner subjective aspect of experience, the "soul," that outlives the body. In Samoa it is the *agāga*, a derivative of the word *aga* (face, persona) that survives, although, not surprisingly, the missionaries mistranslated *agāga* as *soul* (Pratt [1862/1911] 1977:22).[11]

To foreground one element of experience is, inevitably, to background another, which remains relatively undifferentiated. While we are forever making subtle distinctions about inner experience—head versus heart, personal thoughts versus personal feelings, and so forth—among sociocentric Samoans personal thinking, feeling, and willing are not distinguished: one term encompasses all three events (Mageo 1989a:191–92).[12] Further, Samoans are apt to disclaim the possibility of subtle knowledge about subjectivity, saying, "One cannot know what is in another's depths" (Gerber 1985:133). On the other hand, even outside of anthropology Polynesian cultures like Samoa are legend for their highly differentiated knowledge of kinship relations in the form of genealogies.[13] Beyond a relatively small nuclear circle—the outskirts of which are marked by aunts, uncles, first cousins, grandparents, and sometimes great-grandparents—kinship for most Americans is an ink-dark territory and, anyway, not one of particular concern (Stone 1997:248).

If thinly coded and seemingly ignored, experiences that are excluded from a culture's ontological premise are forever subversively impinging on cultural consciousness. While sociocentric Samoans take the persona to be the essence of the person, they are haunted by that dimension of the self they call *loto*. The *loto* is the depths of the person; it may refer to any small deep such as a lake or lagoon, but it is also a comprehensive term for personal thoughts, feelings, and volitions. The *loto* inspires all manner of discomforting sentiments, from arrogance to envy to torrents of grief, which cannot be accounted for by social roles. While egocentric Americans take the inner self to be the person's true nature, the Chinese ethnographer Hsu argues that Americans are haunted with insecurity about maintaining human relatedness, which cannot be accounted for by the notion that selfhood is lodged within us: we are anxious to be liked and about losing our place in status-giving groups (1961:209–30; see also Inkeles et al. 1961:205–6; Newman 1988; Ortner 1991).

Whatever form of experience is marginalized by a culture's ontological premise, this experience is likely to be associated in cultural fantasy with something resembling an "id." Freud (1923) posits the existence of an id, a prerational reservoir of instincts that exists in contradistinction to social values. I question whether there is any part of the self uncontaminated and unconstructed by culture but, building on Freud, suggest that cultures: (1) fantasize that some part of the person is impulsive, that is, animal-like and intrinsically resistant to socialization; (2) associate their version of the impulsive with the body; (3) vary in the otherness they assign to impulsiveness and the body and in the permissiveness with which they regard them; (4) conflate impulsivity with the marginalized element of self.[14]

Thus, in Samoa *loto*, "subjectivity," is the marginalized element of self, and Samoans see the *loto* as resistant to social conditioning, or in their terms as *maʻaʻa*, a word that also refers to a tree that is hard to uproot. While the word *loto*, in itself, simply refers to inner events like thoughts, feelings, or volitions, the derivative word *lotoa* means "passion"; *lotōa* means "passionate." To feel a yearning in one's *loto* (*momo i loto*) is to be carried away by passion beyond all reason. In *Civilization and Its Discontents* Freud, an excellent ethnographer of egocentric cultures like America—associates the id with an "oceanic sense," an inclusive sense of collectivity, "an indissoluble bond, of being one with the external world as a whole" (1961:12). Freud believes this experience to be a fetal memory that can be fleetingly recaptured: "Against all the evidence of his senses, a man who is in love declares that 'I' and 'you' are one, and is prepared to behave as if it were a fact" (1961:13). For Samoans oneness with group members is obvious and commonsensical; in more egocentric cultures oneness is a distortion produced by the transports of passion.

If the aspect of experience that is left out of the ontological premise is associated with passion, then one might say that this experience becomes a cultural symbol for nature, not in the sense of constitutive being but in the Hobbesian sense of that which is antithetical to civil order. Thus, egocentric American fantasies of antisocial behavior are often collective; organized crime is "the Family," run by "the Godfather." Sydney Pollack's film *The Firm* is a contemporary example. Tom Cruise is a young lawyer who joins a firm that appears to be familylike but that actually murders defecting lawyers and serves "the mob." Communism and communist spies were for several decades a key example of this type of American fantasy, although communalistic religious cults are more salient in American fantasies of the antisocial in recent decades.

Moral Lexicons

Whatever experience is left out of the ontological premise is a worm at the heart of cultural constructions of self, subtly contradicting that premise. This experience worms its way more deeply into these constructions through a moral lexicon. This lexicon first reiterates the ontological premise in morally valorized form, suggesting that, whatever one's experience, one's behavior *should* correspond to this premise. Thus, the essayist of early American character Ralph Waldo Emerson equates virtue with self-reliance, which turns out to be a moral valorization of egocentrism:

> The only right is what is after my constitution, the only wrong what is against it. A man is to carry himself in the presence of all opposition, as if everything were titular and ephemeral but he. (1882:29)[15]

Inasmuch as right is equated with the highlighted element of self, the excluded element comes to be seen as a source of antisocial behavior. There was, for example, a Samoan village princess (*tāupōu*) in the 1970s who lived on the main island in American Samoa, Tutuila, and who I will call Sina (Silvery White). Sina was modest and well behaved, all that a village princess should be. When she was twenty-eight she fell in love with a young man of good family from a neighboring village and became his lover; I will call him Tigilau. As village princesses are supposed to be virgins, this situation was irregular, although understandable given Sina's age. Sina became pregnant and told Tigilau, assuming she would give up her title and that they would marry. Tigilau said, "How do I know it's mine?" Sina turned her back and walked away. For her the affair was finished. She felt she had misjudged the man; seeing what sort of person he really was, she no longer loved him.

Samoa being a very small world, Sina's village and Tigilau's village found out what had happened. Tigilau's family did a ceremony of apology (*ifoga*): they sat on the bare ground before Sina's family house, delicately woven, beautifully decorated fine mats upon their heads as gifts of repentance. Sina would not come out of the house. Had she done so would have been tantamount to accepting Tigilau's belated proposal of marriage, which her inner feelings would not allow her to do.

As a village princess, Sina embodied the prestige of her family and village; therefore, Tigilau's insult was felt by the groups to which she belonged.[16] Without a marriage the resulting rift between families and villages could not be mended. Peace between them would be proportionally more precarious. From a sociocentric Samoan viewpoint the problem was that Sina was *failoto*—a word that literally means "to make *loto,*" and that actually means "to insist upon one's own inner thoughts or feelings"—which Samoans see as far too hardheaded and stubborn. When the baby was born deformed, the villagers said it was cursed (*faʻamālaiaina*), meaning that Sina was suffering a divine retribution.

Ontological lexicons have a singular focus on a highlighted area of experience, although they also intimate a territory of shadow. Thus, in Samoa the use of the term *aga* (persona) suggests that people are role players, and this role-playing premise throws a penumbra over inner life; nonetheless, there is a vague, general term for this shadowed territory (*loto*). Moral lexicons are dual; they categorize the highlighted territory as virtue, but they also bring the shadowed territory to light as a source of bad behavior, as Sina's "stubbornness" is attributed to her *loto*. The dual nature of moral lexicons predicates a classificatory activity: separating the proverbial sheep from the proverbial goats—that is, moral discourse.

Moral Discourses

The activity of moral discourse deepens the schism in cultural visions of the self between highlighted and shadowed experience, first articulated in moral lexicons, by underlining a discrepancy between what people think is moral and what they experience as human inclination. At the opening of this chapter I quoted a Samoan song, "Samoan Custom," which said that it is "beautiful" to give respect and support to all people. The song preaches that failure to "stand" on these sociocentric customs brings a loss of prestige but goes on to complain that Samoans "turn their backs on" and "forget" these customs. Indeed, when frequently called upon to support one another—especially when the support desired is of a financial nature—Samoans are apt to exclaim, "No money, too many *faʻalavelave*" (Leai se tupe, tele nei faʻalavelave). I have seen college students wear T-shirts with this message printed across the chest. It amounts to a national slogan. *Faʻalavelave* is the term used to refer to ceremonial events but literally means "to make entangled," as one might be entangled in a net or in a network of social relationships.[17] One might think that being enmeshed was the whole point of sociocentrism, but *faʻalavelave* also means "to bother, hinder, or obstruct" and is generally used to signify "trouble."

In old Samoa the most frequent *faʻalavelave* was the *malaga*. *Malaga* were formal traveling parties that journeyed from village to village for entertainment, to exchange news, and to find spouses or to visit other branches of the extended family on ceremonial occasions.[18] Krämer says, "Like a swarm of locusts the travel-happy Samoans used to descend on various places; for free hospitality is the rule"; Krämer adds, visiting relatives were likely to take away "all that was not too big nor tied fast" ([1902] 1995:101). The values of giving respect and support to others dictated that hosts welcome guests and send them off in ceremony, lavishly feed, care for, and entertain them during their stay, while maintaining a demeanor of perfect graciousness (Wilkes 1845:148–49). As convivial as these occasions sound, Samoan language suggests that *malaga* were experienced as very troubling indeed.

Reading a nineteenth-century dictionary of the Samoan language, Robert Louis Stevenson tells us *lesolosolou* means both "to have no intermission of pain" and "to have no rest, as in the arrival of visitors." *Soua* means "to be overcome by fire, flood or visitors." *ʻAlovao*, literally "to hide in the woods," glosses as "to avoid visitors" (1892:12–13).[19] "So, by the sure hand of popular speech," Stevenson says, "we have the picture of the house deserted, the *malanga* disappointed, and the host that should have been quaking in the bush," rather, I might add, than standing at his or her proverbial post.[20]

If sermonizing songs unfailingly remark on how far people's sentiments are from moral dicta, gossip, the most common form of moral discourse, attributes to others just those inclinations that moral discourse condemns. *Lotoleaga* is the word one hears most in Samoan gossip. Best translated as *envy*, it refers to a personalistic animus that goes against the grain of sociocentric values. And, says one of Shore's informants, "it is the thing you'll find among all Samoans" (1977:284). Explaining *lotoleaga*, I often heard Samoans—for whom height is the premier trope for status—use the American metaphor of crabs in a bucket, each of which pulls the others down.

During the period when Americans were enjoying media gossip about the O. J. Simpson trials, the underlying suspicion was that Simpson had failed to take personal responsibility for his actions. Moral egocentrism—self-reliance, standing on one's own two feet, and so on—means "standing up and taking your punishment like a man," but egocentric moral discourse is obsessed with bringing to light people's willingness to relinquish, and even to deny radically, personal responsibility.

Contextual Discourses

To compensate for the prescriptive shortcomings of moral discourse, contextual discourses recast "moral" and "immoral" behaviors as different genres of symbolic performances, performances that may involve verbal and or gestural language.[21] Behaviors *prescribed* in moral discourse are cast as symbolic performances undertaken by all within the limited parameters of formal contexts, as if in acknowledgment that human beings cannot be expected to act in accord with cultural ethics all of the time but can carry out performances that express these ethics sometimes. Behaviors *proscribed* in moral discourse are also cast as performative and available to all within the limits of informal contexts.[22] I refer to the contextual discourse assigned to formal contexts simply as "formal discourse" and the type assigned to informal contexts as "informal discourse."

The greater latitude granted in contextual discourses is made possible by their rhetorical nature. By *rhetorical* I mean that performances are framed in the as-if mode, so as to indicate that they are not literally meant. Cultural virtues are reconceived as utopian aspirations that are distinguished from everyday human behavior. Cultural vices are reconceived as play, albeit sometimes sedulously cultivated play, invested with meanings as weighty as those of formal contexts. Inasmuch as social contexts are in fact infinitely various, even the distinction between formal and informal contexts itself is an as-if contrivance, linked to an ontological premise. In America our two salient social contexts are public and private, which define a formal/informal gradient in terms of how close the individual is to others. An individual may be with intimately related others, defining the context as private (informal); or an individual may be with others to whom he or she is not closely tied, defining that context as public (formal). Because Samoan society is sociocentric and hierarchical, contexts are constituted not on relations to the subject but by group types: they are peer groups (informal) or hierarchical groups (formal).

In the Samoan epitome of formal contexts, ceremonies, the fundamental virtues of the vernacular morality—respect (*fa'aaloalo*) and generosity (*alofa*)—are performed: one gives flattering speeches, and one makes generous prestations. It does not matter if the participants are truly respectful or generous; they will act *as if* they are by undertaking performances that symbolically convey these values (flattery and prestations). One's capacity to do so is a measure not so much of morality as of social achievement; we will see that contextual discourses involve those activities that the culture associates with achievement and public recognition. When Samoans are being playful, on the other hand, they perform what would be outlandish disrespect outside of informal contexts, joking about things personal and sexual, when respect demands the utmost discretion and modesty. As long as talk is framed in a manner that indicates they are just teasing (*ula*), people generally do not take offense and greet what could be an insult with joyful hilarity and pleasure.

In public talk Americans respect one another's privacy—that is, others' status as individuals—and engage in professional performances that symbolize their qualities as individuals: initiative, an ability to assume personal responsibility and to carry through a task on their own. Although an ability to take personal responsibility is quintessential to moral individualism, in professional (formal) contexts one's ability to do so is indicative not so much of morality as of achievement. In Orwell's film *Citizen Kane* Kane's performative individualism is the measure of his success, even though his morality is dubious. But, if in American professional life the "dependent character" is "thought to be in need of psychiatric help" (Hsu 1961:219), in the private (informal) relations of love and family Americans speak of their needs for one another *as if* they were not really entirely separate and independent, and such sentiments and ways of talk may be deeply appreciated (Quinn 1992).[23]

Strategic Discourses

By taking material formerly defined as "bad"—like dependency in American culture or dominance seeking in Samoa—and calling it "good" under certain circumstances (as in the good marriage in the first case or a good joke in the second), contextual discourses suggest there is nothing inherently wrong with that part of the self left out of the ontological premise and censured in moral discourse. This moral relativity quietly refutes the contextual restrictions previously placed on the exercise of the formerly backgrounded element of self. Undermining these restrictions leads to a promiscuous enlistment of formal and informal discourses and to discourse combinations that better address the real contingencies of lived situations, which rarely fall neatly into formal/informal categories.

In Samoa the orator (*tulāfale*) is an exemplar of strategic discourse. Orators are responsible for the ceremonial recitation of village-specific titles linked to local history (*faʻalupega*). For Samoans these recitations are preeminent demonstrations of respect. Names, in Samoa, both titular and common, are often derived from events and thereby serve to index chronologies. The *faʻalupega* distill village history in the names of the chiefs of the various village families. Woven into the genealogical stories from which these titles derive is a rank ordering of village titles and of the associated families. The *faʻalupega* legitimize this ordering: their relative ranking is (putatively) fixed, just as the past is fixed. But orators are known to manipulate the order of this poetic collection of honorific, subtly elevating the status of some and lowering that of others, for the purpose of forwarding their group's status (Keesing and Keesing 1956:102). Inasmuch as the orator's method is showing respect but his metier is forwarding a set of competitive interests, he amalgamates a talent for decorous role playing (associated in Samoa with moral ideals and respectful discourse) with competitive and aggressive elements of self (associated in Samoa with moral turpitude and joking discourse). In Samoa people generally aspire to the politick form of talk represented by the orator because they believe that success lies in an ability to affect it.

We will see that there is a game-playing aspect to composite discourses like that of the Samoan orator, underlined by the term *strategic*. This does not necessarily imply a Machiavellian relation to culture, at least as Machiavelli is usually understood. What I have in mind is what Dreyfus (1984) discusses in relation to the development of expertise. Dreyfus argues that when people truly grasp a system they no longer experience themselves as conforming to rules but as devising moves. It is at this point that the person acquires a sense of power: actors come to experience themselves as, to a degree, reinventing the system with each move, and that experience is compelling (Dreyfus 1984:30).[24] Notice that the development of expertise also represents an experience of self-realization: Dreyfus tells us that one develops a highly differentiated understanding of one's experience and of oneself in terms of the system and comes to feel the exhilaration of being an agent.

Once again, when I refer to "discourses on self" I do not mean that the subject of these discourses are invariably the self. Sometimes the self is the actual subject. Moral discourse, for example, frequently philosophizes about the self but may also be about spirits or gods, afterlife or genesis, and so on. Rather, all the foregoing discourses are discourse on self in the sense that they realize and, in an important sense, are about realizing cultural construals of self. We will see, for example, that entertainments are a cardinal example of informal discourse. Entertainment topics are as multifarious as culture itself, but entertainments work on material that constitutes a culturally defined moral underside of self, albeit one that is orchestrated in a socially acceptable and even valued form.

In summary, the ontological lexicon is hegemonic: it naturalizes a set of cultural beliefs about experience. Moral lexicons and discourses are ideological, preaching about the way people should be. Contextual discourses enact conventional protocols for formal and informal situations. Strategic discourses are improvisational and aim at an existential project, albeit one that is culturally constituted, pursued by the person as agent.[25]

Talking about Cultural Selves

In recent ethnographies much important work has been done on the cultural construction of personhood, which poses a critique of the universalistic claims of Western psychological theory.[26] There are three major features to this critique.

1. Postmodernists tend to see unified selfhood—the person conceived of as individual—as a bourgeois illusion (Althusser 1971, Derrida 1978, Hebdige 1988:164ff.). I suggest that cross-culturally there are two common "illusions" of personhood: one that people are egocentric individuals and the other that they are sociocentric role players. People react to the illusory and reified nature of these conceptions by predicating multiple selves, realized in the discourses I have just limned. These selves, being various, are only partially shared and are loose in their interconnections. But this variety does not mean that there are no self systems or none that share recurrent features cross-culturally.
2. Because of the influence of postmodernism, elisions and ambiguities in the identities of cultural subjects have an important place in current ethnography; they have been regarded as illustrating the cultural specificity of selves.[27] I hope to show that these elided and ambiguous aspects of self are predicated by the cross-culturally recurrent features of self systems just as surely as the illusions that are their banners.
3. If Western psychological theorists have privileged egocentric models in assuming the primacy of a unified self—the ego—they have also privileged egocentrism in assuming an individual/society dichotomy. Depicting subjectivity as the basis of identity and problematizing sociality, this dichotomy pictures identity as intrinsically individual and as opposed to sociality in a David and Goliath relationship. Ethnographers have pointed out that this relation to self is by no means universally prominent (Strathern 1990, Wagner 1991, Battaglia 1995). In many cultures sociality is the very basis of identity (Markus and Kitayama 1991). I take identity to be the cumulative result of acts of identification—affirming "That is me"—but it begins in culture with an identification either with the subjective or the social aspects of one's own experience. Cultural self systems encourage people to privilege one type of experience while problematizing the other, although by virtue of its problematical character the other receives much social attention; it is this privileging/problematizing process that offers

grounds for a comparative psychology. Psychologists—most significantly, Carl Jung (1966) and G. H. Mead (1934)—have discussed interrelations between social and subjective experience within the person, but only in Euro-American societies.

Rather than abandoning the search for a recurrent systematicity in cultural psychology, we need to reconceive the scientific project in broader terms, unearthing patterns of more than local significance while remaining sensitive to cultural difference. I seek these patterns in the fertile gap that people everywhere seem to feel between their ways of talking about persons and their experience of persons and in the human need for a concordance between description and experience. This tension between description and experience is also one between the acknowledged and the suppressed and is, therefore, reminiscent of psychoanalytic perspectives. But the tension I delineate is phenomenological—residing between language as a form of awareness and awareness not captured by language—rather than between an ego and a quasibiological id.

I do not mean to be tendentious, denying the importance of biology or that there is biology in desire. It is simply that no one can tell the whole story, and my focus is culture and consciousness. Like existentialists, I take consciousness itself to predicate forms of desire: on the one hand, a desire that experience conform to expectation and the schemata from which it derives; on the other, a desire to go beyond any systematic way of talk that is perceived to belie consciousness and to limit its scope. Cognitive dissonance theorists amply document the former (Aronson 1984). There is a biological excuse for the latter: consciousness makes us adaptive.

Development across Cultures

A theory about cultural self systems inevitably raise questions about the reproduction of these systems. On one level the answer to the question of reproduction is simple: if self systems are embedded in lexicons and discourses, conversation entails their reproduction. While true, this response begs the question. People do not utilize lexicons and discourses merely because they exist but also because they are satisfying, even compelling. I propose that, while the *logical* evolution of lexicons and discourses of self progresses through the recognition of a difference between cultural talk about selves and lived experience, the *acquisition* of these lexicons and discourses progresses, first, through the structural arrangement of early relations and, second, through a recursive contest between elders and children about these arrangements. As structural arrangements and recursive contexts are internalized, they supply experiential basses, as well as motivations, for the reproduction of cultural lexicons and discourses on self.

Acquiring an Ontological Lexicon

A lexicon is satisfying if it resonates with one's experience. Contact and distancing experiences in early relations supply the child with experiences of being a person that resonate with the ontological premise. In egocentric societies early relations are emphatically interpersonal: they are organized as intense one-to-one experiences of contact and distance—the most significant of which is between mother and infant—that afford an experience of being a self in contradistinction to another. Again, I quote from that premier ethnographer of the egocentric self, Sigmund Freud.

> An infant at the breast does not as yet distinguish his ego from the external world. . . . He must be very strongly impressed by the fact that some sources of excitation, which he will later recognize as his own bodily organs, can provide him with sensations at any moment, whereas other sources evade him from time to time—among them what he desires most of all, his mother's breast. . . . In this way there is for the first time set over against the ego an "object," in the form of something which exists "outside" and which is forced to appear only by special action. (1961:66–67; see also Lacan 1968:72)

A stress on contact with one person who is from time to time physically distant brings the idea of difference between bodies to bear upon the infant: physical separateness becomes a trope for psychological boundaries. The psychological sense of the self-as-separate that arises originally from a focus on physical boundedness is the ego.

It follows that when the infant's attention is focused on many people, it is correspondingly less aware of its mother's absences and tends to focus less on the body's boundaries. We will see that in sociocentric Samoa early relations are organized as group relations; they feature diffuse but affectionate physical contact that highlights an experience of porosity, or connectedness, with elders. Elders gradually become interpersonally distant, thereby acquainting the child with the boundaries of the status hierarchy.[28] Here interpersonal rather than physical distance is the salient trope for psychological boundaries, through which one identifies one's tier in the group. In turn one's tier dictates one's roles: roles derive in Samoa most fundamentally from relative rank. In sociocentric societies one's role, or persona, is synonymous with one's identity, just as the ego is synonymous with identity in egocentric societies.[29]

Acquiring a Moral Lexicon

If elders typically distance infants either physically or interpersonally, infants tend to resist distancing. In American society the infant usually sleeps alone and may bewail this arrangement, falling asleep only in the presence of another family member. In a sociocentric case like Samoa infants may bewail their mother's absences, despite the many people regularly involved in their care. While parental figures may be annoyed when infants display resistance to distancing, they are generally tolerant; however, when toddlers continue to resist, elders are likely to interpret resistances as "bad" and to respond with negative sanctions. By *sanction* I mean a coercive measure meant to undercut resistance. When negative sanctions are used consistently, young children come to anticipate an unpleasant measure whenever they desire to resist distancing. These anticipations lead to a deterring hesitancy, that is, to inhibitions in those situations in which children typically display resistance.

In Samoa elders impose interpersonal distance between themselves and children; children are also teased about personal characteristics and become interpersonally shy and embarrassed (*mā*). When *mā*, children seem physically unable to move and will sit silently with their heads bowed. Indeed, immobility is one of the connotations of the word *mā*. Thus, the *manumā*, literally "shy bird," is a bird that, when approached, simply bows its head and becomes immobile.

To summarize, elders distance children in a specific kind of relation (interpersonal or group); children resist distancing; children are sanctioned and internalize these negative sanctions; as a result they manifest inhibitions (rather than resistances) in that kind of relation in which distancing took place. Through sanctioning children, then, cultures create a divided self, divided between resistances to separation experiences and inhibitions in that relation type targeted by these experiences. Resistance is interpreted as corresponding to cultural definitions of "vice," inhibitions to cultural definitions of "virtue," and together supply an experiential basis for a moral lexicon.

Inner division is mediated by pride, developed through appreciative spectatorship on the part of elders. Elders begin playing the role of a supportive audience when the child displays behaviors that express the ontological premise. Thus, in middle-class American socialization parents play the role of appreciative spectators when children display independence (Bateson 1972:99–106). Emphasis is on dramatizing independence, rather than on practically carrying out a wide range of responsibilities for oneself (Whiting and Child 1953:94–8).[30] Appreciative spectatorship helps the child to forge a positive sense of self based upon performative versions of independence.

By way of contrast, Samoans told me that children who become independent cut off their parents' hands and feet. Samoan elders will play the role of appreciative spectators when toddlers perform small tasks for others, even though, in general, younger people are expected to pay attention to older people rather than vice versa. I have seen Samoan mothers give a tiny child an object to take to another adult across the room, who at once became a conspirator in a little play in which both adults smilingly attended to the tot's successful performance. Later serving others is merely expected, as some level of autonomy is among Americans.

In the United States a learned pride in independence converts the ontological premise that persons are separate into a moral premise that they should be. In Samoa a learned pride in service to superiors converts the ontological premise that people are role players within a larger group into a moral premise that they should be. I am not arguing that there are two developmental patterns, the egocentric and the sociocentric. Just as a culture may fall anywhere on the egocentric/sociocentric continuum, so may developmental trajectories; it is the moralization of an ontological premise through pride that I propose as a cross-culturally repeated feature.

Acquiring Moral Discourse

Just as infants resist parental distancing, so also toddlers protest negative sanctions. In Samoa the dominant sanction is punishment. Samoan punishments are physically aggressive; children are typically slapped or beaten with a coconut frond broom, but angry elders may also resort to heavier and more damaging weapons to extract deference. Very small children may protest punishment in kind: they often react aggressively, talking back to elders or engaging in other performances that dramatize patent disrespect. Such defiance is suppressed through redoubled sanctions. Yet around this time children also come to engage in culturally stylized misbehaviors that are reminiscent of protests against negative sanctions but which occur with little apparent stimulus; I call these situationally unmoored misbehaviors "counterreactions."

In Samoa a common counterreaction is cheekiness (*tautalaitiiti*). Cheekiness dramatizes the same urge to challenge the status of superiors, to dominate rather than being dominated, evinced by immediate protests against punishment, and does so through gestures that show a metaphoric resemblance to these protests. Cheekiness, however, often arises quite independently of punishment, as in the case of the village children who happily shouted obscenities at me.

Counterreactions might be mistaken for delayed or displaced protests against negative sanctions. We will see in later chapters, however, that counterreactions are reactions to internalized anticipations of sanctions, that is, to the frustrating feeling of inhibition. Counterreactions are attempts to overcome inhibition, rather than direct responses to events in the external social world; as such, they constitute diffuse desires to engage in censored actions not in response to a particular event in light of which it might be justified but in a general sense. Counterreactions, therefore, create a sense of culpability that challenges the child's developing pride in culturally valued performances. This threat is warded off through moral discourse.

Although moral discourse has a classifying intent, it often assumes a narrative form, particularly in the life of the developing child.[31] Gradually, moral stories and fragments of stories take a place in the child's fantasy life. Like all of us, children tend to identify with the protagonists of these tales and to disidentify with villains. The heroes personify cultural definitions of virtue and enact those kinds of performances of which the child is proud; the villains personify cultural definitions of vice as well as the child's own counterreactions.

As the culture's moral lexicon becomes personified in fantasy, children begin to exercise agency in relation to it by engaging in moral discourse: children tell or act out versions of tales to themselves and with others. By this narrative means the moral lexicon becomes a medium of self-expression, rather than something merely inscribed upon children.

Moral discourse, however, not only allows children to identify with personifications of cultural virtue; covertly, it also permits illicit satisfactions. Thus, in the tales told to children—but also in later forms of moral discourse such as sermonizing and gossiping—there is a tendency to focus on a figure who violates a moral code and to replace this figure with a paragon of virtue, with whom speakers and listeners empathize. Typically, participants state or infer that the object of their empathy should inherit the violator's ill-gotten gains, as in the biblical aphorism about the meek who inherit the earth. This arrogation of the logical fruits of the villain's labors by the hero symbolically fuses hero and villain. This fusion allows tellers and listeners alike—in fantasy—to identity with lauded activities and act out counterreactions all at once.

There is, for example, a Samoan children's story in which the protagonist is a Cinderella figure called Scabby-Oven-Cover who faithfully serves her mother and elder sisters, even though they often beat her and make her live in the cook house, the place of lowest status (Moyle 1981:196–207). Scabby-Oven-Cover's haughty sisters throw themselves at a handsome young chief, who ignores them and marries Scabby-Oven-Cover, giving her an exalted status and making the sisters her servants. Samoan young people are supposed to devote themselves to serving elders; this tale offers them a protagonist who does so, with whom they can identify, but allows this protagonist, in the end, to dominate (rather than serve) others.

By proclaiming moral principles and acting out counterreactions in the same activity, moral discourse temporarily ameliorates disquieting inner conflicts between the two. This is the reason that moral discourse is reproduced: while lexicons are reproduced because they are resonant with experience, discourses are activities, and their reproduction requires more compelling forms of satisfaction.

However satisfying, moral discourse also carries with it a dim awareness that, on the symbolic plane, one has tasted the fruits of violation. The result is a perpetuation of that sense of culpability originally rooted in counterreactions. This sense of culpability creates a need to engage in further moralizing, by which one's ethics may be repeatedly proclaimed and counterreactions further dissociated. In this manner the inner dichotomy produced through sanctioning children, plus the inherent dynamics of moral discourse, insure the reproduction of moral discourse.

Acquiring Contextual Discourses

Cultures further manage counterreactions by providing context-bound activities that I call "cultural projects." Cultural projects sublimate counterreactions, camouflaging them in a socially approved form so that they resemble cultural virtues. The term *sublimation* is from Freudian diction and denotes a socially beneficent transformation of impulses as well as disguise. Often, in formal (public) contexts in American culture, for example, work begins with a young person joining an organization in which he or she must fit in, cooperate, and support the undertakings of superiors. Although fitting in is an avenue for affiliation, it is defined culturally as being "self-supporting" and as becoming independent from one's parents. In formal (hierarchical) contexts in Samoa youngsters are given administrative duties in which they order juniors about. Although dominating a junior is experientially an avenue for self-assertion, in this cultural project it is understood as a form of service rendered to one's group.

While moral discourse surreptitiously allows developing youngsters a fantasized participation in forbidden actions, cultural projects surreptitiously open avenues to perform these actions in daily life; therefore, like moral talk, cultural projects perpetuate a sense of culpability, subliminally stimulated by: (1) counterreactions; (2) the moral discourse in which these counterreactions were secretly expressed; (3) cultural projects themselves, in which counterreaction are acted out in dissociated form. Cultural projects, however, are regarded as socially contributive, and we will see that they are a means to achieve public recognition. Public recognition expands upon the positive sense of self that developed through elder's appreciative spectatorship, assuaging this sense of culpability; however, public recognition cannot eradicate it because culpability is denied, just as the satisfactions delivered by moral discourse and by cultural projects themselves are denied. Therefore, as moral discourse leaves participants with a residual need to proclaim their moral righteousness through further moral discoursing, cultural projects leave participants with a residual need to proclaim their social worth through further participation in cultural projects. We will see that cultural projects have a progressive character, gradually evolving into contextual discourses, which are then perpetuated for the same reasons as cultural projects.

Acquiring Strategic Discourse

As growing children become adept at contextualizing, they discover that situations are not readily sorted into a binary set of formal/informal contexts. In response to the actual fuzziness of social experience they begin to produce strategic discourses that combine contextualized responses. While using contextual discourses implies a conventional application of discourse to situations, using strategic discourses implies a creative adaptation of other discourse types to solve novel problems. Wooing is a compelling instance of a situation in which contextual discourses often prove inadequate: formal modes of address are inhibiting, but informal modes may be read as offensively brusque. Often, therefore, cultures orchestrate the development of strategic discourse within the context of courting.[32]

A Samoan boy who wants to impress a girl shows respect for her, but in Samoa respect implies a deferential silence bespeaking a polite abasement of the personal self. Wooing is muted by this demeanor. To resolve this dilemma Samoan adolescents woo for one another, they *fa'asoa*. The person who courts someone for a friend is a *soa*, which means "double": two socks are *soa* to each other. The double will sing his friend's praises, elevating him in the eyes of the girl, so his talk resembles formal discourse; however, he often carries out his representative wooing as a kind of jocular banter, so it also resembles informal discourse: the double uses a composite discourse that suits the contingencies of a courtship.

By way of contrast, Holland (1992a:66) says that in the America folk model of romance a relationship begins when a boy learns to appreciate a girl's uniqueness as a person (read individual); "Only you . . . ," the song goes. The aim of this special appreciation, however, is intimacy; admittedly, sexual intimacy involves needs for others that are at least in part generic—even "animal" and anonymous. This opposition once again calls for inventiveness on the part of the wooer and for a strategic amalgamation of apparently opposed cultural categories and ways of talk.

While moral lexicons represent an internalized conflict between children and inevitably frustrating parental figures, moral discourses offer a means to allay but not resolve this conflict. By offering less inhibiting ways of subscribing to social morality, contextual discourses offer better resolution. Strategic discourses, however, transcend this internalized conflict; they do so through a changed relationship between structure and agency. Moral and contextual discourses feature delimiting structures: ethical rules in the first case, rules of appropriateness in the second. In strategic discourse there are only "the rules of the game," in which one plays with and exploits cultural tenets rather than merely replicating them and in which one experiences limits as contingent upon one's capacities rather than as set and inflexible.

Society is largely content with those who are morally conforming and who channel their energies into cultural projects: it does not insist upon the full development of strategic discourse, unlike other discourse types. Different people, therefore, effect strategic discourses to different degrees and may fall back on other discourses in most situations. Yet we will see that an ability to combine cultural discourses strategically is generally regarded as the signature of a wholly successful adult identity.

Thinking about Development

My focus here is discursive and eschews essentialism.[33] Essentialist ideas presuppose that fundamental characteristics are possessed by human beings—that there is a human nature existing apart from the discourses through which humans constitute that nature. While the premise-discourse series suggests that, in their ontological view of self, people in a culture tend to be essentialistic, my theory is about selves as constituted in and through recognizable types of discursive practice.

Essentialism denies social actors the existential possibility of resistance and creativity. While I see children's cultural milieu as compelling, I do not view them as passive. Children resist normative codes from their earliest years; their persistent resistance is as intrinsic to enculturation as compliance. As in Foucault (1990), in my developmental paradigm power at first seems to enunciate itself as negative—marking out transgressions and limits—when in fact it is an impelling force implanting vectors of progression, constellating resistances that incite movement along these vectors. Elders help to create a relational environment that inscribes an ontological premise on children and negatively sanction children who resist inscription; however, the consequences of this relational environment and attendant sanctions are certain psychological problems that children come to experience as their own. In reaction to these problems, children exercise agency. If agency seems at first only to further trammel them in the self system, it also promises the possibility of mastery and with it a limited form of transcendence.

This tale of inscription, resistance, and internalization echoes Vygotsky's insight that intrapsychic structures mime and rehearse the social relations of childhood (1981:164–65). It must be said, however, that this reproduction is not necessarily intentional on the part of its practitioners. How much the practices I delineate are quiet adaptation on the level of habitus and how much conscious consideration, and in what order, is moot and individual. My interest is not so much in intentionality—although surely intentionality intrudes itself at many points—but, rather, in a logical concordance between lexicons and discourses on the one hand, and antecedent practices on the other, albeit a concordance so exact it might be mistaken for a product of intentional crafting.

It also must be said that socializing practices continue to be applied in altered forms throughout life. They are simply more blatant in childhood because the power adults hold over one another is subject to greater mediation and restraint than that which parental figures hold over children. This continuity insures the continuing reproduction of a lexicon-discourse series.

I appropriate a number of developmental ideas from the psychoanalytic tradition—Freud, Erikson, Bettelheim, Lacan, and so forth. Along with Obeyesekere (1990) and Kurtz (1992), I believe that this paradigm, while not adequate in its present form, is rich in insight that can provide a stepping-off place for cross-cultural perspectives on self. Like psychoanalysts, one of my principal interests is the channeling of culturally shared needs, although, like those in critical theory, I see these needs as culturally shaped.[34] Nonetheless, any discussion of cultural practices in terms of "need satisfaction" raises the specter of functionalism. Functionalists tend to assume that cultural subjects act to amend "society's needs," leaving one at a loss to explain individual motivation. What I am talking about, however, *is* individual motivation, albeit occasioned by a specific sociocultural milieu.

Contra psychoanalysts, I am hesitant to assign specific ages to initiatory periods and would not foreclose the possibility that the timing and even the serial sequencing of these periods differ between cultures. In a culture in which one type of discourse is particularly stressed, adoption of a simplified form of that discourse may be encouraged earlier than it would be elsewhere, and a pedagogy facilitating accelerated acquisition may be embedded in child-rearing practices. Then, two forms of discourse on self may be acquired more or less simultaneously. In this vein Shore suggests that contextual discrimination are focal in Samoa (1982), and Ochs shows that training in these discriminations begins early in childhood (1988). To an extent, however, discursive development may parallel growing intellectual capacities.

Ontological lexicons are conveyed through the structure of a relational environment and involve experiences that precede language acquisition. The development of a moral lexicon, however, presupposes an ability to make the simple binary distinctions upon which language is based (as between good and bad). The development of moral discourse presupposes the more complex ability to understand narratives and to recount narratives or at least narrative fragments to oneself or to others. We will latter see that contextual discourses presuppose an ability to use tropes and, therefore, the ability to distinguish between symbols and things. Strategic discourse involves an improvisational use of discourses and, therefore, some understanding of the principles upon which discourses are based.[35]

Politics of Self

While full development in any culture presupposes progress through the entire lexicon-discourse series, cultural subgroups may be attributed a specific lexicon or discourse type; then the group is expected to develop through the series only up to this point. It is not that people lack innate capacities, but the domination of one group by another is usually justified by ideologies about the innate incapacity of dominated groups. Further, inasmuch as dominated groups can be discouraged from development—cobbled, so to speak—they are more manageable.

When a group is attributed only the ontological lexicon, its members are thought capable of little development: an enslaved group or an untouchable caste are examples. It is admitted that members of this group share minimal understandings of personhood (ontological premises in my terms) with the dominant group. Being a person at all means being a role player in some cultures and an individual in others, but this state of affairs is merely a given, assumed to be human nature in the constitutive sense. In American jurisprudence, for example, all are assumed to be separate people, ultimately responsible for their own actions, but not all are thought to act in a manner that reflects a developed sense of moral responsibility. In traditional Samoan jurisprudence all are assumed to be group members, responsible for the actions of everyone in their group, particularly those beneath them in the hierarchy. A family with an incorrigibly miscreant member would be exiled from the village, its house ravaged, its trees ringbarked. Although in Samoa all have a post—that is, a role in the group—not all are thought to stand at their post.

An enslaved or untouchable group may be thought to lack the capacity for moral discourse, a lack believed to justify the group's subjection. Thus, in India, the members of the lower untouchable castes are thought to engage in incest and prostitution, activities that connote a lack of moral capacity (Trawick 1990a). In Fiji a similar lack of moral capacity was attributed to indentured Indian laborers (Kelly 1991).[36] When a group is believed to be incapable of moral reasoning, the behavior of group members is judged on the basis of their obedience and cooperativeness with those who dominate them.[37] Of course, not everyone in any cultural milieu will share this view of the dominated group, but, when most do not, justification for their disenfranchisement is undermined, and their social position becomes vulnerable to change.

When gender is a basis for the attribution of limited developmental capacities, moral discourse is often attributed to females.[38] In mid-nineteenth-century America, for example, the dominant view of middle-class white women was that they developed the moral character of their children and husbands, helping husbands to maintain moral integrity in a heartless and unstable industrializing world (Canaan 1990:217, Ryan 1975, Welter 1966).[39] When moral discourse is attributed to females, their behavior is judged primarily in moral terms, on a basis of whether or not they keep the rules: the rules specify personifying their society's moral ideals and supporting the achievements of the dominant group. Dominant male groups usually attribute contextual discourses to themselves, a view to which people generally may subscribe and which is hegemonic in Gramsci's sense of the term.[40]

Contextual discourses are associated with cultural projects. We will see that cultural projects are avenues for achievement; therefore, when these discourses are attributed to a group, members are judged in terms of what they do or do not achieve. When I was growing up in the United States, for example, a women was ruined if she conceived a child out of wedlock; a man was judged more on his achievements (did he make a good income, was he well-known in this profession, and so forth), rather than on whether or not he was a faithful husband. It was not that moral rules did not apply to him; they simply did not constitute as consequential a basis for social judgment as they did in the female case. Strategic discourse remains a social ideal to which people aspire; however, members of the dominant group, of whom achievement is expected, are thought more capable of realizing this aspiration than others.

I do not mean to say that people always conform to attributed developmental levels. Slaves and women in sexist societies often craft strategic discourses for themselves. Rather than being regarded as civic paragons when they do, however, slaves who strategize tend to be looked upon as tricky or sly; women who strategize are regarded as manipulative. In cultures that attribute inferior developmental levels to a slave class or caste or to women, the good slave/untouchable is simple and docile; the good women is a testament to cultural morality, not an ambitious Lady Macbeth.

In their putatively lessor capacity for development such groups will be perceived as relatively uncultivated and, therefore, closer to what culture members imagine to be impulsive—and to that part of the self which is conceived as impulsive—namely, the backgrounded part of the self. Thus, in egocentric America, Kohlberg finds a moral discourse of individual rights among males, in line with an egocentric ontological premise (1973:29–30). Gilligan finds a moral discourse of social responsibility among middle-class white American women, which is more sociocentric (1982), although Kondo points out that these women are still "solidly within a linguistic and historical legacy of individualism" (1990:33–34). My point is that, when people are attributed lower developmental levels, they are likely to be seen within the confines of the defining culture not only as less capable and more impulsive but also as closer to that dimension of experience elided in their culture. This closeness, furthermore, will be linked to their attributed developmental limitations. Kohlberg does not think women incapable of moral development, but in his early work he attributed them a more limited capacity for moral development than males and linked these limitations to women's putative sociocentrism.[41]

Even in societies that do not ascribe lower developmental levels to females, contextual discourses (formal and informal) may be gender marked, men tending to specialize in formal contexts and their associated forms of talk and women in informal contexts and talk. We saw that in egocentric (but not sociocentric) cultures the salient social contexts are public and private, with the domestic realm being definitive of private life.[42] American culture again provides an example: until recently men tended to be specialists in public forms of talk, while women specialized in the modes of talk associated with private life, so much so that many women were mute in public and many men in private (Tannen 1990).

Contextual discourses and their associated cultural projects are avenues for achievement and aim at social recognition. Social recognition is by definition public and related to larger social contexts. Therefore, when a culture's informal context is private life—and when contexts are gender marked—woman's place tends to be moralized. By this I mean that: (1) moral discourse is attributed to females; (2) they are thought capable of moral development but not of high achievement; (3) they are expected to devote themselves to personifying moral ideas and to supporting the achievements of males. Davidoff and Hall (1987) trace a moralization of women's roles concomitant to a new definition of social contexts as public (formal) and domestic-private (informal) in England over the course of the late eighteenth and nineteenth centuries. Postcontact Samoa provides another illuminating example of this redefinitive process.

Samoan Selves in Historical Refraction

Although gender was an important marker of social role in old Samoa, status trumped gender as a marker of social difference. Despite pretensions to a well-established social hierarchy spanning families, villages, and districts, in old Samoa status was constantly negotiated, and attributions of certain developmental levels by one family, village, or district to another could not be fixed. The intensity of status competition was such that, although age was a significant marker of status (and therefore of license for achievement), by adolescence all were responsible for furthering the status of their respective groups, and their actions were judged on what they achieved in this regard.

In pre-Christian Samoa the girl furthered family status by serving as a lure, inducing high-status males to sire children with important bloodlines (*tama'āiga*). This aim dictated different courses of action to high-status and ordinary girls. High-status girls were to remain virginal, allowing their family or village to arrange a marriage of state with the scion of another high-status family. Ordinary girls were to raise family status through informal matings and marriages with boys whose family had greater wealth or status than their own and enjoyed considerable sexual latitude as long as their actions forwarded these interests.

Missionaries to Samoa were predominately members of the London Missionary Society (LMS), a conglomeration of evangelical sects (Perry 1974:11, Gailey 1993:295). They first appeared in Samoa circa 1830 and brought with them an English eighteenth- and nineteenth-century debate about the ethics of human sexuality. Evangelicalism represented one side of this debate, romanticism the other. By *romanticism* I do not refer to the entire romantic movement. Indeed, evangelicalism was inspired by romanticism in the broadest sense of the term, with its cultivation of emotional intensity focused on individual identity (Davidoff and Hall 1987:27, 158, 160; Davies 1961: 247, 256, 277). Rather, I refer to that narrower range of beliefs and practices articulated in the period's literature on romantic love, such as the novels of the Brontë sisters and the poetry of Lord Byron.[43] If the tempestuous passions of the Brontës' characters were antithetical to evangelical ideals, romantic relations such as those personified by Esther Summerson in Dickens's *Bleak House,* for example, were much less so. Nonetheless, for evangelicals the reading of novels itself was suspect because so many of them dwelled upon passionate feelings (Davidoff and

Hall 1987:90, 437). Missionaries' moral discourse was, however, in certain respects kin to that of the romantics: both discourses registered a new emphasis on inner sentiment as the definitive ethical issue in human sexuality.

Sexuality and marriage had been for the English—as for Samoans—a matter at once having to do with economic practicalities and deeply implicated in the negotiation of status (Marcus 1966). Evangelicals advocated "free-choice" marriage, entered into for reasons of spiritual compatibility (Davidoff and Hall 1987:179, 219–21, 323–24, 327). English nineteenth-century novels, for example *Jane Eyre*, likewise stormed against marriage for considerations of family wealth and status and advocated free-choice marriage, albeit for romantic love. Thus, evangelicals and romantics shared a common accent on inner sentiment, from which they drew diametrically opposed conclusions. Nonetheless, a communality of topic, a shared ontological premise about the primacy of inner experience, together with an opposition in argument, made romantics subtextual interlocutors in evangelical sermons.

Missionaries used evangelical moral discourse on inner feeling as grounds to oppose informal matings and marriages among Samoans, along with the polygamy of high-status males and serial monogamy practiced by both sexes. Missionaries, however, not only sought to banish what they saw as permissive sexual practice but also to controvert the sex/gender entailments of Samoan sociocentrism, just as their brethren at home were doing in their own society. In these efforts missionaries fancied themselves enlighteners and liberators, bringing "heathens" out of a moral darkness into the light, but their weapon for doing so—an advocacy of free-choice marriage, with its privileging of personal volition, personal thoughts, and personal feeling—was a two-edged sword. Missionaries drew a narrow set of implications from their emphasis on inner self in marriage about sexual decorum and sexual fidelity; Samoan girls often took the presumption while demurring at the narrowness, as if they could read romantic texts between the lines of evangelical arguments. These moral undercurrents, set in motion by missionaries, reached critical force in World War II.

Samoa had been a crossroads for whalers, adventurers, and other Europeans since the mid-nineteenth century. Despite a plethora of foreign visitors, however, Samoans managed a high level of cultural immunity. Although itinerant Westerners came and went, for the most part foreigners were ghettoized in the environs of ports. While the missionaries infiltrated the villages, established schools, and gained influence, much of their "message" was co-opted. By the late nineteenth century there were many Samoan ministers, and their version of Christianity was in accord with the *fa'aSāmoa* (the Samoan way); their "good news" reorchestrated the Bible for Samoan ears (Gunson 1978:320–22). World War II, however, vitiated cultural immunity, as the Samoas became a scene of transit of nonpareil proportions.

There was a plague of American serviceman: during the early 1940s on some islands there were two American servicemen for every Samoan. We will see that for Samoan women American servicemen represented a loophole in Samoan sexual rules. Further, the idea of romantic love—which had long been seeping into Samoan understandings of sex and gender through the subtextual elements of missionary discourse—was expanded by servicemen's discourse on sexuality and romance. American military garrisons became localities of cultural subversion. Samoans called the gates of the garrison on the island of 'Upolu, for example, the "gates of hell," the new foreigners being framed in terms of a confluence of missionary and hereditary Samoan values. In the disruptive climate of encampment, missionaries' moral discourse found new purpose: Samoan sex and gender rules became more adamantly Christian, rigidifying in an attempt to reassert decaying controls on female sexuality.

In the old Samoan village contextual discourses were gender marked, formal discourse being the particular province of men and informal discourse that of women. These were not, however, discourses of public and private life, as were their English counterparts, but of hierarchical situations and peer situations. Probably the most important event in which women practiced informal discourse was the Joking Night, which missionaries misnamed "the night dance." Joking Nights involved a risqué theatrical and choreographic banter characteristic of Samoan informal discourse; girls were leaders of jest. Joking Nights were intimately linked to girls' sexual identity: on these occasions those informal marriages by which girls forwarded family status were apt to come about. Both girls' Joking Night roles and the often temporary unions that ensued from them came as a shock to missionary sensibilities.

During the nineteenth and early twentieth centuries, under missionary scrutiny, Joking Nights migrated from the village center to the bush; in the decade after World War II Joking Nights seemed to disappear even there. The marginalization and gradual disappearance of Joking Nights was indexical of the muting of girls' participation in informal discourse in other venues, as well as of a moral cacophony about girls' sexual identity. Concomitant to the demise of Joking Nights was a rise in the incidence of spirit possession among Samoan girls.[44] As experienced by twentieth-century Samoan girls, however, possession was not only reactive but also innovative. Throughout the early part of the century a reconfigured form of spirit possession had been developing that resembled girls' precontact informal discourse in many respects but that placed this discourse in a censuring frame and laced into it colonial images and problematics.

When Joking Nights were exiled from the village limelight, their choreographic and theatrical elements were split; each part generated a colonial entertainment that remained within the village and that was more in keeping with the values and interests of Christian Samoans. One of these entertainments—colonial dance—retained female stars but was formalized, its once raucous character becoming sub-rosa. The other, colonial comic theater, carried on the raucous and wild social commentary that had characterized Joking Nights but shifted the gendering of these performances from females to males:

in Christian Samoa boys became the star proponents of that informal discourse that had formally been feminine. Gender-bending Christian glosses for formerly female discourses, together with twentieth-century socioeconomics, opened the way for a destabilization of gender categories. If the sexual identity of girls was put at hazard by colonization, the gender identity of boys suffered similarly.

When the male comedians of colonial Samoa replaced the pre-Christian female comedic dancers of Joking Nights in popular entertainments, traces of the substitutive nature of their role remained. Girls had been the featured comedians of Joking Nights; the persona most frequently affected by comedians in colonial theater was that of the transvestite (Shore 1981; Sinavaiana 1992a, 1992b). In postcolonial Samoa there is a rising number of real transvestites who appropriate the girlish persona and the entertainment role of colonial thespian transvestites. These now genuine transvestites are favorite entertainment impresarios. Through this entertainment history we will see that informal discourse Samoan style mutated its presentational forms and topics, while retaining its precontact grammar, a *plus ça change, plus c'est la même chose,* for which gender was the salient trope.

Contemporary anthropologists note that cultural change is often traditionalized: natives are apt to claim that innovations are traditional. Anthropologists call these claims the "invention" of tradition (Hobsbawm and Ranger 1983, Hanson 1989, Jolly 1992). In entertainment, as in spirit possession, Samoan "inventions" are usually reconfigurations—bricolage of past and present—made in response to the changing contingencies of historical experience. In their role as impresarios the jesting of postcolonial Samoan transvestites is reminiscent of Joking Night girls of yesteryear and of the thespian transvestites of colonial comedy theater, but it is also innovative: modern transvestite routines use a distinctly Samoan informal discourse to exploit the humorous potentialities of Western notions of personalized sexual sentiment and romance. Sporting with foreign ideas about the self, these routines constitute a cultural borderland that buffers Samoan culture while offering a venue in which a still-novel premise about self as inner, and a concomitant moral discourse, can be explored.

Cultural reconfigurations, however, do not take place only in shared social institutions such as possession or entertainment. Culture is also reconfigured by individuals enmeshed in the fabric of their personal histories and relationships. In the final chapter, therefore, I investigate the reconfiguration of Samoan discourses on self by a Samoan woman in her autobiographic monologue, a woman who encounters the moral-historical problems explored throughout the second half of the text.

More often than not, cultural historians concern themselves with the passage of events or, recently, with how natives make meaning retrospectively of historical passages (White 1991), that is, either with history as a sociopolitical sequence or with history as the imaginings of the subject, projected into historical narrative. The changing representations of cultural selves, however, is a real history in time and can be documented. Foucault's work on sexuality in Western civilization—which is also a history of person and of gender (1986, 1990)—is an obvious model in this regard, but few in psychological anthropology have taken inspiration from it. This hiatus is matched by another: Scheper-Hughes rightfully complains that within psychological anthropology power is a neglected topic (1992a:222; see also Holland 1992b).[45] Like Foucault's, my focus is discursive, but I eschew those ghostly Foucaultian discourses that construct the persons of which they speak. In *Theorizing Self* women and men, as well as persons of uncertain gender (and even more dubious sexuality), are, sometimes before our very eyes, writing a history of self, gender, and sexuality in their ever-changing discourses: they are agents, and their motives are more or less accessible, having to do with a politics of self.

Self Systems and Development

> *There are no relations of power without resistances; the latter are all the more real and effective because they are formed right at the point where relations of power are exercised; resistance to power does not have to come from elsewhere to be real, nor is it inexorably frustrated through being the compatriot of power.*
>
> Michel Foucault, *Power of Knowledge*

2

Ontological Lexicons: Essentializing and Eliding

First let me take a moment to review and expand upon the Samoan ontological premise as a prelude to considering how it is acquired. Ontological premises are coded in the words used for the nature of people, and even of things, as humans anthropomorphize the natural world in line with their assumptions about people's nature.[1] The Samoan idea of nature puzzled me for sometime. I knew that Derek Freeman had argued that nature is denoted by the Samoan term *aga* (1984:249), and my Samoan friends seemed to confirm this account. In 1987, when Hurricane Tusi virtually demolished the island of Manu'a, for example, the Samoan librarian at the little college where I taught remarked philosophically, "That's the *aga* of the wind!" I stood there looking uncomprehending. "That's the wind's nature," she said in English. I resolutely maintained my uncomprehending look. She added "That's the wind's character."

But, antithetical to our idea of character, *aga* are also social "faces": they are affectations, put on as one might put on lipstick or a seductive manner. When an older relative sees a girl from his family painting her lips red, he might well say "Whose *aga* is that?"[2] He means, "Where did you pick up that painted face, down on the docks perhaps?" The older relative might answer his own question about whose *aga* the girl wears; if a notorious lady of the night called Mutu is currently the talk of the town, he would say "Look at Mutu's *aga*."[3] In this manner the older relative alludes to the role Samoans associate with painted faces. We think of a person's real character as inimitable, but, when I asked an American Samoan college student about the relation between *aga* and imitation, his response was, "Isn't that what *aga* is?"[4]

In egocentric America character is thought to be interior—sometimes clearly reflected by a person's behavior and sometimes obscured by it: one must know the person's motive to read the character behind the act. But if you simply ask Samoans, "What is *aga*?" they usually say "behavior" because for them character is performative: *aga* consist of performances believed to be con-

37

stitutive of the person or thing in question.⁵ *Aga a le ʻapogāleveleve*, "the *aga* of the spider," for example, refers to those performances that are constitutive of the nature of spiders such as making a web or trapping and devouring prey (Freeman 1984:249).

We think people's character is unitary and singular: the real me, the real Jeannette, is one person, however diverse and even contradictory my behavior (or social performances) may seem. When character is construed as social, however, the person is not so much individual as "dividual," divisible into loosely associated parts (Marriott 1976, Strathern 1990, Wagner 1991). These parts, like parts in a play, are also social roles, and people enact several. In Samoan the possessive pronoun *your* can be plural (*au*) or singular (*lau*), depending on whether what is possessed is plural or singular. When one tells a youngster to behave well, "Faifaʻalelei au aga"—literally, "Make nice your *aga!*—one uses the plural form of *your*. The admonition does not refer to one unified character but, rather, to character as an assortment of parts realized in an assortment of social relationships.⁶

I, like Samoans, use the term *persona* (*aga*) for the form of self that derives from identifying with social experience, but various terms have been used by anthropologists and psychologists for sociocentric and egocentric selves (Markus and Kitayama 1991:226–27). This variety necessitates justifying, or at least explaining, my terminology. One of the first anthropologists to investigate the sociocentric form of self, Mauss ([1938] 1985), uses the term *persona* for them; however, more recent anthropologists use the term *person* for the sociocentric self and *self* for the egocentric self.⁷ I eschew this usage because a general term is needed that refers to sociocentric, egocentric, and other possible forms; borrowing Jung's usage (1966:155–59), I employ *self* as the term for this encompassing category. I use *persona* for the sociocentric self because I believe this term provides useful information about this self, namely, that it consists in roles, is performative, plural, and so forth.⁸ Following Freud (1923), I use the term *ego* as a simple and logical way to denote the egocentric self.⁹

Elided Experience

The ubiquitousness of subjective and social experience is one of the arguments against extreme cultural relativism in regards to the self (Spiro 1993), and yet there is copious evidence that people tend to essentialize one of the two, seeing it as definitive of being a person (Markus and Kitayama 1991). If people have both kinds but privilege one, the obvious question is: What happens to the elided form of experience? Yet this is a question little investigated in the literature on self.¹⁰

In the introduction I proposed that essentializing one dimension of experience in an ontological premise presupposes eliding another. We also saw that: (1) this elided experience remains out of focus in cultural consciousness and lexically undifferentiated; (2) because Samoans see personas as the essential aspect of people, they tend to elide inner experience; (3) therefore, although there is a Samoan term for inner experience, *loto,* it is highly general; and (4) this undercoded aspect of experience tends to represent an unsocialized and intractable side of the self in cultural symbolism.[11]

Undercoding

I stumbled upon the generality of the term *loto* in an early language lesson. A knowledgeable and genteel Samoan from the governor's office in American Samoa had decided to teach the class some Samoan songs as a language-learning device. Here is one of the songs he gave us.

Wriggle, Wriggle, Wriggle,	Mīgoi, Mīgoi, Mīgoi,
Wriggle like an ant.	Mīgoi pei se loi.
If dancing wriggle like an ant	'A sivasiva 'ua gāoioi.
Rich as dipping in coconut cream,	Lololo pei se pe'epe'e 'ua loiloi,
Sweet, sweet like banana poi.	Suiti, suamalie pei 'o se poi.
My pigeon, pigeon e	Lā tā lupe, lupe ē
Is crying, crying alas!	'Ua tagi, tagi auē!
This is my loto,	*'O lo'u loto lea,*
May it be like this,	Tau 'ina fa'apea,
May there be making dear.	Tau 'ina fa'apelepele.
Wriggle, Wriggle e,	Mīgoi, mīgoi e,
Wriggle, Wriggle e,	Mīgoi, mīgoi e,
Wriggle, wriggle e,	Mīgoi, mīgoi e,
Wriggle, wriggle more.	Mīgoi, mīgoi tele.
Wriggle here my dear.	Mīgoi mai la'u pele.

My language teacher rendered the line "This is my *loto*" as "Here is what I think," but I remembered that Shore, in his book on Samoa, glossed *loto* as "feelings" (1982:318). Confused, I took the song to several other Samoans proficient in English. Some translated the line as "This is what I think," like my teacher; some as "This is what I feel," like Shore; yet others translated it as "This is my will." When shown the variant translations, all informants told me those too were correct. *Loto* is the Samoan word for thinking, feeling, and willing because these are all aspects of inner experience, and, while we make subtle discriminations about kinds of inner experience (qualifying it, elaborating multiple categories for it), Samoans do not.[12]

Intractable Sides

Samoans do see *loto* as generally intractable and as resistant to cultural patterning. The *loto* is an organ located in the chest. As there is no equivalent organ in English, Samoans sometimes gloss the word as "heart." The literal term for heart is *fatu*. Like our English word for heart, but unlike *loto*, *fatu* is associated in contemporary Samoa with romance. There was a Samoan crooner named Mr. Fatu who toured American Samoa in the 1980s. Mr. Fatu is an apt stage name, while Mr. Loto is an unromantic thought: Mr. Willful or Mr. Stubborn would be the meaning.

While Americans, dieters and tycoons alike, believe in the moral import of having "willpower," the connotations of the word *loto* suggest a picture of the will as innately refractory. *Galuega,* for example, is the noun for "work"; *faigāluega* means "to do work." When one adds *fai* to *loto* one gets *failoto; failoto* does not gloss as "to do one's will" but, rather, as "defiant." Should a child show reluctance to carry out a parental order, the parent is apt to say—"Don't *failoto* to me," meaning "Don't try to defy me"—because they see inner life as what stands in the way of docility and cooperativeness on the part of the child. But I am getting ahead of myself. Long before any Samoan child defies an elder, that child has been deeply encouraged to forget rather than to insist upon his or her personal inclinations.

Acquiring Ontological Lexicons: Contact and Distancing

Ontological premises are embedded in lexemes like *aga* through which people index personhood. The task of reproducing ontological premises is to provide developing children with experiences of persons that are resonant with these lexemes. Then one finds their usage apt, and this is what people look for in a lexicon. Resonant experiences are supplied through relations of contact and distancing in early life, experiences that constitute the self and draw its boundaries.

Contact

Freud argued that we first construct a sense of self by identifying with positive experience and dis-identifying with negative experience (1961). Building upon this idea, Erikson says trust is an incorporation of positive experience and supplies the initial basis for identity (1963; see also Bowlby 1969). Trust also implies an openness to experience. By providing certain forms of supportive contact, early relational environments foster an openness to either interpersonal or social experience. Interpersonal experience is quintessentially between a self and another and supports the premise that the self is individual. Social experience supports the premise that the self is a role player. In other words, trust places an accent on a type of experience that confirms the culture's ontological premise. Trust is a precondition for attachment. In Ainsworth's seminal work, attachment is defined as an interpersonal bond between individuals: "One can be attached to more than one person," Ainsworth says, "but one cannot be attached to many people" (1973:1). Contra Ainsworth, I argue that there are intrasocial forms of attachment among groups of people.

Distancing

In the Western psychiatric tradition, while trust and attachment are necessary to development, too much attachment is believed to blur the boundaries of personhood, creating "boundary confusion"; boundary confusion is a failure to maintain "a consistently individuated sense of self" (Chodorow 1974:58). I propose that, because different cultures bound the self in varying ways, they also have varying forms of boundary confusion, although all are wary of these confusions. For Samoans porous boundaries between persons accurately reflect cultural conceptions of self and do not constitute a confusion; rather, porous boundaries between levels of the social hierarchy constitute boundary confusion.

I further venture that people in cultures avoid blurring the boundaries of self by actively distancing children in certain types of relations, thereby creating "insecure attachment" in areas of experience outside their ontological premise. *Insecure attachment* is the Western psychiatric term, coined by Ainsworth, for an inadequate interpersonal bond between mother and child that undermines later attachment, indeed even the capacity for attachment (1973). Where there should be attachment, there is distance. Distance tends to create mistrust—mistrust in others, whose unavailability implies they cannot be counted upon and mistrust in the self because of the alarming hostility felt toward those frustratingly unavailable persons upon whom one still depends. Again contra Ainsworth, I suggest that parents and other elders in all cultures actively forge some form of "insecure attachment"—some form of separation trauma—as a way of creating a valued form of distance in human relations and thereby avoid whatever relational blurring that each culture considers boundary confusion.[13]

Belonging and Early Identity

Early contact experience is probably universally a profound source of sentiment, and people tend to be sentimental about it, but it is also a matter of property. The child is a form of inalienable property who belongs to certain categories of people. In the United States, for example, adopted children may later seek out their "real" parents. If children have only one set of real parents, their biological ones, it follows that they "really" belong to only these people, however laws may attempt to controvert this relationship. Samoan children belong to the extended family ('*āiga*), rather than to individual persons. In old Samoa and to a lesser extent today they are, therefore, distributed on the same two principles as other forms of family property: (1) the discretion of elders; and (2) an ethic of sharing, particularly among siblings but also among relations generally.

In old Samoa paternal grandparents simply took the first child, especially if it was a son. Maternal grandparents had rights to the second child. These rights reflected responsibilities. Later we will meet Laulii Willis, a Samoan woman living in the 1870s who migrated to England and wrote an autobiography. Flying back from Samoa in 1991, I happened to be seated next to one of her descendants, Ruthanne Crawford, Laulii's grandniece. Ruthanne told me her grandmother had died in childbirth. Her great grandmother (Laulii's sister) had a new baby but gave her own baby to another relative to raise so that she could raise her deceased daughter's child. One of my married students in Samoa had parents living on another island. For several years her parents kept all her children there, although both she and her husband very much wanted to have the children with them. In fact this intergenerational traffic in children is a two-way street: one of my Samoan sisters (in-law) took her mother's last child to raise.

In the nineteenth century children also traveled from brother to sister: they were considered *tōga*, the term for sacred goods in a ceremonial exchange (Turner [1884] 1984:83).[14] In diluted form this arrangement persists, not as a presumption but as a possibility. In an American Samoan family, for example, a married sister had no offspring, whereas one of her brothers and his wife had many but were quite attached to them. The husband would go out drinking, and the wife would fret angrily at home. One night, when the wife had reached a frenzy of anger, the childless sister said the wife should give her one of the husband's favorite little girls. The wife did, bemoaning her decision all the next day, along with her husband. The sister left with the girl for Western Samoa the next afternoon just to be sure her brother and sister-in-law would not wheedle the child back out of her.

The nineteenth-century missionary Turner says: "the custom of adoption was not so much the want of natural affection as the sacrifice of it to this systematic traffic. . . . Hence, also parents may have . . . adopted children, and their own real children elsewhere" ([1884] 1984:83). The terms *natural affection, sacrifice,* and *real children* betray Turner's deep-seated beliefs in the proper ownership of children and in the emotional bonds attendant upon this proprietorship.[15] Likewise, in the literature on development in Polynesia the distribution of children among family members has been termed "adoption," but this term implies the gift of a child to someone to whom it does not belong: *adoption* is a misnomer for a non-Western economy of the affections.[16]

Contact and Trust

The security predicated by inalienability presupposes certain types of contact and fosters that sense of belonging with others we call bonding. In our society early contact experiences are primarily with individual parent figures, fostering interpersonal bonding. In Samoa an exchange of children within the extended family conveys the idea to children that they belong to everybody who is their relative, rather than specifically to parents. Early relational life confirms this idea: it is a continuous stream of familiar presences. Traditionally, at birth the house was full of people who sat up all night if need be, making the event a party. Everyone, male and female, still plays with and fusses over the newborn, and much personal sentiment flows in his or her direction such that mothers sometimes hold the baby only when it is breastfed or put to sleep at night.[17] As the Samoan child develops, it will constantly touch, groom, or lean up against another member of the family, replicating the time when it was always carried by others.[18]

If grandmothers no longer confiscate babies, they still take a managerial role in early care. Workaday responsibility for care devolves upon older siblings, who are enjoined to "take care of your *tei*," referring to their little charge. *Tei*, however, is simply a word for "younger relative," and any older child can be requisitioned for babysitting if it is proximate. A collectivizing attitude toward early care extends the length of the village such that still in more rural villages

> a child of three can wander safely and . . . be sure of finding food and drink, a sheet to wrap herself up in for a nap, a kind hand to dry casual tears and bind up her wounds. Any small children who are missing when night falls, are simply "sought among their kinsfolk." (Mead [1928] 1961:41–42)

Basking in a continuity of care, Samoans come to trust in and identify with their groups.

Corporate Identity

By *corporate identity* I refer to a tendency to experience oneself as a member of a corporate body, rather than as an individual rigidly bounded by one's own skin. There is a Samoan proverb that alludes to a woman who hid her food rather than sharing it with relatives. When the village discovered her vice they "hacked off one of her fingers, buried it . . . and erected a little mound as a warning to others" (Schultz [1949–50] 1985:54). The village's response could be seen as an assertion that the woman had not correctly assessed the boundaries of her person: her little finger stands for her family, and she loses it because she acted as if her family were not a part of herself. Samoan family members tend to see themselves, figuratively speaking, as organically related. Children may be referred to as a "limb" of the family. Family members are apt to say that they are "as one body," or "one body with one blood."[19] A proverb, for example, tells of two royal brothers, one legitimate, one illegitimate, who courted one high-ranking girl. The illegitimate brother secured her love. The other said, "Since we are brothers, it does not matter whether the lady marries him or me." The proverb is used to allude to relations among persons of the same extended family or village (Schultz [1949–1950], 1985:97–98).

Parents contribute to this sense of continuity with others by minimizing

Children, contact, and caring for a younger sibling, Fagaloa village, Western Samoa, 1988. Photo by Sanele.

Children, contact, and caring for a younger sibling, Fagaloa village Western Samoa 1988. Photo by Sanele.

individual differences. When I taught Samoan Studies classes in American Samoa, the class often did interviews in Samoan villages. One question we repeatedly asked parents was: "What are the differences among your children?" The typical response was: "My children are good; there are no differences among them." Occasionally, an adult would say one child was different, indicating that the youngster was particularly naughty. My students put this question to their informants in Samoan using the Samoan word 'ese. 'Ese signifies any kind of difference, including differences for the better. Nonetheless, informants heard 'ese as signifying a departure from a laudable conformity to collective values. Adults are looked upon in much the same light. When I first arrived in Samoa and spoke only English, a Samoan colleague would jokingly remark, "You are so bad!" In later years she said this to me in Samoan, but the Samoan word she used was not *bad* (*leaga*) but 'ese.

The individuated boundaries thought proper to the self in Western culture are based upon a model of the body as a closed, self-contained unit. In the Western psychiatrist tradition boundary confusion is often associated with a fuzziness about where one's own body stops and that of another's begins, for example, when a mother is overly concerned about her daughter's sexuality (Chodorow 1974). But many societies have a model of the body as porous.[20] This difference does not imply that people anywhere actually fail to perceive where their bodies end and those of others begin, anymore than that people anywhere are unacquainted with the body's porosity, but the features of the body upon which people fasten (separateness or porosity) are tropes for their conception of self and, in circular fashion, validate them. Ontological premises are hegemonic: they are based on beliefs that wear the guise of biology.

Secure Attachment and Dependence

Ainsworth (1973) terms trust "secure attachment." Securely attached infants explore more. In our egocentric society, which valorizes independence, exploration is equated with independence and a lack of exploration with dependence (Lamb 1987). I propose, however, that all cultures cultivate a type of dependency, and that trust actually presumes stable dependencies, dependencies that are supposed to endure throughout life and that can be counted upon. Thus, Scheper-Hughes points out that we assume it is natural for mother love to endure through all forms of disaster and deprivation (1992a). Even when we acknowledge that mothers do not always live up to this assumption, we regard them as lacking if they do not. The absolute reliance we place in our mothers Samoans place in their families.

Once a dean of the small college where I taught in Samoa conceived a dislike for me. I worked on two-year contracts, and one was about to expire. He moved to redefine my position so that I would not qualify for it and would have to leave the college. When my Samoan family found out, they took me, via an appropriately placed family member, directly to the lieutenant governor, who immediately resolved the matter such that the dean's own job was temporarily in jeopardy. I have seldom in my life felt so supported and had never realized I could depend on my family, trust it to take care of me. It was a new experience in not being alone. A cynical student of mine later remarked that they had to do it; otherwise, people would have said, "Has she no family?" Samoan families who do not take care of their own are regarded as severely negligent, just as are mothers who fail to care for their children in our society.

One manner in which dependencies are evinced is by asking things of others. While we will ask our parents for what we need, Samoans beg things from others in their extended families or villages.[21] Robert Louis Stevenson tells us that in the nineteenth century this begging was endemic, such that

> the dictionary teems with evidence of its abuse. Special words signify the begging of food, of uncooked food, of fish, of pigs, of pigs for travelers, of pigs for stock, of taro, of taro-tops, of taro-tops for planting, of tools, of flyhooks, of implements for netting pigeons, and of mats. It is true the beggar was supposed in time to make a return, somewhat as by the Roman contract of mutuum. But the obligation was only moral; . . . as a matter of fact, it was disregarded. The language had recently to borrow from the Tahitians a word for debt. (1892:14)

O'Meara catalogs the many forms of begging that still pervade daily village life: people begging money from those they know have some cash, traveling begging parties, begging for food, and so forth (1990:196–202). Within the immediate family property is often treated as common; begging is regarded as a courtesy that may or may not be observed. The Samoan to whom I was married for many years, Sanele, still laments a large opalescent pearl kept in his mother's chest that one of his younger brothers simply took and gave to a friend. This attitude toward property is particularly pervasive among siblings. Ideally, siblings growing up together ask if they may take one another's clothes or money or other goods, but they far from always do and in any case such requests cannot be refused, especially from older siblings.[22]

Distance and Bounding the Self

Distancing experiences canalize attachment and place boundaries on the self. These experiences, furthermore, play upon an ensemble of relations that might be coded as presence/absence, closeness/distance: the proximity and accessibility of significant others fosters closeness; their relative absence or inaccessibility fosters distance. We will soon see that this ensemble can also be understood as a continuum (between presence and closeness, on the one hand, and absence and distance, on the other) along which there are three relevant dimensions: affect, attention, and communication. In the introduction I suggested that in societies in which the mother provides fairly exclusive care, the child's attention is focused upon her. Her absences tend to make the child acutely conscious of its physical separateness (Freud 1961:13–14; 66–67; see also Lacan 1968) and may be further dramatized by frequent departures and by customs of leaving infants alone generally (LeVine and Miller 1990). Being distant from the one body on whom the infant depends is our trope for individual separateness, one that is embedded in the palpable emotional experiences of the infant. There is, however, a hidden absence in the mother's absence—the absence of the plethora of related others who constantly care for, fraternize with, and, in some cultures, even nurse infants. This second absence, so taken for granted as to be invisible, leaves a lacuna in place of trust in wider social relations.

In Samoa the group is ever present, but around the age of two children begin to be cordoned off from parents and other significant elders.[23] This distancing experience—being socially separated from those to whom one initially felt closest—is their trope for a separation between levels of the social hierarchy. In the coming chapter we will see that, however much they are cared for by others, children form a strong early attachment to parents; therefore, distancing is keenly felt and status differences thereby embedded in the palpable emotional realities of infancy. Within the social distance between parents and children there is another absence, that of an interpersonally engaged other who relates to, recognizes, and communicates with the child as an individual. This absence leaves a lack in the place of trust in others as individuals.

Affective Distancing

Beginning at around six months of age, parents begin transferring care of the child to older siblings. This transfer is more or less complete by weaning, which occurs between the first and second year.[24] At weaning it is common to send the child to relatives in another household or village (Freeman 1983:203). Following weaning, parents suspend most physical and verbal demonstrations of affection.[25] It is not that parents cease to feel emotionally responsive, but to lavish love and care upon a child—*fa'apelepele,* literally "to make dear"—as one might on a favorite pet is believed to be bad for growing children. In American culture the child/pet relationship has long been an early model for interpersonal attachment and is, therefore, regarded as sacred, at least to a degree. In Samoa, too, the child/pet relation illustrates the cultural attitude toward interpersonal attachments. A village pastor recalls the turtle he kept and cared for as a child.

> His father noticed his . . . delight in his possession and used this as the basis for a never-forgotten lesson. One day his father announced that the time had come to kill the turtle and share it with the village by giving it to the council of chiefs for their feast. (Sutter 1980:39–40)

Ironically, personally distancing children, rather than "making dear," is dictated by the Samoan definition of love (*alofa*). The problem is that *alofa* connotes giving service to others, as Samoans do when they love you. For example, the word for "true love" is *alofafaifutu. Futu* is the name of a difficult boat passage in Savai'i; safe passage through it requires the services of the local people (Pratt [1862/1911] 1977:28). Inasmuch as love is demonstrated by service, demonstrativeness implies solicitously serving children. Rendering service, however, is a primary means by which Samoans show respect for a hierarchical superior. Demonstrativeness, therefore, reverses roles within the family hierarchy. Should parents show *alofa*, children might infer they are of higher status than elders and that they can do whatever they like. This confusion about the boundaries of the social hierarchy is the Samoan form of boundary confusion. Because Samoans, like ourselves, see the need to acquaint the child with those boundaries constitutive to their sense of self, they believe that, if one has *alofa* for one's children in the sense of sincerely wanting to aid them, it is necessary to hide one's loving desire to serve and defer.[26]

Attention Distancing

Samoans respond to infantile tears with alacrity and concern, but beginning at around six months of age parents will hesitate to pick up a crying baby. Explaining this reluctance, parents will say that, should they be solicitous, the baby may become *matanana*. In the infant to be *matanana* is to be inclined to plentiful tears, which indicates a child is spoiled, but in reference to an adult *matanana* means "boastful" (Milner 1966:137). This semantic range implies the baby's wailing comes to be regarded in the same light as adult boastfulness. Both are perceived as evincing a desire to call attention to oneself, rather than to take one's place quietly within the group. So strong is this shift in reaction to infantile tears that, especially in rural areas where Samoan culture has been slower to change, weight gain drops significantly after six months of age.[27] This admixture of attitudes toward feeding and attention is no surprise: Berne argues that attention is psychological food (1968).

A distancing scenario around food/attention is repeated in early childhood. Very young children will be allowed to eat beside a parent at meals, but after the age of three or four the child must eat last, with the other children. The child who goes on trying to eat beside parents may be called "fialaui'a." *Fia* is a prefix meaning "to want to" and connotes acting a part. A *laui'a* is a large fish; *fialaui'a* means "You want to be [*fia*] a big fish [*laui'a*], rather than a small fry."

The term *laui'a* evokes legends of cannibalism. In old Samoa young people were sent from tributary villages for the feasts of high chief Malietoa Uilamatutu Faigā, until, in sympathy for two of the victims, his son had himself trussed as a *laui'a* and was presented to his father (Stuebel 1976:66–70). In both the word *laui'a* itself and its history lie a vague, funny, but also threatening innuendo that the child is the stuff of which meals are made. This innuendo might be seen as encouraging children to distance themselves when parent's eat; it is reinforced by parental threats to eat children when they are disobedient such as, "I am almost coming over there to crunch your head." The word for *to crunch* and for a crunching sound is *pa'agugu*. It is used in a range of situations, from the crunching of toast to the noisy mastication of bones by dogs (Milner 1966:171). Alternately, parents use the term *gali*, which means to tear off a piece of food with the teeth, especially when the food is tough and requires special masticatory exertion.

Around the same time that elders no long eat with little ones, they also disaccustom them to attention more generally.[28] In old Samoa everything the infant did was gaily applauded by adults. There were celebrations when the baby first sat up, when it crawled, stood, walked, danced, sang, "and when the child was shameless" (Krämer [1902] 1995:60). The baby's early performances are still met with admiring attention. With the transfer to sibling care, however, elders suspend the applause and become less welcoming (Gardner 1965:154).

Communicating Distancing

A similar progression from solicitousness to distance is evident in language learning. Samoan elders may make sounds that imitate those of their babies, stimulating the baby to repeat its vocalization.[29] But around six months of age Samoans begin to treat the imperfect utterances of toddlers as nonsense and prompt them to imitate the speech patterns of elders. In Euro-American parent/child communication parents focus upon the child, trying to interpret the intention of ambiguous verbal utterances and to answer appropriately; this interactive style teaches the child that they have their own individual viewpoint (Ochs 1982).[30] The Samoan interactive style teaches the child to assume a viewpoint coincident with that of its elders, who represent the group. Around the time when Samoan children begin to become verbally competent, vertical communication within the family age-grade system becomes unidirectional. Parents begin to communicate primarily through orders; question asking is discouraged; often orders are given to children as a group rather than to an individual child.[31]

Grounding a Lexicon

One might see the project of the first stage of enculturation as twofold: (1) to create certain trust experiences that encourage the infant to identify with supportive aspects of a relational environment as a positive basis for a sense of self; (2) to mark the boundaries of the infant's sense of self by providing certain distancing experiences that inevitably create mistrust. Where one mistrusts, one tends to withdraw; therefore, creating mistrust through distancing can help to insure that a culturally selected form of separateness will be maintained. In egocentric societies a close mother/child bond teaches the child to trust interpersonal relations. The absence of a network of people upon whose care the child can depend—along with recurrent absences of the one person upon whom the child does depend (mother)—encourages the development of a premise that people are isolated islands of personhood, individuals who touch one another but may lose touch as well. Just the opposite is true in Samoa: supportive intragroup relations teach the child to trust and identify with the group, coming to see itself in terms of a role played within the group. Increasingly distant parents leave in their wake a lack of trust in interpersonal relations and an awareness of the steady presence of hierarchical boundaries that is as deep-seated as our sense of separation between bodies.

Thus, the Samoan data offer a critique of two Western psychiatric concepts fundamental to the comprehension of early development, boundary confusion and insecure attachment: one culture's boundary confusion is another's capacity for bonding; what one culture considers mistrust in human relations is another's sense of appropriate distance. Rather than Western psychiatric versions of boundary confusion and insecure attachment being intrinsically pathological—cultural mistakes in cultivating children—the Samoan data suggests that cultures cultivate inclusive and exclusive boundaries in a manner that reflects an ontological premise and dims contradicting experience. But in the coming chapter we will see that this diminished experience, remaining like the sand that makes the pearl, is only ineffectively forgotten, intrusively reentering consciousness at the first opportunity. Likewise, the socialization practices that would place the intaglio of an ontological premise upon the self are merely a point of departure and the beginning of an inevitable contest between elders and children.

3

Moral Lexicons: Negatives and Double Negatives

In the last chapter we saw that ontological premises highlight one type of experience and downplay another; by virtue of its exclusion, the neglected aspect of self is seen as intrinsically at odds with social order and is associated with passionate behavior. This neglected aspect, therefore, becomes a focus of social anxiety and cannot be ignored, thereby challenging the descriptive completeness of the ontological premise. In the face of this challenge, ontological premises about what people *are* like become moral premises about what they *should* be like. The Samoan ontological premise that people are role players becomes a moral premise that they should "stand at their post," that is, play a role that conforms to their status and rank within the group. For simplicity's sake, hereafter I will refer to the morally idealized version of an ontological premise simply as the "idealized premise."

By what vehicle does one make this transit from tacit assumptions about the nature of people to moral precepts about their behavior? One answer is the image. From the psychoanalytic perspective the earliest form of conscience consists in images of idealized parent figures (Freud 1923; Lacan 1968, 1977). These idealized images also consist in cultural archetypes who display the idealized premise. In Samoa the idealization of the notion that people are role players, standing at their post, is represented by the high chief (*ali'i*) and by the noble style of role playing he embodies.

Figures representing the idealized premise can be segmented into attributes—internal attributes in the case of more egocentric cultures, performative attributes in more sociocentric ones—which in cultural imaginings evoke these figures. In Samoa the high chief is *fa'atamāli'i*: *fa'a* meaning "to act in the way of," *tamāli'i* meaning "those of chiefly lineage." Chiefly action Samoan style can be broken down into three aspects: acting with dignity (*mamalu*), with loving generosity and compassion (*alofa*), and, above all, with respect (*fa'aaloalo*).

There is, however, a problem with acting in line with attributes that actualize the idealized premise: the excluded element of self resists compliance and fosters contradicting tendencies. In response people segment this resistance into a second set of attributes that hinder acting in line with the idealized premise and that are understood as vices. In Samoa the personal self, or *loto*, gets in the way of idealized role playing. Samoans, therefore, articulate a set of interfering vices built on the base *loto* that stand in the way of chiefly acting: emotionalism (*lotovaivai*) can wreak havoc with a dignified demeanor, personalistic animus (*lotoleaga*) interferes with loving generosity, and egotistical pride (*lotofaʻamaualuga*) with respecting others.

Moral lexicons, however, not only condemn tendencies that gainsay the idealized premise but also laud a compensatory set of virtues. These virtues are tantamount to the elision of the excluded element of self; this is not the innocent elision predicated by an ontological premise but an active moral elision of contradictory experience. Thus, Samoans also articulate a set of compensatory virtues that denote a recantation of the inner self: emotionalism is curtailed through personal restraint (*lototele*), animus by personal effacement (*lotomamā*), and egotistical pride through personal abasement (*lotofaʻamaualalo*).

For added clarity let me reiterate this logical transit (from an ontological premise to an idealized premise, personified by larger-than-life figures, and then to moral lexicons) with an example from American cinematic mythology. In America our ontological premise specifies that people are egos; everyman is an island. The figure of the lonely cowboy hero, Clint Eastwood for example, makes this ontological premise a moral one by standing alone, indeed often standing against everyone else, which represents standing for his personal beliefs or principles and which moralizes the stance of the ego (idealized premise). Idealized individualists, however, inevitably summon up others who represent a failure to honor individualism: (1) outlaws who violate the rights of other individuals; (2) the average citizens and inept lawmen of the western towns through which Eastwood rides who are all too often "yes men," accepting the status quo (interfering vices). Given these human tendencies, it is judged a particular virtue to "stand on one's own two feet," resisting social pressure in the forms of money, position, or brute force (compensatory virtue), as the townspeople learn to do under the influence of the cowboy hero and sometimes continue to do so after he rides off into the sunset.

According to this model, there are two layers to moral lexicons: the first consists of attributes of those figures who represent the idealized premise; the second layer consists of interfering vices and compensatory virtues, and shifts focus to the formerly obscure element of self. The tonality of this second focus is negative: both interfering vices and compensatory virtues convey that this obscure element of self should not exist. Let us, then, explore these lexical layers in Samoa, beginning with an aspect of chiefly action and then delineating an associated pair of dispositions, one that interferes with the realization of this ideal and one that compensates for interference.[1]

Dignity (Mamalu)

For Samoans to behave with dignity is to be the very image of respect. Figuratively speaking, that image is straight: a dignified bearing is called *sa'o*, "straight." Because a straight bearing is the signature of honor and status in Samoa, a common term for dignitaries is *sa'o*. The head of the extended family is the *sa'o* of the family. The principle chief of the village is the *sa'o* of the village, and so too the village princess. The term *sa'o* also applies to talk that is straight in the sense of being direct and true. So "Sa'o lelei lava" (Properly straight!) means "How true!" Straight comportment is also equated with a poise that is unruffled by personal reactions to interference and difficulty in the performance of social roles. When the village princess performs the final and most dignified dance in entertainments, her dance is a *sa'o*. Others may clown wildly around her, but if the girl is a good dancer she does not react. Her posture remains erect, her movements even, and her poise unaffected. The problem with this ideal is that Samoans are apt to be carried away by inner feelings that are at odds with dignified poise and antithetical to playing a part.

Emotionalism (*Lotovaivai*)

When loved persons depart upon or return from a journey, reactions tend to be extreme. When the missionary Powell returned to Samoa after a lengthy absence, his parishioners wept so copiously they were "unable to utter a single word" (Freeman 1983:214). At funerals too, the missionary Turner recorded, "the most frantic expressions of grief, such as rending garments, thumping the face and eyes, burning the body with small piercing firebrands, beating the head with stones till the blood runs" ([1861] 1986:133), a description to which Pritchard added further details, such as the tearing out of hair "by handfuls" (1866:148). Today in airports Samoans often sob at the departure of a relative, piling innumerable garlands around the wayfarer's neck and foisting money upon him or her. At funerals Samoans—particularly women—still behave with considerable abandon, kissing the corpse, throwing themselves upon it or collapsing beside it, so that they must be dragged away. Such feeling is believed to be dangerous: it can literally stop the heart from beating.

For Westerners, inner feelings are a testament to authenticity, and, under appropriate circumstances, their public expression shows that the individual can be trusted. Thus, in Camus's novel *The Stranger* the protagonist is sentenced to death for an ambiguous homicide because he shows no feeling at his mother's funeral. Lacking this testament, his actions are distrusted and misinterpreted. In Samoa such feeling, while acknowledged to be human, is imagined as a dangerous emotionalism that evinces moral weakness.

Personal Restraint (*Lototele*)

The paragon of Samoan virtue, on the other hand, is *not* overcome by the exigencies of inner sentiments, retaining always a calm demeanor and encouraging others to do the same. Sanele, for example, had to tell his mother something he knew would make her unhappy: one of her unmarried daughters was pregnant. Sanele and his mother were very close. She cried. Instead of holding her, he sat quietly. I asked Sanele why. He said that he was waiting for her to regain her composure. To have held her, he explained, would only have made her cry more, rather than making her strong. *Tele* means strong.

Love (*Alofa*)

If Samoans disapprove of the display of personal sentiments, this does not mean that they disapprove of expressing sentiment generally. *Talofa,* meaning "We have love [for you]," is the Samoan "hello." The base word here is *alofa*, a loving generosity and compassion. The plural construction of this conventional greeting ("we") indicates, however, that *alofa* is an ideal form of sociality, rather than an individual feeling. Remember that Samoans express love through service (*tautua*.) *Tautua* is the rendering of goods and services to a hierarchical superior, but Samoans gloss the word as "to serve," using this English term as an inclusive category. When someone has *alofa* for you they serve you food, they make a shelter for you, they help you with your work, and they would be aggrieved to go against any of your wishes.

Personal Animus (*Lotoleaga*)

While Samoans believe that it is noble to be hospitable and generous, they also believe that the *loto*—in the form of animus (*lotoleaga*)—inspires a competitiveness at odds with this ideal. Most generally, *lotoleaga* refers to the desire to insult or injure another, either openly or more commonly through gossip. Samoans who are bilingual tend to gloss *lotoleaga* as "jealousy." By jealousy they mean envy, albeit envy in which the envied possession may be a desired person.[2]

Lotoleaga, however, does not index feelings we would consider jealous or envious or possessive per se; it refers only to personalistic sentiments that counterpose proper role playing. Sanele gave the following example. Let us say a wife insults her husband's mistress. This is not *lotoleaga* because the wife's actions are congruent with her social role as a wife and are, therefore, judged not to be personal. On the other hand, let us say that there are two young women, Tuli and Ita, interested in one handsome man. Tuli has long hair, a mark of particular beauty in Samoan culture, and she is preferred by the man. Ita has two sisters, who pursue Tuli and cut off her hair. While such action might be proper for a wife and her sisters, Ita's actions would be construed as *lotoleaga* because the bachelor does not belong to her: her possessive behavior goes beyond the bounds of her social role, betraying feelings that are entirely personal. We would consider both the wife's actions and Ita's as jealous, but for Samoans only Ita's are *lotoleaga*.

Personal Effacingness (*Lotomamā*)

Exemplars of Samoan virtue do *not* feel animus toward others, because they efface all personal concerns (*lotomamā*). One woman gave the following example. A girl is courted and later rejected by a boy. She sees him with another but does not take this event to heart and remains friendly to all parties. Another source of animus in Samoa is a lack of adequate reciprocation. Thus, at ceremonial exchanges participants keep careful track of who has given what to whom and respond to participants accordingly. But those who are *lotomamā* have *no* thought for themselves and, failing to worry about a return, "give with all their heart." They are people who do the impossible, in Derrida's sense of the term (1994), giving gifts in which both gift and giver are erased, along with the personal side of the self.

Respect (*Fa'aaloalo*)

The Samoan communal order is hierarchical; therefore, among Samoans respect is for status rather than personal in nature. Nonetheless, Samoans believe one should give respect for status to all people whether they actually have it or not. It is for this reason that they often address one another as "Lord this" and "Lady that." Love (*alofa*) and respect (*fa'aaloalo*) might seem to entail the same actions, but in *alofa* such actions are a gift, while in *fa'aaloalo* they are just acknowledgment of another's status. In fact, the Samoan version of respect implies a bountiful generosity rather than mere justice, albeit in attributing status to others. The *loto*, however, in the form of egotistical pride or arrogance (*lotofa'amaualuga*) stands in the way of such courtesy.

Egotistical Pride (*Lotofa'amaualuga*)

Fijians, Cook Islanders, Tongans, Rotumans, and other Pacific Island neighbors are wont to complain that "Samoans have too much pride." They mean that Samoans arrogantly challenge others' status. Literally, *lotofa'amaualuga* is "to raise the personal self above others." Height is the Samoan trope for status, and people's *loto* drives them to elevate their own.

Because status is acknowledged by service, challenges to status often consist of a failure to serve. Within the American Samoan and Western Samoan governments, for example, a bureaucrat processing forms, or a secretary or janitor, may more or less neglect to serve patrons, unless encouraged by someone of high rank. Here again the Samoan concept of egotistical pride includes only behavior that is incongruent with one's public role, revealing its personalistic source. Because it is the bureaucrat's role to process forms, the janitor's to clean and so forth, a failure to perform these roles betrays private feelings. On the other hand, for a parent to be imperious with a child is not arrogant, nor is it arrogant for a chief to act forcefully with a commoner. Should the parent's imperiousness or the chief's forcefulness be abnormally overbearing, however, these reactions may be judged to be arrogant; carrying a behavior that is, in principle, congruent with one's role to extremes also intimates personal sentiment.

Personal Abasement (*Lotofa'amaualalo*)

Literally, *lotofa'amaualalo* means to lower the personal self beneath others. If Samoans have a regional reputation for arrogance, paragons of virtue among them assume a lower place than is rightfully theirs. While chiefs will use respectful address when referring to others, implicitly giving them status, they use common language when referring to themselves. One Samoan woman who headed a government agency regularly took out her own trash. The janitor, an old lady who had her own desk in the office, rested a lot, and the agency head did not want to offend the janitor's dignity by beleaguering her with repeated entreaties about such a menial task.

Moral Lexicons

Once again, my theory suggests that moral lexicons are composed of a unitary image that valorizes the ontological premise, coded lexically as a set of ideal attributes, and a lexical pair of vices and virtues that descends from each of these ideal attributes. In this descendant pair, vices are negatives of the idealized image. There is, furthermore, a tendency to judge these interfering attributes to be innately passionate and disproportionate. We, who cultivate the subjective self, might think that private feeling, in moderation, can lend a luster to dignity or that personal pride, again in moderation, can add piquancy to gestures of respect. In the Samoan view subjectivity is the source of what is hysterical, mean, and arrogant; it is precisely that aspect of personhood erased in people of real character. If, in the secondary layer of moral lexicons, vices are negatives of the idealized premise, virtues are double negatives: they represent the absence or abrogation of those vices and, with them, the interfering element of self.

In the ontological premise an element of self is shadowed; in the idealized premise this element is still obscure; however, once one begins to speak of vices as well as virtues, one is speaking about the excluded element of self. A relative lack of terms for qualifying and making subtle distinctions about the nature of this experience in the ontological lexicon, therefore, is replaced in moral lexicons by a plethora of terms related to this experience. There is, for example, a poverty of Samoan terms to characterize the varieties of personal experience, but Samoan language abounds with *loto* terms that class the inner disposition of the subject—also referred to as *loto*—as reprehensible or laudable: dispositions may be kind (*lotolelei*) or obstinate (*lotoma'a'a*) or proud (*lotomitamita*) or polite (*lotoali'i*), and so forth, ad infinitum. So extensive is the terminology for moral and immoral dispositions—all classed as orientations of the *loto*—that Samoan/English dictionaries do not try to enumerate them all, giving only common examples of such constructions. This excess—like those of obsessive-compulsive behavior that often entail tendencies to overcategorization—might be seen as indexical of widespread anxiety about the formerly unacknowledged aspect of self.

Reproducing Moral Lexicons

We have traced a logical evolution of moral categories; however, children are often not so logical. How, then, are they led to subscribe to moral versions of self systems? The answer, I argue, is through culturally crafted versions of pride and shame.

Pride

By *pride* I mean a culturally elaborated form of primary narcissism. Early trust experiences are introjected by the child as a feeling that the self is lovable, and this feeling is primary narcissism (Erikson 1963). We saw in the preceding chapter that early relational experience is arranged to convey and validate an ontological premise. It follows that early trust experiences are structured by this premise and direct the initial focus of self-love. Further, in narcissism we love who we think we are, and who we think we are is shaped by our culture's ontological premise.

Because primary narcissism is derived from trust experiences, it brings with it a sense of the self as trustworthy—that is, a sense of goodness (Erikson 1963). By giving positive recognition to behaviors that express a highlighted aspect of self—in the form of praise or thanks or simply by playing the role of an audience and attending to certain intentions or attitudes—elders build upon this sense of goodness to create pride in the self, however the self is culturally defined. Thus, pride expands the form of narcissism instilled through contact experiences. Samoan children are recognized for playing a role that expresses identification with the group, which means acting as a "limb" of the group through service. Remember that as soon as Samoan children can walk elders begin training them to perform small services for others and that toddlers receive attention and even thanks for these little performances. In the coming chapter we will see that as Samoan children develop service comes to mean taking considerable responsibilities within the group, both of a practical and an administrative nature.

Shame

By *shame* I simply refer to feelings of inhibition: like shame in the broadest possible sense of the word, inhibitions are anchored in anxiety about the responses of others to the self. I see inhibition as a culturally elaborated form of insecure attachment. The preceding chapter argued that early distancing experiences stimulate insecure attachment in targeted forms of relationship. Studies show that insecurely attached infants tend to be either resistant or avoidant in their relationships with mothers (Lamb 1987). Resistant children mix contact seeking with angry or rejecting behavior. Avoidant children ignore mothers rather than seeking contact. Thus, insecure attachment decreases positive involvement in the first case and all involvement in the second; the second type might be regarded as a more extreme form of the first.

In experimental studies of American infants and children, it is unclear if insecure attachment has similar long-term effects, compromising the individual's readiness and availability for interpersonal attachment in adulthood (Lamb 1987). Existent studies are focused on insecure attachment in interpersonal relations. This form of insecurity is not supported in Western cultures and is, therefore, probably mitigated by later cultural experiences: even if particular infants and children are not given the interpersonal experience they need with mothers to form strong interpersonal attachments, these experiences are likely to be supplied by others later in life as well as being broadly supported and encouraged. The Samoan data suggests, however, that insecure attachment lays a basis for resistance/avoidance in later relations. I propose that when the insecure attachment experienced by the child is culturally patterned—that is, when (1) a certain form of insecure attachment is the rule rather than the exception in early childhood, and (2) that form of attachment is not later supported and encouraged, then (3) insecure attachment first inspires resistant behavior, which negative sanctioning converts to avoidant behavior that endures in adulthood.

Let me lay out this scenario somewhat more fully. I argued in the introduction, and we will see in this chapter, that children resist parental distancing. In very young children resistance is usually tolerated, but as the child develops elders usually respond with negative sanctions. Negative sanctions tend to deepen the insecurity initially fostered by distancing and result in avoidance in that type of relationship targeted by culturally prescribed distancing. Inhibition can be seen as a culturally stylized form of avoidance: a child who is inhibited in certain kinds of relations is either withdrawn or avoidant in these relations, withdrawal and avoidance being different versions of the same reaction. The Balinese offer an example. According to Mead (1942), Balinese children are constantly teased by elders. They become shy but also come to skirt groups of elders who tease them.

If inhibitions are cultivated through negative sanctions, different sanctions encourage different inhibitions in the child. Probably the three negative sanctions that people most commonly employ with children are scaring, teasing, and punishment, although in any particular culture one, possibly even two, of these sanctions may be deleted. While primary narcissism is given an initial form by an early relational environment that highlights either the social or the personal self, primary narcissism is a diffuse emotion that probably tends to contaminate backgrounded aspects of self as well. Negative sanctions further focus primary narcissism by undermining narcissistic feelings about the unwanted aspect of self.

Scaring threatens children with imagined harm, often carried out by a third party—for example, a bogeyman. The dangers summoned up by scaring practices tend to be either vague or ultimate, such that it is difficult for the child to address them with normal coping skills. Frequent scaring makes children phobic, undermining the comfortable feeling of trust that derives from early contact experiences. Phobia is likely to play upon and intensify that form of insecure attachment cultivated by early relations.

Teasing checks an unwanted behavior by making children feel foolish about it. Teasing conveys that some aspect of the child is worthy of derision rather than acceptance, undermining the feeling that the self is acceptable, which is early narcissism. We will see that teasing focuses on that aspect of self downplayed in the culture's ontological premise and censured in the moral lexicon. When children are made to feel embarrassed, they want to hide, specifically to hide the exposed portion of the self that is the source of derision. What begins by hiding an aspect of the self from others may end by hiding it from oneself. Thus, teasing inspires shyness and a tendency to dissociate the culturally excluded aspect of self.

In contrast to scaring and teasing, punishment involves real pain inflicted by an authority figure. Punishment tends to focus on either the child's attitude or intent, attitude being the social frame in which a deed is carried out and intent being the subjective frame. Thus, in Samoa a disrespectful attitude is always reprehensible, no matter how trivial the action through which it is communicated, just as for us malicious intent is the gauge of a crime's seriousness. Unlike other negative sanctions, punishment seems to focus on the highlighted aspect of self. Actually, it focuses on the recrudescence of the excluded element within the highlighted domain of experience. In Samoa punishment is aimed against personal willfulness, which appears socially in cheeky attitudes. In our own culture punishment is aimed against desires to violate the rights of others—to ignore the proper boundaries between individuals in theft, for example—which appears internally as motive. Punishment conveys the message that the child's volitions are not necessarily laudable, and this message undermines the sense of goodness that accompanies early narcissism. As a result of frequent punishments, children become passive and allow themselves to be directed and controlled by others.

Inhibition denotes contradictory tendencies in character—namely, a desire to act and an anxiety about doing so. These contradictory tendencies correspond to binary moral taxonomies of "vice" and "virtue" and provide a ground for the second layer of the moral lexicon. We will see that resistance to distancing routines resembles those aberrations from the morally idealized versions of the ontological premise that are culturally defined as vice; inhibitions resemble compensatory virtues.

Exploring these ideas through the Samoan example, I link a form of distancing explored in the preceding chapter to a pattern of childhood resistances, amended by a specific sanction. In truth the application of sanctions is general, and any untoward behavior may call forth any sanction or none at all, depending upon circumstances. The grouping here is logical rather than practical. It is logical in the sense that specific negative sanctions can be seen as reinforcing avoidances initially stimulated by certain distancing routines. My effort here is to distinguish strands of process that are in reality interlaced.

Resisting Affective Distancing and Scaring

We saw that around six months of age Samoan elders begin transferring the infant's care to its older siblings and suspend expressions of affection. Children, however, are apt to be disconsolate when parents, particularly mothers, withdraw. Freeman (1983:203) documents a case of a thirteen-month-old infant taken to his maternal grandmother in another village for the purpose of weaning who became so severely depressed he had to be returned to his mother. After that "he would cry whenever his mother made to leave him." Gerber says "One of the most frequent sights in a Samoan village is a child having a tantrum when his mother gets on the bus to go to town, even when his usual caretaker is standing right beside him" (1975:107). Tantrums constitute struggles on the part of the child to maintain contact with the parent.

> One time a usually indulgent mother wanted to do some work in the *matai*'s [family chief] house. Her young son came to the house when he saw her there. She picked up the broom [threatening to beat him] and he cried but lingered at the outside of the house. The woman called her five year old daughter to take him back to the house. The girl tried to lift him but was unable to do so because he hit her and then sat down, but finally she half carried and half dragged him to the house. He cried for more than half an hour until he fell asleep. (154)

Sanctioning

Resistance to emotional distancing is amended by scaring practices. Scaring is begun early and not necessarily tied to objectionable behavior. Rather, it is employed randomly to create a model situation in which a message about the display of inner feeling is conveyed: this display is ineffective in provoking any rapprochement with elders.[3] In Samoa objects that frighten the infant, perhaps a small animal or doll, may be used to beleaguer the child or to surprise him or her. This routine is likely to produce a tantrum and may be prolonged until it does, much to the amusement of family members.[4]

As the child becomes ambulatory, scaring is used more directly to produce cooperation. Should the child begin to wander out of prescribed bounds within the house, the adult may shout, "Death comes now," or tell tales of ogres and kidnapping spirits, stories that often take the form of village-specific legends.[5] In Afono village, American Samoa, for example, two little girls, Salote and Malie, are rumored to have been "taken" by spirits, and there is a song villagers and others sing about their disappearance.[6] Probably the fear provoked by scaring scenarios plays upon and deepens the insecurity predicated by emotional distancing in early childhood. The result is that resistant behaviors—tantrums, for example—are likely to be replaced by inhibition, that is, by behavior that eschews interpersonal involvements with others, not only in parent-children relationships but in later relations as well.

Inhibition

Mead observes that in Samoa "excessive emotion, violent preferences, strong allegiance are disallowed. The Samoan preference is for ... a moderate amount of feeling. ... Those who care greatly are always said to care without cause" ([1928] 1961:128). This bias against intense interpersonal affect is also reflected in the behavior and the locutions surrounding emotion-laden relationships. In old Samoa open affection between husbands and wives was considered unseemly. They never touched in public, and the wife always walked a few paces behind her husband. The English phrase *in love* has no real Samoan translation. When my husband was growing up in Samoa, cheeky boys, boasting of their sexual prowess, would say, "Watch it or you will speak English," meaning "I'll make you say you love me." Nonetheless, inhibition never wholly replaces resistance. Emotional distancing is likely to make a child feel interpersonally abandoned. Remember, Samoans are apt to become emotional about departures and funerals. Departures and funerals likewise excite a fear of abandonment by a particular individual. Thus, emotionalism survives as an occasional protest against interpersonal withdrawal and as a trace of the feelings experienced in the face of it.

Scaring and Moral Categories

In Samoa the withdrawal of parental care initially provokes resistant behavior in the form of emotional display through tantrums. Samoans curtail this display by scaring practices likely to intensify insecure attachment. By doing so, they convert resistant behavior into inhibition about expressing personal sentiment. This "avoidant" behavior is culturally supported. Rather than being defined as a liability, it is characterized as virtue: to restrain the expression of inner feelings is to be strong and brave (*lototele*). The withdrawal of affection and scaring could, then, be said to inspire contradictory traits: on the one hand, an emotionalism that survives as an occasional protest against parents' interpersonal withdrawal; on the other, interpersonal inhibition that is lauded as an ability to restrain oneself. These two traits together are coincident with Samoan moral categories for the management (and mismanagement) of private feeling.

Resisting Attention Distancing and Teasing

We saw that Samoan parents gradually cease to pay attention to individual children and that this distancing is played out around food. While very little children eat besides their parents, older children eat last and may be called "Want-to-Be-a-Big-Fish" if they demure. In Samoa "to want to be" (*fia*) suggests egotistical pretense—showing off in a manner calculated to capture (or in the child's case recapture) an audience. There are many *fia* terms that suggest children do what they can to attract individual attention. Children are said to: *fiapoto*, "want to be smart"; *fiasili*, "want to be the best"; *fiafaʻalialia*—the meaning of which is clear in its modern and semi-English equivalent *fiasiō* (pronounced *fia show*), "want to make a show"; or they may be dubbed *fiapalagi*, meaning "to want to be a Western European"; and so forth.

This unsatiated desire for individual attention also tends to take the form of envy. Envy may be seen as a desire for attention expressed in the negative, as ill will against anyone who attains it. Youngsters are often jealous of their parents' regard, as is evident in their penchant for telling parents about one another's misbehavior (Gerber 1975:169, 244). Tale bearing is meant to diminish the parents' regard for the other child. The envy of siblings whose parents openly favor one child is proverbial. Schultz ([1949–50] 1985:94–95), for example, recounts a fable in which a couple have ten grown sons and one boy whom they favor, reserving their fine mats—the indigenous equivalent of wealth—for him. The ten throw their brother into the sea.

Sanctioning

One method Samoans employ to check the rampant desire for attention is teasing. Teasing gives the child attention in an unpalatable form. While early trust experiences represent a positive form of attention that indicates acceptance, by suggesting that certain parts of the self are worthy of derision, teasing teaches the child that attention may not be desirable. Like scaring, teasing is applied broadly and not necessarily tied to objectionable action; it is simply a playful style of relating with children. Nonetheless, it is focused on a certain aspect of the self, that aspect excluded in the ontological premise. In Samoa teasing focuses on personal things.

Elders often *faipona* children. *Faipona* is composed of the words, *fai* and *pona*. *Fai* glosses as "to make" or "to do." *Pona* refers to nodes found on an otherwise smooth surface. *Faipona* means "to point out what is not smooth," either aesthetically or socially, and to make a joke of it.[7] *Faipona* is directed either at personal shortcomings and deformities or at the private side of experience. It may consist simply in making up a funny or obscene name for someone. Thus, one adopted girl, whose mother came from rural Savai'i, was often called "Savai'i" by her new mother, meaning she was a hick. Another girl's grandmother would call her Pipi. *Pipi*—literally, "the lips of a small clam"—is a euphemism for female genitals.[8]

Inhibition

Teasing converts resistance (in the form of showing off or envy) into avoidance. Samoan children develop an inclination toward embarrassment (*mā*). The child who is *mā* resolutely conceals inner thoughts and feelings. This habit of hiding an aspect of the self from others leads to hiding it from oneself: Samoans are generally indefinite about their own interior life and forswear the possibility of fathoming anyone else's. They are apt to remark "with the full force of self-evident conventional wisdom," says Gerber; "We cannot know what is in another person's depth" (1985:133). In Samoa another person's "depth" is their *loto*. *Loto* is derived from the word *loloto*. *Loloto* is the word used for depths in general and in particular for the depths of the sea; a *loto* is a small deep, such as one finds in a river, a lagoon, or a person. What one cannot fathom in oneself cannot be shared with another. Both inabilities imply degrees of dissociation.

Moral Categories and Teasing

In Samoa the withdrawal of parental attention produces resistant behavior in the positive form of showing off and in the negative form of envy. Samoans curtail the desire for individual attention through teasing. By teaching children attention may be painful, Samoan teasing converts resistant behavior into inhibition: children come to hide their personal side. By making children inhibited about drawing attention to themselves, teasing prepares them to be personally effacing. The withdrawal of attention and teasing together could be said to stimulate contrary traits in character coincident with the Samoan moral lexicon concerning social regard.

Resisting Communicative Distancing and Punishment

We saw that by the time the child can talk Samoans withdraw from two-directional communication with children, addressing them mainly in the imperative form. Youngsters resist this withdrawal through *musu*. Most simply *musu* means "to refuse," either verbally or through noncompliance, but *musu* also refers to a passive-resistant attitude conveyed by social performances—from grimacing to stomping the feet—through which a person asserts his or her opinion in the negative.[9] During a meal, for example, young people wait in the back of the house to be available to serve elders in the front.

> They will talk together, play guitars and sing quietly, the girls may comb each other's hair. When a call comes from the front room, all this pleasant interaction ceases; the look of annoyance can be plainly read on all faces. Typically, the girls will arise clumsily with an exaggerated show of exhaustion, and sometimes they will whisper "Alas." Genuine anger may flash briefly as the servitors grimace and quietly mimic the words of the command. (Gerber 1975:67)

Musu is a reaction against being dominated and is, therefore, especially common during childhood and adolescence, when people are at the bottom of the age-grade hierarchy (Freeman 1983:219). Mead associates it with an arbitrary character in action, describing a girl who travels several miles to go on a picnic and then returns home immediately merely because she is "*musu* to the party" ([1928] 1961:124; see also Gerber 1975:231). Whimsicality is characteristic of *musu* but also expresses resistance to domination: behavior that may seem pointlessly mercurial makes the point that no one has sufficient status to exert authority; therefore, no justifications are necessary.

Sanctioning

Samoans counter resistance to respect relations with punishment.[10] If a parental order is not promptly attended to, it is followed by a threat. If the threat does not produce obedience, the child is liable to be struck.[11] Should the beaten child cry, his or her tears are treated as a reprehensible complaint against legitimate authority, and the beating will continue in earnest. Rather than reacting to the beating, children must demonstrate deference through a gestural articulation of their inferior status: sitting down, suppressing their emotions, and bowing their heads. If a child does so, blows are likely to be softened. Gradually, this lowering routine becomes an automatic gestural response to parental displeasure.

Inhibition

Punishment converts passive resistance into a more absolute passivity, which is tantamount to the suppression of the subjective self. The punished child's passivity reflects a psychological posture that endures. The psychological tests Holmes administered to Samoans in 1962 and in 1974 showed pronounced tendencies toward deference (1987:132–33). Samoans show deference in many situations in which we would think defiance more likely. For example, C. C. Marsack, former chief justice of Western Samoa, cites a case in which a murderer announces he should die because "the Chief Judge says that I should be hanged, and whatever the Chief Judge says should be obeyed" (1961:23, qtd. in Holmes 1987:165). This murderer mimics the attitude toward punishment in which the Samoan child is schooled.

Punishment and Moral Categories

In Samoa the withdrawal of two-directional communication between elders and youngsters initially provokes resistant behavior in the form of a willful refusal to service (*musu*). Remember that the pridefulness through which Samoans presume to be above their station (*lotofa'amaualuga*) is often expressed as a failure to serve. Thus, *musu* can be looked upon as a precursor of *lotofa'amaualuga*. In childhood, resistance to the demand for service is corrected by punishment. Punishment teaches children that the results of willfulness are painful and thereby transforms resistance into inhibition. Children come to avoid asserting their own desires in relations with elders and to affect a physical and psychological deference before authority. By making children feel inhibited about asserting themselves, punishment prepares them to be personally abasing (*lotofa'amaualalo*). Communicative withdrawal and punishment together could be said to emphasize traits in character that correspond to vices and virtues that Samoans associate with status relations.

Key Negative Sanctions

When several negative sanctions are employed one may be emphasized beyond the others. In Samoa punishment is the most emphasized sanction, but why?[12] Punishment is aimed at producing submission, playing upon the dominance/submission motif. This motif implies hierarchy. The character of groups in Samoa is hierarchical; that is why respect for status is the paramount virtue. While we considered three aspects of noble action, only one of which was respect, the other two relate back to respect: to be dignified is to embody respect; love, Samoan style, is expressed through the same gesture (service) as is respect.

Samoan teasing and scaring are carried out in a manner that is supportive to the dominance/submission motif implicit in punishment. Like punishment, Samoan scaring practices are often used to coerce service. When my youngest sister-in-law, who I will call Sina, was little and ignored her mother's (Vao) orders, Vao would say, "We are going to the *palagi* [Caucasian] doctor." Sina was afraid of the doctor, and this remark got her to do what Vao wanted. The manner in which Samoan elders administer teasing to children also underlines a message about relative status: *faipona* are put-downs, and, while elders can *faipona* children, the privilege is not reciprocal.

Interestingly, the body language through which the child is supposed to respond to punishment subsumes the three inhibitions inspired by negative sanctions: not only is this posture the very image of passivity; suppressing emotions demonstrates personal restraint; bowing the head obscures the face, enacting personal effacement. Similarly, the prescribed response to punishment in Samoa conflates those inhibitions resulting from scaring and teasing. First, during punishment the child is supposed to sit still. A tendency toward stillness (specifically the slowing of the heart) is ascribed to those who are afraid (Gerber 1975:251). Fear is affected by scaring practices. Second, the punished child is supposed to be silent, politely cloaking any feeling he or she may have about this treatment; however, a tendency to cloak the personal side of the self is also the effect of teasing. We saw that teasing encourages the child to be *mā*. Another important Samoan term for embarrassment is *matamuli*, meaning "eyes behind." Children who are *matamuli* or *mā* tend to lower their eyes and bow their heads; this body language resembles that of the punished child: when punished, children must lower their eyes and bow their heads.

Cross-Cultural Consciences

I posit two layers of conscience. Similarly, Freudians posit the existence of two evaluating agencies: the ego ideal and the superego. In psychoanalytic psychology (Freud 1923; Lacan 1977) the ego ideal, consisting of the internalized parents mentioned at this chapter's opening, is unitary in nature and positive in tone. As I do not see the ego as the universal basis of selfhood, the term *ego ideal* is awkward. Nonetheless, I agree that the initial form of conscience consists in positively toned unitary images, albeit images idealizing an ontological premise. The superego reproaches people and harasses them with guilt; it is rule bound, the rules being that one should *not* do what is defined as vice. Like the second form of conscience described in this chapter, the superego is negative in tone and is language-like: it consists in binary categories, being preoccupied with vice as well as virtue (Lacan 1977).

Piers and Singer (1953) argue that guilt is a tension between the ego and the superego, deriving from violations of the superego's rules; shame is a tension between the ego and the ego ideal, deriving from comparisons of the self to the ideal. An earlier generation of anthropologists typically distinguished between sociocentric "shame cultures" and egocentric "guilt cultures."[13] I argue that the logical unfolding of self systems cross-culturally involves a movement from a type of conscience consisting in idealized images to another that besets the self with notions of wrong and right, regardless of whether the culture is sociocentric or egocentric.

Remember that to perpetuate a lexicon one needs only provide experiences that resonate with its constitutive lexemes; however, binary categories of right and wrong exist by virtue of structural differences. To perpetuate binary categories, therefore, one must create experientially familiar sets of differences. The familiarity with differences requisite to the development of the superego type conscience is provided as follows: (1) parents use a distancing routine that inspires a form of insecure attachment; (2) insecure attachment acquaints the child with the culturally defined boundaries of self by dimming experiences of a culturally shadowed part of the self; (3) children resist this routine; (4) this resistance is answered by a negative sanction; (5) the sanction is gradually internalized as an inhibition; (6) the initial resistance, plus the inhibition, represent a dichotomy in character parallel to the culture's binary moral categories and supplies an internalized referent for them. Different sanctions, and probably different styles of employing the same sanction, allow for a range of culturally shaded resistances and inhibitions and, with them, different cultural lexicons of vice and virtue.

4

Moral Discourse: Classification or Narration

Glancing back to the last chapter, one might say that the idealized premise and the moral lexicons that descend from it lead to a recognition that people are just as likely to misbehave as they are to conform to cultural conceptions of the moral: otherwise, why would one need a lexicon of vices? We saw that Samoans preach that one should be humble (*lotofaʻamaualuga*) and free of ill will toward all (*lotomamā*). In fact, Samoan villages are often beset by a poisonous rivalry between their two most prominent extended families (*ʻāiga*). In Sanele's village this rivalry is so volatile that it is the only subject about which he asked me not to write.[1] In Albert Wendt's *Leaves of the Banyan Tree* women of two rival families engage in "an evil, Satan-inspired brawl." The village pastor, Filipo—embodying the ideals and sentiments of the Samoan moral universe—rushes to the scene. Rather than amending the situation, however, Filipo only seems to spotlight the behaviors that Samoans most condemn.

> "It's Filipo!" someone called. . . . "You fatherless whore!" He heard the words clearly, precisely, above the general roar. . . . "Your father was born in a shit-house!" Filipo stopped. The spectators watched him. "Here, see this, you pig," screamed one Amazon, baring her backside, "it's as fresh as the day you were born!" . . . Filipo forced himself down the lane. . . . There before him was one of the worst evils of all: brawling, near-naked women—an obscene battalion of them—on the road and in the ditches, tearing out one another's hair, ripping at one another's faces and eyes and skins and clothes, kicking, biting, and—most unforgivable of all—shattering God's peaceful afternoon with foul, very unchristian language.
>
> "Stop!" he shouted. "Stop, I tell you!" The brawling Amazons took no notice of him.
>
> A massive woman of the Aiga Tauilopepe, right in front of Filipo, hiked up her lavalava, and baring her naked backside in the face of Malo's house

shouted, "There, take that, you motherless, fatherless shit-eaters!" Two of Malo's Amazons jumped on her, toppled her to the road, and clawed and struck at her. Filipo grabbed one of them round the waist and tried to pull her back. She elbowed him in the right eye and pushed him into the ditch. Filipo bounced up, his stinging eye turning blue already, grabbed at his waist, found no lavalava, desperately covered his genitals with his hands, ducked down into the ditch, cursed "Whore!," hitched on his lavalava again, and sprang out of the ditch and into the midst of the brawlers, slapping out at any Amazon who was near him, shouting:

"That's enough. I'll tell your fathers. I'll tell!" His blows and threats had no effect.

So Filipo wept.

His tears didn't touch the brawlers but they elicited aid from the spectators who converged on the grappling Amazons and pushed and carried them toward their homes. Some of the crowd were disappointed that the most colorful fight in years was over. (Wendt 1979:110–11)

These women not only lack those virtues cataloged in the Samoan moral lexicon—dignity, love, and respect—they manifest in abundance all the correlative vices: they revel in the display of personal sentiment; their personal sentiment is ill will toward a rival family; they arrogantly insult their rivals, and indeed all authorities, who, like poor Filipo, would call for civic order. While Filipo blames unruly Amazons for "shattering . . . peace," I suggest that the very existence of idealized premises and moral lexicons have a similar effect: they stimulate cognitive dissonance.

Cognitive dissonance occurs when one has two contradictory bases for belief (Festinger 1957). Idealized premises and lexicons supply one basis for belief about selves; experience supplies another. Studies show that cognitive dissonance is uncomfortable, and people who suffer from it will often distort experience in order to escape it, particularly when dissonance involves their identity (Aronson 1984:113–79). Moral discourse, I propose, is an effort to resolve dissonance by repressing contradictory impulses in the self and suppressing them in others, as Filipo attempts to suppress the "Satan-inspired brawl."

While Filipo, as a pastor, personifies moral discourse, he lacks opportunity to sermonize the "Amazons." The dissonance-resolving teleology of moral discourse is better illustrated by the following incident in a rural village in Western Samoa.

> A nineteen year old girl, Fua, came to stay in Nu'u with her mother, who was married to a *matai* [chief] of intermediate rank. . . . Fua was dark-skinned and not specially attractive by Samoan standards of beauty, but she was charming, graceful and well mannered. A girl of the same *'āiga* [extended family] . . . as Fua's mother's husband . . . was getting married

and indicated that she would like Fua to be her bridesmaid. The bride-to-be . . . was entitled to have only one bridesmaid, as a daughter of the *ali'i* [village high chief] . . . had married in Nu'u the previous year and had two bridesmaids.

Another girl, whom I shall call Sala . . . a blood member of the bride-to-be's *'āiga*, had hoped to be chosen and was very angry when she heard that Fua was chosen. She went around the village telling other women and girls that Fua "was black," she had "a fat bottom and skinny legs" and . . . was "rough" and "talked too much." This . . . got back to Fua and her mother, who went straight to the leader of the village women's committee to complain about "gossip" (which the committee may punish with a stiff fine if a case can be proved). The leader of the committee felt it was a family matter . . . and referred the complaint to the wife of the senior *matai* of the *'āiga*. After consideration, she decided that Sala should be the bridesmaid as was her right as the oldest unmarried female, "*gafa*" (blood member) of the *'āiga*. But she pointed out that Fua was also a daughter of the village, though through adoption, and should be given respect.

The tension between the two girls became a hot topic among the other girls of the village, with the respective behaviour and physical appearance of Sala and Fua being analyzed in great detail. The consensus seemed to be that Fua, though not as attractive as Sala in physical appearance was the more "beautiful" of the two because of her manners and virtue (Sala had an illegitimate child) and charm. (Schoeffel 1979a:141–42)

Moral discourse is a classificatory activity (separating sheep like Fua from goats like Sala). By offering a set of classificatory possibilities—ideals, vices, and virtues—moral lexicons enable moral discourses, but, in using these lexicons to sort out experience, moral discourses tend to problematize these lexicons. We will soon see that the Fua/Sala incident enlists an idealized premise, coded lexically as ideal attributes, and a set of binary vice/virtue categories, but their application—rather than being obvious, as in the case of brawling Amazons—is ambiguous. This ambiguity comes down to three questions.

On the simplest level the problem the episode concerns is: Who should be bridesmaid? Samoans believe bridesmaids should be *tausala*, a word that means "beautiful." If chiefs are male personifications of the Samoan idealized premise, in modern Samoa bridesmaids are feminine personifications of the same. So the question is really: Who best represents the feminine version of the idealized premise?

On the next level the question is: Who is arrogant (*lotofa'amaualuga*), and who is innocent of arrogance (*lotofa'amaualalo*)? Is Sala arrogant for her public remarks about Fua, or is she acting in accord with the prerogatives of her post? Alternatively, is Fua arrogant for presuming to be a bridesmaid?

We will soon see that this second question implicitly invokes a third, namely: Who is gossiping? Are Sala's remarks about Fua gossip? Or, possibly, are the remarks of the village girls' about Sala gossip? In Samoan terms this question is really: What is moral discourse, and what is not? All participants present themselves as engaging in a moral discourse about one another and as aiming at suppressing improper behavior in others. In Samoan, however, the verb *to gossip* is most commonly translated as *faitala,* literally "to make stories," but may also be translated as *lotoleaga* (envy). One of the predominate acting-out behaviors associated with *lotoleaga* is telling slanderous stories about another. To say that talk is gossip, therefore, is also to infer that it is motivated by personalistic animus, rather than proper moral concerns: talk that wears the guise of moral discourse may actually be "making stories."[2]

Sala's remarks about Fua allude to the first two questions. She says Fua is dark and ill formed, intimating that, as the more beautiful girl, she is the proper choice. Sala's other comments, that Fua is "rough" and "talks too much," address the binary level of the Samoan moral lexicon. In the introduction we saw that the most common reproach made to children is that they are *tautalaitiiti,* which literally means "to talk above one's age" and refers to cheeky behavior through which a person presumes to be above his or her station. Sala's accusation that Fua talks too much implies that, like the *tautalaitiiti* child who talks when he or she should not, Fua lacks respect. According to Sala, by aspiring to the position of bridesmaid in her mother's husband's family, Fua would arrogate a post to which her rank does not entitle her. This accusation is also expressed in Sala's use of the epithet *rough,* by which she intimates that Fua is unrefined and of low status.

But, if Fua is entitled to the post of bridesmaid, then Sala's implicit accusations are *lotoleaga,* merely an envious telling of slanderous stories. It is this third question that Fua and her mother place before the women's committee. By humbly placing the matter before them (rather than acting like Amazons), Fua and her mother enact the respect that Sala impugns. The women's committee refers the case to the officiating wife of the bride's family. This wife decrees that Sala is correct in her assertion of rights but has failed to render Fua the respect she deserves as a "daughter of the village," reversing Sala's judgment about who is arrogant. The officiating wife's judgment further implies that Sala's public remarks about Fua were not moral discourse and, therefore, were making stories, which is tantamount to envy (*lotoleaga*). This judgment is confirmed by the talk of the village girls.

The village girls determine that Fua is more beautiful, because Sala's actions (past and present) are *not* indicative of a beautiful disposition. If Fua is more beautiful, it follows that she is the more appropriate candidate for bridesmaid. Here the dignified person is viewed as the very embodiment of respect and as deserving of respect in the form of status and titles. In Goldman's terms (1970), Sala and the officiating wife believe in inherited status, while the village girls believe in achieved status.

If in the Fua/Sala incident the problematical nature of the idealized premise and moral lexicon is the very subject of moral discourse, moral discourse shows itself to be equally problematic. The aim of moral discourse may be to repress impulses and suppress behavior inspired by the discountenanced aspect of self, but its methodology is to discover them. Thus, the discourse of all parties in the Fua/Sala episode aims at suppressing behaviors they see as incongruent with showing respect; however, their method of doing so is to assign blame to some and virtue to others. Sala complains that she is not getting the respect properly due her; Fua and her mother make the same complaint. The officiating wife and the village girls are likewise concerned with assigning blame.

There is yet another problem implicit in the methodology of moral discourse. Moral discourse is not only an exercise in classification; it is also a form of narration. In Sala's tale Fua is a parvenu who lacks respect. In the officiating wife's tale Sala is motivated by personal animus and lacks respect. In the village girls' tale Fua embodies respect in her manners and in sexual virtue; by implication Sala's accusation is empty, and she is acting from personal envy. Yet moral discourse purports to be truth seeking and truth telling: the officiating wife and the village girls seek to distinguish just accusation from envy. Inasmuch as moral discourse inevitably tells tales, its claim to simple truthfulness cannot be entirely veridical. The next chapter will show that in contextual discourse this interpretative, as-if quality becomes conscious.

Reproducing Moral Discourse

If moral discourses are reproduced because they offer the mirage of dissonance resolution, in the introduction I also argued that children's unresolved resistance to distancing routines makes moral discourses compelling. Let me begin by reiterating and expanding this argument. We saw that children resist distancing and that this resistance is amended by negative sanctions; however, children also protest these sanctions. Often their immediate reaction is rage, but rage accompanies a tendency to express whatever the sanction is aimed at suppressing. Children forced to submit through punishment, for example, may belligerently challenge authority in response. Freeman recounts an episode in which an eighteen-month-old Samoan female infant, Sasa, is smacked for going out in the sun after having been told not to do so (1983:207–8). Sasa responds by telling her mother to "Eat shit!" The usual parental response to protests is redoubled sanctions. Sasa's mother proceeds to hit Sasa heavily and repeatedly about the head and body with her open hand. As the child screams, her mother shouts: "Have done! Have done! Shut your mouth!"—finally clamping her hand over Sasa's mouth to stifle her. Parents are more powerful, both physically and socially, than youngsters, so redoubled sanctions usually produce conformity.

But reactions against negative sanctioning also seem to reoccur later without external stimulus. They do so, I believe, because these seemingly deferred protests are actually responses to inhibitions, rather than to negative sanctions.

Inhibitions result from the anticipation of a negative sanction: such anticipation is tantamount to threatening oneself with a negative sanction formerly administered by parent figures. Because inhibitions are interior analogues of negative sanctions, one tends to react against them just as one once reacted against the sanctions. I call these reactions to inhibitions, in contrast to immediate protests against a sanctioning authority figure, counterreactions. Simply put, interactional conflict between child and elder is internalized as a conflict between certain resistances and inhibitions; this internalized conflict itself—without any direct external stimulants—generates counterreactions.

If different negative sanctions foster different inhibitions, they should also foster different counterreactions. Scaring provokes fear but also nourishes a counterphobic attitude. In Tahiti, for example, scaring is the most emphasized negative sanction, and adolescence is characterized by deeds of "daring do" (Levy 1973:448–49). Teasing provokes embarrassment but also stimulates a desire to show off. In Bali teasing is the most common negative sanction, and both children and adults are dedicated to the performing arts (Mageo 1991b:4–11). Punishment extracts submission but also sharpens a desire to dominate. In Samoa, where punishment is the primary sanction, people tend to be preoccupied with acquiring a position of dominance in the form of status and title (Mageo 1988:48–59, 1991b:17–28).

In Samoan childhood the desire for dominance is expressed in cheeky (*tautalaitiiti*) behavior. *Tautalaitiiti*, "talking above one's age," signifies one has failed to take one's proper, lowly place in the hierarchy of the family.[3] *Tautalaitiiti* is the term most frequently used for childhood delinquencies. One explanation for this frequency is that the inhibition of assertiveness—inspired by frequent punishment—provokes cheekiness as a counterreaction. Cheekiness lends a tone to childhood delinquencies in Samoa as well as to adult interpretations of them.

Remember that the Samoan punishment scenario combines the virtues instilled by all three sanctions in dramatic gestures of abasement. Likewise, cheekiness Samoan style combines counterreactions to all three sanctions in dramatic gestures of assertion. In Samoa virtuous behavior is personally restrained, effacing, and submissive; the *tautalaitiiti* child is liable to be an incorrigible who is not only cheeky but also bold and exhibitionistic, despite the best efforts of sanctioning elders. It is not that Samoan counterreactions always take the form of cheekiness. Inasmuch as scaring and teasing are also frequently employed negative sanctions, boldness or exhibitionism are also likely counterreactions, but even these are likely to have *tautalaitiiti* overtones. Thus, when a boy exposes himself to a girl as a joke, his action is said to be cheeky.[4]

The relations between Samoan counterreactions and juvenile misbehavior is illustrated in the following tale, told by a middle-aged Western Samoan in English whom I will call Teʻe (Show Off). Teʻe recalls an episode from adolescence, when he was a paragon of Samoan-style cheekiness.

■ ■ ■

I used to throw rocks very good, even at *matai* [chiefs] of our own village. . . . About 13, 14 . . . one night . . . me and my buddies . . . wanted to see how the *matai* would react when he came out of the pool, and looked for his lavalava . . . so after the curfew bell the *matai* . . . went and took a bath and put his lavalava on the wall, jumped in naked, and I . . . crawled slowly . . . took the lavalava, wrapped [it] around the stone and threw it into the ocean and the *matai* came out trying to feel—cause it was getting dark . . . he didn't even find his lavalava. Seven-thirty, eight o'clock, nine o'clock he was still in the cool pool and when people came to take a bath he moved farther and farther in the darkest spot because . . . no lavalava. At ten o'clock he finally figured there was no one looking. He got out of the pool and took off and went home with nothing on. . . .

The *matai* reported to the village council and Saturday morning . . . we all gathered . . . to have a *tautōga*. . . . My hand on the Bible, I swear I will die tomorrow, if I did it, I will surely die. Everybody, one by one, came in front of [all] the *matai*. I was testing my own strength also, "Will this really happen?" Before I went up in front of the village to swear on the Bible my heart was beating fast. Die tomorrow? Put my hand on the Bible and the minister was there from the Congregational church in his white suit and all the chiefs, they are just looking on this culprit. . . . [Te'e postures a bit now, imitating the minister, and affects mock-seriousness.]

"You swear on the Bible you did not do it? If you are lying you're going to die, you know?"

"Yes I do." [Te'e incants, quoting himself.] I put my hand on the Bible, "I swear I never did it," but they knew. The *matai* had to deliberate . . . and my family was assessed a fine, a few pigs. . . . My father did throw rocks at me and I took off . . . I was the fastest runner in the village.

■ ■ ■

Te'e opens with the theme of throwing rocks. Hitting is the leitmotif of Samoan childhood punishments. Although Te'e does not actually throw a rock at the chief, by wrapping the chief's lavalava in a stone and throwing it in the sea, he places himself in the position of the hitter and the chief in the position of one who is hit. The tale is, therefore, one in which Te'e reverses the authority figure/child relation vis-à-vis a particularly elevated authority figure, not just an older sibling or even a parent but a chief. Te'e's intent is cheeky: he wants to impugn the status of the chief and to forward his own status at the chief's expense, and Te'e gets what he wants. Upon hearing the first part of my taped interview with Te'e, Sanele remarked that, after the truth-telling ceremony, Te'e was surely the leader of the local boys, an observation confirmed by Te'e's comments later in the interview.

In Teʻe's story hitting turns out to be a kind of ridicule, or more precisely a method of denigrating an authority figure through threatening him with ridicule. The joke, however, is also an obvious act of bravado, and its effects necessitate confronting one of the several scaring techniques whereby submissiveness is induced in children and adults, the *tautōga*.[5] In a *tautōga* those who allege innocence of a misdeed must swear on the Bible that they did not do it, believing that to lie after so swearing induces death. The *tautōga*, however, also makes Teʻe a star performer in a drama for which the whole village assembles.[6] Thus, Teʻe's cheekiness provides him with an occasion to behave boldly and to show off, accommodating all three counterreactions under the auspices of status insurrection. Nonetheless, the theme of hitting/punishment frames Teʻe's story. While it begins with a boast about his ability to throw rocks, it ends with Teʻe's father throwing rocks at him. His deed results in a public sanction—a fine of pigs—but this sanction is conveyed to Teʻe in the form of stoning (beating), although this beating too is something of a joke, because Teʻe is so fleet.

Counterreactions and Moral Agency

As in Teʻe's story, counterreactions are apt to result in delinquencies: they expressly involve the acting out of culturally discountenanced tendencies. This potential for delinquency is diminished through the development of moral discourse. Moral discourse succeeds in moderating counterreactions by surreptitiously providing the developing person with an alternative means to express them: moral narratives. Moral tales are not only presented in story form but also in narrative fragments such as clichés, commonplaces, aphorisms, proverbial expressions, and folk wisdom, which borrow from tales and serve as an intertext for understanding them (Kristeva 1980:66). These narrative fragments find a place in children's games and pastimes, such that the child's fantasy life itself gradually becomes an intertext of tales that supplies schemata to organize and interpret experience.

The tales told to children teach morality—not only in the sense that these tales convey explicit moral dicta—but also in the sense that they provide templates for thinking about moral issues (Anderson 1965; Bettelheim 1976; Miller et al. 1996). People tend to identify with those they see as admirable (Aronson 1984:32). The child tends to identify with the protagonists of tales who, like the cowboy in our culture, personify the idealized premise; this identification is tantamount to internalization. Inasmuch as the protagonists of children's stories are objects of admiration, and inasmuch as the child identifies with them, they forge an association between the culture's idealized premise and an experience of being admired. Like praise and recognition, moral stories elaborate on early narcissism. In moral tales, however, those who personify ideals are not merely images, rather their virtues are tried and demonstrated: characters in the stories of childhood often begin as unrecognized persons with whom the hearer can identify and only, in the end, personify cultural ideals.

In Samoa elders tell children legendary tales called *fāgogo* (Moyle 1981). Sanele's grandmother, for example, used to tell *fāgogo* to him and his siblings as bedtime stories. The children were supposed to punctuate their grandmother's tales with exclamations of "'Aue!" (Alas!). When they began to nod off to sleep and failed to "'Aue!" the grandmother would remind them to comment by whacking them with a long stick; whacks are a typical accompaniment to bedtime *fāgogo*. In *fāgogo* the protagonist is often the youngest son or daughter who, in Samoan custom, is least likely to become a chief or marry a distinguished person. These protagonists, furthermore, are often accused unjustly of some form of dereliction, but in the end their worth becomes apparent to all. The Scabby-Oven-Cover story from the introduction is a *fāgogo* and exemplifies these characteristics, but so does the story that the village girls tell about Fua and Sala. From the girls' standpoint, Fua is the protagonist who is initially accused of being cheeky but whose worth is, in the end, attested. The village girls make a heroine of a Fua who represents to them a *tausala* ideal of beauty. People are inclined to subscribe to principles that—for whatever reason—they have defended (Aronson 1984:113–79). Making a character an exemplar of a cultural ideal in telling a tale is much like defending this ideal and probably helps practitioners to internalize moral principles.

I proposed that moral narratives not only allow children and later adolescents to identify with and internalize cultural morality, but that they also allow for the expression of counterreactions. Let us take the village girls' talk about Fua and Sala as an example. The reader will recall that their talk, like the officiating wife, appears impartial and free of ill will (*lotomamā*) toward either girl. The officiating wife validates both Sala's rights and Fua's. Similarly the village girls award Sala the prize for physical beauty and Fua the prize for moral beauty; however, the girls judge Fua to be *more* beautiful. By making Fua the winner of a beauty contest—where beauty is what beauty does—the village girls not only assimilate Sala's and Fua's tale to moral categories but also give it a fantasized ending, "what should have happened" in their terms. They reverse the officiating wife's verdict about who should be bridesmaid, unofficially appointing Fua in Sala's place.

Inasmuch as the girls portray Fua as admirable they are likely to identify with her. A Samoan bridesmaid dresses up in fancy clothes and enjoys the limelight. She has occasion to exhibit herself. Inasmuch as the village girls identify with Fua and, in fantasy, make her the bridesmaid, by way of identification they also make themselves fantasized bridesmaids. Their retelling of the events could be seen as expressive of a desire to exhibit themselves, to show off (*faʻalialia*). In their desire to appoint Fua in Sala's place, therefore, they could be construed as envious of Sala. Their talk, like that of Sala, would then be gossip, and an acting out of envy (*lotoleaga*).[7] In this sense their moral discourse accommodates an exhibitionistic counterreaction (including its negative concomitant, envy), albeit one inextricably intermeshed with themes of "talking above one's age" and respect. After all who will be bridesmaid is not their call, but that of their elders and betters.

There is a parallel, then, between the gossip of the village girls and Teʻe's story. Teʻe puts down a *matai* and asserts his own status. The village girls implicitly put down Sala, elevating Fua by contrast, with whom they identify. Through the joke and the *tautōga* that follows, Teʻe secures an opportunity to show off and to be the star actor in a village drama. The girls secure an opportunity to show off in fantasy; in their minds Fua (their surrogate) should have been bridesmaid.

The gossip of the village girls expresses a counterreaction through a device I call "performative inhibition." These girls demonstrate their lack of ill will (*lotomamā*) by remarking upon both Sala's physical attractiveness and Fua's moral attractiveness, but this appearance of restraint and impartiality is a disguise for their envy (*loto leaga*) toward Sala and for their own desire to exhibit themselves as bridesmaids. Their moral discourse is a means of demonstrating or performing inhibition, and this performance is in turn a way to deny the real meaning of their conversation. Their performance also proclaims their own conformity to moral ideology. Seeing themselves as proponents of Samoan moral ideology is likely to further reinforce and shape the early narcissism that develops into pride. The proponent role seems an especially reassuring feature of moral discourse in the face of the child's newfound desire to act out counterreactions, which threatens his or her sense of goodness and acceptability.

In the case of Teʻe's story one might question whether or not counterreactions actually threaten his sense of self-worth, as he seems proud of his exploit. Teʻe, however, like most Samoans, ultimately derives his self-worth not from being cheeky but from that type of action that is praised and positively recognized in early childhood: service (*tautua*). As an adult, Teʻe would like to advance his status at work but cannot finish the necessary degree because he spends his time doing a modern version of *tautua*, paying for his father's Honolulu hospital bills and supporting his family. His sense of worth is more securely tied to communalistic values than to individualistic assertion. I saw this so often with my students, who seemed to take delight in being cheeky and assertive but who also decided not to go off the island to pursue their education because their grandparents or parents needed someone to take care of them: their sense of self-worth would have been too deeply undermined by neglecting familial obligations. Sanele joined the U.S. army to secure money for an education, but when his father died he came back to Samoa to take care of his mother.

There are two further reasons for this apparent pride in counterreactions. First, as we will see in the next chapter, while moral discourse represses counterreactions in fact and expresses them in fantasy, contextual discourses channel counterreactions into culturally lauded performances. We will further see that these performances are identified with achievement and that, within contextual discourses, the need to express counterreactions becomes a need for achievement, however that is culturally defined. A tendency toward counterreactions can, therefore, sometimes be perceived as presaging achievement and may become symbolically associated with it. Ochs records a village council meeting in which one chief shames another by asking, "Did this little kid throw any stone?" Ochs glosses this query as "Did he ever do anything for our village?" (1988:161), the motif of stone throwing (hitting) arising once again.

Second, Teʻe receives recognition in his stone-throwing story because in moral discourse people not only tend to replace the violator in fantasy with a "worthy" person with whom they identify; they also tend to identify with and valorize the violator. There are, for example, endless American films that valorize outlaws. Not all antisocial behavior provokes this response, but certain deeds, like Teʻe's, signal a surmounting of culturally shared inhibitions. It is not only Teʻe's mood that is mischievous and jocular; one senses this mood among his judges as well, as if they find a degree of surreptitious satisfaction in his deed. Actions and persons who represent an overcoming of inhibition are particularly important in adolescence, for reasons we will consider later.

Moral Economies

Moral discourse serves dual purposes. First, it proclaims the practitioner's conformity to moral principles. Simultaneously, however, it provides a context in which participants can, beneath the level of their own awareness, practice the sins they preach against. The gossip of the village girls gives the appearance of moral behavior, allaying much of the anxiety about attendant consequences while providing at least some of the satisfaction offered by less than moral forms of behavior as well.

One aim of the ego is to mediate between desire and the anxieties attendant upon the violation of internalized precepts (Freud 1961). When the ego is inadequate to this task, as in sleep or mental illness, this medial position is taken up by a dream in the first case and by a symptom in the second. This is not to say that dreams or symptoms consciously integrate impulses and inhibitions; rather, they symbolically concatenate otherwise disjointed territories of the self (Freud [1900] 1953; [1917] 1966:394, 358–60). One might say the same of moral discourse. Moral discourse temporarily unites contrary inclinations—for example, the inclinations to be *lotomamā* (free of ill will) and to be *lotoleaga* (envious)—and gives expression to counterreactions (such as the desire to show off). The greater number of purposes an action serves, the more parsimonious it is of the actor's energy. Although there is not adequate space to consider all forms of moral discourse here, I suggest that they are satisfying because they involve this type of parsimony, combining antithetical inclinations in one activity.

Agency and guilt are both pivotal to the development of moral discourse.

In moral discourse developing young people assume an agenic relationship to moral schemata: they come to use these schemata to think about their experience, as the village girls use Samoan moral schemata to think about Fua and Sala. Moral discourse is a calculus of guilt—assigning it differentially to persons—and is a conduit for counterreactions, which inspire guilt. In the previous example the girls' use of moral narrative amounts to gossip. While this gossip palliates guilt by its moral appearance, it also provides covert satisfactions likely to perpetuate guilt in buried form: the village girls also know that gossip is wrong, and, while ambiguity about exactly what is gossip and what is not provides further camouflage, it is improbable that they entirely escape a sense of culpability, however impartial and "moral" their gossip appears.

Furthermore, the satisfactions that moral discourse develop are only partial and, in their partiality, are frustrating. It seems likely that Te'e, by actually acting out a counterreaction, experiences more satisfaction than the gossiping girls, who only experience satisfaction in fantasy. They will, after all, attend a wedding in which Sala, not Fua, is the bridesmaid. The social actor is driven to escape frustration by replicating partial satisfactions through repeated use of moral discourse, which itself entails further frustration and, therefore, further desire to engage in discourse. Perhaps this is why gossip and like activities seem so addictive.

While moral discourse, if it could, would banish vice and that part of the self culturally affiliated with it, this discourse brings to light vice and virtue indiscriminately, both in the world and in the self. When people discuss, condemn, and gossip about individuals in terms of their moral rectitude or, more likely, the lack thereof, they highlight the excluded aspect of experience—such that this worm at the heart of cultural consciousness seems to breed within the very discourse that evolves in order to curtail it. The next chapter argues that because this emergent element haunts self systems, however fervently it is condemned, contextual discourses accommodate it by assigning to all aspects of the self a proper season.

5

Contextual Discourses and the Tropics of Childhood

The recognition that those behaviors censored in moral discourse are ubiquitous has a transformative effect on its sponsoring principles. In face of the omnipresence of "vice," moral rules mutate into meaning systems aiming less at regulation than at making sense of life. These meaning systems comprise social poetics and also utopian charters for society. American moral discourse, for example, preaches self-reliance; however, "life, liberty, and the pursuit of happiness" represent the American poetics of individualism. This American poetics is eloquently represented in the Bill of Rights, which might be looked upon as a utopian charter for society.

Samoan moralism councils respect. One does not act on one's own behalf but as an ambassador of one's group; therefore, one gives respect in a representative capacity to the ambassadors of other groups. This moral principle is celebrated in the poetic dictum that one should "Teu le vā" (Decorate the space between); the "space between" signifies a relationship, particularly between groups, and is conceptualized as the center of a circle.[1] In *Pouliuli*, a novel by the Samoan Albert Wendt, a circle of white stones around a black stone is an icon for Samoan culture and way of life. Here the black stone can be thought of as a negative space, or *vā*, between the white stones, symbolizing the relationship between them. Even prehistoric Samoan petroglyphs feature this figure (Kikuchi 1964). Furthermore, this figure, symbolizes a utopian charter for society: in every chiefly meeting chiefs representing their respective groups sit in a circle at the posts of a roundhouse; in village landscape great houses of extended families circle the *malae*—an ellipsis, usually of grass, that marks the center of a village.

We will see that social poetics—such as the American poetics of individualism or the Samoan poetics of relationship—become the basis of a *formal discourse* in which the absolute values of moral discourse are replaced by ideals of a rhetorical nature. By "rhetorical" I do not mean that people do not believe in these ideals or in the utopian charters associated with them. In the utopian version of American society, for example, one is advanced on the basis of individual merit—a quotient derived from innate capacity plus hard work—rather than because of social and biological contingencies such as class background, social status, age, race, gender, religion, and so forth. I am an American. Although I am aware of statistical evidence that should make me more than a little skeptical about how consistently this charter actually molds social life, I am bitterly disappointed whenever I am involved in a competition in which merit is not the primary criteria for success, as is John Travolta trying to dance his way to success in *Saturday Night Fever*. For many Americans this charter (as it is inscribed in the Declaration of Independence or on the Statue of Liberty or in the speeches of Abraham Lincoln or in movie classics like *Mr. Smith Goes to Washington*) elicits more loyal belief than does cultural moralism. It is just that the ideals that underwrite this charter are situated in a frame of reference that indicates they are not "the ways of the world" and, furthermore, do not always apply.

Although Americans believe everyone should advance on the basis of individual merit, we expect this principle to apply mainly in public-professional contexts; in private life we are not so strict in our accounting and think children and spouses should be loved despite their failings. Thus, when telling stories about their children, at least when those children are present, American parents will gloss over transgressions and shortcomings (Miller et al. 1996). American wives feel they should love their husbands no less because of mental instability or other weaknesses of character (Quinn 1992:105–6). If we think moral principles like honesty and integrity should always characterize the individual, "merit" is a principle that one can take too seriously.

Similarly, in formal-hierarchical contexts Samoans believe in the utmost decorum, but in informal contexts even titled ladies (*tama'ita'i*) make an art of buffoonery.

> One elderly and dignified *tama'ita'i* is celebrated among the women of her village for a particular dance she does, completely silent and straight faced using eye movements to express passion, resignation, pain, strain, surprise, and release, she parodies a whole sequence of events in sexual intercourse, enacting both the husband and wife roles. (Schoeffel 1979a:217)

While formal discourses would banish the weaknesses of human nature from the republic, the discourses proper to informal contexts situate these discountenanced elements of self in an as-if frame of reference that resembles the frame "play." Bateson says that play in an activity framed so as to indicate that messages do *not* mean what they appear to mean (1972:177–93). When puppies play, for example, a nip resembles a bite but is *not* a bite. In *informal discourse* whatever is construed as vice in moral discourse is framed in such a way as to indicate it is "not that."

Thus, American marriage features a rhetoric of total commitment, which sounds very much like boundary confusion and not very self-reliant. One of Quinn's informants on marriage says that "the way you are supposed to be" in marriage is "in love, kind of losing myself, pu—surrendering your judgement and perspective and stuff like that . . . that's the ideal" (Quinn 1992:105). Yet the rhetorical nature of this ideal is indicated by frames like "private life" or "leisure time." Normally, "total commitments" are not supposed to interfere with the serious business of earning a living (read economic self-reliance); when they do, one goes to a psychiatrist. I know, for example, a professor who, following a divorce, would sometimes cry in lecture. He started seeing a psychiatrist regularly. In this sense informal discourse, too, forwards values that are rhetorical—to be taken with the proverbial grain of salt.[2]

Most significantly, contextual discourses are modes of talk. In the preceding chapter we saw that moral discourse is classificatory in nature. Contextual discourses presuppose classification (situations are classed as if they were either formal or informal) but are explicitly symbolizing activities. Borrowing a distinction from Searle (1969:33–42), one can say that, while moral discourses propound regulative rules, contextual discourses, like games, have constitutive rules: these rules are that communication be through a commonly accepted set of tropes. In this sense contextual discourses are language games, even though they include gestural forms of communication.

Tropes are probably always present in discourses and even in lexicons of self. *Aga*, for example, are not literally faces; they are only figuratively so; the *loto* is figuratively speaking a small deep; and so forth. Moral narratives obviously traffic in tropes. But the task of moral narratives, like other forms of moral discourse, is sorting good from bad. Tropes are explicitly enlisted in this classificatory project, as when one knight wears black and the other white. We will later see that the tropes of moral narratives also have implicit layers and that this dimension of moral tales may work on complex experiences that are not readily categorized. In contextual discourses, however, the discursive project itself is tropic: it is to convey meanings through a set of rhetorical conventions that evoke types of social relationship, relationships that in turn tag and identify social contexts. Lest I strain the credulity of my readers, let us turn from the abstract to the ethnographic and to the constitutive rules of formal and informal discourses in Samoa.

Formal Discourse: Decorating the Space Between

In Samoa "decorating the space between" is a symbolizing activity in which one conveys respect through the following series of tropes: first, a trope of silence; second, a trope of deference; third, a trope of service; fourth, a trope of ceremonial prestations; and, last, an oratorical trope of flattery and flowery allusion. In this series each trope builds upon its predecessor such that tropes become what Baudrillard (1988) calls simulacra, referring to preceding signs within the series of signs, rather than to things in the world.[3]

The Trope of Silence

The utopian credo of Samoan formal discourse, again, is "decorating the space between." "To decorate," *teu*, is also "to hold in": one may *teu* for a feast, but one may also *teu* one's money in the bank. In daily conversation one "decorates" relationships in the negative, by tactfully holding in one's *loto*, that is, by one's reluctance to show one's personal thoughts, feelings, or will, before one's superiors. In a letter to the editor of the *Samoa News* one Samoan, Salu Reed, says that respect "means to hold your tongue, even when the directions given you by your elders are wrong" (May 4, 1989:4). Thus, decorative relating is signified first and foremost by an absence of the personal dimension of self.

The Trope of Deference

Implicit in this silence about one's personal sentiments is deference to those of another, and this deference is explicitly demonstrated by a reluctance to say no. Young Samoan women, for example, cannot politely decline if they are asked to dance. As this deference is demonstrated by the absence of a no, it is still, like silence, respect in a negative tense; however, the Samoan reluctance to say no may have real consequences for the social actor. I have heard a girl explain that she married a man because he begged so often she became ashamed to rebuff him. This feeling is common enough that women use it as a facetious explanation for why they married their respective husbands (Cluny Macpherson, pers. comm.).

The Trope of Service

A reluctance to say no is, implicitly, a willingness to say yes, doing what others ask of you and thereby rendering service (*tautua*). *Tautua* alludes not only to obedient service but also to the products thereof. Until very recently the descendants of the extended family showed respect for their family chief not only by following his orders but also by relinquishing to him all they produced or earned, at home or elsewhere, be it bananas or money. Likewise, villagers rendered certain animals they captured, turtles for example, as well as a percentage of their catch, to village chiefs.[4] This respect given to chiefs, however, was actually something more: *tautua* signified pledges of fealty. For this reason in old Samoa villagers who failed to render goods and services to village chiefs might be fined or even killed: their actions signaled insurrection.

The Trope of Ceremonial Prestations

In ceremonial exchanges decorating relationships is expressed through prestations. These prestations consist in items that signify the service of men (*'oloa*) and others that signify the service of women (*tōga*), the later being decorously crafted. In turn service, *tautua*, symbolizes "pledges of fealty," so, through prestations of these *tautua* symbols, groups take turns treating the chief of a rival group *as if* he were their own chief and pledging simulacra of fealty.⁵ In old Samoa the as-if character of such pledges was underlined by the fact that they might not long outlive the ceremony itself: ceremonies between rival groups were interspersed with wars.

The Trope of Oratory

This as-if sovereignty that groups grant to one another in ceremony is further symbolized by a rhetoric that relies on a symbolism of lowering one's group and elevating the other to a position of dominance. The nineteenth-century British consul Churchward captured the flavor of this oratorical rhetoric in his description of a traveling party's ceremonial greeting. The orator of the hosting group begins

> calling over all the titles . . . of those present, which take no little time [h]e . . . invokes all conceivable blessing on the happy day that has been so fortunate as to give them—a most unworthy set of men—the never-to-be-sufficiently appreciated honour of so distinguished a set of visitors . . . who have so graciously deigned to receive their worthless offerings. . . . [H]e will [then] launch into apologies for the poverty of their gifts, asking the recipients over and over again to be so good as to excuse the poverty of the country.
>
> When the first speaker has completely exhausted all the compliments and apologies that he can remember or invent, he takes a back seat amongst his crowd, giving the other side an opportunity for reply. A decent interval having elapsed, the leading talking-man of the opposite side starts up, and after precisely the same preliminaries . . . which are *de rigueur* in Samoan oratory, he will, elaborately and with care, proceed to return more than verbatim all the compliments paid to his side . . . and of course praise in most lofty terms the prodigal liberality shown in the gifts bestowed; and if he is a visitor, no description of what Utopia should be is sufficiently high-toned to express adequately the appreciation of himself and crowd of the beatific country they have had the good fortune to visit. (1887:101–2)

It seems apt that one should evoke utopias when acting out utopian social charters.

Samoan ceremonial speech conveys respect not only through flattery but also through esoteric allusions to mythology, history, poetry, and, since contact, the Bible (Schultz [1949–50] 1985:vii; Matā'afa Tu'i 1987). These esoteric allusions, like ceremonial prestations and oratorical flattery, are oblique in their symbolism: the esoterica of oratorical discourse conveys respect by presuming upon the knowledge of participants, intimating their refinement and intellect. By comparing the present occasion with mythological circumstances and personages, ceremonial allusiveness also intimates that the current meeting is a "lofty" one, augmenting the dignity of all who attend.

Informal Discourse: *Faipona* and *Ula*

We saw that decorating the space between is initially signified by an absence—the absence of the personal side of the self. This absence is enacted by silencing one's personal thoughts, feelings, and volitions but is also played out in body language by covering private body parts. Sitting cross-legged in ceremonies, for example, I have been given an extra lavalava to insure my legs were fully covered. By the same symbolic logic, to exhibit the personal self, or its Samoan bodily analogues, insults the dignity of the other and is a symbolic bid for dominance or an attempt to redress such a bid on the part of another. Bearing the buttocks, *sigo,* is the ultimate example. Schoeffel provides a graphic depiction of this gesture and its import taken from the Mau, the 1926–29 Western Samoa revolt against the colonial government of New Zealand.

> The women formed a procession and, wearing their uniforms, marched down the main street to Apia . . . but on this occasion the police turned fire hoses on them. At a signal from the leader the women turned their backs on the police, and hoisting their lavalavas, they all with one accord bent and bared their bottoms at the police. (1979a:451)

Outside of the exigencies of colonial intrusion, Samoan moral discourse counsels all humbly to take their post in the group, rather than challenging authority by baring bottoms. The problem is that the *loto* (personal willfulness) impels children to be cheeky, challenging the status of elders, and that a desire to dominate continues to color adulthood. Informal discourses provide a remedy by borrowing the trope of uncovered private parts but adding a playfulness that indicates the insult is not really meant. The nineteenth-century missionary Williams provides examples.

> If a person should jeer a young woman as she might be passing by remarking freely on her person saying she was diseased or ill formed she would instantly throw off her cloth & expose herself in every possible direction & pass on. A respectable young man who had been residing among them some time informed me that when he first went on shore among them the females in great numbers gathered round him & some took off their mats before him exposing their persons as much as possible to his view. Perceiving him bashful the whole of the women old & young did the same & began dancing in that state before him desiring him not to be bashful or angry as it was Faa Samoa . . . or the Samoan fashion. ([1830–32] 1984:232)

Samoans call the genre of humor that Williams glosses as "jeering" *faipona.* Jeering, or lampooning, as it might better be called, gives expression to dominance seeking through exposure: the jeering Samoan, remarking "freely" on the young woman's person, exposes the personal part of her: her actions echo his words. The genre in which the Samoan women tease the young Englishman is called *ula;* the teasing women exhibit their own personal parts to the young Englishman. Both exposure and exhibitionism are tropes for uncovering of the personal self.

The Trope of Exposure

Faipona is a personal remark that points out what is not smooth, either aesthetically or socially, and makes a joke of it. *Fai* glosses as "to make" or "to do"; *pona* refers to nodes found on an otherwise smooth surface. Reading by the pool at the Rainmaker Hotel in Pago Pago, for example, I heard a little boy tell his obese female companion that she had made a *pū,* "hole," in the swimming pool when she jumped in. He added, that must be why Americans call it a "swimming *pū.*"

The Trope of Exhibitionism

In contrast to *faipona, ula* often seems self-deprecating. In the guise of carping upon one's own dignity, however, one says or does things similar to that which one would say or do to insult another: one exhibits private carnal experience. In 1987 a team of government workmen came to cut down a tree that endangered my house on the island of Tutuila. All the chainsaws had been taken to the nearby Manu'a Islands, hit by a hurricane the previous week. The men stood gazing at the formidable tree, their bush knives hanging at their sides, and began to joke. One man recounted how the government truck, in the back of which the others rode, had almost run into a female pedestrian at the local market. He had said, "Watch it or you'll get hurt [*lavea*]." She responded, "What other hurt, I have already been hurt [*lavea*]!" *Lavea* can mean "to be hit" or "to have a cut." The girl who is no longer a virgin is referred to as "cut skin" (*pa'umutu*). Thus, the female pedestrian alluded to her lack of virginity. We will later see that in Christian Samoa the respect accorded a female is deeply tied to her status as a virgin. So the pedestrian appeared to be mocking her own dignity (by saying she was not a virgin) but in this guise exhibited her private parts (her "cut"), indirectly impugning the dignity of the listener.

The Trope of Mimicry

While formal Samoan discourse finds ultimate expression in ceremonial exchange, the most developed examples of Samoan informal discourse are found in entertainment exchanges; in old Samoa the most important of these was the "Joking Night." Joking Nights involved many different forms of entertainment (surveyed later in the text), all of which placed dominance seeking in an as-if frame of reference. While ceremonies further abstracted the trope of service, through which Samoans expressed respect in everyday life, in Joking Nights types of everyday jesting became performance genres.

Mimicry, often in the form of caricature, was featured. Joking Night mimicry can be seen as a trope for *faipona* (lampooning) but took this humor to higher ground. Samoan lampooning is directed at exposing the risible peculiarities of another (and, by implication, his or her family); Joking Night caricatures were not necessarily so: age, infirmity, or animals might be artfully caricatured (Krämer 1995:371–72). When an individual was mimicked, it was usually someone in authority (Kneubuhl 1987), and could, therefore, be seen as joking about authority.

The Trope of Ribald Choreography

Even more salient in Joking Nights were choreographic tropes for *ula*, that exhibitionistic form of jest described earlier. The missionary Williams again provides a description.

> The performers are divided into companies. . . . The young virgin girls taking the lead . . . enter the house entirely naked & commence their dance. The fullgrown women then follow after. Then come the elderly women all of whom are entirely naked. During their dancing they throw themselves in all imaginable positions in order to make the most full exposure of their persons to the whole company. In addition to this there are several persons supplied with flambeaux which they hold as near to the dancers as possible. During the whole of the time of performing the females are using the most vile, taunting, bantering language to the men. . . . The men then enter and being rather more bashful than the fair sex they [wear] . . . a narrow leaf in their hands. . . . The ladies however will not . . . be content with this return for the full & free exhibition they have made & commence a furious attack on them in language suitable to the occasion. The men at length throw away their apology for a covering & make a full exposure of their persons using lights as the females had done before them. (Williams [1830–32] 1984:247–48)

Here the women's choreography paralleled and reiterated their "vile, taunting, bantering language": it was a choreographic form of *ula* and an as-if attack on the dignity of the other through the trope of exhibitionism. Everyday, *ula* takes place between individuals, and in Samoa individuals always represent their family; Joking Night exchanges took place between groups who were ambassadors for villages. They were staged when a group from one village, usually male, traveled to another village and were hosted by a group, usually female, representing the home village.

According an elderly Western Samoan chief, the event began with the women on one side of the house and the men on the other, each side offering a performance that had to be equaled by the other side. As the night progressed, the presentations become bawdy and were responded to by increasingly uninhibited songs and dances. At some point in this rising crescendo a male would shout, rush over, and pick up one of the women, carrying her out into the night. If the couple came back inside after a brief period, the dance was not interrupted, and nothing was said. But, if the couple did not return, the male group shouted, "One wife for our side!"—as if the woman was a point in a game. In Samoan a Joking Night is a *pō-ula,* literally an *"ula* night": by definition then, they were mock attacks upon the dignity of another village and constituted mock competitions.[6]

Contextual Discourses and Binarism

Ontological lexicons presuppose a singular premise about human nature, suggesting that it is essentially one thing, for example, that people are role players. Moral lexicons predicate a binary set of propositions about human *nature:* that people have a good part that conforms to the ontological premise and a bad part that does not. Nonetheless, moral discourse offers a singular premise about *behavior:* whatever one's cultural concept of good behavior is, one should conform to it. Contextual discourses, however, predicate a binary set of propositions about behavior: behavior should sometimes be formal and sometimes informal. But, if contextual discourses suggest a binary view of behavior, they also move toward the transcendence of binarism.

In Samoan self systems one begins with a lexicon of personhood that focuses upon the social nature of the person. In Samoan moral discourse this idea develops into a moral lexicon that categorizes *behavior* as self-serving vice or communalistic virtue. Samoan contextual discourses categorize *persons,* but here categories consist of structural features of identity such as rank, sex, and age, rather than moral qualities: hierarchical contexts are constituted of participants who are different in terms of these variables and peer contexts of those who are similar.

Contextual discourses are judged to be appropriate or inappropriate by virtue of the categories in which their participants reside. Thus, Samoans engage in a respectful discourse in hierarchical contexts and a joking discourse in peer contexts. In old Samoa ceremonies were ideal instances of the former, and entertainments—particularly Joking Nights—were paradigmatic instances of the latter. Yet it is also true that ceremonies and Joking Nights played upon binary categories to transcend these categories. By virtue of a contradiction between the form of these events and their content, both ceremonies and Joking Nights temporarily deconstructed mundane systems of categorization and with them prevailing social boundaries.

In Samoan ceremonies between groups each side was represented by a titled male, and courtesy dictated that their titles be treated as approximate. In terms of structural categories, therefore, intergroup ceremonies were peer contexts; that is, interchanges between persons of the same social category (males) and the same social status (titles of approximate rank). As such, ceremonies should have constituted competitive contexts; however, the content of Samoan ceremonies was an exchange of respect between the sides. Through respectful prestations and flowery oratory each group acted *as if* it was the status inferior of the other, to whom it symbolically rendered humble service. Here the content message, conveyed by an exchange of the tokens of respect, was to be read as encompassing the form message about symmetricality and the implicit rivalry between titles and groups. Perhaps this gesture—the transcendence of rivalry through respect relations—was ritual in nature, symbolically obviating the incessant warring that went on between groups, not only during the ceremony itself but in some general way. This symbolism might explain why in successful ceremonies a radiant spirit of *communitas* seemed to infect participants. The missionary Turner recollects these exchanges as characterized by "a delightful flow of friendship all over the place" and says, "On such occasions parties who have been living at variance had a fine opportunity of showing kindness to each other" ([1884] 1984:183).

We saw that on Joking Nights one village was represented by a group of females, the other by a group of males. Relations between the sexes are respectful in Samoa and probably based upon the prototype of the brother-sister relationship.[7] In terms of structural categories, therefore, Joking Nights were respect contexts; however, the real content of the entertainment was a salacious mock rivalry between two sides.[8] Through bawdy presentations that paralleled ceremonial prestations groups took turns behaving as if they were peers engaged in a jocular contest with one another. This contradiction constituted an ironic frame of reference, in which form and content messages negated one another. The ironic frame conveyed that participants were really *not* brothers and sisters and, therefore, that the sexualized exchange between them was *not* incestuous. This frame further suggested that the rivalry between participating groups was facetious. Perhaps this gesture—the negation of rivalry through jest—was also ritualistic, symbolically dismantling the inherent rivalry between villages in a larger sense. This symbolism might explain the *communitas* that characterizes entertainment in Samoa even today.

Both ceremonies and Joking Nights combined structural features of hierarchical contexts and peer contexts, thereby creating frames that were, in cultural terms, contradictory. In turn the contradictions constituted an implicit commentary on the descriptive justice of binary divisions between contexts, in effect transcending binarism. Just as the as-if character of moral discourse, implicit in its narrative style, becomes explicit in contextual discourses through a play of tropes, we will see that this transcendence of binarism, implicit in contextual discourses, becomes explicit in strategic discourse.

Reproducing Contextual Discourses: Cultural Projects

Contextual discourses are reproduced in response to a problem. That problem is: What does one do with counterreactions? In the last chapter we saw that: children's reactions against parental distancing are held in check, first by negative sanctions and second by inhibitions; counterreactions are a response to inhibitions, rather than to parental behavior per se; and inhibitions have a stimulating effect upon counterreaction and, therefore, do not constitute an adequate defense against them. In Samoa, for example, punishment generates initial conformity and submissiveness to elders, but in the long run punishment also stimulates cheeky (*tautalaitiiti*) behavior in which the person challenges the status of superiors, as Teʻe challenges the status of the village chief by stealing his lavalava.

In the preceding chapter we also saw that moral discourse sublimates counterreactions by providing a narrative form through which they can be acted out in fantasy. We will soon see that contextual discourses also sublimate counterreactions, but are a more satisfying means to do so because they provide a performative style through which counterreactions can be acted out in reality. While developing youngsters are introduced to moral discourse through narration, they are introduced to contextual discourse through "cultural projects." Cultural projects are socially approved endeavors that further transform and camouflage counterreactions so that they lead, not only to social approval but even to a sense of achievement.

Erikson argues that inferiority feelings result from children's awareness that they want to do what parents define as bad (1963). Similarly, I argue that feelings of inferiority are brought on by the child's awareness of counterreactions. Erikson believes that an increasing ability to sublimate energy into industry is the antidote to the developing person's feelings of inferiority. Industry takes culturally scripted forms in cultural projects. Like contextual discourses, cultural projects are performances that employ a system of culture-specific signs.

As there are two contextual discourses (formal and informal), so also there are two cultural projects; one cultural project teaches participation in formal discourse, another participation in informal discourse. I, therefore, distinguish between cultural projects by calling one "formal" and the other "informal." Both cultural projects provide means to act out counterreaction through "performative inhibition," a performance in which one symbolically enacts an inhibition in a manner that disguises a counterreaction.

Remember that in moral discourse performative inhibition has a multi-leveled structure: on one level moral talk expresses inhibition, as the gossip of the village girls demonstrated their impartiality and their lack of ill will; on another it expresses a counterreaction—the village girls' gossip evinces their desire to show off as bridesmaids. We will see that in cultural projects, too, a counterreaction is expressed; however, rather than merely taking the form of talk, in cultural projects counterreactions are acted out, albeit in the guise of an action that symbolizes inhibition. Here again the guise serves as a denial of the nature of the enactment.[9]

Counterreactions replay enraged protests against negative sanctions; the rage that inspires protests is likely to linger on after these protests diminish and disappear. Formal and informal projects transform rage by displacing it through what psychoanalysts call reaction formation, in which an emotion is expressed through exaggerated forms of its own opposite: rage might appear in the guise of love, devotion, or loyalty toward elders who sanctioned the child. I do not mean that emotions such as devotion are not genuinely felt, but, inasmuch as negative sanctioning has been a focal part of the interaction between elders and youngster, elders remain ambivalent figures.

Because counterreactions are responses to inhibition, people have an enduring need to act them out, but the anxiety associated with inhibition is attendant upon doing so. That is why tales about acting out counterreactions, like Teʻe's (in which his heart is beating fast), are also about traumatic encounters with authority. Camouflaging counterreactions as cultural projects assuages some of this anxiety, but cultural projects remain avenues for acting out counterreactions, however surreptitious, and, therefore, they perpetuate some of this anxiety as well. By perpetuating a diminished degree of anxiety, cultural projects insure that the practitioner will need further opportunities to deny through acting out and will become devoted to the cultural project that permits it.

Formal Projects

We saw that in formal Samoan discourse, participants act as if there is a hierarchical relationship between participants. The cultural project that provides patterning for formal discourse in Samoa is rendering service to one's superiors. Training in this project begins as training in obedience to elders. Children are punished when they fail to obey, and punishment is discontinued only when they physically demonstrate abasement by lowering themselves: this act stands in for the missing obedience. Obedience and abasement are thereby defined as positive and negative versions of the same thing. Punishment, that most salient of Samoan sanctions, forges a symbolic equation between the two in the experience of the child.

The posture of the punished child, however, is also a performative version of inhibition. We saw that the punished child is expected not only to lower itself but also to stifle tears and to bow its head: the first gesture connotes the inhibition of assertiveness, the second an inhibition of personal feeling, and the third an inhibition of a desire for attention. If in Samoa the abasement of the punished child is symbolically equated with obedience and is a performative version of inhibition, then obedience is also a performative version of inhibition: obedience provides an idiom for abasement, and abasement equals inhibition.

The initial symbolic equation between abasement and obedience via punishment becomes the basis for a series of symbolic substitutions. As Samoan children begin to master the small tasks through which they provide direct assistance to elders, obedience becomes service: children carry out whole jobs—cleaning up the surrounds of the house, preparing a meal, and so forth—and these performances demonstrate abasement/inhibition just as the obedience of the child once did. As the child becomes a young adult, rendering actual services is partially replaced by rendering goods. Traditionally, girls wove mats and made tapa for the household; boys had their own taro plantation, from which they fed their family. More recently, when young people earn money at a job, they are expected to give their earnings to their parents. Thus, although inhibition denotes the suspension of action, it acquires cultural synonyms that denote forms of work and even of achievement: cultures use inhibition to create a field of endeavor that is symbolic in nature.

At the same time that Samoan young people are learning to perform inhibition through obedience, service, and the rendering of goods, they also acquire younger siblings, above whom they rank. Vis-à-vis this smaller person, they duplicate the pattern of hierarchical relations, becoming conspirators in the system and displacing dominance-seeking tendencies from relations with sanctioning elders to relations with juniors.[10] Mead describes older siblings' admonitions to younger ones as perpetual and says that "no mother will ever exert herself to discipline a younger child if an older one can be made responsible" ([1928] 1961:23–24). Young children should obey senior children without question, serving them as they do any other elder. Older children have the right to exercise the same forms of verbal and physical coercion used by any other elder.[11]

Samoan adolescents reach a middle management position in the administrations in which they participate. The adolescent girl assumes responsibility for administering the household and has as many under her as she has over her giving orders.[12] The adolescent boy enters the village association of young men ('aumāga) and begins helping to administer the village. In old Samoa the assembled chiefs constituted the legislative branch of government; the 'aumāga enforced its edicts.[13] Today members of the 'aumāga serve as a village police force and will occasionally beat, and not infrequently threaten, people who walk or run—Caucasian joggers, for example—or in any way disturb the quiet and the stillness of the village during the evening prayer period (Sā).[14]

The young Samoan's domination of his or her juniors is defined as yet another means of rendering service to the group. Inasmuch as service has become a synonym for abasement in the life of the child, service is a way of performing inhibition. Nonetheless, insisting that another person obey satisfies one's own desires for dominance. Inasmuch as this satisfaction is not coincident with the cultural definition of the situation, it is covert. Covert satisfaction may continue to exacerbate anxiety about censored counterreactions. To allay this anxiety the definition of one's actions as "rendering respect" must be reiterated by further demonstrations of abasement vis-à-vis seniors: the second act compensates for the first and serves as a retrospective denial of its significance.

It seems likely that the demonstration of abasement vis-à-vis seniors through the rendering of services and goods becomes increasingly necessary to youngsters as their authority and correlative opportunities to assert dominance expand. As young people become parents themselves, they are called upon to make contributions to their family chief to support him in his ceremonial obligations. As persons become higher in rank and have few, if any, superiors, abasement continues to be demonstrated by ceremonial prestations that tend to become increasingly frequent and lavish. We saw that each side of a Samoan ceremony symbolically abases itself to the other side through prestations and speeches: each side's chiefs treat those of the other side as if these chiefs were their own, to whom they render humble and obedient service. Thus, ceremonies continue the pattern of abasement vis-à-vis an authority figure.

Embedded in the formal project is a resignification of dominance-seeking tendencies: requiring obedience of inferiors assumes the guise of rendering service to superiors. Nonetheless, because requiring obedience acts out dominance seeking, it is likely to exacerbate instilled anxieties, inspiring new denials in the form of progressively resignified acts of abasement, namely: the rendering of obedience, service, goods, prestations, and, finally, oratory. Thus, in Samoa the formal cultural project feeds into formal discourse. This trajectory would help to explain the almost competitive character of Samoan ceremonial exchange, in which families wildly spend their often limited resources to honor one another.

Informal Projects

We saw that in informal Samoan discourse, participants express an as-if rivalry. The cultural project that provides patterning for this informal discourse is winning respect for one's group through peer competition. Competition is a form of dominance seeking and gives expression to this counterreaction; however, competing with the representatives of other groups is defined as yet another form of service to one's own group. Competitively forwarding the status of one's group displaces dominance-seeking tendencies from family relations to relations between families.

Samoan children are encouraged to express dominance over rivals from other families by physically beating them. My father-in-law's favorite daughter, Pili, was once beaten by the girls of another family. The genesis of the fight was unclear, but undoubtedly the girls felt insulted by Pili and subsequently attacked her. When Pili returned home, my father-in-law divided his eight other children into a female battalion and a male battalion and marched them over to the family of the pugnacious girls, demanding that their family send its children out to fight.

The physical symbolism of competition between families also takes a more rarefied verbal form, lampooning (*faipona*) children of other village families. By the age of five children will make up funny names for one another such as Vae Popoʻu (Legs with Sores), Gutu Felea (Thick Lips), Taepisi (Splash Bowels), Taligafailā (Ears like Sails), and Piliuli (Black Lizard), depending on the other's personal characteristics. Another popular object of jest is family failings. When my Samoan husband was growing up, for example, his uncle initiated a campaign for local political office a few weeks before the day of the election. The uncle's slogan was "Never Too Late!" He lost the election. All my husband's school chums called him "Too Late" for weeks. Perhaps the most common method employed by village children to lampoon each other is calling another child by the name of one of its parents. The teaser means to take the parent's name in vain and, in a larger sense, also the family name.[15]

While lampooning is as-if behavior, these pseudo-assaults so resemble literal assaults that they can lead to fighting. Among children lampooning often does. Fights between children are one thing, but in a Samoan village fights between adolescents of rival families amount to civil war. In adolescence, therefore, status rivalry tends to become formalized in competitive sport events between rival villages, displacing dominance-seeking tendencies from interfamily relations to intervillage relations.

Today a village will typically sponsor a male longboat crew, a male rugby team, a male cricket team, and a female cricket team. In old Samoa feasts between villages were often accompanied by "club and sham fights, boxing and wrestling matches" (Stair 1897:137–38, 236–38), and frequently ended "in broken heads, limbs, and teeth knocked out" (Wilkes 1845:137).[16] Villages also made journeys specifically for the purpose of engaging in these sports (*malaga taʻaloga*). When Samoans adapted British cricket in the nineteenth century, cricket matches were staged as mock battles in which whole villages participated (Churchward 1887:145–46), and cricket bats "looked like battle clubs" (Garrett 1982:278). However belligerent the bats looked, cricket players have long equated scoring with *ula*. Thus, describing cricket matches, the nineteenth-century British consul Churchward says:

> Their antics in the field beggar description. Each ... club would have a distinct method of expressing its joy at the dismissal of an adversary from the wickets; some of them, of a most elaborate nature, must have taken much careful drilling in private to ensure such perfect performance in public. (1887:146)[17]

These choreographic jokes now characterize girls' matches and tend to be led by a male transvestite.

Earlier we saw that *ula* consists in joking about things sexual or scatological, thereby figuratively displaying people's "private" side. This display is inconsistent with rendering respect and, hence, a put-down. In *ula*, however, putting down the other is often disguised as putting down oneself: one abandons one's dignity in order to joke, acts in a manner contrary to one's dignity while joking (by displaying things of a private nature), and jokes tend to refer to oneself. We also saw that Joking Nights resembled a competitive game between villages but differed from sports in an important respect: in Samoan sports, as in fights, boys engage boys and girls engage girls; the two groups exchanging entertainments at Joking Nights were of opposite sexes. This incongruity undercut the rivalrous character of the interchange, making a travesty of intervillage competitiveness.

There is, then, an implied vector in the development of the informal project during childhood and adolescence. The vector moves from lampooning to sports to exchanges of *ula* and represents a progressive resignification of dominance-seeking tendencies that concludes in the Samoan informal discourse of humor. In fact, Samoans *ula* with one another from early childhood. It is just that, while *ula* never displaces more direct forms of competitiveness, it gradually becomes the more common form. Further, the most likely subject for *ula* is sexuality; therefore, although the primary (covert) intent of *ula* is to seek dominance and is aggressive, it assumes the guise of sexual sentiments.

Nonetheless, because *ula* is a form of acting out, it is also likely to exacerbate instilled anxieties about dominance seeking, inspiring new denials in the form of further *ula*. Because *ula* is, *au fond*, a kind of dominance seeking, each act tends to be followed by a more dramatic act in a circular attempt to deny what the act covertly asserts. This trajectory would explain the rising crescendo that characterized Joking Nights in which performances became increasingly bawdy as the night progressed, until finally participants tore off one another's clothes (Krämer [1902]1995:377).

Respect, *Ula*, and Marriage

In cultural projects one progressively resignifies counterreactions, moving from physical tropes to social tropes to linguistic/artistic tropes in the cultural discourse. In brief, the punished child expresses respect for elders by abasing itself physically, but in the formal project this physical symbolism is replaced by more rarefied forms of respect: the rendering of obedience, service, and goods to superiors and ultimately ceremonial prestations and flowery oratory. In the informal project beating someone from another family is replaced by more rarefied forms of dominance seeking such as lampooning, sports, and entertainment exchanges of *ula*. Courtship and marriage represent a transitional point between the physical tropes favored in childhood and the more abstract tropes that hallmark adulthood, exploiting both kinds. In nineteenth-century Samoa there were two types of marriage, corresponding to the two contextual discourses. Formal marriages (*fa'aipoipoga*) were typical between ranking persons and took place in the discourse of respect. Commoners made informal marriages through elopements (*āvaga*) that often came about through an exchange of *ula* at Joking Nights.[18]

Ranking Marriage

In courtship between persons of rank, respect was demonstrated by all through the tropes of silence and deference. Those who married did not speak to each other: arrangements were handled by go-betweens (*soa*). A girl of status did not say no but was expected to marry at the discretion of her family or village chiefs. Even chiefs, however, were expected to bow to the discretion of their orators, who arranged marriages in light of political considerations; chiefs who failed to marry at their orators' behest might well be assassinated (Krämer [1923] 1949; Institutions and Customs of the Samoans [1944] 1954; Henry 1980).

Ranking marriages also trafficked in the symbolism of respect through ceremonial prestations, exchanged between the bride's and groom's families. This mutual rendering of wealth contributed to the prestige of both families. The prestige of the occasion was most concentrated in the bride, specifically in her virginity. Ritual defloration was the apex of the ceremony and involved an elaborate public display of the bride's hymeneal blood. Chief Tuiteleleapaga describes both the operation and the display.

> The old ladies from the maternal side of the bride prepared an elevated bed about two or three feet high, consisting entirely of the best mats purposely kept for such an occasion. On top of the bed was placed a white roll of tapa cloth, exactly on the spot where the buttocks of the bride were to lie, as a receptacle for the hymeneal blood. . . . A selected talking chief [orator], usually from the groom's roster . . . with two forefingers wrapped in immaculate tapa cloth . . . sat by her side or between her legs and . . . broke the hymen . . . the talking chief made a display of his gory fingers. (1980:69)

Alternatively, the groom might perform the operation and, when he did so, "wiped his hands on a white bark cloth which he wore around his waist for the rest of the day as a token of respect for his wife" (Freeman 1983:231).[19]

In Samoa formal marriage was and is popularly understood as a triumph for the bride and her family: she is honored above all. Yet formal marriage songs in old Samoa betray a contrary meaning, celebrating a boy's social triumph rather than that of the girl (Moyle 1988:181–89). The same contrariety is evident in the ritual acts involved in defloration. We saw in the analysis of *ula* that Samoans see things carnal as antithetical to dignity. In defloration the girl was publicly subjected to a carnal operation, in the nude, in which her virtue was publicly tried, and thereby risked public humiliation. In fact, the humiliation could begin before the actual ceremony. Old ladies from both sides might examine the girl by a stream, just to make sure the actual event would not embarrass all concerned. If the woman conducting the examination

> found that the hymen had been broken, she grabbed the girl by the hair and dragged her all over the water, cursing her with a litany of 15-letter words and mentioning the names of her dead aunts and uncles, or she even inflicted severe punishment . . . others followed in materializing their disappointment. (Tuiteleleapaga 1980:69)

In the defloration ritual the boy, or his representative, performed an action that, in any other venue, would be understood as abasing a girl. Further, the defloration was followed by an act of abasement on the part of the boy and the audience: they anointed themselves with the bride's blood. Blood is irremediably carnal. For this reason in the Samoan language of respect the word for *blood* is replaced by a euphemism, *dirt*.[20] By wearing the bride's blood, the groom and the audience together symbolically abased themselves, elevating the bride by contrast. The second act compensated for the first and served as a retrospective denial of its significance. Through a cultural redefinition of the event, and through compensatory gestures, formal marriage, like the formal project, draped dominance seeking in a cloak of respect.

Common Marriage

In the nineteenth century formal marriages provided an occasion for Joking Nights; in turn Joking Nights were a pretext for marriages of commoners. On the marriage day, after the ceremonial exchange and defloration,

> all prepared with anticipation for the *poula,* or night of revelry and lascivious conduct, during which there was a great deal of provocative singing, dancing and contorted acts, as well as all sorts of nocturnal antics and mischief customary to a nuptial night. . . . The night's debauchery usually resulted in half of the girls and boys from both sides eloping. (Tuiteleleapaga 1980:68–69; see also Krämer [1902] 1995:377)

While polite restraint was demonstrated in formal courtship, Joking Nights dramatized the overcoming of inhibition. Those who courted formally refrained from speaking to each other; in Joking Nights youths bantered shamelessly. We saw that, in Samoan childhood, being teased results in inhibitions that compel youngsters to behave effacingly and that these feelings are called *matamuli* and *mā*. *Matamuli,* literally "eyes behind," glosses as *shy*. *Mā* glosses as *embarrassed*. The later stages of the Joking Nights, however, took place largely in the nude, and, instead of having one's eyes behind, one gazed openly at the most private parts of the other. Instead of being shy, one behaved boldly. In Samoan social theory it was the prerogative of elders to arrange their descendants' marriages, but in Joking Nights couples often eloped. Informal courtship, therefore, allowed those involved to exhibit an expressiveness and assertiveness that would be considered cheeky (*tautalaitiiti*) in any other context but at Joking Nights were framed as play, that is, in an as-if mode.

Formal marriage involved physical gestures through which the groom abased the bride and then compensated by abasing himself. In contrast, Joking Nights involved *ula* through which each side playfully abased the other through the exhibition of carnality. Missionary accounts, however, suggest that girls took the lead in abasing the boys' side of the dance.[21] Girls put down boys in the guise of shedding their own dignity along with their clothes. This fictive insult, however, was a pretext for allowing themselves to be abased: the elopements that followed were looked upon as a "defeat" suffered by the girl and her family through her (Schultz [1949–50] 1980:49). Like the "insult" to the boy that proceeded it, however, the girl's abasement was fictive rather than real. A lower-status family had little to lose should the girl elope with the scion of a family rich in land, fine mats, or titles. Thus, a contemporary Samoan friend says of the Joking Nights he witnessed as a boy:

> That's how . . . the traveling party from the other village will intermarry, that's the time they find spouses . . . if [this guy] happens to be high in the social ranks of the village or the district. . . . Or if this guy has plenty of material things to give . . . who cares about what happened during the night. This will consummate social relationships. This will only elevate social status. This will bring prestige. This will bring wealth.

Tropics of Childhood

This chapter is more theoretically difficult than its predecessors, so I will take a moment to retrace it. We saw that moral discourse is innocent of its symbolic content, taking this content to be true. In contrast, contextual discourses are explicit in their as-if character: in these discourses meanings are conveyed, not directly but through culturally shared tropes in which children are trained from their earliest years. Contextual discourses, however, are innocent of their oversimplified form, which divides social life into only two contexts—formal and informal. This binary categorization of social life simply does not do justice to the real variety of social contexts, any more than the binary categories of good and bad do justice to the real moral ambiguity of behavior. In other words, although contextual discourses evince a recognition that they are symbolic modes of communication, they lack recognition of the difference between discourse and experience: contextual discourses (formal and informal) are binary, while experience is infinitely various. It is nonetheless true that the difference between binary discourses and infinitely variable experience is anticipated in the most developed examples of contextual discourse, ceremonies and popular entertainments. In these events, as in ritual in Victor Turner's sense of the term (1977), discursive and other social categories are intermixed and creatively combined, rather than applied in accordance with a simplistic binarism.

Children prepare to participate in contextual discourses (and acquire motivation to do so) through a gradual redefinition of counterreactions and by learning to traffic in a cultural system of signs. In Samoa this preparation begins when children are addressed in imperatives. In reaction to imperatives children tend to become obstinate (*musu*) and are, therefore, punished. By this means they are forced to submit to the will of their superiors. The result of this sanction is an inhibition of assertiveness that makes children passive and submissive but also increases their need for dominance. Initially, children act out this counterreaction by *tautalaitiiti* behavior, that is, by talking back or culturally kindred forms of impudence. Samoans, however, amend cheeky tendencies by embedding youngsters in a hierarchical system in which children demonstrate the inhibition of dominance seeking by demanding this inhibition of others. Demanding that others inhibit their willfulness covertly satisfies the child's own need for dominance. Covert satisfaction helps to canalize dominance seeking but also stimulates the anxiety associated with punishment because in early childhood dominance seeking was typically followed by punishment. This anxiety creates a further need to deny desires for dominance through abasement before authority figures that can be expressed through further acts of obedience, service, and by the rendering of goods that signify obedient service to elders and fealty to chiefs. These renderings, in turn, are replaced by ceremonial prestations that signify an as-if fealty of one group to another. Through this sequence the moral value of respect turns rhetorical, becoming a ritual performance.

In Samoan ceremonies the discourse of respect involves an alternating sequence: sometimes one flatters the other side of the ceremony through complementary address and prestations and abases one's own side; sometimes one is, by the same method, granted a dominant position oneself. This sequence would be psychologically necessary if being elevated to a dominant position carried with it a compensatory need to demonstrate abasement. It also dovetails with the discourse of respect and perpetuates anxieties likely to feed this discourse.

Likewise, the informal project provides acceptable forms in which to act out a desire for dominance: first through beating children of rival families, then through lampooning them, then through competing with young people of rival villages in sports, and finally by "insulting" them in *ula*. In old Samoa *ula*, in Joking Nights, began marriages between villages that amended the dangers of dominance seeking by providing grounds for alliance. This is not to say that young people participated in Joking Nights because they were socially useful.

They did so because Joking Nights were enjoyable, but this was so at least in part because these hilarious volleys of mock insults voiced their desires for dominance.

Like formal and informal discourses, moral discourse permits the covert expression of counterreactions and likewise stimulates a degree of anxiety that must be assuaged by further discoursing. Moral discourse, however, is an occasional activity that requires the excuse of untoward conduct to legitimate it. It is, therefore, largely a retrospective measure that neither circumvents the need for repression nor the correlative danger of antisocial forms of acting out. In contrast, cultural projects combine contradictory tendencies in activities that are ongoing and for which one can receive social recognition. Contextual discourses are extensions of cultural projects: the performances through which counterreactions (dominance seeking, for example) are resignified progress from physical tropes (like beating someone) to linguistic tropes (like joking) and on to artistic copies of earlier tropes in the series. The performances through which counterreactions are retrospectively denied undergo a similar resignification: from physical tropes (like lowering one's body) to linguistic/artistic tropes (like flowery oratory). Cultural projects, therefore, just as contextual discourses, provide a surreptitious means to act out and to deny counterreactions. Here too, however, a residual anxiety attends upon acting out that stimulates repeated performances. This is the nature of the compulsion to engage in contextual discourse and the means by which contextual discourses are reproduced.

Contextual discourses seem a neat solution to the problems produced by an inevitable lopsidedness in the way cultures define the self and its moral properties. These discourses free people from the need for repression, sublimating and channeling energy into culturally defined modes and venues. Satisfaction need not be confined to fantasy (as in moral discourse). Indeed, the very elements of self that were morally suspect become the basis of a sense of achievement in social reality. In Samoan contextual discourses dominance seeking can make one a successful orator or entertainer, and both these figures are objects of public approbation, nay, fame and appreciation.

Surely, contextual discourses offer a better psychological economy than moral discourses, actualizing a broader spectrum of human potentials. But there remains an unsolved problem that harasses people in their use of contextual discourses: life does not always imitate social structure, neatly sorting itself out into preordained contexts. What people do in face of a lack of correspondence between cultural ways of talk and thought and the real vagaries and surprises of experience is the subject of the next chapter.

6

Strategic Discourses and Cultural Antinomies

Cultural life inevitably presents people with situations in which standard prescriptions for contextually appropriate talk are inadequate. At such a pass social actors are apt to mix elements of contextual discourses, adapting them in light of their strategic properties. I call these hybridized discourses *strategic*. In the contextual division of social life into two contexts—one formal, the other informal—each context carries with it a set of protocols, or situational rules, for behavior. We saw that, having constitutive rules, contextual discourses resemble games: they dictate no absolute rights and wrongs but represent conventions that are limiting within certain parameters. The conventions are that one communicate indirectly, through a set of tropes (such as the reluctance to say no in formal Samoan discourse or the exhibition of things private in informal Samoan discourse). Further, in their most definitive forms contextual discourses play with and invert those structural categories that represent their initial presuppositions, as do Samoan ceremonies and Joking Nights. Strategic discourse expands upon the idea of language games and language play; it is as a species of gamesmanship, playing upon all available discourses to achieve a purpose that is practical in nature.

I argued in the introduction that wooing is a universally shared life event that may call for a hybridization of discourse types. Although cultures provide contextual discourses for wooing, and both formal and informal contexts in which to woo, the person's desires range outside these confines. When they do, wooers are likely to encounter contextually enigmatic situations that provoke the development of strategic discourse. Adapting a term from Dreyfus (1984), one might call wooing a "cultural-reference situation," one of those intellectually illustrative but also emotionally charged situations that become culturally coded holistic reference memories, in the present case reference memories for how to do strategic discourse.[1] In Samoa strategic discourse is represented by "dual figures," two figures that are cultural counterparts of each other and that, taken together, interfuse contextual discourses.[2]

Wooing in Samoa

We saw that in old Samoa formal courtship was carried out in the discourse of respect, and the dignity of all parties was protected by the use of go-betweens (*soa*). Informal courtship often occurred on Joking Nights and was conducted in the discourse of humor, in which all parties discarded their dignity and engaged in verbal and choreographic jests (*ula*). In the elopements that often followed, the girl and her family were seen as having suffered a "defeat." While at Joking Nights this defeat was framed as ironic, outside these boundaries it was not. *Moetotolo,* "rape"—literally "sleep crawling"—is an illicit method of scoring against another extended family; it is also a way of diminishing a girl's status (Schoeffel 1978:75, 1979a:178–79, 185).[3] In Samoa an unmarried female is thought of as another boy's sister; sisters have a status above brothers, while husbands have a status above wives.[4] Typically, the sleep crawler attacks a girl in her family house, either placing his hand over her mouth or rendering her unconscious by hitting her in the solar plexus. He then rapes her. Freeman documents cases in which the boy touches the girl's genitals, breaking her hymen, rather than actually initiating intercourse (1983:244–47). By doing so, the sleep crawler acts like the groom in a defloration ceremony. Out of shame a girl who has been abased in this manner is likely to elope with the boy to his family.[5] Even if she refuses, however, in a sense the "marriage" has already come about. Schoeffel tells of a boy who appeared during a wedding ceremony and, holding up the fingers of one hand, shouted, "with this, I have . . . made her my wife" (1979a:185–86).

Given the capacity of sex to diminish girls' status, it is no surprise that, when a Samoan boy speaks to a girl of his desires, the girl is apt to interpret his advances as an attempt to assert dominance (*tautalaitiiti*).[6] My Samoan niece Sina would ride the school bus in early adolescence. She used to complain that some of the boys were "cheeky" (*tautalaitiiti*); what she meant was that they flirted with her.

If some boys are cheeky, many Samoan boys are abashed and tongue-tied in girls' presence and hesitate to display personal sexual sentiments. During childhood Samoan boys are punished for dominance-seeking; the result is likely to be anxiety about their desires for dominance. Boys are likely to have overcome much of this anxiety in cultural projects, but cultural projects presuppose clearly defined contexts. The ambiguity of wooing outside of a clearly defined context often reawakens anxiety. The girl's tendency to interpret advances negatively, together with his own inhibitions, place the boy in a dilemma, for success with women remains a defining element of Samoan male identity. The solution to this dilemma has been an adaptation of the institution of the go-between (*soa*) employed in formal marriages.

We saw that in old Samoa a high-ranking suitor employed a *soa* (go-between) to arrange a marriage with the family of his intended. The ordinary boy, like his ranking counterpart, was also apt to employ a companion to speak for him in marriage arrangements. For the commoner, however, sending a go-between to a girl's family was problematic: not all boys could expect a welcome reception. Samoan parents still tend to be picky about prospective sons-in-law and are convinced of their daughters' ability to lure high-status husbands.[7] The double, therefore, often approached the girl herself rather than her family.[8] While the chief's formal go-between displayed elaborate courtesy to all parties, the discourse of the common *soa* was characterized by ironic impertinence. He still praised his principal but tended to joke with, rather than exalt, the object of his pursuit. Mead provides an example.

> If you wish to know who is really the lover, look then not at the boy who sits by her side, looks boldly into her eyes and twists the flowers in her necklace around his fingers or steals the hibiscus flower from her hair that he may wear it behind his ear. Do not think it is he who whispers softly in her ear, or says to her, "Sweetheart, wait for me to-night. After the moon has set, I will come to you," or who teases her by saying she has many lovers. Look instead at the boy who sits far off, who sits with bent head and takes no part in the joking. And you will see that his eyes are always turned softly on the girl. Always he watches her and never does he miss a movement of her lips. Perhaps she will wink at him, perhaps she will raise her eyebrows, perhaps she will make a sign with her hand. He must always be wakeful and watching or he will miss it. The *soa* meanwhile pays the girl elaborate and ostentatious court and in undertones pleads the cause of his friend. ([1928] 1961:96–97)

Through praising of the prospective lover and teasing the girl, the approach of the *soa* combines the discourse of respect with that of humor. Likewise, *soa* and lover together constitute a dual figure. In this passage the *soa* behaves like a cheeky boy; the real lover sits silent and passive, like a thoroughly cowed child. The *soa* engages in a dominance-asserting type of talk: it is a jocular attack on the girl's dignity (*ula*) and it attempts to turn a "sister" into a "wife." The silence and passivity of the real lover stands as a mark of respect. This doubleness, however, is also represented in the figure of the *soa* itself. *Soa* means "double" and can refer to the members of any pair in which items duplicate each other.

At Joking Nights assertiveness was not an insult because the context was playful rather than serious; gestures were framed so as to indicate that they were not meant literally. Similarly, the assertiveness of the double, *soa,* is not insulting, but for a different reason: the double is not trying to win anything for himself and is, therefore, joking about his own intentions, but he is not joking about those of his friend. Here the definition of the situation as jocular stems from an ambiguity of intent, an ambiguity created by the disjunction between the intention of the double and that of his principal. Remember, in Samoa social attitude rather than personal intent is the usual criterion of moral judgments; therefore, the importance of intent in framing vicarious courtship is a noteworthy anomaly. The double's intent is representation, that is, to play a social role in the service of a friend. If the activity itself is framed as role playing, however, its content is to convey the most personal sentiments. Thus, through the issue of intent the double's discourse mediates between social role and subjectivity and bridges the most fundamental opposition in self systems.

Samoan moral discourse could be looked upon as instructions—a set of dos and don'ts—for excluding subjective elements of experience in order to play roles well. Samoan contextual discourse could be looked on as scripts for two parts, one respectful and one jocular. Playing a scripted part necessitates a disengagement from private emotions in order to portray those conventional sentiments dictated by a role. Thus, we saw the Samoan who plays the role of host always says "*Tālofa,*" glossed as "Welcome," but which literally means "We love you." The host also acts out a script that reflects this conventionalized sentiment, serving guests tirelessly and granting their every request. But conventional sentiments do not correspond to the full range of personal feeling, as attested by Robert Louis Stevenson's should-be host hiding in the bush while his would-be guests search for him. In contrast, the role of the double provides an opportunity to fully express personal feelings by disowning them.

Earlier we saw that contextual discourses are taken up because they secure the freer expression of socially disapproved counterreactions by providing culturally approved forms of acting-out behavior. Furthermore, these forms serve as denials that one is acting out. Contextual discourses are reproduced, however, because the acting out they allow stimulates a degree of anxiety, which must be repeatedly overcome by further denials in the form of further discourse. Strategic discourses offer the same benefits but to a greater degree, while lessening liabilities. They too offer a camouflaged means to act out: the double is performing a service and thus appears to engage in the formal cultural project, which in Samoa is a project of service (*tautua*). But in the discourse of the double acting out is less disguised and denial made by a simpler ruse: the double is actually expressing personal feelings, so his actions are very close indeed to those that are condemned in moral and formal discourses and that are only allowed in highly tropic form in informal discourse. The ruse is that these most personal sentiments, about which the double is so direct, are not personal *to him:* they are not his sentiments—or so it appears—for this ruse is not merely the psychological version of hairsplitting, a trick of rules (or roles); we will soon see it is often a ruse in every sense of the word. Because strategic discourse maximizes expression and manages the need for repression more economically than contextual discourses, the social actor is moved to reproduce it.

However economical, the figure of the double appears to reconstitute the opposition between social acting and subjectivity on a new level. By virtue of the double's role as a representative, distance on private sentiments and a repression of the speaker's personal self is maintained. In practice, however, the double often erases this distance. To illuminate the practice of the double, I turn to a Samoan trope through which courting was traditionally understood, pigeon catching.

Representative Doubles and Decoy Pigeons

Pigeon catching was chiefly sport in old Samoa.[9] It was carried out with decoy birds. Young pigeons would be caught, leashed around the leg, and trained. Chiefs took trained birds, secured by a long string, to a pigeon-catching mound.[10] They then released the pigeons to circle about the mound on the string, as if circling around food or water. Wild birds would be attracted to the area, fly above the mound, whereupon they were captured by the chiefs, who waited in blinds below.

In proverbs that highlight wedding speeches today the captured pigeon is a metaphor for the marrying girl. Thus, in one speech the orator says, "we must rejoice that the bird has entered the cage, for the decision has been reached . . . Thank you, for the pigeon has altered its course because of your desire and our own wish" (Matā'afa Tu'i 1987:47, 48, 60). This comparison is pervasive in Samoan mythology.[11] By analogy the double is a decoy bird with which the groom may "capture" a girl. A decoy pigeon is, after all, likewise a double.

The doubling inherent in the use of decoy birds suggests duplicity. Indeed, in Samoan proverbs pigeon catching may be used as a metaphor for nefarious designs (Schultz [1949–50] 1985:31–32). Duplicity was, in fact, inherent in the methodology of the hunt: birds were lured by a trick rather than openly pursued. The word for luring is *fa'alata*. *Fa'alata* means "to lure" but also "to tame," which was what Samoans liked to do with the most beautiful of their captured pigeons. In 1772 the French navigator Bougainville reported that Samoans "amuse themselves in their leisure hours by taming birds. Their houses were full of wood-pigeons, and they bartered them by the hundreds" (qtd. in Muse and Muse 1982:1, Williams [1830–32] 1984:83).

The word *fa'alata* can be applied to humans, in which case it refers to the capturing of affection. Samoans say that the child, like a small animal, must be lured or tamed. Later this word may be used in courtship, for *fa'alata* is derived from the word *latalata*, which means "near," or "to make someone come near." When boys or girls desire a relationship, they may say "*Fa'alatalata mai si ou agāga*," which means "Make your spirit closer." The double lured the girl by persuading her to meet secretly with his principle, "under the palm trees," as Mead says ([1928] 1961). Clandestine meetings of this sort carry with them an expectation either of sexual intimacy or of elopement.[12] Doubles and the clandestine meetings they arrange, however, can be dangerous for a girl: she may be lured for one boy only to be delivered to another (Goodman 1983). Thus, one of my Samoan friends says:

Sometimes young men who have never had sexual experience . . . and . . . for instance if this guy is not a very nice looking . . . handsome guy—ugly looking—we [are] scared to look at his face, and then what we did in the *fa'aSāmoa* is called the *fa'asoa* . . . means you go between. So we tell the girl, "Hey, [there is] this nice boy," and she knows who you're talking about . . . "We can bring this boy to you." And she fantasizes a lot with that boy and what happen [is] she came thinking she was going to go with this young handsome guy but [it is] not the case, she will end up with the dragon, with the ugly looking thing, but what will she do. She cannot scream, sometimes she [will] get hit on the *moa* [epigastrium]. . . . So then you wake up after it's done. So what would you do, go tell the village or go tell your family that you been . . . to bed with this ugly guy?

The jocular tone of this story highlights the connection between Samoan joking and dominance seeking, and the dark side of *fa'alata*. *Fa'alata* also means "to betray." Judas Iscariot is known in Samoa as Iuta Le Fa'alata, literally "Judas the Betrayer." As a form of betrayal, *fa'alata* refers to someone who treats you with deference but for an ulterior motive. *Fa'alata* people assume a pleasant manner but do not sincerely respect the object of their ministrations and may act to hurt the other through gossip or through more direct means, if they get the chance.[13]

Luring (*fa'alata*) and the duplicitous role playing it suggests are morally ambiguous, and yet *fa'alata* also implies a fully conscious use of Samoan lexicons and discourses on self. In pigeon catching duplicitous acting is put to use by the high chief. The tame bird plays the role of a wild bird but is not. The high chief uses this role playing to capture the wild bird. The decoy bird–plus–high chief is a dual figure that represents a capacity for the strategic deployment of roles and thus for self-conscious role playing. Perhaps it was for this reason that pigeon catching was a major event in old Samoa and the pigeon a symbol of status. Pigeon catching involved month-long excursions in which whole villages accompanied their chiefs into the bush (Pritchard 1866:161, Churchward 1887:141). Samoan social structure is based upon the ranking of titles. The village registry of titles, recited to identify those present at any ceremony, is called the *fa'alupega*. The word *fa'alupega* is derived from the word *lupe*, "pigeon" (Milner 1966:115–16). The term *fa'alupe*, literally "the way of the pigeon," means "to have a title."[14]

The double is a lure who serves the lover, much as the decoy pigeon serves the high chief. Speaking of personal sentiments to a girl, a double also personifies the personal side of the self, or *loto*—repressed or channeled in all former discourses—now virtually free (as the tame pigeon is free to fly in a manner resembling the wild pigeon). Yet, inasmuch as the double acts for another and not selfishly, he embodies a *loto* thoroughly trained to act in the service of sociocentric values.

But, if duplicitous acting can be used to deceive a "bird," it can also be used to deceive one's principal. When speaking of the double (*soa*) in my college classes in Samoa, the older ladies would always giggle and say, "Yes, but he often ends up with the girl!" Mead tells us:

> The choice of a *soa* presents many difficulties. If the lover chooses a steady, reliable boy, some slightly younger relative devoted to his interests, a boy unambitious in affairs of the heart, very likely the ambassador will bungle the whole affair through inexperience and lack of tact. But if he chooses a handsome and expert wooer who knows just how "to speak softly and walk gently," then as likely as not the girl will prefer the second to the principal. This difficulty is occasionally anticipated by employing two or three *soas* and setting them to spy on each other. But such a lack of trust is likely to inspire a similar attitude in the agents, and as one overcautious and disappointed lover told me ruefully, "I had five *soas*, one was true and four were false." ([1928] 1961:90)

This type of courtship was common enough to have a name, *fa'asoa a Talali*, after a *soa* who eloped with every girl he was ever commissioned to woo (Tuiteleleapaga 1980:65).

If doubles are infamous for deceiving lovers, the ability of pigeons to deceive chiefs is also recounted in a story of Tigilau and Sina, the star-crossed lovers of Polynesian mythology.[15] In one of the Samoan Tigilau/Sina stories, Sina desires Tigilau, but her parents marry her to Tupu o le Fanua.[16] In Samoan *tupu* is often glossed as "king" and refers to a particularly exalted chief. So one might say that here Tupu represents the figure of the high chief, who we saw in chapter 3 personifies idealized role playing and with it the primary values of the Samoan sociocentric order.

Tupu's distinctive ability is that he has power over birds, whom he calls as he pleases. Like an idealized pigeon-catching chief, he is able to assemble birds at will. One is reminded of Firth's Tikopian examples of those who have *mana*, for whom fish congregate for capture (1949).[17] Sina has Tupu call the birds and selects a young pigeon to keep. The pigeon is tied around the leg, as decoy birds are, but turns out to be Tigilau in an assumed form. In the dark of night Tigilau, having again become a man, elopes with Sina. Here the tame bird (Tigilau, as a pigeon tied by the leg) makes off with the wild bird (the marriageable girl). In fact Tigilau is no tame bird: he symbolizes the idea that, when one plays roles strategically, one can play them for oneself as easily as for another. In strategic discourse subjectivity escapes its bonds along with Tigilau.

In his escape Tigilau also embodies a new relation to tropes. In contextual discourses tropes are conduits for conventionalized meanings: in Samoan formal discourse silence bespeaks the abasement of the personal self; in Samoan informal discourse exhibitionism bespeaks its assertion; and so forth. But Tigilau, playing the role of the decoy pigeon, reverses this pigeon's culturally given symbolism: rather than representing service to a chief, Tigilau-as-pigeon represents subversion and thus betrays the aleatory, unpredictable property of tropes.

In his relation to tropes Tigilau also brings to light an ambiguity in the analogy between the *soa* and the decoy bird. In wooing, the *soa* is a duplicate of his principle, in that he takes the place of that party. In pigeon catching, however, the tame pigeon is actually the duplicate of the unsecured wild bird. The tame bird attracts the wild bird through resemblance. This parallel suggests an affinity between the *soa* and the girl, who is the wild bird; its innuendo is that there is a residual wildness in the *soa*. With strategic discourse and its embodying figures the experiences of self, lost in a prejudicial ontological premise, are regained, but so is a fantasy of the self's intrinsic wildness and freedom from social constraint, a fantasy with which these experiences were associated. This freedom may be a fantasy, but it is not mere fantasy: the articulation of strategic discourse is also an articulation of creativity and of agency.

The implication for development latent in duplicitous decoy birds is simply this: sexuality and the need for intimacy are apt to bring a problem to bear on the developing person; namely, conformity to moral codes and contextualized rules of appropriateness may not get one what (or who) one wants. If this sounds individualistic, remember that the object of desire is culturally constructed. In Samoa the object of desire is likely to be a prepossessing person of high status (who will, potentially, raise the status of one's group), although in Samoa, as everywhere else, desire is notoriously whimsical, unpredictable, and often at odds with accepted values. Even when young people desire those to whom elders object, however, desire is culturally patterned, just as *lotōa* (passionate desire) is patterned in Samoa. To respond adequately to desire in all its human dimensionality calls for a creativeness not provisioned in foregoing discourses.

All prior discourses portray human nature in terms of binary oppositions, although these oppositions take different forms throughout the series. In ontological premises there is an opposition between one aspect of experience that is emphasized and another that is downplayed. In moral discourse the opposition is between an aspect that should be emphasized and one that should be minimized. In contextual discourses the opposition is between a rhetoric based on social poetics and a rhetoric derived from a suspect dimension of self. In strategic discourses opposition is initially maintained: formal rhetoric is used as a frame, while the informal rhetoric becomes the content. Thus, in the discourse of the double, praising his principle (a formal rhetoric) is the frame for action, while joking (an informal rhetoric) is the content. Likewise, serving one's principle (the formal project) is a frame, while seeking to dominate the girl and her family (the informal project) is the content. Here the frames serve as prophylactic containers of suspect contents. But gradually—as the social actor recognizes the implications of the notion that discourses can be combined to suit contingencies—the actor's preferential relation to the acceptable and suspect elements of self disappears and with it the provincial character of personhood.

Strategic Discourses and Adult Identity

Developing moral and contextual discourses means internalizing preexisting parts of the world, such as moral narratives and cultural projects. In strategic discourses development becomes improvisational: one devises moves as one goes along. Here the person's own desire inspires a relativization and partial transcendence of the self system in terms of which development has taken place. Moral and contextual discourses refer to compulsory forms of behavioral competence: those who are incapable of conforming to local ethics or to local notions of appropriateness are not well accepted by society. But cultures merely offer prototypes of persons who use strategic discourses as exemplifying a method for resolving contradictions inevitably entailed by the attempt to divide social life into contexts. The Samoan prototype of strategic discourses is the historical figure of the orator, a figure derived from the *soa* (go-between).

High chiefs (*ali'i*) were the original hereditary chiefs of Samoa (Kirch 1984). Orators were their executors. Acting as a *soa*, however, was so primary to the role of the orator that the term was used to encompass the broad-ranging services he rendered. Thus, the saying "The orator makes *soa* for his chief" does not necessarily refer to courting but simply means "The orator works on behalf of his chief" (Milner 1966:212).[18] In the political negotiations of old Samoa the high chief, like the lover, could not directly seek dominance. Just as the *soa* who formally courted a high-ranking girl for a marriage of state, the orator muted dominance seeking by flattering those to whom he spoke. Meanwhile, he attributed his principal an exalted status through his oratorical reconstructions of genealogy, a status that legitimated claims to land and titles.

Perhaps it was because of the orator's duplicitous usefulness that oratory may be referred to in proverbs as a "net," such as that used in pigeon hunts, and delivering a speech to capturing a pigeon.[19] The Samoan proverb "The catching place is full of decoy pigeons" refers to "a village that boasts of experienced orators" (Schultz [1949–50] 1985:31). *Tula*, a respect term used for high-ranking orators, was a stick on which pigeons were carried (Schultz 1911:49).

Also, like the double (*soa*), the orator might practice his craft in his own interest rather than that of his chief. Orators arranged chiefly marriages, for which they were paid handsomely in fine mats and through which they found favor with those whose interests the marriage served. Many historical intrigues are attributed to orators' attempts to arrange serial marriages for their high chief with increasingly more powerful and well-born wives.[20] High chiefs often became pawns in a matchmaking game carried on independently of their wishes.

There is an old Samoan saying that "the high chief's wealth decays into orator's hands"; political power has likewise decayed.[21] Keesing remarks, "the talking-men ... passed from managing the chief's affairs to managing the chief himself, determining his successors, deciding his marital affiliations, hedging him about with ceremonial restrictions" (1934:55). Although historically the orator began as a servant who spoke for high chiefs, he ends as an authority who speaks to them. Thus, the missionary Stair tells us, orators "speak out plainly to those above them when needed, often saying very unpalatable things" (1897:70); one is not surprised when Stair adds that these "servants" have the power "of deposing and banishing an obnoxious chief." Indeed, Robert Louis Stevenson describes the high chief as the orator's "gagged audience" (1892:3–4). The right to speak is a metaphor for power in Samoa; those who listen serve. Thus, the figure of the orator represents a reversal of age-old hierarchies and with it the victory of strategy over convention.

In earlier chapters we saw that in moral discourse counterreactions are denied: the apparent impartiality of the village girls who gossip about Sala constitutes a denial of their envy and thus of their own desires to show off as bridesmaids. In contextual discourses forbidden actions are also denied. Indeed, *ula* (teasing) may serve as a straightforward denial that one is acting out dominance seeking. When people are engaged in competitive repartee and one begins to grow angry, the other is likely to say, "I was only teasing you," employing the word *ula* to repudiate the aggressiveness of the interchange. In strategic discourses, however, the darker side of discourse is broadly acknowledged. Everybody admits that orators use courteous address to promote the dominance of their own group: Samoans say a good orator is *kuluku* (crooked), meaning skillfully manipulative (Shore 1977: 437). The more conscious the negative side of a discourse is, the less it resembles a defense mechanism and the more it becomes a technology—in Foucault's terms, a technology of self (1988).

The Vernacularization of Oratory

The manipulative and persuasive use of words is the signature of the offices of the orator, but it is not confined to him. Due perhaps to the efficacy of this form of elocution in Samoan history, oratorical speech—respectful speech for political ends—became the normative style of *fono*. The *fono* is the archetypal Samoan political forum, attended by the heads of all village households.

> "No one," says a part-Samoan, "is to express his opinion freely at the meetings." A chief states: "It is the Samoan custom to go around, not to come straight forward and say what you think." To "go around about in speaking" is denoted by the word *taani'o*; . . . *Malele* means "to say something in a public speech in order to satisfy . . . fellow members of a *fono* without having any intention of carrying it out." "To ponder," *fuafua*, has the significant parallel meaning "to take aim with a spear," but the "spear" may be deliberately aimed so as not to hit the target directly. *Faafisi*, "to entangle" as by a vine, also implies to manipulate a person's words so as to "wrest a meaning" from them for one's own purposes. . . . Maintaining room to maneuver . . . makes the whole interaction process a cautious and devious exercise. (Keesing and Keesing 1956:144)[22]

In the last chapter we looked briefly at formal ceremonial speeches, structured according to certain formulaic rules. *Fono* speeches, however, are freewheeling in their construction, deploying logically prior modes of talk—such as moralizing, or poetical flattery, or joking—strategically.[23] Inasmuch as the strategic enlistment of discourses is not dictated by a set of rules, its crafting lies inevitably with the social actor: agency takes priority over structure.

Analyzing expertise, Dreyfus (1984) offers a possible explanation for the unruly character of strategic discourse by telling a tale from the Socratic dialogues. Socrates asks Euthyphro, a religious prophet and expert on pious behavior, how to recognize piety. Socrates, ever the philosopher, is in quest of a set of rules; Euthyphro can give him none. Dreyfus explains that rules, like sets of instructions, help those beginning to learn a system. When one masters a system, however, one does so on the basis of a "holographic memory," a memory that superimposes innumerable recollections of whole situations seen in light of the system, like memories of chessboard layouts. Moral discourse can be seen as coding a self system as a set of rules; contextual discourses code the self system in terms of whole situations or contexts, understood as formal and informal; strategic discourses superimpose or hybridize formal and informal situations. According to Dreyfus, superimpositions represents a correlative style of thought, out of which emerges intuition, a sense of the possible moves inherent in the actual situation and the differential advantages of these moves. While beginners simply apply a given set of maxims with little or no sense of responsibility for the results, those who have begun to master a system (and I would add a self system) "feel responsible for and emotionally involved in, the results of . . . choice" (Dreyfus 1984:30). This is not the who-is-to-blame type of responsibility associated with moral discourse; rather, it is a sense of one's own potential to affect outcomes and creates a "spell of involvement" (31).

This spell of involvement characterizes Samoan strategic discourse, a discourse most exercised in the pursuit of titles. While the highest titles are typically conferred by orators, each extended family (*'āiga*) has its own titles and confers them at its discretion. One has a claim to titles in the *'āiga* of each of one's four grandparents, more right to titles through paternal lineages, and males have a weightier claim to titles than females. While keeping these considerations in mind, each *'āiga* enjoys a considerable latitude in the selection of a claimant. All Samoans, then, have avenues to titles, and the aim of adult life is to acquire one. Mead says, "Samoans find rank a never-failing source of interest" ([1928] 1961:50). She sees the boy's life as directed toward securing a title: "Only the lazy, the shiftless, the ambitionless fail to respond to this competition" (190–91). Holmes says, "Rank and prestige constitute the focal point of Samoan culture, to which all other aspects of life are secondary in importance" (1987:122). Freeman's work can be seen as a footnote to the emotional intensity that surrounds the acquisition of Samoan titles (1983).

Samoans greatly value the honor associated with titles, but the position itself is political in nature. Titled persons hold discretionary powers over their extended families and a seat on the village council, insuring them a substantial role in governance. Today titles are virtually a prerequisite to government office, and high titles are likely to be afforded special consideration and financial advantage by the powers that be.

Samoans say, "The path to power is through service."[24] This proverb suggests that candidates for titles are assessed on the basis of their selfless devotion to the group, that is, for conformity to the moral and poetical ideals of Samoan social life. In fact, if not in proverb, titles and other positions of power are secured by a politic rhetoric historically associated with the figure of the orator. This bias is evident today in the criteria upon which the High Court of American Samoa selects among rival claimants for titles. The criteria upon which the court bases its judgments are four, established by the Samoan legislature.[25]

First, the claimants must show that they are blood members of the extended family (*'āiga*), with an arguably close lineage relationship to the former titleholder. Second, claimants must have significant support; many *'āiga* have several branches, so different claimants may be supported by rival factions. The first and second criteria, however, are often inconsequential, because there are many people with sufficiently strong blood ties and because, if any one claimant has a clear majority of the *'āiga* on his side, the matter would not usually be brought to court.

The third criterion is "forcefulness, character, personality and knowledge of Samoan customs," and the fourth is the likelihood that the person will render future service to the extended family, to the village, and to the country. All candidates for a title argue a record of service, indicative of their potential for future service. Further cases cited in the *American Samoa Report* (1978:1064) inform us that the criterion of future service to the family, village, and state "depends on forcefulness, character, personality and knowledge of Samoan custom." In short, in many instances all four criteria come down to the third criterion.

In court "forcefulness, character, personality and knowledge of Samoan customs" is typically demonstrated by giving testimony (*American Samoa Report* 1978:695–98). This testimony, like oratory, is a vehicle to display one's knowledge of the history and genealogy of the extended family and sometimes of the ceremonial titles (*fa'alupega*) of villages associated with the title that is sought.[26] *Fa'alupega*, those "way of the pigeon" names that are the signature of status in Samoa, are derived from events and, therefore, represent a "compressed community history," constituting the charters of families, villages, and districts (Keesing 1934:48; see also Meleiseā 1987b:2). Knowledge of these appellations is, therefore, tantamount to a mastery of local precedent. Like a good lawyer, however, Samoans who employ oratorical discourse are wont to use precedent for their own purposes. In court and out skill in lawyer-like specifying establishes those qualities of erudition and eloquence through which power is secured in Samoa. All adult Samoans to an extent, and successful Samoans in particular, are political strategists who jockey for titles and for their family's power and position through a politic discourse that features a knowledge of genealogy.

Under the auspices of civility, and under the cover of ambiguity, Samoan strategic discourse surreptitiously forwards a set of private interests. In this sense strategic talk subsumes the abasing tendencies vaunted in Samoan poetics and the contentious tendencies pervasive in Samoan praxis. As contextual discourse ends in a melding together of persons in a spirit of *communitas,* strategic discourses begin as a melding together of contextual discourses. While the most definitive versions of contextual discourses play upon cultural categories, the most definitive versions of strategic discourses play upon logically prior discourses.

There is a tendency to believe that Samoa represents an undeveloped version of Polynesian political structure: Samoans never evolved the more securely stratified forms of political organization evident in many Polynesian chiefdoms (Kirch 1984). In Samoa the proto-Polynesian hereditary chief was gradually disempowered, but this process was no devolution, nor was it indicative of halted development. A gradual process of "democratization" took place because of diffusions of power and authority that came about through the figure of the orator and through the strategic approach that he represented.[27] This is not the American everyone-is-created-equal version of democracy. In Samoa one's own family is always, arguably, the first family, above everyone else. But the broad affectation of strategic discourse in Samoan social life creates a field of opportunity for families to compete, just as American strategies create a field of opportunity for individuals. These fields are, in both cases, limited but real enough to offer possibilities that give a telos to social life and to personal development.

Implied in Samoan social history is a sequence. The sequence begins with self-conscious role playing (symbolized by the activity of luring) exercised in the service of another and concludes with the tactical use of facades by the social actor as agent. The double and the orator are Samoan social prototypes for strategic discourses. Symbolically, they are decoy birds who, through playing an assigned part, are apt to act in their own behalf. Together they represent a deconstruction of communal hegemony and the development of creativity in Samoa. When one learns to use communal personas for privately conceived aims, one moves from a dutiful loyalty to the sovereign communal order of ancient Samoan society, represented by the high chief, toward a complete relativization of sociocentric role playing and egocentric will within the person. Double and lover, orator and high chief, pigeon catcher and decoy bird, become one.

In light of the historical rise of the orator, it would appear that one arrives at strategic discourses in Samoa through a historical process. This is not to say, however, that earlier epochs of Samoans represented an earlier "stage" in the evolution of the culture's self system. Undoubtedly, earlier generations articulated different styles of talk with their own etiology. Every era casts its own history backward into the past, constructing itself as the inheritor of time-honored understandings of the self: historical perspective sees diachrony as developmental, leading to the present state of affairs. Yet history is also those current events and contingencies that continually reshape discourses. Because discourses and social history are inevitably intertwined, they can provide insight about each other. It is to this mutually illuminating relationship between discourse and historical process that we now turn. But, before we go on to examine the Samoan self system in historical motion, let us take a moment to review and consolidate the gains of this volume's first half.

One begins logically and developmentally with an ontological lexicon, a frame of reference on self that is context free, as the beliefs about self inscribed in this lexicon are essentialized. Moral lexicons can be thought of as offering technical knowledge for the application of ontological premises to daily life: they offer a "how-to" perspective, which is also a how-one-should-behave perspective—in Samoa how to play a role in the group, with dignity, respect, generosity, and so forth. These shoulds, or rules, implicit in the moral lexicon are nonsituational, but situations or contexts come into view by virtue of the issue of application. Moral discourse represents a recognition of the problematicity of application, betraying a necessity for an interpretative, or narrative, process. Here the question of responsibility arises: if application is interpretative, it requires judgment, and one can make a right or wrong judgment. This possibility brings with it a sense of "opportunity, risk, inspiration, threat, etc." (Dreyfus 1984:30), in short all the ingredients of a compelling story. With contextual discourse one moves from an understanding of self systems in terms of abstract rules to an understanding in light of situations, although these situations are presented to the person in a simplified typology (formal or informal), which can be seen as rule-of-thumb examples of the articulation of the self system and actual contexts. Strategic discourses represent the mastery of the self system and the point at which these systems become a transparent language through which to realize agency in response to the challenging novelty of real situations.[28]

As liberating as this scenario sounds, in Samoa its gendering strikes a discordant note. Doubles are figures who represent mastery of the Samoan self system. While girls can be doubles as well as boys, the historical model for the double is the high chief's orator, who used ranking girls as pawns in a political game. It is the girl whose status may diminish through the machinations of the duplicitous double and who is in danger of being betrayed by his charming rhetoric. Samoa is far from solitary in its penchant for gendering developmental scenarios. We will soon see that this gendering represents the historical vulnerability of self systems, a point of ingress for foreign ways of regarding and making selves.

Selves in Culture History

What were the most immediate, the most local power relations . . . How was the action of these power relations modified by their very exercise, entailing a strengthening of some terms and a weakening of others, with effects of resistance and counterinvestments, so that there has never existed one type of stable subjugation? How were these power relations linked to one another according to the logic of a great strategy, which in retrospect takes on the aspect of a unitary and voluntarist politics of sex?
—Michel Foucault, *The History of Sexuality*

7

Bodies, Selves, and Sexualities in Pre-Christian Samoa

My theory as presented so far concerns the acquisition of discourses on self and their emotional correlatives. But self systems are constantly mutating in response to culture contact and historical change. Any useful theory of self must help us understand how people negotiate these contingencies and how their sense of self is affected by them. In this volume's second half, therefore, I put the ideas developed in the first half to work on Samoan history. I argued that cultural self systems have divergent starting points and that these points of departure result in self systems that are comparable—in that they share ontological premises as well as moral, contextual, and strategic discourses—but also radically dissimilar. In the second half of the book I ask: If there are radically dissimilar self systems, what happens when two such systems collide; what kind of accommodations, mutations, and revisions to discourses of self come about, and for what reasons? In partial answer to this question I explore the "positioning" of discourses in social life and how this positioning began to change when Western Europeans began residing in Samoa around 1830. Again, what I mean by positioning is the hegemonic attribution of certain kinds of discourses to specific groups.

In the introduction I proposed that in many societies progress through the full set of discourses is to a degree limited by cultural expectations. It is expected that dominant groups will acquire contextual discourses. In other words, they will be discursively competent in those contexts categorized as formal and informal, respectively. These groups will also master those cultural projects concomitant to these discourse and acquire the talisman and fundament of cultural projects, an achievement orientation; some will also become exemplars of strategic approaches to social life. But this developmental scenario is not likely to be attributed to disempowered social groups, such as slaves, outcasts, lower classes, or in many societies women. Even when discourses on self are not attributed in an obviously discriminatory manner, contextual discourses are often gender marked, men specializing in formal discourses and women in informal discourses.

The Positioning of Discourses on Self in Samoa

Race, class, gender, and age are the categories most commonly used cross-culturally to mark social difference. In Samoa social structure legislated against the consistent use of any differential factor aside from age. Precontact Samoa was racially homogeneous. Although there were elements of class segregation, certain extended families ('*āiga*) having stronger claims to an elevated lineage than others, genealogy was a malleable science. '*Āiga* were and are adept in the interpretation and use of genealogy in jockeying for power and position. Because '*āiga* were of limited size, they simply could not afford consistent or thoroughgoing gender dimorphism.

Both sexes made up the family militia. In feuds with other families accepted practice was and is that girls fight girls and boys fight boys.[1] In the nineteenth century Samoan boxing contests were held for male and female competitors (Turner [1861] 1986:126), and even now both sexes take pride in their ability to win a fight. In the family similar expectations also held for males and females in regards to sexuality. Both genders were demure in the presence of categorical brothers and sisters, and so too were all their companions (Krämer [1902] 1995:62, Cain 1971:177). Thus, Pritchard says of the Samoans:

> Of all their customs, the most strictly observed . . . was that which forbade the remotest reference to anything, even by way of a joke, that conveyed the slightest indelicacy in thought or word or gesture, when brothers and sisters were together. In the presence of his sister, the wildest rake was always modest and moral. In the presence of her brother, the most accommodating coquette was always chaste and reserved. (1866:125)

Unlike extended families, however, villages differentiated people by gender. On the village level contextual discourses were gender marked, males specializing in formal and females in informal discourses, which in Samoa meant that men specialized in the talk of ceremonies and women in that of entertainments. Politics proper took place in formal realm; war, brokering peace, and marriages of state were likely to be controlled by chiefs and particularly by chiefly orators. What this meant was that in Samoa—as in so many other places—girls were often pawns in the strategic games of others rather than strategists themselves. This statement must be qualified: common girls exercised a fair degree of agency, and, at least in Samoan social theory, lineage trumped gender as a marker of personhood, a principle that gave ranking girls a degree of leverage. Nonetheless, girls had deeper use for foreign allies in the Samoan game of jockeying for status than most of their contemporaries, although, when Westerners became a significant presence in Samoa after 1830, people of both sexes sought assistance from them. Further, for the most persistent of the nineteenth-century visitors—missionaries—girls' seemingly unrestrained sexuality was emblematic of the culture's "heathen" state, and special attention was paid to girls' "redemption."

While missionaries saw Samoans sexual relations as practically without rules, these relations simply reflected a set of rules invisible to the missionaries because of their radical novelty. Missionaries could not believe that a society in which young girls were encouraged to dance naked before torches and sing songs about sexual body parts could have any sexual morality at all. Ironically, mission thought and talk about the self were deployed by Samoan girls against the sociocentric hegemony of their own society, in light of which their sexuality had been modulated and directed in precontact times. Girls were a symbol of the sexual not only for missionaries but for Samoans as well and a locus of sexual control—control that began to erode in the cacophony of discourses that characterized Samoa from the late nineteenth century onward. This erosion resulted in a repositioning of girls' discourses on self. This history of the positioning of discourses is, therefore, predominantly their history, but, inasmuch as girls' cultural lives were inextricably involved with those of others, it is also a history of both sexes and the shifting line that demarcated them.

While the point of this volume's second half is to illustrate how my self theory can be put to cultural-historical work, in the process we will inevitably encounter general questions about historiography in colonized societies, in which those leaving written records were the colonizers. Missionaries, who resided for spans of years and mastered the language and protocols, are the best sources on precontact Samoa, but how does one document gendered discourses and their associated sexualities when missionaries wrote mainly of their efforts to change local customs, lauding their own efforts or despairing about them, again and again? My answer in this chapter is that in the various tableaux offered by mission and other early accounts can be found an iconography of feminine bodies. This iconography is part of a gender puzzle that can be pieced together in light of more general ethnographic data: girls' bodies talked, even though their voices fell into the interstices of history.

Deciphering girls' bodily iconography and what it meant about contact and the self will allow me to explore, in the next chapter why Samoan girls and English missionaries, unlikely bedfellows, found common purpose in the circumstances of cultural contact and why postcontact girls and their sexualities made Christianity seem a sensible solution to the problems posed by modernity to Samoans—despite Christianity's culturally discordant premises about the nature of selves.

By the time incorporations of mission ideas began reorchestrating Samoan discourses on self in the late nineteenth and early twentieth century, there were a wealth of writers documenting the culture. Reports from virtually all types of sources, however, document Samoan culture either as static or as the scene of a history of events. Here again the question is: How does one document changes in selves, in their moralities, in their meanings, and in their relations to power when these were not the subjects of those who wrote at the time? The answer I offer in chapter 9, is that one finds documentation for a history of self in the discrepancies between successive synchronic portraits, made as decades follow one another. I read changes to moral discourse in shifting spirit beliefs and practices, as spirits arguably represent a cultural unconscious, a kind of moral refuse bin, which changes its contours and contents as moral discourses suffer historical transformation.[2]

We saw that Samoan ceremonies are the most mature example of formal discourse and entertainments of informal discourse; in this history, however, I will be more interested in entertainments than in ceremonies. In part this is because precontact Samoan girls were specialists in informal discourse, and I am writing their history, but there are larger reasons as well. Ceremonies so often legitimize themselves by conscious attempts to imitate and preserve the past and are, therefore, resistant to rewriting. Entertainments tend to be supple in their responsiveness to innovation and venues for exploring new ideas on self. Further, in Samoa most ceremonial events were not perceived to be at odds with Christianity (though certain ceremonies, like defloration, offended missionaries); indeed, missionaries and other visitors saw the elaborate courtesy and gifting they involved as noble-savage analogues for European civility.

English missionaries came from a highly class-stratified society but one in which, under the circumstances of industrialization, class boundaries were eroding. The London Missionary Society (LMS) reverends who Christianized Samoa were fledgling members of the middle class, having risen from the lower orders of society partially by virtue of their vocation (Gunson 1978:31–100). Many had even higher class aspirations, sometimes realized in the course of their missionary activities (132–47). From the first, missionaries had been granted exalted status in Samoan ceremonial life; they had little reason to complain of a discourse that so generously awarded them their own secret aspirations. Entertainments were another matter: missionaries regarded them as a root of insidious difference and of evil; they were a prime target for missionary complaint. Thus, on May 27, 1842, just a decade after the first sustained contact between Samoa and the European powers, the missionary Macdonald wrote to his superiors in London from his post in Savai'i, Western Samoa, of a "wicked" chief named Popotunu.

> He has long kept up the night dance in order to lead the youth of the lord into all sorts of wickedness. I have endeavored to persuade him to give up such a vile practice but . . . he would . . . put me off by blaming the young men of the place whose hearts were in the dance. This led me to think of attending the dance personally to dissuade them from it. I had an opportunity to do so on Saturday, January 7, 1842. It being late when we were about to retire we heard the noise of the dance, having entered into a small canoe with one of my Teachers we crossed the Bay to the place where they

were dancing, and so much were they taken by surprise that I sat down for a minute or two right in front of the dancers unobserved. I was fully prepared to meet with violence, but it was not so, for as soon as they observed me the dancers instantly fled. . . . there was no more dancing that night.

Changing entertainments spoke about more than the prejudices of mission visitors, being part of a cultural discourse on self that was gendered and through which gender was understood. In chapter 10 I use changing entertainment practices to document revisions to informal discourse and a shift in the gender attribution of informal discourse from females to males. Once again these changes can be traced through incongruities in reports from one period to the next.

Discursive changes were correlatives of shifting power relations, for, as Foucault (1990) observes, power is at least in part a matter of what can be said and by whom. Through the contact experience and the cultural revisions that followed, Samoan girls lost their specialty in the informal discourse of jest that reigned at entertainments but in its place did not gain a specialty in the formal discourse of ceremonies. This loss indexed pervasive amendments to cultural expectations of girls: to a degree girls were expected to relinquish their place in cultural projects and achievement scenarios; many became demurely mute except among themselves or when possessed by spirits. If power is invested in forms of talk, we rewrite power relations by reconfiguring discourses for ourselves, negotiating existing speech rules in creative-strategic ways. In the concluding chapter, I turn to a life history monologue by a Samoan women who creates a voice for herself by reconfiguring Samoan discourses on self. Let us begin this history, then, with missionary tableaux and the feminine bodily iconography they depicted.

Pre-Christian Girls

Although early missionaries were generally shocked at Samoan undress, this amaze applied particularly to the fair sex. Thus, Stair remarks "in their heathen state" Samoans wore "mere apologies for clothing" and were "in little better than a state of nudity" (1897:113), but the missionary Williams complains that Samoan women "are by no means as careful about concealing their persons as the men" ([1830–32] 1984:232).

> On leaving just as I was about to step in the boat a young woman with a fine white mat on made through the crowd & offered her garment for sale. Thinking the lady had made some kind of provision in case of selling her ball dress I gave her the number of beads she demanded when without any ceremony she took off her mat & handed it to me standing *with the utmost unconcern* among the crowd without the slightest covering on her. On my saying that ladies in England did not thus expose their persons a young

friend standing by lent the tail end of her round about the dimensions of which was not such as to afford too ample covering to herself so that when divided between the two they had to stand very close together to derive any advantage from it even to their front parts. However no person present & there were perhaps 200 appeared to offer the slightest insult to her or take any notice than if she had been regularly clothed. As we passed Aborima [Apolima] a canoe came off to us having two men & a young woman on board. The men had their round abouts on formed of leaves which I wanted to obtain as a curiosity. Before I could go below to get a piece of native cloth as a covering for him, he had desired the young woman to give him her mat which she had done & when I came on deck she was sitting in the canoe *with perfect unconcern* without a particle of clothing on. (167; my brackets and emph.)

The apparent lack of "concern" about feminine bodies must have suggested to early visitors a reversal of Western gender categories: it was seen as distinctly unfeminine. Commodore Wilkes writes:

The women besmear themselves with cocoa-nut oil mixed with turmeric, which gives them a shining yellow tint, that is considered as a beauty; on each breast is a spot of reddish brown, of a singular shape, and of various sizes, from that of a dollar to that of a desert-plate. They do not show the least sign of *feminine* bashfulness. (1845:140; my emph.)

Further, female undress seemed to the missionaries strangely purposeful and intended. The missionary Williams notes in his journal after paramount chief Malietoa's five wives joined him for afternoon tea, "The natives appear to take the greatest pride in exposing their persons" ([1830–32] 1984:78). Williams left Tahitian missionary teachers in Samoa. Returning after an absence, he

enquired of the teachers why they had not taught them [the Samoans] to sing. They informed me they had . . . but the females immediately took what they obtained to the dancing houses & sang it to their dances. . . . I asked them [the teachers] if they had not taught them [the Samoan women] to make . . . nice white Tahitian cloth. They said . . . they could not get the women to learn. They were so intolerably lazy. They liked the cloth very well indeed to put round their middles but they could not induce them to cover their persons of which they are exceedingly proud especially their breasts which are generally very large. They are continually wishing the teachers' wives to lay aside their garments & "faasamoa" do as the Samoan ladies do, gird a shaggy mat round their loins as low down as they can tuck up the corner in order to expose the whole front & side of their left thigh anoint themselves beautifully with scented oil, tinge themselves with turmeric put a string of blue beads round their neck & then faariaria [*fāʻalialia*] *walk about to shew themselves.* You will have, say they, all the manaia [*mānaia*] the handsome young men of the town loving you then. (117)³

One wonders, was it missionary biases against a different sexual order that generated these spicy picture postcards? Surely, they would have shocked and titillated in a manner likely to draw a broad readership and sympathetic contributions to the mission for, in Murray's words, "improving" Samoan women's "deplorably degraded condition." This chapter tests the truth of missionary reports through an analysis of the bodily iconography of feminine gender in old Samoa. What I find is that missionaries were accurate observers of actual behavior. What these behaviors spoke about, however, was not "perfect unconcern" but, rather, a set of concerns and a gendered discourse on self. Although this bodily iconography was visible in girls' decorations generally, it was particularly legible in their hairdos.

"I cannot assign a reason why the females crop themselves so close," the missionary Williams remarks, "while the men generally have long hair" ([1830–32] 1984:231).⁴ When the missionaries first arrived in Samoa, pubescent girls, especially virgins of rank, shaved their heads bare except for a *tutagita—gita* for short. The *gita* style consisted of a tuft over the left temple from which a long tail was left to dangle "recklessly" down the cheek, set off by a shorn head, although sometimes there were tufts all round the sides or no tufts but only a tail and, with virgins of particular rank, sometimes two tails (117; Krämer [1902] 1995:325).⁵ Tufts and tails were commonly bleached with lime to a light reddish-brown, reminiscent in shade to the reddish-brown breast markings described by Wilkes.⁶ In order to disentangle this iconography, let us explore the predominate elements of the pre-Christian hairdo: the tuft and tail, the bleached-red color, and the shorn head.

Of Tufts and Tails

In Samoan the word for *head* (*ulu*) can mean "head" or "hair." The head was considered *mana*—charged with spiritual potency—and hair, an outflowing of *mana*.⁷ Across Polynesia spirits personify *mana* (Koskinen 1967). In Samoa female spirits are characterized by long, unbound, streaming hair. Inasmuch as spirits' salient physical features might logically be taken to signify their salient spiritual features, one would guess the hair of female spirits represents their *mana*. An iconic representation of the spiritual by the physical is supported by the case of male chiefs: throughout Polynesia the chiefs genitals are a symbol of his *mana* and their size glorified (Shore 1989:142).⁸

Like genitals, *mana* is associated with sexuality. In Samoa beings replete with *mana*—such as chiefs and spirits—are notorious for their sexual appetites.⁹ If *mana* equals sexuality, and long hair stands for *mana*, it follows that long hair also equals sexuality. This link is confirmed by Samoan ideas of

Village princesses wearing ceremonial headdresses. From the photographic collection of J. L. Dwyer (1908–13). Courtesy of K. A. Wheat (copyright). Original photograph currently stored at the American Samoa Historic Perservation Office.

feminine beauty. Everywhere beauty queens are sex symbols. Beauty pageants began in Samoa in the early 1970s. At one of the first pageants in American Samoa the queen was determined *exclusively* by measuring each girl's hair with a yardstick.

Mana is also synonymous with fecundity.[10] Firth equates *mana* with the fruiting of trees and the multiplication of fish (1949). Hair, as an extension of the head and its *mana*, would also signify fecundity. This conclusion is also verified by custom: in precontact Samoa women allowed their hair to grow long only during pregnancy (Stair 1897:175). As there was no practical reason for doing so, hair must have signified the pregnant, or fecund, state.

Red

The tuft and tail's light reddish-brown color emphasized their significance as outflowings of *mana*. Red is the color of *mana*. Luomala describes the sacred chief as having a "beautiful red complexion . . . so distinctive that the reddish color of certain birds [and] flowers . . . is ascribed to their having acquired some of [his] skin" ([1955] 1986:139–40). A red nimbus surrounds female spirits, or, more precisely, their skin, which glows red "like that of the fisherman returning from the sea" (Krämer [1923] 1949:16a).

Light-reddish-brown hair occurs naturally in a few Samoans and is a mark of aristocratic blood. The headdress worn by the village princess (*tāupōu*) on ceremonial occasion (*tuiga*) is adorned with tufts of reddish hair.[11] Female spirits are often said to have reddish-brown hair decorated with a red hibiscus.[12] As hair is to humans, so feathers are to birds. One of the most important contemporary spirits, Letelesā, who is said to have red hair, may appear in the form of a scarlet-headed parakeet, the *sega*. Red *sega* feathers were used to decorate the finest of fine mats that, like chiefs and spirits, were believed to be replete with *mana*.[13] The *sega* itself is said to have originated as a "clot of blood," the Samoan euphemism for miscarriages (Stuebel 1976:54). Spirits (*aitu*) typically originate as clots of blood. By implication the *sega* is a kind of *aitu*, and the clot of blood genesis of both bespeak their innate redness.

Shaved Heads

The most telling evidence as to the significance of shaved heads can be found in reports from Christian times. Laulii Willis was a Samoan woman, descended from an orator, born in 1865, who came of age in Samoa in the 1870s; she married an Englishman and migrated to England, where she later wrote her memoirs. In precontact Samoa eligible girls had worn the tuft-and-tail style, but by the time Laulii grew up girls wore this style only prior to puberty; in adolescence Laulii and many of her contemporaries grew their hair long (1889:17), influenced no doubt by the foreign fashion.[14] Toward the end of her first marriage Laulii was believed to have committed a sexual indiscretion. An older sis-

Samoan girl with long hair. From the photographic collection of J. L. Dwyer (1908–1913). Courtesy of K. A. Wheat (copyright). Original photograph currently stored at the American Samoa Historic Perservation Office.

ter shaved her head, leaving a lock or two (78). In other words Laulii was forced to return to the tuft-and-tail style, not to symbolize her virginity but as a punishment that symbolized an assertion of sexual control.

Two decades later Krämer says girls' heads were shaved as a punishment or to keep a precocious girl from premature sexual adventure ([1902] 1995:329). In the 1920s girls generally grew their hair long, but, according to Mead, "a stigmatizing shaving of the head" was a recently abandoned punishment for promiscuity ([1928] 1961:273). Thus, while Laulii Willis's sister had left a lock or two, later the head was shaved altogether. Heads are still being shaved when Samoan parents catch a daughter in a compromising situation, so it seems unlikely that this punishment was absent in Mead's day. Nonetheless, Willis's, Krämer's, and Mead's reports all imply that shaving the head signified an assertion of sexual control: it was a method for making sure the girl did not, figuratively speaking, let her hair down.

In Christian times propriety dictated that girls wear long hair in a neat bun. The symbolic intent of this binding is evident in nineteenth-century jurisprudence: taking the comb out of a married women's hair, such that it fell down, was one of the four personal offenses that received public punishment (Stair 1897:95). Today villagers may remark of a girl who wears her hair streaming down, "Look at the hanging of her hair; she is probably a wanton." When Samoan parents warn a girl to behave, they often say, "Be careful, or I'll pull out your hair!" Dragging a girl home by her hair is a punishment common enough to have a name, *futi le ulu*, meaning "pull by" and "pluck out the hair"; parents may still drag girls out of urban discotheques by their hair.

The Do

The tuft-and-tail style (*gita*) displayed the girl's hair. Samoan semiotics affiliates reddish-brown hair with *mana* and also with sexuality/fecundity. If the *gita*—like the flowing hair of female spirits and of girls at beauty pageants, like the long tresses of pregnant women—represented *mana* and sexuality/fecundity, then the girl's bleached locks would have been a kind of flaunting, advertising her potential sexuality and subsequent fecundity. The *gita*'s iconography supports the missionary perception that Samoan girls' believed they should "walk about to shew themselves." In the *gita* style, however, girls' shaven heads iconographically contradicted the freedom expressed by their reddened locks so as to indicate it was not meant literally.

Girls' flaunting, plus this set of cautionary quotation marks, was a discursive practice linked to Samoan informal discourse in which jesting turned upon a figurative and literal exhibitionism placed in a rhetorical frame. By "discursive practice" I mean a particular expression of a discourse on self, either verbal or gestural, by a specific group in which the performative nuances may be different than the nuances of prototypical instances of the discourse but in which structural elements remains the same. In Samoa, for example, informal

Samoan women with long hair. These two older women are surrounding a village princess making ceremonial kava. From the photographic collection of J. L. Dwyer (1908–1913). Courtesy of K. A. Wheat (copyright). Original photograph currently stored at the American Samoa Historic Perservation Office.

discourse is prototypically a discourse of jest; girls' flaunting was not always a joke (even though it was associated with joking contexts, like nighttime entertainments); nonetheless, this flaunting bore a structural resemblance to Samoan informal discourse.

If we now know what reddened locks did not mean—at least literally—what then did they mean about the girl's role? To answer this question let us broaden our view, placing our puzzle piece, feminine bodily iconography, back into the larger picture: gendering in the pre-Christian Samoan village.

Gendered Discourse in the Pre-Christian Village

Samoan village social structure was gender dimorphic, being divided in an *'aumāga,* an organization of untitled males, and an *aualuma,* an association of village-born sisters and daughters.[15] The *'aumāga* served the village council of chiefs (*fono*) by cultivating plantations for them, carrying out their ordinances, and serving as an army reserve (Meleiseā 1987b:7). So clearly was war a male task that the nineteenth-century British consul, Churchward, remarks, "The women, even when the two opposing armies face one another with deadly intent, pass to and fro between belligerents without molestation, visiting their friends and relatives on either side" (1887:47). During their visits women had a reputation for undermining the military campaigns of their own faction by gossiping about them to the rival camp (Pritchard 1866:61–62).

Not only was war a masculine province within the village; the oratorical discourse of genealogy and allusion was as well. Thus, Mead says:

> It is an exceptional girl who can give her great-grandfather's name, the exceptional boy who cannot give his genealogy in traditional form for several generations. While the boy of sixteen or seventeen is eagerly trying to master the esoteric allusiveness of the talking chief whose style he admires, the girl of the same age learns the minimum of etiquette. ([1928] 1961:82–83)

As this discourse of genealogy and esoteric allusions was, and is, characteristic of formal contexts in Samoa, one could say that oratorical performances and the formal discourse associated with them constituted a male specialty.

The female counterpart of the *'aumāga,* the *aualuma,* sponsored two major activities: hosting parties visiting the village and the marriages of village princesses (*tāupōu*), which created further occasions for visits between villages.[16] Receiving guests meant housing, feeding, and entertaining them. For the latter purpose the *aualuma* composed bawdy, jocular songs such as the following.

The Girl's Belly

Kava. The Kava. The man is a sennit-ball maker.
But his beater doesn't stand upright. He takes it and stands it in the groin.
When it spills, it spills. It covers all of the mat.
When they leave, dogs lick it up. They are startled, because it is disgusting.
The two of them are startled when they are discovered.

The clitoris jabs, the clitoris jabs. Get out of the way.
Let my journey proceed. I want to stand over there at the lookout.
I proceed, but not all the way. Now I am erect.
I squeeze in underneath until ripe.
And later the girl's belly is swollen, and lastly fat.[17]

Aualuma welcoming and parting ceremonies also featured comic-exhibitionistic dances in which girls' erotic antics were consistently reported to be more flagrant than those of boys.[18] Commodore Wilkes observes:

> the mode of performing . . . differs from that of the Tahitians, but is like it lascivious. . . . The dance is usually performed by young girls, who stand up before the audience, throwing their arms, legs, feet, and hands, in numerous strange attitudes, which are any thing but graceful. The others who are present sing amusing words . . . the dance of the girls at Upolu consisted entirely of motions of the body, and was so indelicate as to produce disgust. . . . The dances of the men are by no means indecorous. (1845:134)

Probably the comic "indelicacy" of feminine performances derived from girls' role as *aualuma* hostesses: they were responsible for breaking the figurative ice.

Remember that *ula* is a kind of joking that often involves showing off private parts, like "The Girl's Belly," and that contextual discourses are performative, being both verbal and gestural. Hosting featured verbal and choreographic jest and was feminine within the village; therefore, one could say that informal discourse constituted a feminine specialty.[19] Girls' village sex roles predicated participation in a discourse that involved exhibitionism, iconographically represented by her reddened tuft and tail—but what of her shaved head? One might see this clipping as a symbolic analogue for the string fettering the foot of the decoy pigeon. In Samoa luring was not confined to doubles (*soa*). If from the perspective of the boy the girl was the wild pigeon, from the perspective of village and family she was the decoy.[20] As doubles aimed to "capture" girls, girls aimed to capture titles, wealth, and land—the Samoan constituents of status—for their groups. The decoy pigeon, luring in the service of its chief, was a symbol of achievement and even of a strategic orientation to social life. An achievement orientation is the psychological concomitant of cultural projects, so girls' luring in the service of their families participated in a cultural project that aimed at achievement, just as their brothers did. High status and common girls participated in this cultural project differently.

The village's status depended on that of its major resident titles. Virginal village princesses (*tāupōu*) drew high titles into their communities' compass. To this end a *tāupōu* was decorated in a manner that flaunted her charms, even her pubic hair being oiled and combed (Freeman 1983:229). When she married a high chief, she would journey to his estate, but, after becoming pregnant, she often returned to her natal village. When the chief died, a descendant, usually male, succeeded him on the strength of paternal *and* maternal lines. A criteria for the selection of a *tāupōu* was distinguished lineage; therefore, the *tāupōu's* son had a weighty claim and might bring the title back to his village.[21] Like *tāupōu*, all high-status girls were to remain virginal, allowing their extended families (*'āiga*) to capitalize on their attractions through an arranged marriage with the scion of another high-status family.

Similarly, undistinguished *'āiga* deployed their girls to lure scions of ranking families in informal marriages (*āvaga*) because the children that descended from these unions had rights in the father's family estate. A girl who became pregnant from an elopement qualified for a piece of land from the boy's family, which she shared with her group. Her child was a *gafata i luma*, "a genealogic step forward" (Hjarnø 1979–80:91–93). Should she bear a son who was particularly serviceable, as well as bright or talented, he might receive a minor title in his father's family. Should his sons marry well, they had even better prospects.

The emic category for informal marriage, *āvaga* (elopement), referred to all instances of a girl running off with a boy, even when she returned to her family after a few days or weeks.[22] Its encompassing character supported girls' participation in a cultural project of competition for titles and land through bearing high-status offspring. Often *āvaga* included no defloration. After the couple journeyed to the boy's estate, the boy averred, "This girl is a virgin; she has never had a husband," but it was only the boy who need be "satisfied with her virtue," his veracity seldom being put to any test (Stuebel 1976:30).[23] *Āvaga* were often provisional unions in which the distinction between intercourse and marriage was one of degree rather than of kind, the degree gauged by the length of time the girl stayed with the boy. Thus, Turner says, an exchange of property and festivities occurred later, "if the couple continued to live together" ([1884] 1984:95–96). The birth of a child precipitated further exchange and lent a final imprimatur to the relationship (Hjarnø 1979–80:107).

Although in the mid-nineteenth century Pritchard says, "One rendezvous, in the house of the man, makes her his wife, and the child is legitimate" (1866:134), legitimacy does not really seem to have been an indigenous issue. Many of the highest families in Western Samoa trace their lineage to a daughter born to a sixteenth-century female paramount, Salamāsina, to a man with whom she was only briefly involved and whom she never formerly married (Schoeffel 1987). Salamāsina is one of the highest names in Samoa. Genealogies traced to her are by definition exalted and the formality of the union irrelevant.

Governor Schultz, the foremost early expert on Samoan jurisprudence, distinguishes intercourse from marriage: "Sexual intercourse, when the parties do not end by living together does not leave any obligations. The girl especially, called 'fafine ole aso' [girl of a day], is free at once in this case" ([1911] n.d.:29–30). Lack of obligation aside, even here it appears that intercourse constituted a kind of marriage; referring to the philandering habits of chiefs' sons (*mānaia*), Schultz adds that a *mānaia* was "unconditionally free, as it is . . . his duty to contract as many *marriages* as possible for the good of his village."[24] Ranking girls' offspring had better access to titles not because the children of intercourse were viewed as illegitimate but because these ranking girls were likely to mate with ranking boys, such that the children had doubly exalted lineages.

The idea of *āvaga*, then, gave the pre-Christian girl sexual latitude, yet, as in the case of the fettered decoy pigeon, this appearance of freedom was deceptive: she was supposed to act responsibly, in the interest of her family. According to Schultz ([1911] n.d.:22–23), there were two kinds of elopement: elopement in the will of the family (*āvaga i le loto o le ʻāiga*) and elopement in the will of the girl (*āvaga i le loto o le teine*). The girl who eloped merely upon personal inclination—*i le loto o le teine*—was likely to be caught and punished. Lower-status girls, then, were sexual entrepreneurs capitalizing on their attractions to lure high-status partners and thereby enhance family status. This is why Samoan girls schooled missionary wives in decorating their bodies and in *faʻalialia*, flaunting themselves, so, the missionary Williams says, they might attract "mānaia" ([1830–32] 1984:117). Williams glosses *mānaia* as "the handsome young men of the town," but the word actually means "the sons of chiefs."

Gender Dimorphism in Old Samoa

Probably the different roles ascribed to girls and to boys were supported by variations in child rearing. We saw in chapter 3 that in contemporary Samoa the featured negative sanction is punishment. By making children feel one down, punishment inspires a need to be one up and to seek dominance in the form of status and titles.[25] In old Samoa boys were concerned with getting a title, while girls were preoccupied by *faʻalialia*, "flaunting," although flaunting was a means of getting titles for one's descendants. Girls were specialists in the joking discourse of entertainments, *ula*, which was a disguised method of dominance seeking, but the disguise—the exhibitionism on the surface of *ula*—is noteworthy. Counterreactions represent doing onto others what was once done to you. Perhaps, then, teasing was a more emphasized negative sanction for girls, one that may have become yet more emphatic during colonial times.

Decorated Samoan girl (probably a village princess). From the photographic collection of J. L. Dwyer (1908–13). Courtesy of K. A. Wheat (copyright). Original photograph currently stored at the American Samoa Historic Perservation Office.

Decorated Samoan girl, probably a chief's daughter. From the photographic collection of J. L. Dwyer (1908–13). Courtesy of K. A. Wheat (copyright). Original photograph currently stored at the American Samoa Historic Perservation Office.

We saw that by the 1880s a girl's hair might be cut for sexual indiscretion and that by the twentieth century her head might be shaved altogether. While cutting a girl's hair is a punishment, it is also a method of shaming her. We will soon see that with missionization little girls were made to cover up. Today teasing and shaming are used to make children feel embarrassed about nudity. Girls are, therefore, the more likely recipients. Retrospectively, I noticed that the examples I collected of elders lampooning children about some personal feature (*faipona*) were of older women teasing girls about their bodies and their sexuality. Tete'e's story, in which he steals the lavalava from a bathing village chief, centers around themes of hitting and dominance (although shaming and exhibitionism are also salient). The Fua/Sala story, however, centers around shaming (through gossip) and showing off (as a bridesmaid); showing off, or exhibitionism, is the counterreaction concomitant to shaming. We will see that flaunting and the vice I associated with it—*lotoleaga,* or jealousy toward those who get special attention—was key for Samoan girls in colonial spirit possession episodes.

If girls hoped to bear those "children of many families" (*tama'āiga*) who were fated to become high-title holders, bearing children of title could not have been quite the same as bearing titles oneself.[26] The pre-Christian Samoan family was, then, not a site of gender equity, in that it gave its titles mainly to boys, but it also compensated for inequity. While men, as title bearers, had secular authority (*pule*), women as mothers and sisters had cursing power (*mana*). What this meant was that, while male title holders had final word in decisions of import, should a man gainsay his female relatives, particularly his sister, supernatural sanctions were believed to ensue. Even today real fear attends upon displeasing a sister. This relation between a secularly powerfully brother and a spiritually powerful sister sounds like a gender balance, yet so common were brothers' violation of sisters' wishes that, whenever a brother became seriously ill,

> [t]he sister ... was ... closely questioned as to whether she had cursed him ... she was entreated to remove the curse, so that he might recover. Moved by their pleadings, the sister took coconut-water in her mouth and ejected it toward or upon the body of the sufferer, by which means she either removed the curse or expressed her innocence of having called down any malediction upon him. (Stair 1897:180)[27]

In other words, custom implied that the brother was so likely to gainsay his sister that his health was always potentially imperiled.

Conceptual Fetters

If the girl was a decoy pigeon drawing wealth and titles into the family, and if the differential advantages accruing to girls from such endeavors was less than the advantage accrued by title-inheriting boys, how did Samoans insure that the girl-as-pigeon did not take flight? Like the long fetter restraining the decoy pigeon, the Samoan definition of marriage allowed a girl the range necessary to lure but also prompted her to exercise a degree of judgment in mating that boys might forgo.

In formal marriages the girl's feelings were seldom consulted: she was a pawn in a political game. Indeed, Williams describes singing at formal weddings as attempts at "cheering up the feelings of the intended wife for contrary to ladies in civilized countries who look upon marriage as the summit of their ambition . . . the Samoan ladies bridal day [is celebrated] with weeping and wailing" ([1830–32] 1984:255). When Sanele was a boy, a Fagaloa girl—a high chief's daughter—wedded his uncle Ola, an older, highly titled man of Fagaloa. She arrived in her wedding dress and was taken to a welcoming house, where the village children sang to her, while she cried. Such lamentations were unlikely in *āvaga* that girls undertook of their own volition. The social interpretation of formal marriages, however, portrayed them as a public triumph. Inasmuch as Samoans identify with their public persona, girls would have wanted to be eligible for them and to maintain the requisite virginity.

In *āvaga* the girl was usually a principal agent. *Avagaga* is the term for eloping girls: the suffix *ga* refers to the agent of the activity. There was no term for the eloping boy. *Āvaga* is understood as a girl following a boy back to his family estate, and a girl who wanted to marry on her own initiative simply followed a boy (Schultz [1911] n.d.:22). There is, for example, a legend about two brothers, one older and plain, the other younger and handsome. In Samoan thought the older is the likely heir to family titles and should, therefore, be considered the more eligible. Both brothers court a chiefly girl, but she calls to the handsome younger brother.

> "You, sir, come here," . . . Instead, the youth stood up, to go home, but suddenly the girl also stood and followed him. Off they went, the youth being chased back, and the girl following along behind, wanting to become the youth's wife. (Moyle 1981:122–23)

Disgruntled, the old brother proposes a wife-getting contest: both boys are to roam around the village to see who follows them; the girls who do are called "wives."

If girls eloped on their own initiative, we also saw in chapter 5 that elopement was defined socially as defeat. Inasmuch as Samoans are identified with their public persona, most girls were likely to hesitate before this prospect. Thus, the cultural definition of marriage tended to align the girl's interests with those of her family and recommended the sexual restraint symbolized by her shaved head.

Discontinuities

Nineteenth-century missionaries opened boarding schools for Samoan girls. At first the girls would submit to their confinement but, the missionary Bullen

(1847) complains, "began at length to sigh for liberty to range at large with their idle companions." Although the missionaries tried to get free-ranging girls' parents to make them stay, they discovered parents did not have this authority. "After twice correcting a child, I have heard them [the parents] say *in her hearing,* 'Well if this does not suffice, I suppose she must have her own way,'" such that Bullen feared that at the boarding school "it would be necessary to allow them [the girls] to come when they please, remain as long as they please, allow them to do very much as they please, and to leave again when they please." To missionaries at least the Samoan girl looked as free as a bird. Today girls' liberty is placed squarely in Christian categories by parents and preachers alike.

In American Samoa *eva* is the common term for freely ranging. Trysts are called *ēvaga*. Should a girl be away from home too much, people will say "Se vā'ai ia Eva," meaning "Look at Eve." This sentence refers to the biblical temptress, but it includes a pun on the word *eva*. "Eva eva a te'i 'ua fula 'ae mulimuli ane 'ua puta" is a Samoan saying, meaning "Ranging about, suddenly swollen, and lastly fat." Sanele say it refers to a girl getting pregnant "from being *eva*." The saying links sudden swelling to later rotundity and is a variant of a line from the old jocular song "The Girl's Belly," which concludes "And later the girl's belly is swollen, and lastly fat." It is noteworthy that the older version of this line does not employ the word *eva*. Once the swelling girl is compared to the Christian Eve, her condition is no joke. *Ta'a* is the Western Samoan synonym for *eva;* however, *ta'a* can also refer to a lover, and the girl who goes *ta'a* frequently is suspected of having one. *Faita'aga,* literally "to make *ta'a,*" glosses as "fornication." *Ta'a pō,* "to go *ta'a* at night," is an offense for which Samoan-Christian girls are punished by having their head shaved.

In Christian Samoa freely roaming is censured because for girls it is regarded as an expanded version of *fa'alialia,* "walking about to show oneself," which in turn is regarded as luring. I have heard Sanele remark, when seeing a girl roaming about alone at night, that she was "looking for sex." Once girls had roamed about with comparative freedom, like decoy pigeons, to lure chiefs' sons in the service of their families. Doing so was part of a cultural project, and this was why Samoan girls encouraged missionary wives to lay aside their garments and do the same. These girls were not amoral or even "intolerably lazy" (read uninterested in achievement). On the contrary, they were offering their own mode of achievement to their missionary friends. But now, says one of Shore's informants, "boys . . . run around naked. The girl, however, should be covered up" (1982:228). Indeed, in Christian Samoa *fa'alialia* is glossed as vanity (Milner 1966:457) and is grounds for sharp criticism.

What the Christian girl is not supposed to be is *sa'oloto,* free. Disputing Mead's claims about the promiscuity of Samoan girls, a former American Samoa governor, Lutali, says, "There is no girl in Samoa who is taught by her parents to roam about and to be *sa'oloto* [free] to date" (*South Seas Star* 111(45)19/11/87:1). *Sa'oloto* is built on two terms: *sa'o,* meaning "free" or "independent," and *loto,* which we saw denotes the subjective dimension of experience, associated by Samoans with impulsiveness. In Christian Samoa girls' sexual independence, rather than being viewed as enterprise exercised in the service of their families, is viewed as an impulsive assertion of personal freedom against family values. Boys retained their freedom to range. Like brothers *and* sisters in pre-Christian Samoa, they were not expected to behave with great personal restraint except in the presence of an opposite-sexed sibling.[28] Thus, the obligation that once existed *between* brother and sister—to behave with dignity vis-à-vis one another—became a consistent feature of the girl's role.

While girls had been the agents of informal discourse in pre-Christian Samoa, in Christian Samoa they became the emblems of dignified contexts. Unlike agents, emblems do not speak. In chapter 8 we will see that this change signaled a loss for Samoan girls of an ancient discourse on self and of its correlative sexual habitus. But it would nonetheless be a mistake to see Samoan girls as victims of history. Contact presented girls with a host of opportunities and choices, and it is to these that we must look for the answer to why girls traded the alluring decorations of an earlier age for a mantle of dignity.

8

Foreign Incursions on Samoan Discourses of Self

Culture contact recreates a tower of Babel confusion of tongues, where the "tongues" are not only languages but also lexicons and discourses on self. Samoa withstood this confusion better than many Polynesian locales. In part this is because—although Western powers continually interfered in Samoan politics from a few decades after they took up residence—throughout the nineteenth and the early twentieth century most visitors were ghettoized around the major ports, Apia in Western Samoa and Pago Pago in American Samoa (Gilson 1970, Davidson 1967).[1] This chapter focuses on exceptions to this rule, two historical waves in which contact between foreigners and locals was extremely broad reaching: the incursion of English missionaries, who Christianized Samoa in the nineteenth century, and the incursion of American servicemen, who established bases in Samoa during World War II. I trace foreign influence on Samoans in terms of the premise/discourse series, from ontological premises to moral lexicons to moral discourse to contextual discourses. But in a sense this story must begin with strategies, asking why Samoans saw it in their interest to listen to missionary talk about the self.

Samoan Strategies and Christian Visitors

Practically from the day of their arrival circa 1830, missionaries became a chip in a Samoan political game. We saw already that in Samoa everyone politicked for status; the chiefs from whom missionaries sought local aid and legitimacy were no exception. When the missionary Williams first placed Christian teachers in Samoa, for example, he left them with High Chief Malietoa. Williams believed Malietoa to be something like a king and hoped to use him to facilitate rapid conversion. In fact, Malietoa, like his fellow chiefs, was constantly vying for sovereignty and legitimization, and the teachers at once became a means to this end. Samoans were impressed with the efficacy of the Christian god, who produced such fine articles as ships and guns (Williams, qtd. in Keesing 1934:396). They would gladly have heard "the good news," but Malietoa permitted the teachers to speak only to those who first paid him their respects in a formal visit (Gilson 1970:76).[2] Later, when missionaries established themselves in the villages, both chiefs and orators used Christianity to validate their authority by securing positions as deacons and elders in the church (85).

As early as the second decade after contact, Christian education became a means of appropriating status for commoners. Missionaries had begun to train "native pastors" (Keesing 1934:397, Garrett 1982:125). The London Missionary Society (LMS) took primary responsibility for Christianizing Samoa.[3] Generally, English missionaries of the period had a strong egalitarian ethos; often their missionary vocation was part of a project of social self-betterment (Gunson 1978:34–35, 38). This ethos was particularly strong among LMS ministers, who tended to be poorer but better educated than those of other mission societies (86). It is unlikely that they would have excluded enterprising young men without inherited status. Once trained, Samoan pastors often used their ministry to assert political authority. By the 1880s British consul Churchward complains that native pastors "cannot curb their ambition, and beyond their missionary influence assert a sort of temporal authority, ruling the districts in which they live with a veritable rod of iron" (1887:81).

Samoan families were quick to recognize this new source of status and authority. Thus, Chief Tuiteleleapaga tells us that

> [a]fter the missionaries . . . settled on the islands and villages, a new era . . . dawned. Missionaries established schools for boys and for girls. The graduates from the boys' school at first found it difficult in getting a beautiful . . . wife because her parents and the girl herself still looked forward to the chiefs and talking chiefs [orators]. However, after some reluctant marriages . . . the people noticed the superiority of a missionaries' wife over a faletua [chief's wife] or tausi [orators wife]. . . . [Y]oung girls and other unmarried women began to envy the missionaries' wives sitting with their husbands on the dais with deacons during church services. . . . In an assembly in church or any other place, the faifeau's [pastor's] faletua not only receives the first and best share, but priority in salutatory remarks. (1980:45)

In this passage Tuiteleleapaga calls the Samoan pastor a "missionary." Pastorship, it would seem, became a means to identify with and incorporate the status of foreigners. Although this passage concerns the aspirations of mothers and daughters, rather than those of young men, it confirms that the ministry was a means to rival chiefly status, the pastor's wife acquiring the same honorific title as the chief's wife, *faletua*.

This new route to status—Christian education—was an education in literacy, and literacy was universally desired.[4] In 1839, a mere nine years after the

LMS came to Samoa, the missionary Murray writes from Tutuila, "Every village has its own teacher and its own school" (1839). From 'Upolu the missionary William Day expresses his amazement at "the great multitude of persons who have learned and are learning to read and write" (1839). The missionary Hardie says that in his district alone there were twelve schools and a thousand scholars (1839). Like reports are ubiquitous in the missionary record.[5]

Incursions on the Samoan Ontological Lexicon

The London Missionary Society was an umbrella organization of evangelical populist sects—Wesleyanism being the original example—all of them believing strongly in personal religious feeling and experience (Davidoff and Hall 1987, Parry 1974:11). Inasmuch as Christianity found a ready place in Samoan agendas, missionaries were positioned to ask something in return. What they asked was that converts display "much knowledge of their own hearts" (Harbutt 1841). A knowledge of the catechism was a necessary but insufficient criteria for the privilege of Baptism, let alone for church office.

This missionary emphasis on inner experience had a strong emotional impact on nineteenth-century Samoans, whose conversions were accompanied by foreign perspective on indigenous styles of selfhood: Samoans often came to see themselves not only as role players but as hypocritical. In a 1839 letter from Tutuila the missionary Murray quotes a recent convert proclaiming, "Formerly . . . we uttered love . . . with our mouth while our hearts were full of hatred and murder but now we know true compassion" (1839). In a letter dated March 20 of the following year Murray says that one of his Samoan servants

> is still in deep distress . . . I found her exclaiming in . . . poignant grief—"Woe is me! Woe is me" and in answer to my enquires she stated that the words that had gone to her heart were these "where is the hope of the hypocrite when God taketh away his soul," adding that she had just discovered that she had all along been a hypocrite. (1840)

This distressed Samoan accurately judges her own behavior as having been based on a sociocentric premise about self and as organized around a persona. She also appears to be discovering and adopting a discourse of sincerity, a discourse in which inner experience is the locus of veracity, suggesting a radically novel apprehension of self.

The Soul

Mission accounts of Samoan religious "enlightenments" may have been adapted to evangelical modes and categories. Thus, the dramatics that missionaries reported as orchestrating conversion experiences mimicked the "agony of mind and body," and the emission of "hysterical screams and groans" that were hallmarks of evangelical conversion experiences in England (Davies 1961:154). The missionaries occasionally quote Samoans in their own language, and when they do one suspects them of Procrustean tendencies. Harbutt, for example, transcribes a conversation between himself and a woman in which he inquires why she desires Baptism:

> she replied because . . . she wished the salvation of her soul—I immediately said then there is salvation in Baptism is there? She immediately and with peculiar emphasis replied "E leai lava o le faaola o le *atamai* i le toto paia o Jesu lava" No indeed! The blood of Christ alone is the salvation of the soul. (1841; my emph.)[6]

In this passage the Samoan word that Harbutt translates as *soul* is *atamai*, which actually means "cleverness," "mind," or "wisdom." Certainly, it was a new cleverness that scholar-converts sought to acquire. Samoan culture had long valued cleverness and esoteric knowledge in the figure of the orator. For missionaries, however, *soul* was the most important term for self and carried a bulging valise of conceptual baggage.

For evangelicals the soul was one's inner spiritual life, which was taken to be the essence of the person and to be of a contextually transcendent character. It was also a sense of self becoming broadly popular in eighteenth- and nineteenth-century England through evangelical religious belief and practice (Davidoff and Hall 1987:88). Because humans were believed to be sullied by original sin, surrendering the soul to God required a near constant monitoring of the state of one's inner life, thereby expanding a subjective mode of awareness and constituting subjectivity as a site of identification and as a genre of self. As in Foucault's model of Victorian sexuality (1990), a rhetoric of repression served as a strategy of development.[7]

We saw that ontological premises—for example, the self as inner or the self as role player—are evident in cultural lexicons. Missionary lexicons were inscribed back into Samoan language when missionaries began translating the Bible and other religious texts into Samoan. Thus, in chapter 2 we saw that *aga* is a social role, or persona, which Samoans take to be the self's constituent aspect. In old Samoa the term *agāga*, constructed from the root *aga*, was also used for disembodied spirits and ghosts (Turner [1884] 1984:16, Cain 1979:70–143), and thus was what one became after death, still an identity but without a body. Logically, Samoans referred to a disembodied identity (*agāga*) with a compound form of the term for identity, *aga*. Pratt and his missionary colleagues also believed that identity survived after death. Because they equated identity with internal life, they calqued this significance onto *agāga*, defining it as an inner essence, a soul, in the Christian sense of the term, thereby reversing Samoan premises about self (Pratt [1862/1911] 1977). *Agāga* is still glossed as *soul* in contemporary Samoan/English dictionaries, although its meaning is tagged as Christian: in oratory the term is used to give speeches a "biblical flavor" (Matā'afa Tu'i 1987:42).

We also saw in part 1 that, while the word *aga* (meaning a social persona) indexes the Samoan ontological premise, the word *loto* refers broadly to the inner dimension of experience—particularly to individual will—and that this dimension is backgrounded by the Samoan ontological premise. Further, we saw that Samoans tend to regard the *loto* as morally suspect. Nonetheless, when English hymns that sang of raising the soul up to God were translated into Samoan, the word *loto* was often used for *soul; loto* was, after all, the Samoan word for the person's inner life, however differently Samoans regarded it. If one were to translate the Samoan version back into English, one might speak of raising the passions up to God, not that Christian soul, which was for missionaries the very basis of transcendent communion with the divine.

Incursions on the Samoan Moral Lexicon

Sometimes missionaries' tower of Babel mistranslations resulted in a special moral lexicon that Samoans tended to relegate to church contexts. Pratt, for example, glossed the Christian term *conscience* as *lotofuatiaifo*, a compound term based on the root *loto*: in other words, Pratt defined that part of the self that Samoans see as most morally problematic as the very basis of morality. *Lotofuatiaifo*, however, never came to be a comprehensive term for moral sensibility. One of Gerber's informants in the 1970s says, "All I know about that word is, the pastor uses it in Church" (1975:198). When asked for a definition, Sanele game me this example.

> Let's say a pastor ... received generous donations from his parishioners, but he asks for more funds for some special purpose. He will tell his flock to go deep into their *lotofuatiaifo* and then decide what to give.[8]

In other words, by using the word *lotofuatiaifo,* the pastor admits what he asks is above and beyond those social expectations that are the normal guide for conduct in Samoa and, therefore, a matter of personal choice.

There were, however, other evangelical glosses that secured a better foothold in the language. Pratt translated virtue and vice as forms of *āmio*. *Āmio* is behavior that stems from the *loto*, that is, from the individual's own will. Thus, one of Shore's informants says, "It's your own choice: your *āmio* is your option" (1982:154). While Samoans tend to speak of behavior in light of its social consequences (Duranti 1984a), Pratt's translation implies that the inner self—the soul, particularly its personal volitional aspect—is the definitive moral consideration.[9]

Evangelicals had archetypically Western ideas of agency and intention. Constitutive of the watchful evangelical conscience and the confessional praxis through which it was enacted was the idea that individual agency could and should be read in every nuance of personal thought and feeling (Davidoff and Hall 1987:86–89). Self-surveillance and confession were underwritten by a belief in original sin, which predicated that thoughts and feelings tended to be reprehensible. The Samoan word *sala* was in Christian times taken to mean "sin" but previously referred to something like a slip-up in a performance and to matters of face rather than interiority. Thus, the traditional expression "O le sala e tau'ave i le fofoga" means "The fault is carried in the face" (Milner 1966:197–98) and refers to the custom of covering one's face with a fine mat in token of ceremonial apology.

I do not mean that Pratt and his colleagues, by converting Samoans to Christianity, succeeded in replacing indigenous lexicons on self with their own lexicons. Rather, missionary epistemes found an enduring place in local language because, through much of the nineteenth century, missionaries alone offered to sate newly literate Samoans' appetite for books. Just a decade after their arrival missionaries, writing even from remote areas, remark that "the people were everywhere enquiring for books" (Pratt 1840). By 1844 the LMS had established a printing press on 'Upolu, and by 1850 there was more or less universal access to the Bible (Garrett 1982:125, Huebner 1986:399). Missionary glosses were littered throughout the prayerbooks, primers, catechism, and dictionaries that prolix missionary translators produced in the decades following contact (Huebner 1986:401). The Bible was a nineteenth-century best-seller partially because, like Samoan oral traditions, it was chocked with proverbs and stories that came to provide fresh material for those esoteric allusions that were the hallmark of Samoan oratory. Conversely, church sermons and speeches were used for the demonstration of oratorical skills (Holmes 1974:60–62). In Christian contexts missionaries and Samoans alike expected orators to be familiar with Christian terms and usage.[10]

Incursions on Moral Discourse

In Samoa girls have long been lexically marked with a missionary insignia. In contemporary Samoan there are two styles of pronunciation, *tautala lelei*, "good speech," and *tautala leaga*, "bad speech."[11] Good speech employs the /t/, /n/, and /r/ sounds and is sometimes referred to as T-language; bad speech employs the /k/, /ng/, and /l/ sounds, is sometimes referred to as K-language, and is most commonly used by contemporary Samoans. A girl, for example, is a *teine* in good speech but a *keinge* in ordinary speech. Speaking *tautala lelei* is a way of being dignified (*mamalu*); it is associated with written language—a missionary import—and with Christian and colonial contexts generally. Not only is T-language the language of church, Samoans are apt to insist that Western Europeans use only T-language, putatively because it accords with their inherent dignity but also effectively placing them in a linguistic ghetto.

It seems likely that, after contact, the Samoan language began to drift toward bad speech but that the missionary version of the Samoan language—frozen in Pratt's dictionary, early editions of the Bible, and other missionary publications—preserved the older speech style (Shore 1982:269). Interestingly, it is also the speaking style associated with girls in Christian Samoa (Ochs 1988:57). Perhaps this association originates in the special attention missionaries focused on Samoan girls. As early as 1844, missionary boarding schools had been founded for girls. Thus, the LMS missionary Mills says:

> Mrs. Mills commenced a boarding school.... [I]t promises to be very useful in raising the character of Samoan females. In commencing we feared that after the novelty had passed they would soon get wearied of the restraint and return to their families but instead ... they appear to have an increasing attachment to the school ... and more are seeking admission than can be accommodated.... [T]heir ages are 7 to 13. In Reading, Writing, Arithmetic, Geography, Sewing ... they make respectable progress, but the great advantage of such an Institution is the Moral and Religious Education.... Our energies need to be directed as much in raising up pious and educated teachers' wives as in preparing Native Male Teachers for the Work. (1844)

According to Mrs. Mills, "Moral and Religious Education" aimed at saving girls form "the corrupting influences of other natives," that is, at changing their moral consciousness about their sexuality. The *aualuma* was, after all, the association of village-born females who put on Joking Nights and other bawdy entertainments. In old Samoa girls slept in the *aualuma's* greathouse, where *aualuma* entertainments were likely to take place, but that was also called "the house of the group of pearls," referring to its young residents.[12] Many Christian pastors believed that the virtue—read virginity—of the "pearls" was inadequately protected in the *aualuma* house and desired that Samoan girls reside with them. For young Samoan women residing with missionaries gradually became a marker of status and respectability.[13]

In late-eighteenth- and nineteenth-century England it was broadly argued that woman was a uniquely moral being and that her delicacy and sensibility made her society's moral barometer (Millar 1806, Wheeler and Thompson 1825, Wollstonecraft [1787] 1993, Ellis 1842). Further, missionaries' own claims to status and position were based on spiritual meritocracy (Gunson 1978). Surely, a moral discourse on virtue/virginity as an entitling form of merit was central to the "Moral and Religious Education" missionaries offered girls. A conflation of virtue and virginity in Samoan moral discourse on girls is evident in the Fua/Sala story analyzed in chapter 4, in which Sala is viewed as being less entitled to social position because she has born a child out of wedlock. To understand why this discourse on virginity took root in Samoan minds it is necessary to trace the changing morphology of marriage.

Changing Marriage

In the last chapter we saw that *āvaga* (elopement) was the common form of marriage in precontact Samoa. In his early work on Samoan jurisprudence, Schultz insists that even in the highest-ranking marriages the term for giving the bride to her suitor was *āvaga*, because it was "the essential thing, everything else only accessory" ([1911] n.d.:22–25). If in ancient Samoa the idea of marriage was coincident with that of *āvaga*, this idea may have posed problems for establishing lineage. One of the guarantors of lineage is a bride's virginity, but *āvaga* itself has connotations of consummating a relationship; after an *āvaga* no such proof could be obtained.

Throughout ancient Polynesia the primary means of establishing status was genealogy: to claim status was implicitly to assert lineage. The Samoan game of jockeying for status was a negotiation about genealogy. When being polite, one treated others as if they were of exalted lineage; in ceremony one attributed lineage and ancestry to them, and they responded in kind. Exploiting the polite attributions of ceremonial exchange, orators attributed ever more exalted lineage to their own chiefs. Repeated lineage claims, defended in war, gradually gained legitimacy. Goldman makes a distinction between inherited and acquired status in Polynesia (1970). Samoans, blurring this distinction, achieved status in the guise of inheriting it. Samoans also achieved status through a biopolitics.

Orators' arranged marriages that mingled eminent bloodlines, creating candidates for high title in the form of *tama'āiga*, "offspring of many families," infants who distilled alliances among ranking families and villages in their persons. Reconstructing changes that predate practices recorded at contact is speculative. Nonetheless, it is tempting to suggest that at some point in Samoan history three changes in high-status marriage ceremonies came about so orators might better establish lineage. First, the exchange of property became increasingly ostentatious. The property, particularly fine mats, was material proof of lineage, requiring considerable extended family connections to assemble. Possessing certain named fine mats was prerequisite to possessing certain titles, on the model of King Arthur's Excalibur. Second, the wedding exchange came to proceed the *āvaga* in order to provide a venue for the third change, a defloration ritual. Because the ranking girl's guarded virginity was central to those marriages that created children of lineage, it was a badge of lineage.[14]

Samoan Glosses for Christian Ideals

In Samoan terms Christian moral discourse on girls and virginity implied that all girls wore this badge of lineage. Just as everyone could go to heaven in the Christian paradigm—whereas the *lagi*, "sky," had formally been a preserve of the higher gods and the defied spirits of chiefs—so also in Christian Samoa all extended families might validate their claims to genealogy symbolically, through the virginity of their daughters.¹⁵ To this end a new concept of marriage needed to be invented (or imported). Just as in precontact times a unitary concept of marriage had probably been splintered by the invention of formal marriages that included deflorations, in Christian times the enduring concept of marriage as elopement for common people was further undermined by the importation of a new version of formal marriages, church weddings. These weddings were called *fa'aipoipoga*, a term borrowed from Rarotongan because there was no Samoan term that clearly demarcated formal and informal unions (Schultz [1911] n.d.:22).

Church weddings were a kind of formal marriage to which all families could aspire. If they supplied only one of the imprimaturs of formal marriages—virginal daughters—capitalist economics has since supplied another mark, ostentatious display. Today, as Samoan families become wealthier in American Samoa, Hawai'i, New Zealand, and elsewhere, they engage in more and more ostentatious demonstrations of wealth at weddings. Macpherson says that Samoans in New Zealand often mortgage their homes to fund the weddings of their extended family's daughters (1991). When I resided in American Samoa during the 1980s, brides from middle-income families might have as many as three $500 wedding dresses, worn successively over the course of the marriage day. These dresses combine the display of wealth and putatively virginal girls in one figure, democratizing claims to lineage in capitalist style.

Christianity, however, did not simply offer families new means to appropriate status through daughters; it made the same offer to girls themselves. Virginity was an affectation of the practices of nobility and an appropriation of their names. In precontact Samoa the virginal daughters of chiefs were called "O Tausala" (Stair 1897:115). Freeman's report in the early 1940s suggests that a virginal standard for conduct had come to be applied to all girls (1983:226–53), and Schoeffel says that in the 1970s *tausala* was the term used for this "conceptual ideal of the adolescent girl" (1979a:139). In American Samoa "Miss Tausala" is now the title of the girl who wins the local beauty pageant, a competition open to all unmarried females.¹⁶

As all girls became emblems of their family's hypothetical claims to lineage, Samoan parents became increasingly interested in the aesthetic realization of the *tausala* ideal in their daughters, and, to this end, girls came to be treated by their families as persons of status. In Samoa status is embodied in physical stasis: those with status do not serve others but are served by them. Schoeffel describes Samoan parents of the 1970s as valuing chiefly qualities in their daughters above and beyond "serviceable attributes" (1979a:139). For this reason, she says, "In large households girls often manage to push off most chores on to their younger siblings and male peers" (1979a:138). This parental preference is remarkable, as it goes against the grain of Samoan attitudes toward children, who are appreciated for their services. "You should have children," my Samoan mother-in-law used to say to Sanele, "so that they will take care of you."

Not only did being *tausala* become a means to acquire status; ironically, a Christian augmentation of the girl's status was likely to have played into girls' roles as lures because in Samoa status is a defining aspect of attractiveness. When a girl wants to be attractive to a young man she may avoid doing her chores, pretending that she is waited upon rather than that she serves others. So common is this predilection that there is an expression for it. When a girl avoids her chores others may remark "Who are you *te'e* to?"[17] The question means something like "Who are you trying to impress?" A *te'e* is a pole that holds up a clothesline. The idea is that avoiding chores is like standing up very straight, which in Samoa is the bearing affected by those of high status.[18]

Today there is a Samoan word for *not* being a virgin, *pa'umutu* (cut skin); the missionary-linguist Pratt, however, records no such word, although the topic was of obvious interest to missionaries. There is still no Samoan word for anatomical virginity. While the nineteenth-century Pratt glosses the English word virgin as *tāupōu,* the word for "village princess," the mid-twentieth-century linguist Milner glosses virgin first as *teine,* the Samoan word for "girl," and only secondarily as *tāupōu* (1966:458), the change in nuance telling a historical tale.

Christian Moral Discourse and Sexual Liberty

Girls had yet further reasons for receptivity to the missionaries' moral discourse: again, ironically, it served girls as a wedge against the moral hegemony of their own cultural order. When missionaries instructed their charges in the importance of virginity, they inevitably relied upon the moral discourse surrounding female virginity in their own culture. Virginity was the site of an argument about marriage topical in English society during the late eighteenth and nineteenth centuries (Maynard 1993:36). Liberal currents in English society had become vociferously critical of marriages entered into for political and economic reasons. From the birth of the romantic novel in Richardson's *Clarissa* ([1748] 1985), the idea that girls should marry for love rather than for the advance of family wealth and status was a radical theme. Likewise, evangelicals advocated "free-choice" marriage, albeit for reasons of spiritual compatibility (Davidoff and Hall 1987:219–21, 323, 437).

Despite what appears, in historical perspective, to be a common advocacy of the importance of subjective sentiment and freedom of conscience in intimate relations, romantics and evangelicals saw themselves as adamantly opposed. One can find their antagonistic positions represented in English nineteenth-century romantic novels. In *Wuthering Heights,* for example, Kathy can be seen as symbolizing the soul, irredeemably torn between these two arguments on the meaning of free choice in marriage, represented by the Dionysian Heathcliff on the one hand and Apollonian Edgar Linton on the other. These antagonistic positions were also insinuated in evangelical sermons in which "motives for marriage" were a major theme (Davies 1961:156).

From the days of their arrival missionaries referred to economically practical and political marriages among Samoans as "works of Darkness" that "the light of the glorious gospel will chase away" (Williams [1830–32] 1984:77). Missionaries saw the exchanges that marked Samoan marriages as a means through which older chiefs "purchased" comely young women (Wilkes 1845:148–49), linking chiefly marriages to slavery, a missionary cause célèbre in other colonial locales.[19] The missionaries' idea that girls' personal inner feelings should be a prime criterion for marriage created a moral cacophony in late-nineteenth-century Samoa. Many girls seemed to be marrying for reasons that took little account of family status. Earlier I referred to the memoirs of Laulii Willis, a Samoan who married an Englishman. Although Laulii Willis was an orator's daughter, she married at her own insistence at age fourteen, threatening to elope if she was not given her way. After a brief marriage she did elope (unsuccessfully) with a European. Shortly thereafter she married Mr. Willis, with whom she left Samoa (Willis 1889).

By the 1920s missionary discourse on the importance of inner feeling in marriage was taken up not only by girls but even by parents. Parents sometimes even refused "to make their daughters *taupo* [village princesses] because the missionaries say a girl should make her own choice, and once she is a *taupo*, they regard the matter as inevitably taken out of their hands" (Mead [1928]1961:101).[20] According to Keesing, by the 1930s even village princesses disappeared on brief elopements, after which they returned to their families (1937). Keesing suggests that the institution of the village princess was close to being abandoned in part because, quoting an informant, "it is nowadays too hard for a girl to be a virgin" (1937:8).[21] With the incursion of American servicemen in the 1940s, this incipient revolution in the Samoan sexual system became volatile.[22]

World War II and Samoan Moral Discourse

Seductive foreign males had visited Samoa since contact. Whalers, for example, had anchored in Apia and Pago Pago, particularly during the 1840s, and the missionaries complained that the men induced girls to go aboard their ship (Murray 1839; Gilson 1970:165, 183). The early 1940s, however, witnessed a visitation of nonpareil proportions. In some Samoan locales foreign men outnumbered the indigenous population of men, women, and children. In American Samoa the expansion of the Tutuila naval station was most intense between 1942 and 1944. In 1942 there were 14,371 marines on Tutuila (Franco 1989). According to the sixteenth census of United States Department of Commerce, in 1940 there were 12,908 Samoans in all of American Samoa, a territory including Tutuila, the Manua's, and several other small islands. Between 1943 and 1944 in Western Samoa there were between 25,000 and 30,000 troops in a Samoan population of approximately 62,000 (Stanner 1953:325). The troops were concentrated on the island of 'Upolu, however, which had a considerably smaller Samoan population.

> A great deal of sexual promiscuity . . . between Samoan or part-Samoan women and American troops. . . . Romantic, at least friendly, liaisons were very common. One mission society reported that in Upolu alone there were 1,200 known instances of illegitimate children by American soldiers from Samoan girls. . . . With troops so widely dispersed in an area so densely settled it was impossible to prevent familiar association. Many soldiers regularly visited girl-friends within the villages . . . the entrance-gates to the airport . . . became known among the Samoans as "the gates of sin." (Stanner 1953:327)

In part sexual laxity during World War II probably derived from the anomalous character of American servicemen. Within Samoan moral discourse incest is not only a limiting sexual principle but a principle deployed to place limits on budding relationships. Family is broadly defined in Samoa and is inclusive of relations with the most distant and tenuous of relatives. People, therefore, require extensive genealogical expertise to know when they are committing incest. Parents' genealogical expertise far exceeds that of their children. Still today, when parents want a relationship terminated, they often tell young people that they are related. This genealogical talk about the morality of sexual relationships is likely to have been used extensively in old Samoa, when the young person's circle of acquaintants was more circumscribed. It would not have worked, however, as a means of limiting relationships with American serviceman: GIs simply were not relatives.[23]

Romance

To the increasing moral cacophony of the twentieth century, servicemen probably added yet another moral discourse. "GI Joe" may have had cavalier attitudes toward Samoan girls, but he also carried with him his own culture's discourse on sexual relationships. This was a romantic discourse evident in America cinema of the 1930s and 1940s, such as the films of Busby Berkeley or those starring Nelson Eddy and Jeannette Macdonald, Fred Astaire and Ginger Rogers, Greta Garbo, Marlene Dietrich, and the list goes on. The servicemen who populated Samoa with an epidemic of illegitimate children during the war would have employed this discourse, if only as a rhetoric for seduction. In chapter 3 we saw that the English phrase "in love" has no real Samoan translation and that when Sanele was growing up in the 1960s cheeky boys, boasting of their sexual prowess, would tell girls, "Watch it or you will speak English," meaning "I'll make you say you love me." The American servicemen of World War II were probably those fellows who originally made Samoan girls speak English by teaching them to say "I love you."

In American romantic rhetoric choices about mating and marriage were to be made on the basis of personal sentiment, just as in the missionaries' moral discourse. While affairs with American GIs were not what English missionaries had in mind, missionaries had inscribed in Samoan language, and imprinted in every text that the ever-growing population of literate Samoans read throughout the nineteenth century, a basis of understanding for the romantic talk of American military visitors. In other words, although the explicit message of missionaries' moral discourse to girls was "Be virginal!" the sub-rosa message was "Be virginal because that alone accords with the purity and seriousness of your inner feelings, that is of your soul." But inner feelings in love have implications that do not always accord with virginity.

American talk about romance, like missionary talk about virginity, found an enduring place in Samoan moral discourses about relations between girls and boys. The Samoan word for "love" is *alofa,* and Shore tells us that boys who have *alofa* for girls do not make love to them (1982:228–29). This "do not" makes cultural sense: we saw in chapter 5 that seducing a girl in Samoa is a way to defeat her and her family and, in chapter 3, that "compassion" is the strict meaning of *alofa.* But Sanele says that all the Samoan popular songs about girl/boy relationships he heard growing up in Samoa (since 1958 or somewhat thereafter) used the word *alofa* for romantic love. Here again contact gave Samoan lexicons new meanings with profound implications for how people thought about the self.

In childhood Sanele heard an old recording of Samoan songs about sexual relationships, sung by women, that were humorous rather than romantic. These Rabelaisian songs were those once sung at *aualuma* entertainments. Similarly, the ethnomusicologist Moyle, working in Samoa during the 1960s, found that adults (who presumably had grown up during the 1930s and 1940s) knew the funny-bawdy type songs that Sanele had heard but most young people did not (1975:239). This cultural forgetting reminds me that I have only been telling half the story, for Christian moral discourse on virginity did more than liberate girls' personal sentiments: this discourse had implications for Samoan contextual discourses, erasing the precontact positioning of informal discourse.

Incursions on Contextual Discourses

In England eighteenth- and nineteenth-century evangelical Protestantisms played an important role in the articulation and separation of public and private contexts, particularly in the definition of private life and of women's place within it (Davidoff and Hall 1987). I have argued that in many Western societies private life is the informal context par excellence. In chapter 7 we saw that pre-Christian Samoan women, like their English sisters, were associated with informal contexts and specialized in informal discourse, but Samoan informal discourse involved physical and sexual exhibitionism, which came as a great shock to missionary sensibilities. While the more urbane of foreign visitors did not vehemently object to indigenous sexual practices, all seemed to share missionaries' shock at girls' participation in the informal discourse of jest. Thus, the British consul Churchward says,

> Any stranger to Samoa... on his first introduction to such a party of girls, seated in front of him so demurely and properly, would require but slight provocation to persuade himself that he saw an eightfold incarnation of all that is modest and good. Alas for such a man's feelings should he... remain too long, and witness the very extravagant performance of these same damsels, when fairly roused and hounded into delirium by the approving shouts of the audience!... [T]hese same quiet-looking... damsels are quite capable of becoming so excited... as really to lose all command of their actions, distorting their countenances in the most hideous manner, and performing such undesirable antics, that... they appear at last more like a lot of demons let loose from below, than the angels upon earth they at first appeared. (1887:229–30)

Exhibitionistic songs and dances featured such silly posturing, expressions, and outrageous banter that even missionaries understood them to be forms of jest, at least when performed by males. Williams says of males, "Hands & arms, legs & knees are all requisitioned & many of their anticks are both funny and clever." But when females engaged in facial antics, for example, "throwing their upper lip from side to side to an astonishing distance producing a singular... distortion of the features," Williams calls it "hideous," "disgusting," and a "perversion of taste" ([1830–32] 1984:247).

The Western reaction against what was perceived to be girls' unfeminine behavior was gradually incorporated in Samoan-Christian moral discourse: the ideal of everygirl as *tausala* (virginal and dignified) was incongruent with girls' specialization in the antics of informal discourse. For many decades girls resisted the move to Christian bodily decorum and all that it conveyed. Indeed, according to the missionary Hutton, they were more "intractable" than their men and "addicted to pleasures, and obstinately refusing to cover the upper part of their persons" (1874:149). Nonetheless, by the end of the nineteenth century only old women still danced naked throughout the second half of Joking Nights. Maidens would "once in a while undo their lavalava only to fold it back together very soon" (Krämer [1902] 1995:374). Yet Christian decorum remained but skin deep and was shed by the conclusion of the dance. Writing of Joking Nights in the 1890s, Krämer says, "everyone dances in an ever more unrestrained, uninhibited manner until morning dawns, and when all are gone but the visiting young men and the girls of the host village, the boys in high spirits tear the lavalava off the girls amidst laughter and screeching" ([1902] 1995:377).

Changing Contexts and Marriage

In chapter 5 we saw that contextual discourses rely upon cultural projects and that both formal and informal projects represent culturally legitimated avenues for achievement. Remember that in old Samoa girls' cultural project was making highborn offspring through an informal discourse of flaunting and luring. This endeavor relied upon the scant distinction Samoans made between formal and informal unions, there being no word to distinguish them. Church weddings (*fa'aipoipoga*), however, were clearly distinguished from marriages out of church. Out-of-church marriages, most of which were *āvaga*, came to be called *fa'apōuliuli*, literally "the way of the darkness," making them symbolic of heathen benightedness. Babes born from them were "babies of the night" (*'o le pepe o le pō*), or "children of the night" (*tamapōuliuli*).

Implied in the idea that only formal marriages were valid was another, that marriage and intercourse with a female virgin were, at least potentially, different events. Foucault (1990) suggests that via an ethic of prohibition and confession, people in nineteenth-century Western societies learned to speak about private practices, which then became defining elements of sexuality and self. From the viewpoint of self theory, this shift in discourse amounts to an articulation of cultural contexts as "public" versus "private." It appears as if in Samoa the missionary concern with private sexual experience brought to light this alternative set of contexts, such that it became possible for Samoans to commit the private act of intercourse without committing the public act of marriage.

The new contextual distinction between private and public, and with it a distinction between intercourse and marriage, began to undermine the status of informal offspring. The missionary term *fa'apōuliuli* is still used for "marriages" conducted by young people without the sanction of church or family. Often in *fa'apōuliuli* families later recognize the marriage and then the couple wed in church, but when recognition is denied the girl returns home, and a resulting child is illegitimate. Milner translates *tama fa'apōuliuli*—literally, "child of a *fa'apōuliuli*"—as "illegitimate child." In Samoa marriage implies contractual obligation between families (such as the granting of land to a descendant and his or her accompanying relatives). If, however, the girl who vanished with a boy for a few days or weeks on an *āvaga* did not marry, and if her offspring's claims were illegitimate, then elopements were no achievement: families could not capitalize on mere promiscuity. This shift in the Samoan sexual calculus must have made girls' discourse of flaunting seem selfish and would explain Samoans' increasing compliance with missionary disapproval of girls' role at entertainments, particularly Joking Nights. As a result, as Samoans became increasingly Christian, the old practice of flaunting (*fa'alialia*) was compromised for girls.

The contextual implications of the Christian sex/marriage distinction developed slowly. In the first decade of the twentieth century Schultz believed that the introduction of Christianity had "brought about important changes in the domain of the laws regulating marriage," but the old views had "not yet disappeared" ([1911] n.d.:30). From this report in 1911 to Mead's in 1928 portraits of girls' roles were, in major outline, resonant with nineteenth-century reports. Two sorts of marriages existed: high-status marriages, preceded by a test of virginity and an elaborate exchange of wealth; and common marriages, or *āvaga*, in which virginity was moot and which were acknowledged by an exchange occurring sometime after the beginning of cohabitation, often at the birth of a first child.

Changing Attitudes toward Informal Discourse

In pre-Christian Samoa both the discourse of hierarchical contexts (in which males specialized) and the discourse of joking contexts (in which females specialized) took place in the village. Chiefs and their liege men (*'aumāga*) staged ceremonies, while the village women's association (*aualuma*) staged bawdy entertainments, like Joking Nights. By the 1930s, however, Joking Nights had migrated. Sloan reports on a dance he witnessed in Manu'a during the 1930s that took place within the village that, while energetic, did not end in elopements (1940:106). "Along in the small hours of the morning," Sloan adds "the younger folk quietly slipped away to hold an impassioned dance of their own in a deserted house far down at the other end of the village." Joking Nights were an important venue for girls' discourse of flaunting. The migration of Joking Nights to the village periphery represents a shift in social feelings about this discourse, feelings that became intense in World War II. Consider, for example, the following song.[24]

Girls of Samoa[25]

You girls of Samoa,
I didn't think your heads were stupid.
The boys from the military arrived
And all of a sudden you paint your lips,
Looking for your heels and put them on.
You were never of that habit while you were growing up.
You will end on the breadfruit plantation,
Picking breadfruits for the cooking pit.

Vanished are all the sailors of the military
Abandoning you on mainstreet,
Sitting everywhere along mainstreet
With your hair disheveled.

Finished are the days of showing off
Next to a guy from the military.
I told you not to flaunt yourself.
You will end with no status whatsoever.

Deserting your family and vanished,
Vanished and live at Satapuala,
You lived next to the gates of sin
Lived everywhere on the mainstreet,
Like a girl from downtown,
But you knew full well
That you come from a back village.

In the opening lines the "Girls of Samoa" are called "stupid" because they adopted modern and foreign forms of flaunting: painted lips and high heels. The last two lines of the first verse suggest that these new forms of flaunting were presumptuous (*tautalaitiiti*), for the Girls of Samoa who showed off next to a military guy ended on the plantation, picking breadfruit. Cultivating and preparing staple foods like breadfruit is the lowest-status role in Samoan culture; it is normally the brothers' role, not that of higher-status sisters. In the second verse I use the phrase "flaunt yourself," for *mateletele*, a word with no real analogue in English but which means "to walk fast and swing your hips." It is a self-advertising style of walk today confined to transvestites and prostitutes. This verse reiterates the consequences attendant upon flaunting implied in the first verse, asserting that the girls who do "will end with no status whatsoever."

Remember that in old Samoa Williams tells us girls' flaunting was thought to attract the favor of chiefs' sons, but, rather than acquiring status by luring a boy who had status, as American servicemen did from the Samoan point of view during World War II, in the second verse the Girls of Samoa end with disheveled hair.[26] We saw in chapter 7 that in old Samoa: hair symbolized sexuality; hanging hair flaunted sexuality/fecundity; shaving the head or, in missionary times, arranging hair in a neat bun signified sexual control. In the song the girls' disheveled hair reflects the promiscuous sexual climate of the war. This hair "style" also pictures girls' flaunting very differently than the *tuiga*, the tuft and tail that symbolized flaunting in pre-Christian Samoa. Rather than being a lovely display, ordered by the frame of a shaved pate, it is mere disarray, disorder, and an absence of control.

A Samoan, explaining the place name Satapuala, tells me, "The Samoan girls dropped many Samoan boys and go after those *papalagi* [Caucasians].... Womens went crazy. Some went over to Satapuala, where the servicemen were stationed and hung around the gates." The song calls these "gates of sin." Stanner, quoted earlier in the chapter, says the airport gates were also called gates of sin. Perhaps this phrase was used for many portals of foreign and military ingress, evoking the missionary "gates of hell." The phrase not only condemns foreign but also indigenous practices, reorchestrated by the circumstances of dawning modernity.

In "Girls of Samoa" the word *vanish* is repeated three times: in the second verse the GIs vanish; in the third the girls vanish and then vanish again. Vanishing was one of the GIs more noted features: the bastard children left in their wake were called "lost marines," referring to the belief that their fathers had been lost in the war. The Samoan term here is *sola,* which means "to run away or escape," like a darting fish, Milner says (1966:213), or perhaps like a pigeon? In the girl's case running away evokes the idea of *āvaga,* but in the song girls do not return to their family, remaining instead on the streets of a port town. The different sorts of vanishing represented by GIs and girls, respectively, evoke the dangerously transitory character of modernity in which Samoan families lost not only access to wealth and status from a boy's family, and the promise of high-status offspring, but sometimes even girls themselves.

There is another between-the-lines sense to this song. The portrait suggests that the Girls of Samoa are making fools of themselves and fools of their countrymen in the bargain. Thomas points out that, in Samoan colonial history, sexual ethics became a sign for Samoan difference, and difference is a foil upon which cultural identity is constructed (1992). But here *sexual ethics* should be really be read as *women's sexual ethics,* because from contact onward in Samoa, as in so many other places, it was girls' and women's sexual ethics that were made the issue by missionaries and that were importuned by foreign visitors. Girls' sexual ethics—as a sign of Samoan difference—was a likely focus of feelings about cultural identity. The songs' first words, "Girls of Samoa," imply that these disheveled girls have a representative status.

Perhaps the hostility in the song can best be understood by reference to a more contemporary song, often sung to English-speaking foreigners soon after their arrival.

Savalivali

Savalivali means "go for a walk."
Tautalatala means "too much talk."
Alofa ia te 'oe means "I love you."
"Take it easy" *faifai lēmū.*

Inscribed in this song is an enduring reaction to and reversal of relations of sexuality and power predicated by World War II. This song is sung as a mnemonic to learning Samoan, but it also traces the typical progression of a contemporary Samoan seduction. The boy will first ask the girl to go for a walk. He does not, however, just want talk. He will tell her that he loves her, and the last line of the song I take to be a request for gentleness in lovemaking. Remember that when Sanele was growing up cheeky boys, boasting of their sexual prowess, would tell a girl, "Watch it or I'll make you speak English," meaning "I'll make you say you love me." In *Savalivali*, rather than an American serviceman teaching a Samoan girl (whom he seduces) to speak English, a Samoan boy is teaching an English-speaking girl (whom he seduces) to speak Samoan. I am not saying this meaning is explicit or even wholly conscious, nor could it be, as it violates both Christian values and the traditional Samoan value of *alofa* as selfless hospitality to wayfarers. It is sung innocently, but it has a historical undercurrent.

What Sanele's boasting cohorts actually said in Samoan was "Vā'ai 'oe tei va'e nanu"—literally, "Watch it or you will speak a foreign language," although here *foreign language* is a euphemism for English. *Nanu*, "to speak a foreign language," also means "to mispronounce badly," suggesting some level of difficulty and incompetence. Language competence is an important theme of Samoan humor about cultural contact and, furthermore, one that works cultural identity issues. There are many Samoan jokes about speaking English in which Samoans are caricatured as stupid, as in the following joke told to me by Sanele. At the market in Western Samoa a male tourist is looking at a stingray. A women is selling this fish with her friend. The seller speaks only Samoan and so cannot ask him if he wants to buy the ray; her friend acts as an interpreter. In Samoan stingray are called *fai; fai* also means "to make" and is a euphemism for intercourse. A boy might jokingly say to a girl, "Sau tā fai," "Come let's make it," meaning "Come let's fuck." Translating for the seller, the friend says, "Do you want to buy some fuck?" The insulted tourist replies "Shut up stupid!" Translating his comment back into Samoan for the seller, the friend says, "The man says he likes your *fai*, but he doesn't have any *tupu* [money]." To the Samoan ear *tupu* sounds a lot like "stupid." In this caricature of commercialism, female promiscuity—or the Western perception of promiscuity (but it is all a mistranslation)—plus feeling stupid are metaphors for the experience of culture contact.

There are, likewise, Samoan jokes about speaking Samoan in which foreigners are caricatured as stupid. Shore records a sketch from twentieth-century Samoan comedy theater in which the prince of Wales is portrayed as an idiot unable to pronounce or to speak Samoan (1977:321–24). In all these instances language is a tower of Babel metaphor for a meeting between the local and the foreign. In the war the meeting was on American terms, but in *Savalivali* it is the foreigner who must learn to speak an unfamiliar language and who presumably ends up feeling stupid.

Here language is also a metaphor for discourses on self and for the intrusion of foreign discourses, indexed by "I love you." Through much of the twentieth century Samoans were developing a national identity: Western Samoa in particular was deeply involved in nation making (Davidson 1967, Field 1984). These efforts probably exacerbated local sensitivity about girls and their lost marines.

After the War

Despite wartime reactions to girls' flaunting, in the bush Joking Nights endured even after the war, but they were strictly word-of-mouth affairs among young people. A Western Samoan, whom I will call Vavau (Past), was a boy in the 1950s and gives the following description.

■ ■ ■

There is a thing called *'ale'aleaitu*. You know what that means? . . . There is a traveling group, a malaga . . . and they have these so-called *pōula*. Especially when a boy and a girl elope to go somewhere in the woods, or to the boys family, the whole *'aumāga* would come and entertain . . . at night . . . they sing and they dance and tell all kinds of jokes, sexual jokes, and into the night, 2 o'clock in the morning . . . that's when the *'ale'aleaitu* phenomenon will take place, which means whoever you are dancing with at that time, you will take off the lavalava and you can run off, elope, at that time we say you're going to "Tear off the eye of the aitu [spirit]," "Sasae le mata ole aitu." It's . . . planned. . . . The lavalava come off, nobody cares. The words of the song [songs] are explicit telling you what to do . . . you have a group of the malaga over here and then the host over here and they exchange items, back and forth. . . . There goes your lavalava, there goes your dress, you don't care. . . . This night we're going to tear off the eyes of the aitu . . . we expect something very interesting.

■ ■ ■

Vavau's description of *'ale'aleaitu* shows strong continuity with Krämer's description of Joking Nights of the 1890s but also indicates a continuing shift in location. In precontact Samoa Joking Nights were staged by the village women's association (*aualuma*) and would, therefore, have taken place in the *aualuma*'s greathouse, one of the greathouses that ringed the village's open center, the *malae*. According to Sloan, by the 1930s Joking Nights had migrated to the village margins; by the 1950s they had migrated into the bush. What is done in the proximity of the *malae* is visible to all; the *malae* represents the highlighted aspects of the self, prominent in Samoan lexicons and discourses. The bush symbolizes what one might call a "cultural unconscious."[27] Inasmuch as Joking Nights were key occasions for Samoan informal discourse and migrated to the bush, the bush became a domain of partially forgotten discourses on self.

This "unconscious" resembles that discussed by Jung, who believed that dissociated elements of self could be shared by members of a culture and that shared dissociations had a historical dimension (1970:179–226, 413–17). In Jung's analytic psychology dissociated elements of self may be symbolized by, or projected as, spirits (1963:8–22, 1971:330–555). In societies in which spirit beliefs endure, repressed/dissociated aspects of experience are associated with spirits. In Samoa, for example, the inner self, or *loto*, tends to be dissociated. One is more aware of inner experience when alone, and it is in these circumstances that Samoans are most wary of spirits. Until recently people who were ill or in a weakened state were never left alone, as their solitude was a lure to spirits. A Samoan proverb says, "The bush is full of spirits" (Schultz [1949–50] 1985:83, Shore 1982:49). In pre-Christian times the inhabitants of the bush, spirits, supplied a means to deny responsibility for reprehensible behaviors. Stair, for example, complains that erring Samoans "cloak over their delinquencies by attributing them to gods. Many a faithless wife and many a murderer have secured themselves from punishment in this manner" (1897:216). This migration from the *malae* into the realm of spirits implied that girls' exhibitionism and informal marrying were: to be hidden; behaviors for which girls wanted to abjure responsibility; moving into a cultural unconscious.

By Vavau's youth Joking Nights had vanished even from the bush, at least in the environs of his village. Recall, however, that flaunting by Joking Night girls led to elopements. Elopements had by no means vanished, but young people came to employ spirits to conceal them because eloping had become increasingly illicit. Vavau tells of a young man, a taxi driver in the 1960s, who

■ ■ ■

took off with one of the young girls from our village and we went out and told the story that she was picked up by an *aitu* [spirit] . . . but we knew exactly where she was, we knew who she went with, what house they stayed at up in the bush. We went up to take them food and water and to visit them and return to the village. The family was looking everywhere, they even went to the faipele. You know the faipele is . . . like a palm-reader, use the deck of cards and that person . . . will tell you what exactly happened . . . he didn't even know the truth. . . . We laugh at the whole thing because . . . we knew where this girl was . . . and I don't think the family will even accept it today if you tell them that she was with this taxi driver two weeks . . . and that was not the only case.

■ ■ ■

At the end of the nineteenth century an elopement of a couple of weeks was not an overly distressing event for parents. Krämer, who resided in Samoa during the 1890s, says that the morning after a Joking Night a few girls would go off with the visiting boys who attended the dance, "although they often returned several days or weeks later, disenchanted and sobered" ([1902] 1995:377). Recall that in pre-Christian Samoa a boy's status would have mitigated a girl's culpability for elopement. The taxi driver incident took place when taxi drivers were tinged by the glamour of modernity and had status as people with a cash income, probably a car, or at least access to a car. By the time of this incident only kidnapping spirits could mitigate the girl's culpability.

On Erasure

The invocation of spirits to cover elopements was indexical of a widening rift between increasingly Christian standards for overt sexual practices and covertly continued precontact practices. Eventually, overt standards impinged upon covert practices, eroding girls' specialty in informal discourse, which in turn undermined girls' avenues toward achievement. While discourses of self have historical tenacity, discursive practices are vulnerable to historical "erasure." Recall that discursive practices are isomorphically linked to a discourse on self: girls' flaunting and luring, plus the limitations signified by their shaved heads, were structurally isomorphic with Samoan informal discourse.

Erasure is a process with discernible phases. In the first phase of erasure everyone knows the old discursive practice continues, but, because of incongruence with a new moral discourse, people come to feel that it is a subject about which one must exercise discretion. The discursive practice is, therefore, relegated to peripheral situations. In pre-Christian Samoa flaunting was a discursive practice in which girls specialized; as virginal ideals once applied only to chiefly girls came to be broadly applied, girls' flaunting became suspect, and occasions that featured flaunting—Joking Nights—moved from the village center to its periphery, as in Sloan's 1930s report.

In the second phase of erasure people become critical of those who maintain the old discursive practice. In Samoa people became critical of girls' flaunting, as evidenced by 1940s songs about girls and servicemen in World War II. The practice and its occasions, therefore, move from the periphery of cultural consciousness to a cultural unconscious and may begin to take on spirit symbolism. For Samoans spirits and the bush had long represented a twilight territory of cultural consciousness; it was into this territory that girls' flaunting at Joking Nights began to migrate. In this phase of erasure the discursive practice and its occasions are also hidden from those in authority. Vavau says that when he was a boy news of Joking Nights circulated only among young people.

During phase 3 discursive covers develop to conceal the surviving remnants of old practices. In Vavau's youth in the 1960s elopements, which were understood as concomitant to flaunting, survived under the cover of stories about girls being kidnapped by spirits. Discursive covers work because authority figures begin to deny the existence of the practice at issue. Vavau suggests that the "kidnapped" girl's parents would not believe that she had eloped, even if the truth were put to them. No wonder the fortune-teller is at a loss for an acceptable explanation. The discursive practice is denied because it has come to be seen as a moral negative and as indicative of impulsivity. In pre-Christian Samoa flaunting was a discursive practice through which a girl mated and married in the service of her family. In Christian Samoa flaunting became a symbol of license (*sa'oloto*), and joking (*ula*) in the presence of boys came to be defined as cheeky—that is, as a presumption upon the privileges of a girl's elders to arrange her marriage. At this point even very diminished forms of the old discursive practice may be criticized. Thus, in contemporary Samoa, when a girl laughs too much, elders will remark censoriously that "she is looking for a husband!" meaning "she is looking for sex!"

The fourth phase of erasure is the subject of the coming chapter, but I will add an anticipatory word here. In this phase desires that were associated with the discursive practice are dissociated. Samoan women had expressed sexual desire through a discourse of flaunting. Holmes went to Samoa in 1954 and reported frigidity and other symptoms that indicated that some Samoan women had begun to lose awareness of sexual desires (1957, 1958). Fragmented scenarios of the former discursive practice still exist, but in cultures with spirit beliefs—rather than covering delegitimated practices—spirits assume authorship for them: these now fragmented discourses are expressed in states of possession.

In regard to possession Shore records an interesting 1960s report delivered by an older informant (1977:313–15, Shore 1978:179). Krämer's and Vavau's depictions of Joking Nights included a wild dance in which clothes were torn off called the *'ale'aleaitu*. In chapter 10 we will see that this dance was a form of mock possession in the sense that participants imitated spirits but did not go into trance states. Shore's informant, however, sees the *'ale'aleaitu* as a form of actual spirit possession and says that the dance was interrupted at this juncture: everyone fled in terror of spirits. What had once been a trope was taken as true because what the trope represented—its identity as symbol—had been dissociated.

If discursive practices can be dissociated and take spirit form, in the coming chapter we will see that this does not mean they are easily forgotten. What appeared to be lost discursive practices and their gender markings were layered into cultural images and into the unread nuances of stories. In Samoa girls still had a tendency to let down their hair, to decorate it with pretty flowers, and to wear red, but these metonyms for the old discursive practice of flaunting tended to provoke spirit possession. Being "taken" by spirits became not an excuse but a danger. As one of Goodman's informants says of a notorious Samoan spirit, "Telesā gets angry at . . . any girl who goes into the forest and puts down her hair" (1971:470), literally or figuratively. Yet Samoan spirits also preserved traces of erased discursive practices, traces that could be ritualistically disclaimed and exorcised, even while they continued to haunt the Samoan cultural order.

9

Possession and Reconfiguring Moral Discourse

In Samoa, as Christianity was indigenized, girls were expected to style themselves after a moral ideal. This moral ideal, however, did not correspond to those considered in chapter 3, which applied to males and females alike. Rather, it was mapped upon an erasure of informal discourse for girls. Unlike contextual discourses, which are characterized by constitutive rules, this discourse involved a set of regulatory rules about the teasing, often exhibitionistic form of jest called *ula*. As the century wore on, girls might still jest in undertones among one another, but they were not to do so openly with boys, nor were they stars at bawdy entertainments like *pōula,* Joking Nights.

With missionization girls' status and dignity increased—symbolically associating them with formal contexts—but girls did not trade a specialty in the informal discourse of entertainments for a specialty in the formal discourse of ceremonies. Missionary ideas about premarital chastity implied to Samoans that all girls were like village princesses. The village princess is a girl with a central role in ceremonies—but as a token sister figure whose appearance is representative rather than full-fledged. The special character of her presence is indicated by her muteness. The substance of Samoan ceremonies is giving speeches; the village princess gives none. Rather, she prepares kava served to participating chiefs. Similarly, Samoan-Christian girls were to convey their virtue through a dignified reticence and a circumspect manner, through muteness rather than speech.

What changes in the moral landscape result when women are reduced from a contextual to a moral discourse? Moral discourses are gateways to cultural consciousness. In dividing the licit from the illicit, they mark out a domain of the repressed, for humans lay claim only to a limited portion of thoughts and feelings branded as illicit. The remainder becomes to one degree or another forgotten, disowned, and dissociated. Banishment from cultural consciousness, however, does not mean that newly illicit remainders of discourses on self cease to exist. Like the part of the self left out of the ontological premise, these remainders still seek expression. What I suggest over the next few pages is that discursive systems exist in larger penumbras of meaning that can sustain morally banished aspects of these systems and can also be drawn upon. One domain in which these meaning penumbras are evident is narratives. Moral discourse is, after all, often a narrative practice: it tends to take story form particularly in the life of the developing child. Banished discursive practices continue to be tropically represented in narratives.

It is an old presumption in psychoanalysis that our stories are replete with submerged meanings, inaccessible even to ourselves. How can meanings play this game of presence and absence? The answer is tropes. In psychoanalysis the unconscious dimension of mind is characterized by "primary processes" that employ symbolic or tropic logics rather than sequential logic, for example, the logic of metaphor, metonymy, and synecdoche. Spiro (1992) points out that Freud is mistaken when he calls this figurative mode of thought "unconscious," as tropes are laced throughout normal discourse and often consciously employed.[1] Tropes, however, have a capacity to carry latent meanings, which the ratio-sequential elements of a discourse lack. We will see that these latent meanings reside not in any specific use of tropes but in an intertext of stories that deploys them.

Images in stories are often associated with themes. By themes I mean action scenarios that tend to occur with the image. Images and themes together constitute what I call "narrative tropes." Narrative tropes are symbolic versions of idea/emotion clusters in cultural consciousness that recur in tales. "All images," Barthes says, "imply underlying their signifiers, a 'floating chain' of signifieds, the reader able to choose some and ignore others" (1977:38–39). Narrative tropes have the floating chains of signifieds that Barthes attributes to images: when these tropes appear, they have plain meanings and a plenitude of subtle resonances that derive from similar stories the listener has heard. This chapter argues that, existentially, "the reader" may be "able to choose" among possible signifieds, but there are cultural rules against reading some of the subtle resonances of narrative tropes, specifically those resonances that threaten current cultural identity.

Some distinction needs to be made here between cultural identity and the self. By *self* I refer to those cultural conceptions of what it means to be a person embedded in lexicons and discourses, plus the phenomenological experience that evades and contradicts these conceptions. Identity refers to all that with which a person identifies. By cultural identity I refer to those aspects of culture that people view as representative and identify with for that reason.

Narrative practices extend beyond simple storytelling, including dreams and the recounting of dreams and, in some cultures, spirit possession episodes and their recounting. There are possession institutions in which spirits speak little and mainly inspire performances; however, in others, Samoa among them, possessing spirits—if properly coaxed—will tell their story, just as will the gossips who later elaborate it.² In twentieth-century Samoa girls' flaunting posed a threat to cultural identity and was buried in the unread resonances of narrative tropes in possession. The narrative tropes of possession stories also harbor the morally transgressive, and, we saw in the last chapter, there is often a considerable overlap between the transgressive and practices at odds with cultural identity. Inasmuch as possession does cultural work on what is morally problematic, historically generated moral cacophony tends to stimulate it.³

In Samoa the moral cacophony provoked by missionaries plus marines precipitated a possession epidemic. My Samoan in-laws grew up in the decades following World War II (the 1950s through the 1970s). None of the boys were ever possessed, but half of the family's girls suffered repeated episodes. During the 1980s I collected possession stories in Samoa, and all of the tales told to me date from the 1950s to the 1970s. Horst Cain, present in Samoa during the 1960s, is the first to document a large incidence of female possession (1971). The Samoan linguist John Mayer first visited Samoa from 1970 to 1973; people he spoke to from the villages along the road to the airport in Western Samoa (Saleʻimoa, Faisota, Faleasau) were still full of stories about possessed girls who had behaved in some mildly exhibitionistic way—such as wearing a hibiscus—with an American serviceman in World War II and of stories of American serviceman who had been found dead, reputedly because of possession by a female spirit (pers. comm.).

These reports are not congruent with those of the nineteenth century. The missionaries Turner ([1861] 1986, [1884] 1984) and Stair (1897) tell of spirits and even possession, as does the late-nineteenth-century ethnologist Krämer ([1902] 1994, 1995), but none of them lead one to believe possession is the particular affliction of young women. Neither does one find the possession of young women in early-twentieth-century travelogues, in which the bizarre holds a particular appeal (Grimshaw 1907, Sloan 1940). In the 1920s Mead says that young women may be kidnapped by spirits ([1928] 1961:92) but does not describe episodes in which a spirit speaks through a girl or in which a girl, not herself, acts in the guise of a spirit. Mead had abiding interest in all things psychological, making it unlikely that she would have ignored a preponderance of possession cases among young women.⁴ Freeman, who initially worked in Samoa from 1940 to 1943, documents a possession episode suffered by a boy (1983:222–25), but he does not mention a high incidence of female possessions. The possession stories I recorded speak vociferously of a repressed erotics. It seems likely that, had there been such an incidence in Freeman's fieldnotes, he would have used this data to support his case for the prohibition of young women's sexuality.⁵

The demise of Joking Nights, discussed in the preceding chapter, coincides with the beginning of this twentieth-century epidemic period. We will see that the displacement of the teasing/flaunting practices of Joking Night girls continued—from the village center to its periphery and to the bush—finding a terminus in possession episodes. Possession episodes and their associated stories offered a venue for a moral mediation on these practices but also a venue in which foreign discourses about sexuality and the self—first implanted by missionaries then cultivated by World War II servicemen—could be explored. Possession episodes and stories represented a new moral discourse in which women were specialists, as it was girls who were most likely to be possessed and girls and women who were most likely to gossip about the episodes. Although Sanele has recounted to me certain incidents of possession that took place in his own family, all the other stories I have heard of possession in Samoa have been told by females.

Reconfiguring Possession

I propose that possession is culturally crafted through narrative practice. To explore this proposition, I put to you a historical question: How are institutions of possession rewritten? To answer let us explore the rewriting of Samoan possession over the course of the nineteenth and twentieth centuries. In old Samoa there were two primary forms of contact with spirits, one malevolent, one benevolent. Most illnesses were attributed to the malevolence of spirits.[6] One class of spirits, *aitu*, communicated with humans through mediums called *taulāitu*, "*aitu*-anchors."[7] Spirit anchors were high status, either because they were chiefs or chief's sisters or priests or because of their oracular abilities.

Contemporary Samoans say that one may be *ulufia*, "entered," or one may be *fasia*, "hit," by a spirit. It seems likely that in old Samoa mediumship was understood as being entered, as spirits spoke out of mediums' mouths and would have had to enter them to do so. It also seems likely that sickness—which was said to result from spirit malevolence—was understood as being hit. So, in old Samoa there was mediumship, on the one hand, and, on the other, physical ailments. Now there is an afflictive form of possession and there are ailments with a spirit provenance, which are distinguished from ailments with a physical origin. One might be tempted to think that today being entered causes possession, and being hit causes spirit ailments, but being entered is in fact a synonym for possession: possession may be called *Ma'i Fasia*, literally "Hitting Sickness," meaning "an illness caused by a spirit-inflicted blow."

Being hit has also become possession's introductory phase. When a person becomes ill or behaves strangely and there is no apparent physical cause, people say that he or she has been hit. If the person's condition does not improve, relatives seek out a healer specializing in the treatment of spirit ailments. While in old Samoa spirit anchors were professional mediums, in colonial spirit possession they became healers.[8] Thus, while in old Samoa one form of spirit contact was benevolent, one malevolent, now all contact is afflictive. I say afflictive because it is not that contemporary possessing spirits are necessarily malevolent; ancestral spirits may possess young people out of a concern for their well-being. Whether precipitated by spirit anger or spirit concern, contemporary possession is a dangerous illness visited upon the subject via an external agent.

Spirit anchors typically assume that, when victims were hit, they were also entered. Inasmuch as being entered is now regarded as a sickness, contemporary possession combines the benevolent and malevolent forms of pre-Christian contact with spirits; however, it also resembles an early Christian intermediate category of contact. In the late nineteenth century one finds accounts of female spirits seducing handsome boys.[9] Krämer says that the next morning the boy's skin looked "all aflame" and Mead that it was "suffused with a strange rosy flush," "as if," Saeu Scanlan (a former Samoan college president) told me, "he had been working in the sun" (Krämer [1923] 1949:16A–17, Mead 1929:269). However glowing his appearance, the red flush was a fever, and the sickness could be fatal. If the boy had a human lover, the spirit might drive her mad or kill her. Sexual congress is now a common possession theme, although we will soon see that it is often subtextual.

The contemporary victims of Hitting Sickness, rather than being dignitaries or handsome boys, are usually young women of no great status.[10] Remember that being hit, *sasa,* is the most common form of negative sanction in Samoan childhood. The term *Hitting Sickness* suggests possession is a punishment. Indeed, Samoans actually describe possession as a spirit punishing the person (Goodman 1971:469). The frame "punishment" associates possession with morality. Further, spirits typically reproach the girls they possess for flaunting and luring, marking possession talk as a species of Samoan-Christian moral discourse.

If Samoan possession has undergone such extensive revision, I ask again: How might it have done so? Retrospectively, possession becomes a focus of gossip and other forms of creative retelling. Repeated narratives are inevitably selective and interpretative: narrators retell tales that are of particular interest to them and to their audiences; their repetitions, like oral formulaic poetry, are a form of mimesis, varying and elaborating the schemata embedded in stories in ways that speak to their own pressing concerns. Episodes and retellings occur within an intertext of spirit lore and possession tales; retellings articulate new ideas about possession with older scenarios, feeding the transformation of those scenarios and feeding back into the future contours of possession experiences.

Possession, Consciousness, and Agency

Possession, like the dream, partakes of a liminal form of consciousness, where *liminal* refers to a betwixt-and-between form of knowledge. Narratives always carry a range of meanings, but some stories, like those of childhood, give an impression of transparency. Dreams and possession bear the signature of liminality through their air of mystery and opacity, which says: this event is replete with meanings it declines to deliver. For this reason dreams and possession are often linked to hermeneutical practices such as ethnoanalysis.

Passive possession is also characterized by a repudiated form of agency. In the possession episode itself agency is repudiated through the supposed absence of the agent. Possession narratives purport to be truth telling. Agency is repudiated by the claim that the narrator is merely documenting events or accurately repeating an account told by others. The ethnoanalyst putatively exercises agency only in the service of returning the victim to the social world of discursive rules.

Repudiated agency is necessary to the moral work of possession narratives because of their sub-rosa transgressive character, their obsession with what is morally problematic in culture. In his analysis of Western nineteenth- and twentieth-century moral discourse on sex, Foucault discovers that, while moral discourse appears to concern itself with suppressing transgression, it is generative of thought about precisely that which is marked out as transgressive (1990). In Samoan possession girls could express and think about the discursive practice of flaunting, while abjuring responsibility for doing so. After all it was not they who spoke but the inexorciseable remnants of the "heathen" world, those spirits who lived on after the demise of the old religion. I do not mean that girls' participation in spirit possession was in any sense cynical; girls experienced themselves as spirit victims, and so it had to be, or the necessary license to talk and think about all that had become so morally complex in their cultural universe would not have been extended to them. We will see that girls did so by creating layered tropes in which one layer indexed flaunting and luring practices, discountenanced by Samoan Christianity, and others indexed those discourses on the nature of sex and marriage that missionaries and then American GIs had introduced.

In their antiagenic character possession narratives differ from the typical moral tales of childhood, possibly because they represent cultural thought about the moral in process, and their resolutions are uncertain. In children's moral tales a protagonist—often against the odds and sorely tempted to act out of line with cultural virtue—exercises heroic agency, albeit often with the assistance of tutelary spirits. In Samoan possession stories an unwitting, erring antiheroine is rescued (usually) but is also punished for her waywardness, as if to compensate for irremediable traces of agency.

Possession and Cultural Identity

The liminal thought that takes place in possession is about the morally problematic, but I also suggested that possession tropes include in their resonances high-voltage cultural identity issues. In colonial Samoa possession was a venue for thought about cultural identity. Thomas argues that representations of cultural identity tend to be oppositional or reactive (1992:213). It follows that, when cultural material has an oppositional or reactive character, this diacritic marks it as potentially significant for cultural identity. Contemporary Samoans also refer to spirit infirmities and possession as Samoan Sickness (*Ma'i Sāmoa*). The distinguishing feature of Samoan Sickness is that it will not respond to Western medication. Indeed, one test of whether or not an illness is really *Ma'i Sāmoa* is to give the sufferer Western medicine. If the medicine does not work, people conclude it is Samoan Sickness.

Diseases that, by definition, cannot be treated by Western physicians represent a counter colonial discourse on cultural identity. The Pacific is full of these "diseases," practically every island group having its own spirit-inflicted illness, called after the word for sickness plus the name of the nation or—when the nation encompasses more than one ethnic group—plus the name of the ethnicity. This disease/medicine symbolism is particularly significant as medicine is the version of Western "science" that is most likely to touch people's lives. Science is the allegorical star in the Western Myth of Progress, so fundamental to Western colonial projects, which were underwritten with an Enlightenment justification of "bettering" the natives (Chatterjee 1993). Samoan Sickness and its Pacific analogues mark a domain that can neither be touched nor bettered by the West.

Possession is also oppositional vis-à-vis Christianity. In Samoa, for example, possessing spirits are called *aitu*. They may be either nationally known spirits or dead relatives. Indeed, Samoans typically gloss *aitu* as "ghost," even though the category includes parts of the pre-Christian pantheon of spirits, many of whom never were human and never died. But, while *aitu* can be used to denote the deceased who return to haunt the living, so can the term *agāga*. We saw earlier that *agāga* is the Samoan term for the essence of the person, which the missionaries mistakenly glossed as "soul." *Aitu* and *agāga* would then appear to be synonyms. The Catholic Holy Ghost, however, is called "Holy *Agāga*." To call this ghost a "Holy *Aitu*" would be an oxymoron and a sacrilege. This is because, despite the term's application to *agāga*, *aitu* strongly connotes "heathen" spirits who Christianity defined as "devils."

Spirits have long been an insignia of Samoan difference, flagging aspects of Samoan culture that missionaries regarded as irredeemable and wanted to cast out. As an insignia of difference, spirits have counter colonial nuances. The female spirit Telesā, for example, is a member of the Matā'afa family of Western Samoa. While Telesā has been one of the most potent spiritual entities during the colonial period, in nineteenth-century Western Samoan history the Matā'afas were leaders of the resistance to colonial designs (Gilson 1970, Meleiseā 1987a). Recall that in Samoa the brother has *pule*, "worldly power," and the sister has *mana*, "spirit power." When Telesā possesses someone, the victim's family seeks aid from the current holder of the Matā'afa title, who then persuades the Telesā to leave the victim's body. One might say the Matā'afa/Telesā relationship is an idealized version of the brother/sister covenant, in which a brother represents secular resistance under circumstances of colonization and a sister represents spiritual resistance under the same circumstances.[11]

Colonialism typically inspires ambivalence about cultural identity among the colonized, for example, a negativity toward custom and defensiveness about it, both of which may hamper an adaptive sorting out process in which people keep whatever parts of the past they find useful and integrate new ideas that are likewise useful. Samoan possession is a venue in which the anxiety normally attendant upon an awareness of the infiltration of cultural otherness into local minds and hearts and bodies does not debar a semiotic play with old and new ideas.[12] Possession's liminal-tropic nature can accommodate contradictions between the old and the new. Liminal opacity provides a space in which contradiction is less visible; the "floating chain," or layered quality, of tropes can carry a multitude of contradictory meanings, different meanings being evoked by different intertextual resonances of the same trope.

Narrative Tropes in Samoan Spirit Stories

There are veritable thickets of tropes with their constituent themes and images in the stories to follow. Further, I use these stories to elucidate the Samoan intertext from which they take their meaning, an intertext that expresses the moral problematics created by Christianity and colonization. Intertextual meaning resides in the connections between stories; to show these connections will entail brief references to further stories, with their own thickets of tropes/themes/images. These narrative tropes, rather than being separate and distinct, tend to intermesh and to reference one another. To help the reader navigate this trope thicket, I hierarchicalize its presentation. Sections will be devoted to major tropes, while their constituent images and themes will be italicized when they first appear.

Because possession stories are delivered as reportage, narrators do not give them names, a practice usually associated with self-consciously fictional narration. I have, however, given all the possession narratives recounted in this chapter names for easy reference. I begin illustrating and extending the thoughts presented here with a possession story told to me by a Samoan sister-in-law, who I will call Tuli (Curlew).

■ ■ ■

Miss Blue Eyes

Tuli took a group of Sunday School teachers on a trip from the island of 'Upolu to Savai'i. One of the teachers had blue eyes because she was part German. The group bathed in a pool. Later they could not find the blue-eyed girl. Tuli finally found her nude, sitting on a rock facing the pool. She had Spirit Sickness. Later several more teachers got Spirit Sickness.

■ ■ ■

The Flaunting Trope

Nudity is an example of a flaunting trope and is common in Samoan possession stories: as in "Miss Blue Eyes," possessed girls often shed their clothes. Human women can be distinguished from spirits by the shame they feel when nude; spirits, and humans when possessed by them, feel none.

The flaunting trope represents an idea/emotion cluster about the discursive practices of pre-Christian girls. Remember, those girls—preaching their own cultural practices—counseled missionary wives to "lay aside their garments," gird only a "shaggy mat round their loins," and then "walk about to shew themselves" (Williams [1830–32] 1984:117). Flaunting is also a catalyst for the onset of possession episodes. Horst Cain says that "beautiful vain women and girls" are particularly likely to be possessed (1971:178). This detail is reminiscent of stories recorded by the nineteenth-century German consul Stuebel in which spirit girls injured real girls who were involved with the boys they seduced; however, here the menacing jealously of female spirits has expanded, encompassing all who are "vain." *Fa'alialia*, "flaunting," can also be glossed in English as "vanity." If spirits hit real girls who are vain, and if vanity Samoan style is a remnant of the discursive practice of flaunting, then Cain's report suggests that spirits hit real girls who engage in it.

Bathing is a flaunting trope theme. In possession stories bathing in pools, springs, and rivers is a common precursor to possession. In "Miss Blue Eyes" the Sunday School teachers bathe in a pool, and the possessed blue-eyed girl sits facing this pool; later several more bathers become possessed. In another possession story, which I have discussed at length elsewhere (Mageo 1996a), a girl scout troupe bathes in a remote pool, and later several scouts become possessed. The female spirit Telesā is said to hit girls who bath at the river by her village (Goodman 1971:470), meaning that she possesses them.

The bathing theme evokes the flaunting trope because bathing may entail partial undress. Bathing girls *let down and comb out their hair,* which we will soon see are also flaunting trope themes. Another is *going eva*, that is, wandering about, particularly alone or in a spirit's haunt, which is associated with walking about to show oneself, mentioned above. Although "Miss Blue Eyes" is not actually accused of going *eva*, roaming about alone is signed by her disappearance—by the temporal hiatus between her bath with the other girls and her later discovery beside the pool. Evidently, she wandered off from the group.

The Cultural Identity Trope

A major idea/emotion cluster figuratively represented in Samoan possession stories has to do specifically with cultural identity. A theme that evokes this trope in "Miss Blue Eyes" is *traveling to Savai'i*. In The Girl Scout possession story a trip to Savai'i was likewise the possession locale. The two major islands of Western Samoa, 'Upolu and Savai'i, are not only places in the world but also signify moral-historical periods. Thus, despite an actual peppering of old and contemporary cultural elements throughout the archipelago, Samoans often remarked to me that cultural practices that had died out elsewhere still existed in Savai'i. More urban 'Upolu, with its nightclubs and fancy tourist hotels, is symbolic of the high life, foreign influence, and modernity. To Samoans, as to people everywhere who are modern or becoming so, "tradition" and "modernity" themselves signify different and conflicting moral discourses: tradition now tends to be equated with the sexually conservative discourse of Samoan Christianity and modern with the more relaxed sexual morality of young people in contemporary Apia. Trips to Savai'i may, therefore, allegorize a historical regression in which the "present," symbolized by a contemporary girl, encounters a ghost of times "past," in the person of a spirit.

Another cultural identity trope image is the *half-caste*, *'afakasi* in Samoan, literally "one half." In Tuli's rendition of "Miss Blue Eyes" she identified the victim as blue-eyed rather than by name or by any other characteristic. The half-caste girl is most likely to be painted as fair-haired. In "The Girl Scout" the possessed girl had fair hair, which she wore down; a spirit marine, who crashed in Savai'i during World War II, had run after her to touch it. Unlike blue eyes, fair hair is referentially ambiguous: it implies aristocratic genealogies but also genealogies that incorporate the foreign. Fair hair is an old genetic strain in Samoa said to be the mark of aristocratic blood, so much so that, when children of common families have fair hair, they are suspected of being love children of a philandering aristocrat. Fair hair is at least as frequently associated with mixed blood. Sanele had a tendency to imagine that we would have fair-haired babies, even though I am a brunette; this fantasy is typical of those Samoans have about mixed marriages. Ambiguity allows the half-caste image to encompass contradictory meanings as different intertextual resonances.

As in "Miss Blue Eyes," half-caste features in possession stories—most commonly fair hair but also blue or green eyes—are usually explained by German rather than American ancestry. Germany was a major colonial presence in Samoa during the latter part of the nineteenth century, and Western Samoa was a German colony from 1900 until 1914. German planters, unlike American servicemen, sometimes stayed in Samoa, marrying local girls and starting families. German ancestry is respectable, whereas being a "lost marine" is not.

Getting Samoan Sickness is itself a cultural identity trope theme. We saw that possession is Samoan Sickness and thus diacritically marked as expressive of cultural identity. In possession stories girls who have half-caste features are particularly likely victims. Inasmuch as these stories bear even a minimal relation to demographics, this proclivity for possession reflects the likelihood that half-caste girls are objects of community ambivalence about foreignness: they embody the incursion of foreigners into local experience. Samoan Sickness is a way to affirm their cultural identity to themselves and to others by identifying with the spirit, or in this case the spirits, of Samoana.

Fair-haired village princess leading a sitting dance. Charles Kerry Studio (sitting dance), after 1890. Historisches Fotoarchiv, Rautenstrauch-Joest-Museum, Koln.

The Appropriation Trope

Appropriation figuratively represents an idea/emotion cluster about the nature of possession itself. The possessed Miss Blue Eyes sits on a rock by the pool. Spirits are said to have *resting rocks* and may possess those who inadvertently sit on the wrong rock. Because possession stories exist in an intertext of spirit lore, Miss Blue Eyes' seat on the rock suggests the appropriation of a spirit rock.

Often, when spirits possess a person for bathing, the victim bathed in a pool belonging to the spirit; this *spirit pool* theme is implied in "Miss Blue Eyes." Meanings in possession stories tend to be "overdetermined." This term, from the psychoanalytic study of dreams, refers to a meaning that is redundantly supplied by a number of symbols: not only does the spirit lore intertext suggest that Miss Blue Eyes sits on a spirit rock but also that she bathed in the wrong pool.

Appropriations often mark the onset of possession. Pili, one of my sisters-in-law, was possessed because she picked a large red hibiscus from a bush at Utulei village. This village is the home of a spirit known as LeTeinesusutasi (The Girl with One Breast), who lives across the road from the sea and was believed to go fishing with one breast slung over her shoulder. When she fished, nobody else caught a thing. The day Pili picked the hibiscus a strange woman came into the village store where Pili worked and said: "I take care of those hibiscus and you have taken the most beautiful one." The accusing woman took the flower and flung it to the ground, grinding it with her foot. Pili got a terrible headache and became possessed.

The catalytic nature of appropriation suggests that possession is the appropriation of a spirit identity. To better illustrate the spirit identification signified by the appropriation trope I enlist my next possession story.

■ ■ ■

What's In a Name?

When one of my Samoan sisters-in-law (whom I will call Losi) was in high school, she had a girlfriend, Telesia (Terry). Because Telesia was very pretty, her school chums would sometimes tease her by calling her after the female spirit, Telesā. Normally Telesia and Losi walked to school together down a lane haunted by Telesā; one day Losi took another route. Losi's and Telesia's school uniform consisted of a frock worn over a blouse. When Telesia reached school, she was wandering in a daze without her blouse. She had Spirit Sickness. When Telesia returned home, she told her father to get a glass of water for herself and one for her friend. Telesia's father asked her what was the name of her friend. "Telesia" said the girl. "And what is your name?" the father asked. "Telesā-ā-ā," she replied. When Telesia was treated by a spirit healer, Telesā spoke through her, accusing her of: stealing her name, wanting to be pretty, of wanting to be the best girl in town, and of trying to lure a boy on a visiting tour boat in whom Telesā herself was interested.

■ ■ ■

In "What's In a Name?" Telesā accuses Telesia of a list of vices, but the first one is summative: appropriating Telesā's name is an act of identification, and for girls identification with a female spirit is possession itself. Girls may be possessed by spirits, male or female, young or old; however, a Samoan dean of the college where I taught told me that the possessed girl resembles a generic spirit girl. Samoans refer to these spirits simply as "girls," *teine*, which I capitalize below to distinguish spirit girls from human girls.

"When a person gets *Ma'i Aitu* [Spirit Sickness] they get very smooth and pretty."
[You mean their face gets smooth?]
"Yes, smooth and clear."
[You mean like a *Teine?*]
"Well they usually are young girls."
[I mean like *the Teine?*]
"Yes."

In "What's In a Name?" identification is dramatized by Telesia's teasing girlfriends and by her father's misrecognition of Telesā. Stealing Telesā's name frames identification with a female spirit as a theft and hence as illicit and presumptuous on the part of the victim, which I take to symbolize that to identify with a spirit is also to identify with morally transgressive thoughts-feelings-desires.

Another appropriation trope theme is *spirit jealousy*. Samoans often attribute possession—which is after all defined as being hit by a spirit—to the jealousy of female spirits, which the spirit in turn attributes to a girl taking what rightfully belongs to the spirit. The last on Telesā's list of reproaches to Telesia is that Telesia wants to lure the same boy in whom Telesā is interested. In "The Girl Scout" the victim is actually hit by a female spirit, the girlfriend of the deceased marine, because the marine wanted to touch the victim's fair hair. Spirit girls are prototypically ascribed fair hair, and we saw that fair-haired girls are the particular victims of possession, which Samoans attribute to spirit jealousy.[13]

In chapter 3 we saw that in Samoa an inhibited desire for personal attention tends to be expressed negatively as *lotoleaga*, ill will. Samoans somewhat imprecisely gloss *lotoleaga* in English as "jealousy." I suspect this imprecision stems from a contemporary tendency to see romance as an occasion for *lotoleaga*. Telesā's reproaches to Telesia include "wanting to be pretty" (*fia-aulelei*) and "wanting to be the best" (*fia-sili*). In chapter 3 I listed a number of *fia*, "to want to be," terms with which Samoans sanction the child's need for personal attention, a need repressed (in the short run) and exacerbated (in the long run) by teasing. Remember that those who are *lotoleaga* are envious of others who receive attention and are wont to gossip about them. We saw that Samoan girls' socialization probably makes a hunger for attention and its negative concomitants piquant. This problem is remedied, to a degree, by moral discourse, which channels envy into fantasy (as in the case of Fua and Sala), but more substantially by contextual discourses, which provide disguised forms through which a desire for personal attention can be sated in reality. This need was once assuaged in girls by starring in Joking Nights and by flaunting generally. Telesā is correct when she attributes Telesia's possession to these want-to-be desires, for in Christian Samoa these desires were channeled into possession.

Note that the form of possession itself—as a punishment in which one is hit—reaffirms the general primacy of punishment as a negative sanction in Samoa and with it the need for seeking dominance through status and titles. We will see that, by identifying with a female spirit, the possessed girl temporally becomes an idealized village princess, the feminine version of a titled dignitary. But within this "punishment" frame possession intimates that the need for attention is accented for girls. We saw that this need is accentuated through teasing/shaming. The song analyzed in the last chapter, "Girls of Samoa," is itself a kind of shaming and was related to a larger body of talk during and after the war in which girls were aggressively and sometimes cruelly teased about their sexuality. People said of a girl with children of uncertain paternity, for example:

Roam, roam with the army guys,	Eva, eva foʻi ma tama ole ami,
The guys leave and left them with a little army.	O tama ole ʻae tuʻu ni tamaʻi ami.

Notice that here roaming about, *eva*, is a target of jest as well.

Identification with a female spirit underlines girls' status as stars in possession episodes. Still, it is unlikely that, in terms of frequency or breath of participation, possessions are as sufficient a venue for desires to flaunt as Joking Nights were, or even as were pre-Christian girls' everyday forms of flaunting. One might predict, therefore, that in Christian Samoa girls would be beleaguered by *lotoleaga*. In this case female spirits, who seem very *lotoleaga*, would embody a morally problematic side of real girls.

The Spirit Girl Trope

Female spirits themselves are an extensively layered figure that alludes to much of Samoan cultural history. First and foremost, spirit girls embody the figure of the girl in Christian Samoa. We saw that Samoans refer to the female spirits of possession stories as "girls" (*teine*). Remember, in colonial Samoa the word *girl* came to be glossed in English as "virgin." This girl-as-virgin identity is enshrined in the sister. In their role as sisters, females are referred to as *teine*, "girls"; in their role as wives they are *fafine*, "women." Inasmuch as female spirits are persistently called *teine*, they are symbolically affiliated with the sister.

In pre-Christian Samoa sexual respect was a value having to do with incest avoidance and was acted out between categorical brothers and sisters. In Christian Samoa sexual respect became a value the sister emblematized by acting like a village princess, that is, by being virginal and dignified. The most notorious female possessing spirits are Telesā and Sauma'iafe. They were reputedly extraordinarily beautiful village princesses, one might say archetypal village princesses, in high-ranking families before they were taken by spirits.[14] Recall that the ceremonial headdress worn by the village princess consists of human hair bleached to a light-reddish color and that spirit girls naturally have this hair color: by implication they are the model that village princesses imitate. Village princesses were the centerpiece of the precontact sex and gender system. Inasmuch as spirit girls are spoken of as if they were idealized village princesses, they also stand for this system. If spirit girls are idealized village princesses, to be possessed is to appropriate village princess status, however temporarily; therefore, identification with spirit girls is also a way to actualize the democratized Christian-Samoan ideal of everygirl as village princess, and spirit girls also stand for this ideal.

Nonetheless, spirit girls have long had a reputation for following handsome boys home at night and will follow American Samoan boys visiting Western Samoa on the airplane to do so. The elopements of old Samoa (*āvaga*) were thought of as a girl following after a boy. Related to the idea of following a boy is ranging about, usually denoted as *eva* in American Samoa and *ta'a* in Western Samoa. Areas that a spirit girl haunts are called *e ta'a ai le teine*, literally "the walkabout of the girl." In old Samoa girls were at liberty to range (like the decoy pigeon), and ranging was part of their role as lures to high titles. Female spirits evidently never reside but always range and are themselves a trope for the activity: they embody the lost liberties of common girls.

Layered in the meaning strata of spirit girls are also ideas and feelings about missionization and colonization. Spirit girls are either a colonial invention or a reconfiguration of older figures that were far less salient. Spirit girls' fair hair is described as long and loose; they are often seen combing it out. Indeed, long trailing hair is a synecdoche for spirit girls themselves: those who "see" spirit girls sometimes report seeing only moving hair. In colonial Samoa long hair was so dangerously evocative of spirits that girls might be possessed if they combed their hair in the middle of the night or if they wore their hair down in villages associated with possessing spirits or in any village at night outside the house, especially at twilight. Until recently, mothers feared even very young daughters might be possessed merely for going from house to house at night with their hair down.[15] Long hair was a missionary import. Furthermore, spirit girls do not correspond to any category of numinal described in reports made during the first decades after foreigners took up residence in Samoa.[16] The first record I have found of them is Stuebel's, a German consul to Samoa in the 1880s, fifty years after missionaries arrived on the scene. Inasmuch as fair hair evokes chiefly genealogies but also half-caste genealogies, and inasmuch as spirit girls typically have fair hair, they layer mixed feelings about the foreign in images of chiefliness.

Remember, spirit girls were reputed to have killed American servicemen whose bodies were found in villages during the war. This type of story is intertextual with older tales of Samoan boys who died because they resisted spirit girls' seductions. Further, spirit girls desire foreign boyfriends, as does Telesā in "What's In a Name?" So spirit girls evoke contact experience as well as the romantic discourse associated with foreign boys, although, unlike the World War II girls with their "little armies," spirit girls are no one's victim. Finally, spirit girls have a distinctly modern flavor: they travel about in motorcars and on the airlines. Not only do they follow boys on planes from one Samoan island to another; they even catch the plane to Hawai'i to call upon the goddess Pele.[17]

The *Tausala* Trope and the Cheeky Trope

Remember that *tausala* refers to the colonial idea that every girl who is virginal and dignified qualifies as a village princess. Possession stories tend to feature the image of a lovely girl, whom one might call a romantic figure, and who is by implication virginal. Miss Blue Eyes is a Sunday School teacher. Similarly, Telesia in "What's In a Name?" attends a Catholic girls' school. But, while girls who are possessed are portrayed as *tausala* figures, when possessed they are portrayed as cheeky. *Tautalaitiiti* (cheekiness) literally refers to impudent talk. Possessed girls often use foul language or swear. For a girl *tautalaitiiti* is the opposite of *tausala* and demonstrates the capacity of narratives tropes to carry contradictory meanings.

Cheekiness is enacted disrespect and is kindred to both the spirit girl trope and the flaunting trope. Although *tautalaitiiti* is a term liberally applied to the vices of boys and girls, in spirit talk it identifies girls with spirits: for a girl to be compared to a spirit is the same as being called cheeky, either in the impudent or in the sexual sense. Should a girl be very impudent, elders will say, "The real spirit, that little girl there."[18] Nothing similar is said of boys. When a girl associates too much with boys, people are apt to say, "She mingles where the boys are, like a spirit."[19] Should a girl wander alone, people will suspect her of sexual impropriety; however, they also remark, "Just like a spirit" or "Must be a spirit."[20]

In "What's In a Name?" Telesā accuses Telesia of being cheeky in the sexual and hierarchical sense: Telesā says Telesia wants to be pretty, which suggests a cheeky flouting of sexual respect; Telesā also says Telesia wants to be the best, which suggests an impudent aspiration to achieve above her station and a reversal of hierarchical respect. Both of these accusations are warranted by Telesia's behavior during the story. Telesia appears at school without her blouse, reminding one of cheeky boys who expose themselves to embarrass girls but also of nineteenth-century girls who "obstinately" refused "to cover the upper part of their persons" (Hutton 1874:149). Telesia also orders her father to serve her two glasses of water. For a Samoan child to order her elders is impudent.

Another cheeky trope theme is *kicking an animal,* as in the following story.

■ ■ ■

Kicking a Toad

Sanele has a cousin who I will call Sei (Flower). Sei spent her adolescence in Pago Pago. When Sei was seventeen, she used to walk to choir practice at dusk across a park. At noon one day the family heard footsteps on the pebbles outside their house, although they saw no one. A moment later Sei was possessed by TuiAtua. When she was treated, TuiAtua spoke through her; he said "I was the toad that you kicked," "You came on the park with your hair down," "You came over and picked a hibiscus [for your hair]."

■ ■ ■

Samoan youngsters may be told to say "Tulou" if they see an animal on the road, particularly later in the day or early evening, because it may be a spirit.[21] *Tulou* is the simplest form of respectful address. Sometimes, instead, kids act out disrespect by kicking or otherwise abusing an animal; indeed, this relatively discrete rebellion against the constant imposition of hierarchical relations is invited by the interdiction. Sei, however, is actually accused of three instances of disrespect: kicking the toad, letting her hair down, and decorating it with flowers in a spirit's haunt. While the first is cheeky in the hierarchical sense, the second two behaviors—having to do with hair—are cheeky in the sexual sense.

The Flaunting Trope Revisited

TuiAtua complains that Sei crossed the park with her hair down and picked a hibiscus for her hair. *Letting down, combing, and decorating* one's hair are probably the most salient themes constituent to the flaunting trope. Long hair itself is a flaunting trope image and is extensively layered. Long hair is the Samoan-Christian analogue of the tuft and tail that displayed the pre-Christian girl's sexuality-fecundity, so hair embodies the pre-Christian practice of flaunting. Inasmuch as missionaries taught Samoans to appreciate long hair, it represented the Christian view of femininity, laced into which was a discourse on the importance of personal feeling in sexuality and marriage as well as on personal feeling and the self. We also saw in chapter 7 that in contemporary Samoan beauty contests long hair has been a measure of one's conformity to this "Miss Tausala" ideal of everygirl as village princess but also to a Western romantic ideal.

Remember that the pre-Christian girl's tuft and tail were bleached red and that this color symbolically underlined its sexuality/fecundity significance. We saw that having fair-reddish hair, as some Samoan girls do, is an invitation to possession; adorning oneself with *the color red* is likewise an invitation and is another constituent of the flaunting trope. Like hair, red has both image and theme characteristics. The native form of hibiscus is red, and, when the color of a flower adorning the hair is mentioned in spirit lore or possession stories, it is typically red. Telesā comes from the village of Lepea; Saumaʻiafe comes from Saleʻimoa. They are reputed to wear red hibiscuses and to hit girls who wear a red hibiscus when crossing the *malae* in Lepea or Saleʻimoa.

Before I knew much about Samoan spirit lore, I used to swim with my head above the water and a hibiscus, often red, in my hair every evening in Pago Pago Harbor. Evening is a spirit-charged time. The Samoan woman who ran the Department of Education had a husband who also swam at that time. He would stare at my red hibiscus–bedecked floating head; I would stare back; he would disappear beneath the water. His wife later told me he had thought I was a spirit girl. In "The Girl Scout" the possessed scout had reddish hair, wore a red flower in her hair, and was dressed in red. A college student of mine told me of a case of recurrent possession in her village, Aoloau, between 1977 and 1978. The girl wore new clothes every day, which were often red, and she painted her fingernails and toenails red (I thought, like the girls in the World War II song who painted their lips). While TuiAtua does not mention the color of Sei's flower, the Samoan intertext of spirit lore and possession stories would have evoked this color.

The Seduction Trope

Probably the most important image constituent to this trope is *the spirit chief*. In possession stories spirit chiefs are almost as recurrent and almost as layered as spirit girls, representing an idea/emotion cluster about the discursive practice of flaunting and luring. In "Kicking a Toad" TuiAtua plays the role of a high title who is lured. We saw that a colloquial term for possession is *ulufia*, "to be entered"; *ulufia* has connotations of a sexual entering (Shore 1977:342–50).[22] Reputedly, spirit chief possession typically begins with tropic forms of flaunting: the girl is roaming about alone, particularly in the bush, letting her hair down, wearing flowers, and so forth. Spirit chiefs are said to seduce lovely girls, but, inasmuch as the onset of these episodes are marked by flaunting, subtextually they portray the luring of a high title.

The most notorious contemporary male spirits are Tui-Atua and Tui-Fiti. *Tui* refers to a very high chief, and Samoans often gloss it as "king." TuiAtua means "King of Atua." Atua is a major district on Western Samoa, and in old Samoa the paramount of Atua had jurisdiction over Tutuila, the main island of American Samoa that TuiAtua is now said to haunt. TuiFiti means "chief of Fiji," an important character in Samoan mythology and legend.[23] Unlike spirit girls, these male spirits are found in early reports, in which they are called *tupua*

(Stair 1897:211, Powell 1845), although the category has changed. In pre-Christian times *tupua* were specific high chiefs, deified after their demise; the spirit chiefs of contemporary possession episodes and stories are generic high chiefs and are no longer called *tupua*. Indeed, the missionaries glossed *tupua* as "idol," as in the biblical edict "Thou shall not worship idols." Again, missionary translations embedded Christian meanings like viruses in the Samoan cultural order. Inasmuch as TuiAtua is reputed to seduce girls and appears in the guise of a toad, he also represents a cross-cultural theme that Bettelheim calls the *animal groom*, which symbolizes girls' ambivalence about male sexuality (1976:277–310).

In "Kicking a Toad" TuiAtua layers images of chiefliness with images of foreignness, just as spirit girls layer images of village princesses with fair-haired foreigners. "Kicking a Toad" is set in Pago Pago, American Samoa. There are an abundance of toads in American Samoa. When it rains (almost daily) they congregate on the roads in vast numbers and end up splattered along the pavement in the wake of cars. Samoans frequently told me that the American army imported them in World War II to cut down on mosquitoes. Like their sponsors, they bred with great success. TuiAtua's toad persona, therefore, subtly evokes not only the luring of high titles but also American servicemen. Given that Samoans still hear biblical sermons throughout childhood, it is tempting to suggest that toads evoke biblical plagues as well; a conflation of the two would picture American servicemen as a plague of biblical proportions.

The toad is thus associated with another seduction trope image that I call the foreign boy, which we found in "What's In a Name?" in which Telesā and Telesia liked the boy on the tour boat, and in "The Girl Scout," in which the spirit marine pursues the victim to touch her hair. I suggested earlier that the foreign boy image symbolizes the newly personalized relation to sexuality associated with foreign boys like marines and indexed by "I love you."

If possession for girls is often "entry" by a male spirit who is lured, being "entered" does not necessarily involve a dissociated state. Spirits may cause swellings rather than dissociated behavior, but it is male spirits who do so—specifically Moso or the Nifoloa, who are sometimes said to be one and the same (Schoeffel 1979a:381). *Nifo* means "tooth." Nifoloa swellings are believed to result from a splinter in the flesh that is actually the Nifoloa's tooth, which has entered its victim. The healer extracts the tooth, or some analogy for a tooth, from the victim's body, as in the following story.

■ ■ ■

Wearing Perfume

Sanele says that one of my Samoan sisters-in-law, whom I will call Pese (Song), was possessed by the Nifoloa because she was wearing perfume when she crossed a bridge he haunted. Pese felt she had gotten a splinter on the bridge, which hurt when she returned home, but which none of her siblings could find. That night her foot and lower leg became swollen. A spirit healer was asked to come but did not because he could not find the requisite leaves to treat her in the darkness. In the morning he sent the siblings to two places where he had seen the leaves. The leaves could not be found at the first location—according to the spirit healer because the Nifoloa had hidden them—but were at the second location. The spirit healer made a herbal smoke that he blew on Pese's foot. There was a loud popping sound, which one of Pese's sisters said was the sound of the splinter exploding.

■ ■ ■

Obviously, *wearing perfume* is another flaunting trope theme. Samoans love heady perfumes. Sanele was always buying me perfume and lavished cologne on himself. As in "Kicking a Toad," in "Wearing Perfume" there is a subtextual framing of Spirit Sickness as the consequence of flaunting and luring: one seduces a being of high status and is entered by him. This entering results in swelling, as does intercourse in the song "The Girl's Belly." Pese's swelling could be seen as a displaced pregnancy. I have heard of another case of possession by TuiFiti in Savai'i in which the girl's belly would repeatedly swell and then deflate, but this is not a common symptom. In Nifoloa Spirit Sickness sexual body parts are migratory, as is so common with hysterical symptoms: it is usually legs or feet that swell, not bellies. The splinter is an analogue for the Nifoloa's phallic and detachable tooth; like many phallic symbols, it also signifies semen.[24]

The Liminality Trope

Spirits often hit people who are making a crossing, which I think represents an idea/emotion cluster about living betwixt and between historical worlds. In "Wearing Perfume" it is the perfume plus the bridge location that provokes the spirit. *Crossing a bridge* is a common liminality trope theme. My father-in-law, Toa, for example, was once riding his bicycle around midnight in a particularly spirit-stricken suburb of Apia. Crossing a bridge, he noticed that the bicycle had ceased to make progress despite his energetic pedaling. At once Toa began to spew forth insults, and the spirit let him go.

Crossing a malae can be equally dangerous. Again, *malae* are those open spaces at the center of villages. *Malae* usually look like parks. In "Kicking a Toad" Sei crosses a park with her hair down and places a flower in her hair. Spirits often hit girls who cross a *malae* thus arrayed. Spirit girls themselves are normally arrayed in this fashion and are associated both with bridges and with *malae*. Schoeffel records a story of a boy suffering from a fever (1979a:397). He traces his fever to having seen a beautiful girl standing on a bridge combing out her hair. A spirit healer is summoned and on her way sees this strange girl, but she is standing on the village *malae*. Putting these observations together, the healer says, "Then we knew who it was," meaning it was a spirit girl.

Layered into *malae* are at least two historical versions of Samoana, one associated with day and the other with night. The *malae* has long been the focus of Samoan-Christian respect. Charles Alaʻilima, a Samoan lawyer and former judge in American Samoa, says today people often build their houses away from the *malae*, back in the mountains where formerly there were only village gardens, because when one lives around the *malae* everyone sees what you do (pers. comm.); there "traditional" Christian-Samoan mores are strongly felt. Yet in some villages on moonlit nights a spirit girl will drag her hanging hair across the *malae*.[25] Village boys visiting friends will then stay the night, rather than crossing the *malae* back to their own dwelling. Crossing the *malae* one comes across a terrain of historical contradictions.

A liminality trope image in "Wearing Perfume" is *disappearing leaves*, which are proverbial in possession stories: healers are forever seeing the leaves they need to heal Spirit Sickness at certain locations in the bush, but, when they return later to get them, a spirit has hidden them. Like the leaves in Pese's story, they are eventually found, so these leaves are neither present nor entirely absent but floating between the two categories. Like deeper meanings in possession episodes, they are obscure, must be sought, and invite the effort. In "Wearing Perfume" not only leaves but the splinter—the "tooth" itself—is invisible: none of Pese's siblings can find it.

The Solicitude Trope

The solicitude trope expresses an idea/emotion cluster about close interpersonal relations and the family. "Wearing Perfume" is a family drama in which the siblings, by seeking the healing leaves, express solicitude. Remember that within the Samoan family interpersonal distance is a corollary of hierarchical respect; therefore, Samoans distance their children interpersonally. Opposite-sexed siblings replicate this distance for reasons of sexual respect. If there is a marked difference in age between same-sex siblings, they tend to replicate parental distance; if there is not, they tend to joke with and tease one another, creating yet another form of interpersonal distance. But, when youngsters are hurt or sick, family members become solicitous. Spirit Sickness—not usually feigned but exquisitely sensitive to psychological needs—invites solicitous performances in which a more intimate mode, historically associated with missionaries, can be practiced. Intimate family feeling is still actively fostered by foreign missionaries. Mormons, for example, encourage Samoan nuclear families to have evening gatherings in which members talk about their personal feelings.

A primary solicitude trope theme is *listening*. If Samoan Sickness does nothing else, it almost always buys the victim an attentive audience.

The Dead Mother

■ ■ ■

A man whose wife died later formed a relationship with another woman. They stayed together with the man's family. One of the man's older children, a girl called A . . . became ill and weaker. . . . She would only talk of her mother. . . . One day the girl woke up. . . . But it was not her voice. It was her mother's voice and . . . she chastised her husband for settling down with another women who was not looking after their children properly. The husband recognized the wife's voice and was listening to the girl, but the other woman became very angry and told the family the girl was lying to . . . get rid of her. (Macpherson and Macpherson 1990:199)

■ ■ ■

Reproaches have a proper vector in the Samoan status system, going from higher to lower. Living wives are lower status than their husbands. Spirits, however, are higher status than humankind. As a spirit, therefore, this dead wife's reproaches are legitimate, and A, in the personage of her dead mother, can reproach her father and expect a hearing.

In "The Dead Mother" the father's solicitude is matched by his consort's jealousy and reflects an oedipal triangle. This triangle reflects sociohistorical shifts in Samoan family structure toward a more nuclear model. According to Mead, in the 1920s youngsters had an escape when interpersonal relations within the family became difficult; they moved to the household of another relative. Relatives were bound by the ancient tradition of giving sanctuary to runaway members of their extended family (1928 [1961]:24). These alternative homes were grouped close together. Samoan houses lacked walls, and the divisions between families within an extended family were negligible. Within Samoa's generational kinship system aunts and uncles were referred to by the same word as parents; in old Samoa they were so regarded.

Today, escape from one's nuclear family is no longer as simple as once it was. Adoption is still common, and often children will grow up with near relatives other than their parents, but now aunts and uncles more often shut their doors to runaways. Within the tightening net of a more limited family, hierarchical and sexual respect probably have more oedipal overtones than once they did.[26]

The Authenticity Trope

The authenticity trope represents an idea/emotion cluster about the reconfigured nature of Samoan traditions, like spirit possession. The most recurrent theme constituent to this trope is *real versus false possession*. Narrators, and narrated characters who play the role of spectators, often query whether or not the victim has actually been entered by a spirit or is just acting, as does the consort in "The Dead Mother." Samoans have and improvise numerous methods for differentiating real possession from feigning. In one possession story the "possessed" girl—in a spirit persona and with a spirit's authority—began asking for things that her father had formerly denied her. Her father told her siblings to bring nettles and to rub her with them as a cure. The girl spontaneously recovered. Doubters generally believe in the importance of antiagency in demonstrating the genuineness of possession. The idea is to create is situation in which, were the person as agent present, she would not choose to be possessed.

Partially, this theme derives from a modernist skepticism, probably exacerbated in my own data collection by telling spirit tales to me—an educated Western person who Samoans presume does not believe in spirits—but it is also closely linked to the cultural identity trope. When the authenticity trope appears, possession itself seems to play the role of Samoana, and skeptics represent people's wavering faith in it, wavering between Western and indigenous perspectives. In "The Girl Scout," for example, the possessed girl's Westernized family did not believe in possession and took her to a German physician. His pills had no effect. Subsequently, their girl exhibited preternatural knowledge twice over, speaking fluent German without training or experience and predicting a death that did occur two weeks later. Preternatural knowledge is, along with antiagency, a demonstration of the genuineness of possession. It also testifies to the superiority of local knowledge. Westerners often assert cultural hegemony by virtue of their putatively superior scientific knowledge. Preternatural knowledge in possession presupposes a cultural form of knowledge that surpasses science.

Possession Remedies

Perhaps the best evidence that Samoan possession is about discursive problems lies in its cure: the fundamental rule for curing possession is that the spirit be made to speak; when spirits fail to do so, the victim may die (Shore 1978).[27] In Spirit Sickness, after the spirit speaks, the ethnoanalyst begins a negotiation to get it out of the girl's body. These negotiations typically entail two promises to spirits. If the possessing spirit is a dead relative, the spirit is likely to be angry at the girl's relatives for their abuse or inattentiveness to the girl; then the relatives must promise to reform. If the possessing spirit is a spirit girl or a spirit chief, the spirit is usually angry at the girl herself, and the healer often promises to cut off the possessed girl's long hair, as in the following story.[28]

Haircut

A Samoan friend, whom I will call Lau (Leaves), told me that when she and her sister were adolescents, their parents made them wear their hair up around the house and in the village. Whenever Lau and her sister were going to the family plantation, however, the sister let her beautiful straight black hair down her back as soon as she was out of sight of her house. Subsequently the sister was possessed by Sauma'iafe. The attending healer promised Sauma'iafe to cut off the girl's hair at ear's length, and the operation was performed immediately after the spirit left her body. Thereafter her hair was kept short.

The Visage Injury Trope

Possession itself is often signified by a visage injury: being hit may result initially in *red marks on the face,* a visage trope image reminiscent of spirit-seduced boys' flaming skin. The face may become "bent" in consequence.[29] Most commonly, as in "Haircut," the visage injury is simply cutting off a girl's hair. In demanding that a girl's hair be cut, spirits signify an identity problem. Remember that the basic sense of self in Samoa is referenced by the word *aga,* which is a social role or persona but also a face one wears; similarly, the English word *persona* is derivative of the Latin term for the masks (and roles) of theater. The visage is, therefore, an identity symbol, and the visage injuries characteristic of possession may represent the morally problematic nature of girls' identity in Christian Samoa. It was, after all, the girl's image that was problematized by missionaries who seemed to want all girls to be virginal village princesses and which was problematized again in World War II, when deserted girls hung about in town, their hair disheveled. The song "Girls of Samoa" from the preceding chapter, furthermore, suggests that during World War II girls were felt to be cultural ambassadors, for better or for worse.

Cutting a girl's hair is a standard parental punishment for sexually indiscreet behavior. Like punitive parents, possessing spirits who demand a haircut temporarily injure a girl's ability to flaunt. Recall that long hair was thought so attractive that beauty contest could be won or lost on its measure. We saw that long hair is a synecdoche for spirit girls themselves; cutting it also seems an apt sign for breaking that identification with spirit girls that is possession.

From a psychological viewpoint, however, possession events are authorial: spirits are dissociated parts of the "victim's" personality. If it is the girl who speaks through the spirit, why might she demand that her hair be cut? Cutting one's hair frames flaunting as "punishing oneself," deflecting censorship as well as assuaging guilt through a dramatic denial that events could be authorial: until recently there were few Samoan girls who willingly cut their hair. Long hair also emblematizes the moral and psychological conundrums that colonial history visited upon girls. When a girl cuts her hair, all is bracketed in one gesture, an economical gesture indeed—and this bracketing affects not only the girl's own feelings but also her family relations. Parents think long-haired daughters beautiful. Consequently, they are icons of family face; however, they are also seen as alluring and thus as potential avenues of family shame. Further, they are favorite spirit victims. For all these reasons long-haired girls are closely watched. A girl who cuts her hair can better avoid parental scrutiny.

The Departure Trope

Sending a girl away from Samoa, for example, to relatives in Hawai'i, California, Washington, or New Zealand is a standard possession remedy and a departure trope theme that often concludes possession stories. The departure trope probably represents an idea/emotion cluster about how to manage the transgressive elements of self that possessed girls enact and embody. Actually, Lau's sister was possessed in Hawai'i some years after the events to which her possession was attributed. In her case getting Spirit Sickness—a Samoana symbol—may have reaffirmed her cultural identity in circumstances that threatened to dilute it. But possession is just as likely to distance girls from Samoan culture. One fair-haired teenage girl I interviewed in Hawai'i was riding in the back of an open pickup truck in Samoa, as Samoans often do, when the truck passed a spirit haunt. She blacked out, wakening up perplexed in Hawai'i. In Hawai'i her Samoan relatives explained to her that they had taken her away from Samoa because she had been hit by a spirit. She is now in her early twenties and has not been allowed to return to Samoa.

This "geographic remedy" probably does to a degree distance girls from their problem by placing them in cultural milieus in which Samoan-Christian moral discourse about flaunting is abated. Samoan girls who live in Hawai'i, for example, may be allowed to wear shorts; when they come to Samoa, relatives tell them to put a lavalava over their shorts. The efficacy of the geographic remedy may also derive from its psychological affinity with possession itself, which can be seen as maintaining distance in its effects.

Possession entails the departure of the normal persona. Possession is more likely in societies in which identity is based on the persona because it is tantamount to a substitution of a social actor's normal persona by the persona of a spirit. Such a substitution would produce a dissociated state when conscious identity is synonymous with the persona: a dissociated state is by definition one in which conscious identity is absent. Possession also allows social actors to enact the distance on subjectivity that is the concomitant of a sociocentric ontological premise. When people's premise is that the self is social, their conscious identity is rooted in acting out social roles, expressing only what is appropriate to those roles, as does the actor in a theatrical performance.

An ensemble of different roles offers opportunities to express a range of role-appropriate thoughts/feelings/desires. Sometimes, however, this range may fail to encompass particularly powerful thoughts/feelings/desires. Then tension can be relieved by a state in which the normal role player departs—that is, in possession—and in which a spirit expresses those ordinarily transgressive sentiments that are deemed appropriate to the role of a spirit. In other words, possession allows the person to go on role playing, maintaining theatrical distance on subjectivity. In the geographic remedy real distance is substituted for theatrical distance.

Another possible explanation for the geographic remedy is that Polynesian value systems are inherently public and social (Levy 1973:347–54, 1974; Shore 1982:158–67). If Polynesians do not internalize their moral discourse but sustain it socially, leaving the sustaining society should rid the individual of those conflicts predicated by this discourse. But the fact that girls can no longer escape Samoan-Christian moral discourse by hiding in the bush—as did the taxi driver's girl—suggests internalization. While girls' acute symptoms may disappear outside Samoa, one wonders: Can they so easily escape the moral discourse of self and gender with which they have constituted their identity? Samoan moral discourse is largely public and social, albeit now interlaced with individualistic colonial discourses, yet sociocentric moral discourses in themselves do not constitute a reason to believe that Polynesians internalize their values any less than egocentric societies internalize theirs. My argument in chapter 3 and throughout the first half of this book is that moral discourse is always internalized, as are all discourses on self, whether the premise from which they spring is social or individual.

The geographic remedy is also a logical extension of the progressive marginalization of the discursive practice of flaunting. Over the last three chapters we have watched this discursive practice move from the village center to its periphery to the bush to the unconscious. In the geographic remedy it is banished from Samoa altogether. Banishing girls with a penchant for possession protects Samoan-Christian moral discourse, which is stamped with a World War II rejection of flaunting. Although relatives who send girls away are deeply concerned for them, they are also likely to be embarrassed by having a girl around who is not only an important representative of family face but who in possession acts "just like a spirit," with its connotations of heathen impulsiveness.

Retrospective

Possession narratives are bespeckled with narrative tropes. These tropes feature surface meanings, which are patent, and latent meanings, fenced off from full awareness by cultural reading rules. Further, these latent meanings themselves are layered, carrying wide bands of culture history in their resonances. These meanings lie not so much in the tropes themselves as in the spirit lore intertext in which possession is embedded. While there are cultural rules against reading meanings about the morally transgressive and against reading meanings that pertain to sensitive areas of cultural identity, these reading rules actually allow for a liminal form of thought about such topics. In Samoa, when girls were restricted to moral discourse, the result was an increased incidence of possession. Possession offered an opportunity to think about all that was excluded by Samoan-Christian gender morality and from changing conceptions of cultural identity, most saliently the erased discursive practices of girls.

Possession constitutes a special discursive practice in which those elements normally present in moral discourse under the sign of transgression are granted greater play in tropic form and in which the character of moral thinking becomes liminal. Liminality permits new and old ideas, to which history has lent emotional power, become the focus of an evaluative process that is narrative in character. In Samoa a passive form of possession offered an alternative moral discourse but one that probably appears in many places when standard forms of moral talk are beset by the contradictions in ethos produced by historical experience.[30] In the coming chapters we see that this greater range of moral thought was concomitant to the creation of reconfigured contextual and strategic discourses on self.

10

Entertainment and Reconfiguring Informal Discourse

When Christian reverends sought to import their style of mind, or spirit or spirituality, Joking Nights—those wild entertainments that missionaries misnamed the night dance—were among those customs they first sought to change. As early as 1840, just ten years after the arrival of the London Missionary Society, Pratt brags, "The night dance with all its abominable accompaniments has been put to a stop in my immediate neighborhood" (1840).[1] During the several decades after contact, as Samoans rapidly converted to Christianity, Joking Nights' various facets fell to pieces, what survived in the bush being one of them.[2] The pieces of Joking Nights that remained within the Samoan limelight were rewritten along lines acceptable to Christianity and became new entertainments. But remember that Joking Nights were cardinal examples of informal discourse, so a rewriting of Samoan entertainments was also a rewriting of a discourse on self; because Samoan contextual discourses were gendered, a rewriting of informal discourse was a rewriting of gender as well. Once again, when I refer to a discourse on self, I mean a discourse that realizes a part of the self as it is culturally construed, rather than a discourse on the *topic* of self.

Preeminence in Joking Nights was a feminine prerogative in old Samoa. By this I do not mean that women were the only entertainers of note. Everyone from tiny children to revered chiefs participated. Just as a village princess (*tāupōu*) had a key role in kava ceremonies, a conductor-clown (*faʻaaluma*), probably male, had a key role in Joking Nights. Nonetheless, entertainments were sponsored by the *aualuma,* the village's organization of sisters and daughters (Shore 1977:318). Because females were the normative hosts, theirs was the basal responsibility and theirs the basal role.

In chapters 7 and 8 we saw that female sexuality was symbolically privileged in the missionary encounter, coming to represent the unredeemed "heathen" state; therefore, missionaries, in their attempts to redress this state, regarded the schooling of Samoan girls in Christian ideals about sexuality and marriage as particularly important. The missionary ideal of girls as virginal meant to Samoans that every girl should be like the virginal village princess, whose role as an emblem of respect took on new significance. This new village-princess ideal was culturally coded in the figure of the unmarried girl (*teine*) as *tausala*, a word with aristocratic connotations, denoting a lovely, dignified, virginal girl. Virginity, however, was part of a larger set of missionary ideals that harped upon the value of personal sentiment in matters of conscience generally and in marriage in particular. This genuinely foreign value was useful to girls in contravening traditional guidelines for mating and marriage, but it also suggested a novel idea about the self: the self was subjective and inner, rather than social.

Spirit Sickness stories, considered in chapter 9, demonstrate that these potentially disruptive foreign ideas became textual elements in colonial images of girls. A missionary privileging of the virginal girl (*teine*) as a cultural icon was refracted in the figure of the spirit girl, who was also referred to as a *Teine*. It was as if the discursive muting of girls in Christian Samoa was matched by their newfound vocality as symbolic figures. This symbolic privileging also characterized reconfigured entertainments: we will soon see that the figure of the girl was regnant even in colonial comedy theater, despite the fact that the actors were all males.[3] In Spirit Sickness spirit girls became an idiom to think about the cultural complications and concatenations effected by missionization and colonization; in colonial entertainments the figure of the real girl played this same role.

In Joking Nights, dances were often theatrical, and skits were highly choreographed. A Christian rejection of the ribald aspects of precontact girls' roles generated a colonial split between dance and theater.[4] Dancing became a separate entertainment and less bawdy. A new comedy theater evolved in which the lead role migrated from females to males, although older women maintained prominence in everyday joking practices.[5] This new theater, Spirit House, became a venue for boys and men to express and think about problems of gender history and, in this respect, resembled Spirit Sickness for girls.

There was no widespread need for males to become possessed. The issues that colonialism visited upon them were not moral in nature, having more to do with a confusion in gender codings; therefore, males did not require the moral cover afforded by the liminality and antiagency of possession.[6] Their gender confusion centered around colonial reversals of female roles, first in relation to informal discourse and later in relation to status. By playing the part of lead comedians, boys took girls' place as the major practitioners of informal discourse. Although colonial girls' role became morally restricted, girls also gained access to education and, as they became women, to money. Both education and money were status variables in colonial Samoa that could reverse culturally-predicated relations to husbands. Feelings about these reversals were explored in Spirit House.

A capacity to traffic in transgressive ideas and anxious feelings is a feature that informal discourse shares with possession. Like possession, informal discourse typically reverses the values of the hegemonic moral order. Inasmuch as informal discourse is a contextual discourse but shares commonalties with spirit possession—which I argued is in Samoa a species of moral discourse—it may be helpful to reiterate the distinction between moral and contextual discourse.

I associate moral discourse with classification and narration, and contextual discourses with cultural rhetorics and performance. Narratives, however, may have a performative character, as when children act out stories or when spirits speak through possessed girls. On the other hand, cultural performances may involve narration, as in theater. The fundamental distinction between moral and contextual discourse is simply this: when the operative cultural work is classificatory—having to do with sorting out actions and characters along lines of virtue and vice, rewarding or rescuing the innocent and punishing the guilty—the discourse is moral. When the operative work is placing cultural values and their antinomies in as-if, rhetorical frames—in which the metamessage is "This is not literally meant"—the discourse is contextual.

Even when possession has a performative emphasis—in the trance dances of Bali, for example—it lacks those as-if quotation marks that characterize contextual discourses. At least when possession is a viable and vital institution, people believe that spirits *really are* appearing in the bodies of those possessed. The as-if rhetorical quality of contextual discourse presupposes conscious use of tropes as tropes: the discourse itself turns upon a shared understanding of their symbolic nature. In possession there are rules against reading the deeper meanings of tropes, although the ethnoanalyst has a privileged position in this regard, but even his or her interpretations tend to be encoded and cryptic. In "The Girl Scout" possession story, for example, the marine was simply a spirit who spoke with a foreign accent; it was the ethnoanalyst who declared it was a marine. Samoan ethnoanalysis often involves figuring out who the possessing spirit is. This marine identification had great tropic resonance in colonial Samoa, but this resonance was unread by the ethnoanalyst; only the spirit's accent was read.

The Informal Discourse of Joking Nights

Let us return to this chapter's project, tracing a reconfiguration of Samoan informal discourse through the fragmentation of Joking Nights. I begin with a brief review of the Joking Night program. Although it is likely that programs varied, all sources describe a prototypical progression. In what follows I combine and interpret various sources to sketch this progression, leaning heavily on Krämer, who provides the most telling and clearly documented version ([1902] 1995:366–81).[7]

Joking Nights were organized as exchanges between two groups or sides, one from a hosting village, the other from a visiting village. Each entertainment group occupied one end of a long, open, oval house; between them were two fireplaces that spotlighted performers, their bodies shimmering with lavishly applied coconut oil (Pritchard 1866:78). Torches were held near to the performers for the same purpose and possibly passed back and forth between the sides (Williams [1830–32] 1984:247–48). To exchange entertainments was to "Pass the Fire." Rather than being jocular throughout, Joking Night had a two-part contrapuntal sequence. Each part had three moments, or phases, which successively realized this contrapuntal architecture.[8]

Joking Nights: Program

Part 1: Synchronized Dances   Part 2: Comic Dances

Leader: Village Princess [*Tāupōu*]   Leader: Clown [*Faʻaaluma*]
and High Chief [*Aliʻi*]
1. Sitting Dances   1. Mimetic Theater and Dances
2. Standing Dances   2. Exhibitionistic Dances (*Sāʻē*)
3. Top of the House [*Taualuga*]   3. Spirit Frenzy [*ʻAleʻaleaitu*]

Part 1

Joking Nights were held the evening after major ceremonies.[9] Part 1 was a choreographic version of a ceremony. In chapter 5 we saw that Samoan ceremonies consist in an exchange of prestations signifying the service of men (*ʻoloa*) and the service of women (*tōga*); in turn, offerings of service sign an as-if bestowal of fealty in which each group grants the other as-if dominion. Part 1 of Joking Nights made the same gestures, exchanging entertainment presentations that (like the prestations of ceremony) spoke an idiom of respect. First were sitting dances led by a village princess, in which movements of hands, arms, face, and torso were complex and synchronous. Second, the dancers rose to perform synchronized standing dances. Third was a dance, unnamed in early accounts but resembling a dance today called the *taualuga*, led by the highest-status person present, usually a high chief; indeed, *taualuga* may also refer to high chiefs (Moyle 1988:209, 233; Guernsey-Allen, pers. comm.). The *taualuga* dancer was surrounded by others, who circled in a stately accompaniment.

Like ceremonial prestations, in Samoa entertainments are a kind of service and, therefore, symbolic pledges of fealty. Thus, within the village it is usually children and youngsters who entertain their elders. At Joking Nights, having the highest-status person of one group rise to entertain the other group was, therefore, a great condescension: by dancing, the chief offered service and reiterated the pledge of fealty made that day in ceremony. There was, however, a contradiction in Joking Night exchanges, particularly in the chief's performance, that subtly belied respect and with it the similitude of part 1 to ceremonies.

Although entertaining is normative for Samoan young people, it is also a reversal of the rule of respect: those of inferior status are not supposed to call attention to themselves, but they are stars at entertainments (Mead [1928] 1961:112). Young people do not normally call attention to themselves because to do so is to assert dominance. For the same reason high chiefs usually do not speak in ceremonies; like the polite young person who will not contradict an elder, they are silent, although spoken for by an orator. To do otherwise would have dominance-asserting nuances and could invite intervillage strife. So, a dancing chief at a Joking Night conveyed a double message: on the one hand, he pledged fealty through service; on the other, he asserted dominance by taking the starring role, reversing the rule of respect. By doing so, he placed his pledge of fealty in those ironic quotation marks that characterize informal discourse.

There was a similar ambiguity in the ascending choreography of part 1. Elevation is a symbolic correlative of status in Samoa; deference is conveyed by placing oneself lower than others. Thus, the penitent child and chief alike express deference by sitting down, the child before its elder and the chief, in ritual apologies (*ifoga*), before the titled heads of an offended village. Part 1 began with a sitting dance, progressing to standing dances and the *taualuga*. *Taualuga* refers to a top or ridge; Samoans often gloss the word as "the top of the house," and thus it continued the choreographic elevation from sitting to standing and countered the message conveyed by chiefly condescension.

Part 1's difference from ceremonies was further underscored by a gender transposition. In ceremonies chiefs are represented by orators. At the opening of Joking Nights it was the village princess who took the chief's place as leader of a side. That an adolescent girl should be a high chief's surrogate inverted not only the gender bias of titles in Samoa (toward males) but even the age-grade system that was the terra firma of all status relations. There was a similar double entendre to the Joking Night as a whole, for part 2 rescinded the representations of respect articulated in part 1 and likewise positioned Samoan ideas of respect within a playfully deprecatory frame.

Part 2

In part 2, first, there was a theater of caricature and comic mimicry, which in Samoan could be called *faipona*. Recall that *faipona* is a signature form of Samoan informal discourse and refers to a type of joking in which one harps upon or caricatures another's potentially humorous features, disparaging that person's dignity and reversing hierarchical respect. The contrapuntal structure of Joking Nights also insinuated a deprecatory comparison, much like *faipona*, so *faipona* was an apt opening for part 2 and lent an initial definition to the rest of the evening. While at the opening of part 1 entertainers sat deferentially before their audience, at the opening of part 2 entertainers put down others through caricatures, which might even be directed at the audience.[10] Dancers sometimes mimed innocuous objects such as animals but mimicked social superiors as well.

These often hilarious performances led, in the second phase toward a ribald dance called the *sāʻē*. Although exhibitionistic, the *sāʻē* featured such silly posturing and facial expressions as well as such outrageous banter that even prudish missionaries understood them to be jest (Williams [1830–32] 1984:247–48). Samoans call this jest genre *ula*. In chapter 5 we saw that *ula* refers to a verbal and bodily burlesque in which one harps upon or exposes things sexual or scatological and that, like *faipona*, *ula* is a signature form of Samoan informal discourse. In review dignity is the bodily idiom of status in Samoa. Inasmuch as *ula* entails undignified antics, it appears to be joking at the expense of one's own status, but *ula* appropriates a standard Samoan insult to the dignity of another—self-exposure; therefore, in *ula* one actually jokes at the expense of the other's status and playfully assaults hierarchical respect. Inasmuch as the tropes one tends to use in *ula* are sexual or scatological, *ula* also assaults sexual respect.

Recall that in Samoan a Joking Night is an *Ula* Night; although part 2 of the evening was probably peppered with *ula* throughout, the *sāʻē* was the beginning of uninterrupted *ula* and set the tone for the remaining performances. The *sāʻē* dancers paralleled the synchronized dancers of part 1, their mirthful-sexual posturing counterpointing the ordered harmony of the sitting and standing dances. *Sāʻē* choruses were led by a *faʻaaluma* (conductor-clown); his antics counterpointed the grace of the village princess, who led the choruses of part 1.

In the third phase everyone but the young people departed, and then came the *ʻaleʻaleaitu*. *ʻAleʻale* means "hasty" or "rash," and referred both to the increasing tempo and wild tenor of the dancing. An *aitu*, you recall, is a spirit. We saw in chapter 8 that *ʻaleʻaleaitu* dancers "Tore off the eye of the spirit," meaning that they shed their clothes. The *ʻaleʻaleaitu* provided occasion for elopement, and we saw in chapter 5 that elopement was looked upon as a "defeat" suffered by the girl and her family through her, although the loss was usually not in earnest.[11] The *ʻaleʻaleaitu*, then, was the climax of a "contest" in which one group "scored" against another, counterpointing the apparent condescension of the *taualuga*-dancing high chief in part 1. The spirit, symbolically "torn" or dismembered in the dancers' divestment, took the place of the high chief who was honored in the *taualuga*; chiefs were often said to be part spirit and might include a spirit in their genealogy (Cain 1971).

If part 1 of Joking Nights resembled a ceremony, part 2 resembled a sports competition in which one side "won" and another "lost." On festival occasions in old Samoa, villages staged sports events from wrestling and club matches to javelin throwing; competitors represented their village.[12] Likewise, Joking Nights elopements stood for points in a game between villages. Nonetheless, the difference between part 2 and sports was underscored by a gender transposition. Samoans conceive of competition as a same-sex undertaking. A "sports competition" between persons who would rather mate than fight made a mockery of the whole business of competition for status, converting competition into an occasion for mutual pleasure.

In summary informal discourse Samoan style had a fractal quality, containing formal and informal poles within itself.[13] Part 1 had a formal flavor, resembling a ceremony, even though it was orchestrated so as to convey "not really a ceremony." Part 2, which resembled a sports competition, took informal discourse Samoan style to its logical extreme, making an unqualified mockery of hierarchical and sexual respect. In Joking Nights the rhetorical as-if nature of informal discourse was signed through a repeated intercalation of contradictory elements between apparent analogues. The semiotics of part 1 suggested an analogue to ceremonies but included symbolic assertions of dominance that contradicted this analogy. The semiotics of part 2 suggested an analogue to sports but also contradicted this analogy through a heterosexual symbolism. The program as a whole suggest a parallel (through structural isomorphism) between part 1 and part 2, but the contrapuntal contents (dignified dances vs. disrespectful antics) likewise contradicted parallelism.

Colonial Entertainments

Missionary references to Joking Nights as "the night dance with all its abominable accompaniments" suggest their disapproval focused more on dirty dancing than comedic theater. Part 1—sans the dirty dancing—became the colonial synonym for Samoan dance; the comic theater from the first phase of part 2 continued as a separate entertainment. Both dancing and theater carried on the informal discourse of old Samoa but with a difference. In Joking Nights the contradictory framing of informal discourse was put to work creating reflective distance on the key moral opposition of the Samoan cultural universe: respect/rivalry. From the perceptive of Samoan courtesy rivalry is comically crude; from the perspective of Samoan rivalry courtesy is but an invitation to defeat. In colonial entertainments rhetorical quotation marks were put to work framing historical experience as well, providing a reflective distance and social commentary on this experience.[14] Let us consider these two entertainments consecutively.

Dance

In reaction to the ribald character of those Joking Night dances called the *sā'ē* and the *'ale'aleaitu,* missionaries tried to ban Samoan dancing altogether. Samoans, even Samoan ministers, resisted; they argued that restrictions be "made dependent on the character of the dance" (Stevenson 1925:218, qtd. in Moyle 1988:206). This stress on "the character of the dance" gave rise to dancing of good character, which Samoans called *siva; siva* became an encompassing term for the dance. In old Samoa the word *siva* referred to singing rather than to dancing (Moyle 1988:232). Was it, then, a Samoan euphemism that played down the dancing about which missionaries expressed such chagrin? Did Samoans lead missionaries to believe that they were only going off to a songfest: "A dance? Why heavens no—only *siva!*" Neologisms, however, not only provided covers but new directions.

Most obviously, *siva* is composed of synchronized dances from part 1 of Joking Nights, for example, sitting dances and standing dances in which a large group of people, in orderly rows, move in union and which, while energetic, are not sexy. *Siva* conclude with that dignified dance called *taualuga*, as did part 1. But this surface scenario is used to smuggle in the old informal discourse from part 2, albeit in a condensed and camouflaged form, that revolves around the *taualuga*.

Today the participants who encircle the *taualuga* dancer, like their Joking Night counterparts, may move in a stately manner, but, unlike their predecessors, they are more likely to *'ai'aiuli* this dancer. To *'ai'aiuli* is to engage in wild choreographic jesting. The *sā'ē* was choreographic jest; the *'ai'aiuli* is a contracted and displaced version of the *sā'ē* that, like dancing itself, got a new name to bypass missionary censors. The word *'ai'aiuli* itself carries on the work of disguise. *'Ai'aiuli* means "to humble oneself so as to draw attention to another" (Milner 1966:10), and Samoans will tell you that the *'ai'aiuli* accompaniment is a way of paying "respect" to the central dancer (Shore 1982:257–59). Yet this cultural definition is camouflage for the layered character of the event. Even the name *taualuga* itself is euphemistic: this dance might more fittingly be called the *taualuga-'ai'aiuli*, as it is most often a choreographic duet. Calling it *taualuga* is a way of highlighting the respect elements of a dance that in fact layers the less than respectful segments of Joking Nights into a Christian style of dancing.

In contracted form the *taualuga-'ai'aiuli* duet replicates the parallel-plus-counterpoint program of Joking Nights. Rather than stately performances followed by joking performances, in this duet one finds stately performances accompanied by joking performances. The parallel resides in a two-part choreography rather than a two-part program and suggests a likeness to participants: Samoans say both parts are methods of expressing respect. But, because of the contradicting content, an *'ai'aiuli* comic circling the *taualuga* dancer places the values that she embodies in ironic quotation marks. The comic, too, is set in ironic quotation, for his choreographic style alludes to a form of jest (*ula*) that itself refers to rivalry, but the *'ai'aiuli* dancer typically throws himself at the *taualuga* dancer's feet for her to step upon his back. Thus, in the *taualuga*, *ula* wears the guise of its own opposite—willing subordination.[15]

The informal discourse of *siva* not only secreted a ribald pre-Christian past within a colonial present; it also became a mode of thinking about foreign ideas and historical problems, namely: (1) a colonial transposition of gender roles; (2) a Christian democratization of status, albeit one that carried on

Village princess dancing a *taualuga*, with *'ai'aiuli* accompaniment. From the photographic collection of J. L. Dwyer (1908–13). Courtesy of K. A. Wheat (copyright). Original photograph currently stored at the American Samoa Historic Perservation Office.

indigenous tendencies, and; (3) a new individualism, associated symbolically with girls as romantic figures.

Transposing Gender

Two gender shifts that characterized *siva* are critical to understanding the dance's colonial transformation. The first concerned the choreographic role of young women in general and the second that of the village princess. Nineteenth-century visitors to Samoa were wont to remark that on Joking Nights girls performed the most "undesirable antics."[16] In *siva* the joking role (*'ai'aiuli*) is danced by anyone but girls: boys climb the house posts; older women shriek and beat the ground with a palm frond; men holding orator titles may even expose themselves. At Joking Nights the highest chief present would dance the *taualuga,* and chiefs were usually male. By the time Milner worked in Samoa in 1959—even though the highest-status person still graced an occasion by condescending to dance—the *taualuga* was conceived of as the village princess' special dance (1966:248).

The colonial ascription of the *taualuga* to the village princess changed the register of her body language. In body language Samoans gloss status as restraint. The dances led by a village princess on the Joking Nights were synchronized. Synchronized choreography implies control but not necessarily a high degree of restraint. Today, for example, Samoan boys do synchronized slap dances that are energetic and fast, their hands flickering in unison over many planes of their bodies. In the *taualuga,* however, technique is demonstrated by succinct and understated inflections of movement. Village princesses were virgins. By making the restrained body language of the *taualuga* the village princess' highlighted style, colonial dance emphasized the virginal aspect of her choreographic identity.

This shift in the village princess' body language was accompanied by a privileging of her choreographic role. In Joking Nights the village princess' role was key but circumscribed; in *siva* her dance role became paramount. As early as the 1880s, Churchward says that the village princess "takes the leading part in all Sivas or native dances" (1887:348). Samoans seem to have redeemed the dance in missionary eyes by making the village princess its central figure. While Joking Nights featured sexual display and elopements, *siva* featured village princesses, who became symbols of the ideal of female premarital chastity that missionaries promoted.

In part 1 of Joking Nights the village princess had taken the place of the chief in the sitting and standing dances, a placed reclaimed by him in the finishing *taualuga*. Inasmuch as in colonial times the *taualuga* became the village princess' special dance, she had become the high chief's trace. Previously, the chief was the ultimate emblem of status, and the *taualuga* was one of his synonyms. His choreographic displacement speaks volumes about virginal girls' status ascent.

Democratization

We saw in chapter 8 that, in suggesting all girls should be virginal, Samoan Christianity implied that all girls were *like* village princesses. During colonial times this symbolic appropriation of village princess status was executed in the body language of the dance. If by the late nineteenth century the *taualuga* had become the village princess' special dance, by the 1920s all girls' movements had taken on a *taualuga*-like style (Mead [1928] 1961:118). No more did dancing girls perform absurd antics that in colonial eyes made them resemble "a lot of demons let loose from below." Rather, they were those "eight-fold incarnations of loveliness" that the British consul Churchward, with his Western gender presumptions, desired them to remain when they sat before him demurely in their costumes of leaves and flowers at the opening of a Joking Night (Churchward 1887:229–30).

Today, any girl may play the choreographic role of village princess, her genealogy notwithstanding. At the small college where I taught there was a "Samoa Day" each year in which every college club (and there were many) would pick a girl to dance the *taualuga* and decorate her, just as villages once decorated their village princess, to be the centerpiece of their dance. To pick a girl to dance the *taualuga* is to make her an honorary village princess. Thus, through the *siva* being a village princess has become like being a beauty queen. *Siva* is now a subtle contest: at contemporary beauty contests each of the participants will dance a *taualuga* as a criteria for selection. The "title" they win is the modern facsimile of a village princess title.[17] Thus, while girls did not develop a new specialty in formal discourse (they did not take a leading role in ceremonies), neither were they muted altogether. If they lost their voices, their dancing feet continued to speak a performative language.

Individualism

In old Samoa the *taualuga* dancer performed in a stately manner, encircled by a stately accompaniment. This arrangement connoted harmony and connection between the central and peripheral dancers. In colonial Samoa the *taualuga* dancer almost always elicited an *'ai'aiuli* accompaniment, explicitly contrapuntal in character. Her role in relation to this accompaniment was to be aloof and abstracted—to dance as if dancing alone—to be utterly unruffled by the outrageous antics that many danced around her. Even when not dancing with an *'ai'aiuli* foil, by the 1920s girls had a tendency to perform in solo, seemingly oblivious to all:

> Each dancer moves in a glorious individualistic oblivion of the others, there is no pretense of coordination or of subordinating the wings to the center of the line. Often a dancer does not pay enough attention to her fellow dancers to avoid continually colliding with them. It is a genuine orgy of aggressive individualistic exhibitionism. (Mead [1928] 1961:118)

There were virtuosos who performed in part 2 of Joking Nights, but most people danced in chorus, albeit a chorus that disassembled into couples during the night's last stage (Moyle 1988:231). In contrast, *siva* was a performative discourse in which girls could explore an individual way of being a self. Remember, an emphasis on elements of individualism—personal conscience and inner experience—had been associated with their virginity in the missionary encounter and with their new status as quasi village princesses.

Theater

Despite missionary boasts to the contrary, in a sense Joking Nights were not discontinued. Joking Nights took place in the great house (*faletele*) of the *aualuma* (organization of village-born females). For the purposes of the evening's entertainment, this great house was called a Spirit House, *Faleaitu* (Shore 1977:318). Probably this place name had been a synonym for Joking Nights. The comic theater that opened part 2 and that survived the demise of "night dances" took this place name as its title. Inasmuch as this comic theater was still a night of jests, Spirit House was in effect a Joking Night.

Part 2 of the Joking Night began with mimesis and caricature. Spirit House begins and ends with mimesis and caricature, yet initially Spirit House resembled the later phases of the Joking Night as well, for it featured sexually explicit skits with "scantily clad actors" and "obscenity in word and gesture" (Sinavaiana 1992b:197). We will see that, more than any other colonial entertainment, Spirit House holds the former place of Joking Nights both literally and symbolically. Far more explicitly than *siva*, Spirit House skits continued the informal discourse of Joking Nights and put this discourse to work providing critical commentary on those changes in Samoan cultural consciousness effected by missionization, colonization, and modernity.

"Spirit Girls"

Actors in Spirit House were called spirits (*aitu*). We saw in the preceding chapter that in Spirit Sickness agency was bracketed: the deeds performed during possession episodes were attributed to a spirit. Spirit House enlisted the trope of possession to bracket authorship: Spirit House skits were likewise performed by spirits, although in theater the idea of the spirit was used as a rhetorical device, rather than literally meant. Nonetheless, here again the spirit was a way to claim as well as disclaim, for it hallmarked this entertainment as heathen and thus as a sign of Samoan difference in the context of Christianization. Under this sign of Samoan difference it became possible for the spirits of Spirit House to author a new informal discourse about all that threatened hereditary modes of talk and thought about selves.

Spirit House is now a male genre, but this sex segregation seems to be of fairly recent vintage. Chief Tuiteleleapaga, who was Mead's assistant in the 1920s, reports both boys and girls participating (1980:50). Jill Samuelu married a Samoan and lived in the village of Afega on 'Upolu from 1958 to 1966. She also remembers both boys and girls performing (pers. comm.). By the time Sanele grew up in the 1960s, however, girls no longer performed. It is likely that this theatrical segregation was an adjustment to tightening moral regulations for girls. Sex segregation meant that boys had to play female parts. Transvestism became the favorite device of Spirit House actors, perhaps in deference to this necessity.[18] The rise of Spirit House "girls," who are after all spirits (and, therefore, in effect "spirit girls"), would then have been more or less historically concurrent with the Spirit Sickness epidemic, with its omnipresent spirit girls. Like Spirit Sickness, Spirit House revolves around the figure of the village princess.

Village Princesses

"Often the only performer in costume is the lead comedian," says Sinavaiana, and "he may wear the ceremonial headdress [*tuiga*] and leaf skirt of the Samoan princess" (1992b:197). It is as if Spirit House is a black-and-white photo with one figure in color, giving this figure a subsuming quality. But Spirit House "village princesses" are the proverbial Mona Lisa with a mustache. Thus, Sinavaiana describes one girl as having an obviously male physique, mustache, and prominently tattooed biceps (Sinavaiana 1992a:102). By hybridizing mustaches and ceremonial headdresses, Spirit House girls made a mockery of the village princess and parodied the Samoan-Christian ideal for which she stood.

Spirit House girls framed the figure of the village princess in ironic quotation through a second contradiction as well. Village princesses embodied the Samoan-Christian ideal of everygirl as virginal. Spirit House girls do not simply act like girls but like Samoan transvestites. In Samoa male transvestites are called *fa'afafine*, literally "the way (*fa'a*) of women (*fafine*)." Remember that in a wifely role a female is a *fafine*, "a woman"; in a sisterly role she is always a *teine*, "a girl." In relation to one's own family one is a *teine*, that is, somebody's sister; in relation to one's husband's family, one is a *fafine*, that is, somebody's wife.[19] The word *fafine*, therefore, suggests the subject is sexually active. Thus, when a transvestite—who is after all a *fafine* (sexually active)—mimes the persona of the village princess (who is by definition not), it places her "virginity" in ironic quotation, making it a sign belied by its theatrical portrayal. This contradiction was further exploited by sexy performances. Flaunting their sexuality, as Joking Night girls once did, Spirit House girls engaged in "flirtatious exchanges with the audience . . . wagging a hip or waving coyly" (Sinavaiana 1992a:102).

Spirit House antics not only hybridize colonial village princesses and ribald Joking Night girls; they also interlace this composite figure with modern/foreign elements. In one skit a male actor (playing a feminine part) dresses to go to church, instructing "her" son to get her makeup. "Now go to the safe and get me my *mascara*. . . . Then go on behind our pigsty and get me my *lipstick* . . . then go to the chest and get us the *Camay*" (Sinavaiana 1992a:111). This tableau pictures the contemporary Samoan feminine persona as an absurdist pastiche, linking this persona to Western imports generally and to disturbing Western ideas, like an economy based upon hoarding (in safes and chests), and with an image of pollution (a pigsty), as if a reorganization of social space along foreign lines was experienced as a cultural pollution.

Recalibrating Gender

If Spirit House's transvestite face reverses the colonial version of sexual respect (embodied by the village princess), Spirit House plots reverse the colonial version of hierarchical respect. These plots may straightforwardly burlesque colonial authority: Samoan schoolchildren poison their Caucasian teacher, for example, or a Samoan interpreter ridicules an English royal visiting Samoa (Shore 1977: 321–24, 329–31; Sinavaiana 1992a, 1992b). Even more frequently, however, caricatures of indigenous authority figures are made via a colonial context. Thus, Shore records a skit in which Samoan sons exploit (rather than serve) their foolish father (1977:324–26); they do so by asking for his money, not only reversing age-old expectations about the respect due to superiors but implicating colonialism and its economy in this reversal. A caricature of Samoan husbands as authority figures via colonial contexts came to be a favorite Spirit House theme and explored a colonial recalibration of gender relations.

Missionaries had long stressed the importance of women as wives. In post-Renaissance Western countries women had been induced to control their sexuality in order to be preferred marriage partners, in part because they had status predominately as wives (Kelly 1984:19–50). In Samoa, although women could hold status through marriage, fundamentally they held status through their own cognatic genealogies and as sisters. In relation to Samoan brothers, sisters are objects of respect; however, in relation to wives, husbands are objects of respect. Thus, brothers should serve their sisters food, eating only after they have done so, while wives serve husbands. The female organization of old Samoa, the *aualuma*, was composed of the village's native girls, excluding in-marrying wives. In contrast, the female organization of Christian Samoa was the ladies' church auxiliary, consisting of all adult women of the village, implicitly incorporating and elevating the status of the wife.[20] While the elevation of girls' status had a muting effect, elevating that of wives' seems to have made them vociferous.

In the Spirit House skit "Jealousy II," for example, a husband is suspicious that his "wife" has a lover (he finds a strange pair of slippers in the house, the slippers themselves standing as a marker of colonial culture). His wife rejoins his accusation of infidelity with "her" own. Invoking the scores-of-the-trip ethos described by Chief Tuiteleleapaga in chapter 2, the husband counters that his infidelity is "just a man's game; he goes there and here, but ends up with you Mama" (Sinavaiana 1992a:104–5). In Spirit House, however (unlike in Tuiteleleapaga's story), wives' good-for-the-gander infidelities are a popular theme, and in "Jealousy II" it is not the wife who is unable to contain her jealousy but the husband.

In old Samoa whole families cared for babies; in rural contexts they still do. But the burden of childcare, as well as a gender identity rooted in it, has contaminated Samoan understandings of the wife as a cultural figure. In "Jealousy II" the English usage *Mama*, pigeonholing the wife in the maternal role, tags the husband's argument as an invocation of colonial "tradition."[21] For the most part, however, in this repartee it is the wife who speaks English. "She" scores against him by this invocation of the language of education and status in colonial Samoa, while the husband does his ineffectual best to insist that she just speak Samoan (Sinavaiana 1992a:104–6).

In the context of missionization speaking English stands for a Christian education, which girls often received in missionary contexts. While this schooling must often have seemed like a language class, it was also an education in a new discourse on self. If imported through the figure of the girl, however, this new discourse seems to have turned argumentative in the figure of the wife. We saw that in Samoa those with authority speak; those without should not "speak above their age." By their vociferousness Spirit House wives reverse the respect relations prescribed between husband and wife. Their joking is about a colonial recalibration of husband/wife roles that places colonial versions of the wife (as Mama and as asymmetrically faithful) and of masculinity (as sexually dominant and of authoritative stature) in ironic quotation.

Informal Discourse in Postcolonial Entertainments

While Christianity compromised girls' *ula* at Joking Nights, modernity has had a similar effect on the *ula* of both sexes. This vignette shows why.

■ ■ ■

Satan the Anus[22]

One night Sanele and I were dancing at a Pago Pago bar. The power went off. Deprived of Western music by a lack of electricity, the bar crowd began to sing the Joking Night "Pass the Fire" song that is still sung when Samoans exchange entertainments. The song goes,

'Ua alu atu le afi.	Here goes the fire.
'Ua alu atu le afi e.	Here goes the fire hey.
Fai fai pea, fai fai pea	Do it do it again, do it do it again hey.

Soon the lyrics of the last line changed from "Fai fai pea," to "Fia fia mea." *Fia* means "to want to." *Mea* means "thing" but also refers to male and to female genitals and to sex. Thus, the new line meant, "Want to want to make sex, want to want to make sex, hey."

Then the group began adapting the words to a Samoan-Christian tune sung for *taualuga* dancing. The first line was "Satan is the yam that was planted," which the crowd changed to "Satan is the asshole that was planted," by substituting the word *ufi*, "yam," with the word *ufa*, "asshole." A fight broke out because, Sanele later told me, one boy was there with his female cousin (a categorical sister), and the boy sitting next to her began singing the scatological version of the song.

■ ■ ■

Like part 1 of Joking Nights, like colonial dance, this nightclub evening ends with a *taualuga*, but here the *taualuga*—that choreographic and, in the present case, melodic synonym for respect—has become *ula*. Like all other *ula* we have encountered since Christianization, but in a new context, the second song places Christian-colonial values in ironic quotation through an intercalation of opposites. Here *Satan*, a key player in Christian religious discourse, stands in for this discourse but is intercalated with *anus*, which connotes the opposite of respect: recall that mooning is the penultimate gesture of disrespect in Samoa. The effect is to change a typical invocation of Samoan-Christian respect (the condemnation of Satan) into a photographic negative of respect (a joke about religious discourse). If the second song is a good example of *ula*, why does it end in fighting? At Joking Nights and other age-old rituals of hospitality, *ula* had a key role in defusing a volatile rivalry between villages and the titles who represented them. While Satan the Anus, like its jocular predecessors, succeeds in positioning respect in an ironic frame, it fails with rivalry. This failure can be laid at the door of modernity.

Joking Nights consisted in an exchange of items between a hosting village and a visiting village, and often the group representing the hosting village was composed of girls while that representing the visitors was composed of boys. This arrangement insured that matings that followed the frenzied phase of the dance would be village exogamous and probably not incestuous. This arrangement, however, was proper in another sense as well, for we saw that Samoans not only abhorred actual incest between categorical brothers and sisters but even the hint of sexual fact or feeling when both were present. To cross this line was and is to impugn the honor of another family and thereby to ignite an incipient rivalry. This Samoan sense of propriety has become problematic in contemporary entertainment, in which, like the boy who sings about Satan, participants are likely to be oblivious to the presence of opposite-sexed relatives.

Postcolonial Stars

Today Spirit House is performed at annual national celebrations. Like spirit possession, it has also migrated to remote rural contexts that Samoans look upon as traditional cultural reserves. But, if this theater is not as popular as once it was, its favorite device still is. In postcolonial entertainments—at nightclubs, at parties, at beauty and talent contests—a male transvestite often takes the role of impresario and stand-up comic.[23] These rising stars represent a necessary amendment to Samoan informal discourse, which is yesterday and today a discourse of *ula*. While a girl would be offended should another say or do anything off-color in her categorical brother's presence, the transvestite is no girl. Likewise, boys must beat another who says anything indelicate in his categorical sister's presence, but—by social agreement—the transvestite is no boy. Slipping in between the cracks in discursive categories, transvestites can *ula* before mixed-sexed groups and allow audiences to *ula* vicariously.

In Joking Night comedy girls took the leading role. Spirit House girls are a remembrance of Joking Night girls and abbreviated representations of bygone Joking Nights; likewise, transvestite impresarios are abbreviated representations of Spirit House. It is as if the girl, having become the subsuming figure of Spirit House, has subsumed the theater itself. In Samoan a real girl is a *teine moʻi*; *teine moʻi* translates back into English as "virgin." One might say, then, that, while the real girl became a colonial emblem of respect, the postcolonial "girl" became not only the proponent but also the emblem of Samoan joking. Samoan informal discourse's migration from girls to "girls" was also a rewriting of Samoan gender. Let us trace this migration and its gender implications on a more personal level.

Reinvented Gender

Transvestism is not mentioned by early visitors to Samoa. Missionary prudery did not bar them from commenting repeatedly on what they saw as unusual sex and gender practices, neither in Samoa nor in other Pacific locales; in Tahiti, Hawaiʻi, and the Marquesas missionaries and others commented both upon heathen heterosexuality and upon transvestism.[24] Lack of comment in Samoa, therefore, suggests that Samoan transvestism is innovative. Yet it is not plausible that Samoan transvestites sprang full-blown, like Venus arising from sea foam. Early records of transvestism among Samoa's Polynesian cousins evince an ensemble of behaviors that resembles contemporary Samoan transvestism; therefore, I suspect that in old Samoa transvestism was merely an extremely marginal practice that suffered a historical drift into the cultural limelight. Lack of transvestites in early reports on Samoa is more likely to reflect a contemporary increase than a precontact absence: today male transvestites are conspicuous in their numbers. If in contemporary Samoa boys have an increased tendency to become transvestites, it follows that historical factors have contributed to a destabilization of the Samoan sex-gender system.

Status is, perhaps, the primary feature of identity in Samoa: it not only dictates but *is* one's role in the group. A decline in status, linked to gender, therefore, would increase ambivalence about gender identity. While the girl's role has been idealized in Christian Samoa, the boy's has moved in the reverse direction.[25] We saw in chapters 3 and 4 that in Samoa status is associated with directing the actions of others; serving others is associated with a lack of status. While adolescent girls' newfound dignity was correlated with a decrease in demands for service, elders made increasing demands on boys. Decreasing agricultural productivity in recent decades, due to erosion and soil depletion, has increased the time and energy that boys invest in subsistence; so have their elders' desires for ever more expensive foreign goods (O'Meara 1990, Macpherson and Macpherson 1985). There is a legend that captures the feeling accompanying this increasing asymmetry. Two parents on their deathbed tell their several sons to care for and serve their daughter. She does nothing but stay in the house and look pretty. Eventually, the brothers kill her, turn into pigeons, and fly away.

Colonial shifts in the status and responsibilities of adolescent males and females were likely to give an additional message about boys' declining status, exacerbating boys' ambivalence about masculine gender. Evidence of this ambivalence can be found in boys' joking practices. Samoan boys employ mock effeminacy to entertain their friends. When boys assume a formal clowning role (*faʻaaluma*) in an entertainment, again they are apt to act effeminately (Shore 1978:178). At the American Samoa Community College Flag Day celebration in 1989, for example, one clown posed like a model then danced ballet steps then made sexy feminine motions then *taualuga* gestures then boxing motions then tiptoed and, finally, began singing in falsetto voice. We saw that dignity is the bodily synonym for status in Samoa and that *ula* is a joke at the expense of another's dignity that appears to be a joke at the expense of one's own dignity. But *ula* may also carp upon the dignity of a cultural figure, such as a chief, a pastor, or a village princess. By acting like girls, boys appear to attack their own dignity, yet their fakery portrays the figure of the girl as undignified and is an implicit attack upon the status of sisters.

Bettelheim suggests that we all feel body envy for our sexual opposites (1976). In Samoan boys' effeminate joking body envy is compounded by status envy, and the former becomes the medium of the latter. This joking, however, is double-edged, for mocking the figure of the girl (*teine*) also privileges her, just as she is privileged in Spirit Sickness, in Spirit House, in beauty contests, and, we will soon see, by transvestite impresarios. One wonders if this back-handed privileging effectively assuages boys' envy or—like the discursive remedies to counterreactions explored in this volume's first half—offers partial satisfactions that rekindle need and anxiety in the very act of satisfaction. Furthermore, if boys' effeminate joking derives from a historically exacerbated status envy, effeminacy does not ameliorate their status.

In Samoa important titles are normally given to brothers, but sisters may hold titles, and this is no disgrace. Homosexuals may also hold titles. *Faʻafafine*, however, are seen as jesters, and families will not invest their status and dignity in them. To become a transvestite is, therefore, seriously to compromise one's opportunities for status. Transvestism, at least in Samoa, is like Derrida's version of the gift: it is a choice that subverts any reason that calculates advantage (1994). Although, once made, this choice, like every other, becomes part of a patterning of satisfactions.

Samoan male transvestites often deny that they have made a choice, taking the position held by many gays and lesbians in the United States, that they are captives of their biology: they were born and not made. Some have identified with a feminine persona as far back as they can remember. The captivity transvestites feel, however, may also be understood as a role. Transvestism is the adoption of a social persona, that is, of a role. A role consists of scripts. Samoans have a script for the loss of a girl's virginity, one that many transvestites seem compelled to reduplicate again and again. The girl is said to become the emotional thrall of her first lover. Like the freshly deflowered girl, the transvestite is said to deny her lover nothing; she also gives him money or whatever he asks. In Samoan social theory, however, the girl (*teine*) marries, thereby becoming a woman (*fafine*) and immune to girlish follies. The transvestite, however, acquires no such immunity; humor is her only exit.

Gender is a powerful form of self-definition, and in our need to define ourselves we make choices. But we are also captives, captives of a collective cultural imagination—an imagination that is invested in cultural figures. In colonial Samoa girls have been symbolically privileged and have tended to capture the local imagination in spirit possession, dance, theater, and in other areas as well. Perhaps because of this privileging, the feminine persona is now more likely to capture boys' imaginations and to present itself as a bewitching possibility. This persona also captures the imagination of audiences. Inasmuch as dignified Samoan Christian girls cannot appear in ludicrous performances, audiences are likely to appreciate boys who address Samoa's postcolonial preoccupation with the legacy of colonialism—symbolized by the figure of the girl—by representing girls in comedy and as stand-up comics. This appreciation is public support for a choice that often requires support.

If the transvestite role derives from boys' joking, the transvestite is a boy who does what most Samoan boys do, but does so consistently rather than intermittently and acquires paraphernalia to accompany this jesting role. One

Samoan drag queen I interviewed alleged that he is heterosexual, has a girl-friend, and affects a girlish style and enters drag queen contests for fun. He even made a pass at me during the interview. This unserious affectation of the transvestite role is atypical but underscores the fact the role itself is conceived of as jest (*ula*). It is in this sense that *ula*, informal discourse Samoan style, is the signature element of transvestite identity and the transvestite a contemporary emblem of this discourse. Indeed, an intercalation of opposites—which this chapter has argued is constitutive of Samoan informal discourse—is their very name.

A Rose by Any Other Name?

Earlier we saw that the word for transvestite is *fa'a-fafine* and builds on the base *fafine* (woman), implying that transvestites fall on the wifely side of the Samoan sister:wife::virginal:sexual ensemble of oppositions. This implication is confirmed by a number of jocular names that tag *fa'afafine* as sexual: they may be called "eat planet" or "eat carrot," both of which allude to fellatio. Another term is *fagufagu,* which refers to someone who wakes you up from sleep, in this case a male who wakes another male by initiating sex. Nominal contradictions pile upon contradiction when it comes to *fa'afafine,* however, for, if the base *fafine* suggests they are sexual-biological in their femininity, the prefix *fa'a* redundantly tags transvestites as cultural.

Fa'a is a polysemous prefix if ever there was one in which, Milner says, the multiple meanings are not mutually exclusive (1966:43). As a prefix, *fa'a* mediates extreme cases. Thus, while *leai* means "none," *fa'aleai* means "not very much." So, it would seem, *fa'a* makes femininity, as an absolute and contrastive difference, less different, suggesting a devolution of gender categories. We will soon see that *fa'afafine* humor plays upon the possibility of just such a devolution. *Fa'a* also means "to make," as in *fa'a'ata,* "to make laugh" (as *fa'afafine* often do) and turns an intransitive verb transitive. Thus, *fa'afafine* make gender into something made or invented. *Fa'a* can also signify something facetious or pretended, as in *fa'aalofa,* "false love." *Fa'afafine* are often referred to as *teine pepelo*—literally, "lying girls"—but *pepelo* can also mean false, as in faux pearls. Perhaps most significantly, *fa'a* means "a way" as in the expression "a way of life." "The *fa'aSāmoa,*" the Samoan way, is the Samoan term for culture, and one so characteristic that the missionaries cite Samoans invoking it to legitimate local custom. *Fa'afafine* are often called *fa'afs* for short, emphasizing the prefix and thus the cultural part of their name.

If *fa'afafine's* categorical name imply that they are cultural (*fa'a*) women (*fafine*)—as opposed to girls—their referential name contradicts this implication: typically, *fa'afafine* are referred to as girls (*teine*). One of their jocular names is "talking *pipi.*" *Pipi* is a Samoan euphemism for a girl's (that is, a virgin's, as opposed to a woman's) genitals. In anal intercourse *fa'afafine* are sometimes reputed to exclaim, "Oh my *pipi,* oh my *pipi.*" Thus, one might say that *fa'afafine* are those displaced or wandering genitals found in the idea of hysteria, and their own wandering genitalia potentially provide an expanding set of sites at which to ironize the cultural concept of virginity. In the transvestite body, as in colonial dance and Spirit House, one finds an intercalation of opposites that places the figure of the virginal girl in ironic quotation.

Recall that informal discourse in Christian Samoa was preoccupied not only with the ideal of the virginal girl (*teine*) but, more broadly, with foreign ideas embodied in the figure of the girl. *Fa'afafine* tend to take foreign names. As a rule, they adopt fancy girls' names from English, usually those that begin with the same letter as their Samoan names, although sometimes they choose a name beginning with a letter that does not exist in Samoan. There is no *c* in Samoan; one of my informants is Chiffon, another Cherie. The letter *r* occurs only in words of foreign origin (Milner 1966:194); in Samoan *r* is pronounced as *l*, yet a famous Pago Pago transvestite is Rosie. While it is true that Samoan names are often unmarked for gender, some names are marked, such as Sina, and so are many indigenized Christian names, such as Mele (Mary). It is uncommon for transvestites to choose these names.

Beauty Contests, Transvestite Village Princesses, and Informal Discourse

If, in Christian Samoa, the village princess is a democratized ideal to which everygirl aspires, transvestites are no exception. One of my transvestite informants, who had attended Marist Brother's, a boys' Catholic high school in American Samoa, boasted to me that "she" always took the part of the village princess when the school put on entertainment performances, dancing a *taualuga*. At Samoan boys' schools a transvestite often plays this part.

The ideal of everygirl as a village princess is an ideal of everygirl as virginal. In mock seriousness transvestites will insist that they are virgins, provoking laughter and protests from the girls and women who are their companions. This joke is *ula*. Like the *ula* considered earlier, not only is it a surreptitious attack on the dignity of companions that appears to be a kind of self-mockery, but this joke also mocks a colonial ideal. By insisting that they are virgins (who are called "eat carrot" and "talking *pipi*"), transvestites make a mockery of virginity itself and the Samoan-Christian ideal for which it stands.

We saw that the *tausala* ideal of everygirl as a village princess is today celebrated in beauty contests. *Fa'afafine* are apt to stage beauty contests, as this episode illustrates.

The Beauty Contest

Sanele and I were at a wedding shower in Samoa. Showers are a borrowed institution and so, as in our own culture, they are female affairs. Somehow Sanele had come to believe that he was included in the invitation. He was, therefore, the only man attending, in a manner of speaking; out of approximately forty women, there were half a dozen *fa'afafine* at this shower. The party games that the hostess had planned, such as passing an orange around without hands, hinged upon no "man" being present. The *fa'afafine* decided to stage a beauty contest in which they competed and that Sanele judged. They paraded. Then each sang or danced a love song, giving such spicy and exuberant interpretations that one "girl" managed to fall out a window in the course of "her" performance. In fear of the consequences of any girl losing, Sanele awarded titles to all of them.

■ ■ ■

Samoan beauty contests are of recent vintage. The first annual girls' beauty contest in American Samoa took place in the early 1970s. The image of the beauty contestant in Western countries is that of an idealized feminine partner in a romantic relationship. Samoan beauty contests were, of course, a Western import, constituting evidence that a foreign discourse on love was layered into Christian and Samoan models of feminine gender and of a continuing seep of foreign ideas about the self into the Samoan cultural universe.

When I arrived in the 1980s transvestite beauty contests were not much in evidence. These days, just as there is a proliferation of transvestites, so too is there a proliferation of beauty contests. The transvestite versions are often called by the American term "Drag Queen" pageants. *Faʻafafine* relish the idea that they are "queens." Just as their simulation of virginity makes a mockery of sexual respect, their simulation of aristocratic status makes a mockery of hierarchical respect. As in Joking Nights, high-status people who personify respect are likely to be in the audience: everyone who is anyone goes to the bigger transvestite pageants, including former governors and their wives, the current Samoan representative to the U.S. Congress and his wife, and so forth. Drag Queen pageants—as Joking Nights of old—are full of verbal and choreographic antics that reverse sexual respect. In the 1990 beauty pageant in Pago Pago, for example, one girl joked by acting as if she was going to expose her "breasts"; another would lift her skirt and flash her underwear.

Samoan beauty contests include a talent section like their "Miss America" or "Miss Universe" templates. As in "The Beauty Contest," transvestites impersonate pop vocalists like Whitney Houston who sing romantic songs. These vocalists and their songs signify the Western scenario of romance that entered Samoa with the missionaries, was embodied in the figure of the girl dancing a *siva* in solo, and was cultivated by seductive Western visitors, especially in World War II. It is also a scenario that transvestites satirize. Thus, a tune that I have heard them sing repeatedly is "Quando, Quando." In the American version this song is sung by a stereotypical Latin male and is based upon the repetition of the line "Oh my darling tell me when?" which is hilariously gender ambiguous when suggestively repeated, again and again, by a "girl."26

As in "The Beauty Contest" transvestite pageants award many titles. These titles applaud two sorts of accomplishment, both of which were evident in the mimetic phase of Joking Nights. While most Joking Night skits were funny, some were more straightforwardly imitative in intent. Krämer gives an account of a girl who does a choreographic imitation of a butterfly, breathtakingly evocative of real butterflies ([1902] 1995:372). Likewise, sometimes the winner of a transvestite beauty contest is simply the girl who gives the most stunningly accurate imitation of real girls, such that even Samoans would be at a loss to tell the difference; sometimes the winner is the most brilliant comic. Given that many prizes are awarded at every contest, representatives of each category are likely to appear in the ranks. *Fa'afafine,* then, are not only caricatures but doubles. We saw in chapter 6 that in Samoan to be a double is to be a *soa,* a go-between, for *soa* means "double." If the transvestite gives new meaning to the figure of the village princess, she also gives new meaning to that of the double.

Doubles and Deconstructing Colonial Gender

Remember that the boy and his doubles constitute a strategic composite and that formal discourse in Samoa is as likely to be conveyed by a dignified reticence as by speech. In Mead's 1920s portrait of the courting boy and his double, the real lover sat quietly, while the double joked flirtatiously with the girl. Today girls, hanging out with transvestites, will whisper a sexual comment about a passing boy, possibly mentioning some feature of his anatomy or that she loves him. While the girl sits demurely, the transvestite turns the murmured discourse into *ula* and calls it out to the boy. Like the doubles of yesteryear, however, counterfeit girls act as much for themselves as for their sponsors, and, just as in the case of the double, their status as representatives is often a facade. As a proxy for the lover, the double (*soa*) was compared to the tame pigeon who lured a wild bird in the service of a chief. In the modern forgery of this antique practice—in which the transvestite jokes flirtatiously, while the real girl is mute—the boy is the wild pigeon who is lured. So *fa'afafine,* like the thespian transvestites of Spirit House, enact contemporary role reversals that imply a feminization of males but also a devolution of colonial gender categories.

We saw that the most developed examples of contextual discourse, Joking Nights for example, play upon and transcend binary/oppositional cultural categories. *Fa'afafine* joking seems to aim at a deconstruction of oppositional/colonial cultural categories of femininity and masculinity, as these categories are mutually signified in relation to the idea of virginity. The following joke, for example, was told by transvestites during my years in Samoa.

■ ■ ■

Exchanging Farts

Two transvestites hitch a ride with a truck driver. One transvestite asks if "she" can fart. The truck driver says okay and there follows a soft "pu." The other transvestite makes the same request, gets the same answer, and there follows another "pu." Then the truck driver asks to fart, after which follows a high pitched "e-e-e-e." The transvestites squeal "He's a virgin, he's a virgin."

■ ■ ■

This is a jest genre Samoans call *poka*. *Poka* is a pidginized version of the English term *poker* and is a form of humor: rather than exchanging choreographic jokes as participants did at Joking Nights, in *poka* people exchange narrative jokes on the Western model of "telling a joke." Joking Nights dancers might proclaim, "One wife for our side"; in *poka,* when a narrator tells a really good joke, other jokers are apt to say, "You win for today."

While preoccupied with the colonial encounter, Spirit House (*Faleaitu*) defined itself against Western forms: it was a house (*fale*) of spirits (*aitu*). *Aitu* are explicitly heathen, representing everything about Samoans that missionaries wanted to exorcise and, therefore, were an insignia of Samoan cultural difference. In contrast, *poka* is inclusive; it is an informal discourse that self-consciously hybridizes the Samoan and the foreign. Nonetheless, *poka* is culturally distinctive; neither *poka* nor poker are a joke type in the United States.

"Exchanging Farts," furthermore, is probably imported; American male students tell me that was a locker-room, gay-bashing joke in the early 1980s. In the American version, however, the riders are not transvestites but homosexuals, and a derogatory term is used to specify them. I suspect the American joke also "bashes" gays by comparing them to females: in our culture, as in Samoa, virginity is not a category normally applied to males. When the riders of "Exchanging Farts" call the truck driver a virgin, they feminize him and themselves with him, implying all their anuses are analogous to vulvas. But in Samoa the comparison of girls to "girls" does not bash; indeed, girls make it as frequently as possible. Further, in Samoa this joke is typically told by transvestites and was probably imported by them; a fair percentage travel to the United States, where they may become temporarily "gay" in the American style.

The popularity of "Exchanging Farts" among *fa'afafine* is surely related to its capacity to play upon Samoan prototypes of informal discourse. Joking Nights opened as an exchange of respect in a bodily idiom that was an ironic copy of ceremonial exchange. Likewise, "Exchanging Farts" opens as if it were a respectful exchange between the sides: everyone shows respect for the other side by asking, "May I?" In Samoa polite exchange is a social synonym for respect, but in this joke the exchange is not of speeches (like Samoan ceremonies) nor even of entertainments (like Joking Nights) but of farts. The intercalation of a contradicting content places exchange-as-respect in ironic perspective: an exchange of farts can be no more than "courteous."

Joking Nights were exchanges between a hosting group and a visiting group. In "Exchanging Farts" the host is the truck driver, while the transvestites are guests. This host's "village," however, is no longer even a residence but what Clifford calls a "traveling culture" (1992). In the truck/village parallel the truck can be read as a sign for the mutating shape of social structure in circumstances of modernity. There none of us reside, Samoans included, all being on the way somewhere else, locked into a perpetual state of change, and harried by that sense of being forever transitory we call history. But this temporal location—modernity—this village, is not all tragic decay of traditional forms; in "Exchanging Farts" modernity is simply a new excuse for a good laugh and yet another reorchestration of an old discourse.

In Joking Nights the hosting side initiated the exchange and then "passed the fire" to the visitors, but here it is the transvestite guests who do so: they ask for a ride, and they first ask to fart. Thus, the transvestites counterpoint the usual sequence of Samoan exchange. This counterpoint is underlined by a gender transposition. At Joking Nights the hosting group was normally feminine and the visiting group masculine, but in "Exchanging Farts" the hosting side is male, and the visiting side is "female." This gender transposition suggests a modern confusion of sides, one that pivots—like all the informal discourse of the colonial period surveyed in this chapter—on the question of virginity. Here the question of gender itself becomes one of virginity: the two *fa'afafine* are revealed to be "false girls," that is, *not* virgins, but also by implication boys, while the truck driver is revealed to be a virgin, which in Samoan is a *teine mo'i*, "a real girl."

In colonial times the girl-as-virgin was a democratized version of the precontact village princess but was also linked to the foreign idea of individualism. "Exchanging Farts" opposes a group, a gang of two, to an individual; like the girl dancing a *siva*, our truck driver stands alone; like her, he seems "in a glorious individualistic oblivion" to the social context in which he moves, a context that is his downfall.

In Joking Night "competitions" girls might lose their virginity. "Exchanging Farts" parallels this scenario: the girls' side gives (up) their simulated virginity by way of the fart. In other words, the way they respond to the truck driver's fart makes a bodily comparison (*pu*'s to *e-e-e*'s). In this comparison their virginity suffers by contrast: their bodies admit that they do not lack sexual experience. It is, in effect, as if they had suffered a seduction and are, in body logic, virgins no longer. By giving their Janus-faced virginity, however, the transvestites—like the double who captured a virgin for his chief—capture the truck driver's virginity. Implicitly inviting him to follow their lead, giving permission by asking it themselves, they lure him into giving up (admitting) his real virginity. In contrast to Joking Nights, in "Exchanging Farts," the girls constitute the winning side, while the truck driver is deflowered.

This joke's legerdemain operates by focusing the ear on a body part that, as we saw in "Satan the Anus," is lumped together with sexuality in the discursive version of the Samoan incest taboo but that—unlike the genitals—is of uncertain gender. The anus' uncertain gender implicitly undermines the certainty of those Samoan-Christian values that are genderized. Freeman says Samoans have a virginity cult (1983:226–53). In old Samoa this was a village princess cult, which in colonial Samoa became a cult of everygirl as village princess. In postcolonial Samoa the dilation of the borders of this cult seemingly will not stop until it encompasses everyone, genital anatomy notwithstanding. The joke, like transvestites themselves, takes advantage not only of the truck driver but of Samoan-Christian ideals, which are taken for a ride. Thus, in the person of the transvestite informal discourse offers a deconstruction of cultural concepts, a deconstruction that is turned upon the remains of colonial ideals.

Taking a moment to tie threads together, one might say that, when the colonial encounter compromised girls' role in informal discourse Samoan style, it was a loss both to themselves and to their culture. Not only did girls' muting compromise their own hereditary freedoms and avenues toward achievement, their cultural consociates had relied upon them as leaders of jest in Joking Nights and other entertainments. In these venues informal discourse co-opted the intense desire for dominance created by Samoan socialization, which contributed to social fission—fights, wars, and so forth. Doing "the work of culture," girls and their Joking Nights turned these counterreactions into a basis for alliance. This is not to say that girls participated in informal discourse because it was socially useful. Why girls were so motivated is a question we have already take up; my point here is that this discourse had a pivotal place in the Samoan self system, and so the loss of its star performers was likely to be felt by others and to fissure Samoan social life. This fissuring opened the way for the intrusion of imported discourses with radical implications for the manner in which Samoans talked and thought about sexuality, gender, and the self and led to changes in the gender ascriptions of indigenous discourses on self.

In entertainments these intrusions became the subject of a reconfigured informal discourse; they were framed with ironic quotation marks made through the intercalation of contradicting opposites, quotation marks that were a constitutive part of hereditary informal discourse in Samoa. While much about informal discourse changed with changing times, its symbolic grammar remained the same.

If boys took over girls' roles as specialists in the informal discourse of entertainments, memory of the older gender marking of this discourse remained. Informal discourse still showed traces of being girls' specialty, but the girls themselves acquired quotation marks. In colonial Samoa Joking Night girls were replaced by the thespian girls of Spirit House; in postcolonial Samoa transvestite girls assumed their mantle by playing the role of stand-up comics. The latter came to be both proponents and emblems of informal discourse and to star in those entertainments in which this discourse was employed to think through the implications of culture change and to dismantle colonial ideals.

Much of the rewriting of informal discourse and of gender surveyed in this chapter was authored by those who were, at least anatomically, males. But what of girls themselves? Were they content with the occasional *siva* and with the vicarious satisfactions offered by transvestite companions and transvestite performances? We will see in the coming chapter that girls were as busy as their colonial and postcolonial doubles rewriting Samoan informal discourse and their own genders with it.

11

Lives and Reconfiguring Strategic Discourse

Let us begin this final chapter with a backward glance. All along I have argued that in every society there is a dominant sense of self that emphasizes some element of our common humanity to the exclusion of another. Normally consigned to the background of the psyche, this discarded element remains—relative to other virtues and capacities—in a state of nature. When it does emerge in behavior, it retains a wild appearance, validating the social perception that it is intrinsically uncouth and deserving of suppression. What follows is an inevitable lopsidedness. In the course of development, however, the excluded element is gradually introduced into a moral framework and then supplied with contexts in which it can be exercised. Finally, the excluded element is integrated in strategic approaches to daily life. This progression, I have argued, is requisite cross-culturally to becoming a fully realized human being. Yet attributions may impede development through the series for some culture members. These groups lack access to the full scope of their own talents, which may be associated with elements of self that they are expected to eschew.

In Samoa the dominant sense of self is social, and, therefore, people identify with social personas, or roles. This focus tends to exclude the subjective dimension of experience. Because this dimension is not the object of conscious consideration, it is apt to remain uncultivated and becomes symbolic of unsocialized human nature. As such, subjectivity is a topic of moral reasoning in Samoa, reasoning that condemns various forms of individualistic assertion. Assertive behavior is, however, also given social place in administering the group and in forwarding the group's status vis-à-vis other groups. Eventually, assertiveness comes into its own as people learn to politick, adopting a social persona to assert a set of personal interests.

As in many other places, the Samoan self system changed with missionization and colonization. Samoan girls came to be confined to a moral discourse. What this meant was that, to a degree, girls lacked contexts in which to exercise assertiveness. I stress the proviso "to a degree" because girls still administered younger siblings and participated in certain competitions, for example, athletic competitions between villages and later, in more urban areas, beauty competitions. But the pre-Christian Samoan project of furthering family status by bearing a child of status had given girls a broader band of opportunities for assertiveness and for achievement. Christian girls came to sustain their family honor through a demeanor that was, in many respects, passive and unassertive. The mantle of dignity they were supposed to wear in lieu of the decorations of an earlier age was problematical for them, as twentieth-century possession episodes demonstrate. Girls in these episodes dramatized a conflict between a Samoan-Christian conscience that demanded consistent dignity and restraint and a more assertive and sexual dimension of their being affiliated with showing off and luring behaviors, which once had been the rule at entertainments.

This final chapter is about one of my Samoan sisters-in-law, who I will call Eseta (Easter), and Seta for short. By rewriting discourses on self and her gender role with them, Seta offers a solution to the problem that Samoan Christianity poses to the achievement of a powerful form of identity for girls. Appropriately, Seta's tale begins with a possession story. I was collecting possession stories at the time. Sanele told me a possession story about Seta, and I wanted to get it from Seta herself. Possession, however, is not the end but the beginning of Seta's tale. Her story is also that of the Samoan *teine* (girl) becoming thoroughly self-possessed through a reappropriation of voice from the realm of spirits.

There is a progression in Seta's tale and one that retraces the developmental sequence that, I argue, characterizes discourse on self in childhood. Seta begins by rewriting moral discourse but goes on to rewrite contextual discourses and, finally, in the events that following the interview, begins to employ discourses strategically. Seta's personal development suggests that change in adulthood follows a course resembling that of childhood development. This is obviously my interpretation, but it should be added that I had not yet hit upon my theory of the self when I conducted this interview with Seta in the summer of 1990.

A word about Seta's rewriting process is a necessary preface to the following analysis. We have seen throughout this text that discourses on self build upon, and sometimes transcend, binary pairs of cultural concepts, in Samoa pairs like social personas (*aga*) and subjective experience (*loto*), or respect and cheekiness, or hierarchical and peer relations. Seta, rewriting cultural discourses on self, is really rewriting this paired series, along with those additional concepts that colonialization and Christianizing superscribed on it. Seta rewrites, at least initially, through narrative. I view the narrative as a relational mode of thought: that is, a mode in which characters embody elements of a binary set and in which problematic interactions constitute intellectual queries about the relations between the members of this set. Such queries are addressed through the substitution of new characters. Each new character is symbolically identified with one character from an original interaction but is also representative of a larger idea ensemble, bringing this ensemble to bear on the query at issue.[1] We will soon see that by virtue of a reorchestration of the original set in terms of this ensemble, characters reverse themselves: a character who signified one side of a conceptual pair comes to signify the other side. The cultural categories that these characters represent are thereby deconstructed, reshuffled, and rewritten.

As to Seta's background, her mother gave birth to fifteen children, adopted four, giving four of her own in adoption. Seta's father had many talents and several vocations, the most important of which was that of a Catholic catechist. The priestlike role of the catechist has been a way for the Catholic Church to accommodate an unwillingness among many Samoans to renounce sexuality, marriage, and children. Seta has no children of her own but adopted several. She has recently become a catechist, and her husband has followed her in this vocation. Seta knew that I was interviewing her with a view to publishing the results; she had corrected Samoan spellings and contributed accounts of spirit possession to previous articles. Several of the possession stories that I recounted in chapter 9 derive from her reports. The tape recorder sat practically in her lap on the floor before her; from time to time I would readjust its position to better catch her voice and to make sure she realized what we were doing. Nonetheless, I know the situation made Seta unwittingly vulnerable, not only to me but also to herself, and it is only one of her many selves that took possession of Seta that day, one evoked spiritlike by the circumstances surrounding the conversation and by the particular alchemy of our personalities.

Seta's story consists of episodes from her personal history, related in one long, continuous interview, delivered in English, and in certain events following that interview related to me by Sanele in which Seta was the star performer. The story is complex; to clarify it I treat its various vignettes as the scenes of a play. Rather than burdening the reader with remembering Seta's entire story, I intersperse my analytic commentary between the scenes. Because Samoan families are large, talking about them involves many characters, which can be confusing. To address this difficulty I begin by providing a cast of characters, giving nicknames as Samoans are wont to do.[2]

Running Order

Act 1: Seta's Interview

Scene 1	Grandmother Possession
Scene 2	Father Ifi
Scene 3	Burning Ifi
Scene 4	The Healer
Scene 5	Grandfather Spirit

Act 2: Events

Scene 1   Family Meeting
Scene 2   The Curse

Characters

Eseta (Easter), Seta
Ta'avao (Roam-in-the-Bush), Vao   Eseta's mother
Ifilele (Tree), Ifi   Eseta's father
Sanele (Chanel)   Eseta's brother
Samuelu (Samuel)   Eseta's brother
Manulele (Bird)   Eseta's brother
Lima (Five)   Eseta's brother
Kapilieli (Gabrielle)   Eseta's brother
Talo (Taro), Kalo   Eseta's brother
Mose (Moses)   Eseta's brother
Eleni (Canned Fish)   Eseta's brother
Talosia (Pray), Sia   Eseta's sister
Fe'e (Octopus)   Eseta's sister
Sina (Silvery White)   Fe'e daughter, Vao's adopted daughter and, therefore, Eseta's sister
Tutu 'Āiga (Light-of-the-Family)   Eseta's uncle, a title name
Tutu 'Āiga   Eseta's deceased grandfather, a title name
Tama'i (Small)   Vao's son and Eseta's adopted son
Taunofo (Trying-to-Sit-Down), Nofo   Kapilieli's wife
Ifilele (Tree), Ifi   Kapilieli's son
Mataalofa (Helpful), Fa   Sia's daughter
Semisi (Siamese)   Sia's son
Temete (Demeter), Meke   Sina's baby, named after my dissertation
Vaeleaga (Hurt Foot), Vae   Seta's husband

■ ■ ■

Act 1, Scene 1: Grandmother Possession

Seta: Maybe [it was] when I was 13 . . . that was the time I was attending high school. . . . Well actually I don't think I know much about it. I know I was lying there. . . . I think she [Seta's mother, Vao] was scolding me. . . . I was so scared. . . . I was inside the Samoan fale [house] and . . . I was just staring out.

. . . They [her siblings] couldn't tell if it was my voice . . . and I was giving them the different answers. . . . She [Vao] said . . . when I was back again . . . it was her mother. . . . [I] was telling about things that were happening long ago. . . . It was really my grandmother that was talking out.

My mom was scolding me while I was outside . . . picking rubbish . . . and then she said I was just blanked out . . . the next thing, I was in the middle of the house. . . . She [the grandmother] was really telling my mother not to treat us like that. . . . She [Vao] gets angry . . . usually pulls our hair and gives us spanks. [Sanele was never hit by his mother and only once by his father.]

To me, I didn't think it was *Ma'i Aitu* [spirit possession] . . . but to them, they said . . . my grandma was really in me and talking about those things my mom . . . has to do. . . . They only splashed water on me when I fainted. . . . The only thing I remember was . . . I was all wet. . . . She [Vao] must have smacked me . . . with something that really hurt me. [Sanele recalls Seta was talking to a fruit tree. His brother, Samuelu, and his sister, Sia, boiled water to splash on her head].

My mom . . . really tells us what to do. . . . Even if you don't know where you put your hair ribbons, the only thing she has to do is cut your hair. [Sanele says Seta had beautiful hair, reaching down to her knees].

For example, 'cause every day you go to school [we] have to plait our hair in two . . . on Monday you have to wear white ribbons, on Tuesday blue ribbons, Wednesday white ribbons . . . cause we have long hair, me and Fe'e [one of Seta's younger sisters]. So during those days, when you come back on Monday, you have to put your blue ribbon or your white ribbon so that you'll be able to get it on Wednesday. . . . Some days we might forget where we put the ribbon or we put it in a misplace . . . or else somebody must have grabbed it . . . one of my brothers . . . and then in the morning my mom was going to plait our hair . . . she just got the scissors and cut it short 'cause we just couldn't find the ribbon. . . . And she's always like that, cause she wants us to do this and do this and do this.

Commentary

This opening scene begins to problematize the binary terms of the Samoan moral lexicon in childhood—respect (*fa'aaloalo*) and cheekiness (*tautalaitiiti*)—in which the younger person personifies the violation of respect and the older person personifies the rule of respect. Seta tells us that throughout her childhood her mother, Vao, treated her as if she were cheeky, scolding her angrily, pulling her hair, spanking her, and so forth. In "Grandmother Possession" the deceased grandmother takes Seta's place in opposition to Vao, thereby reversing the Seta/Vao relation: here it is Vao who has displeased her own mother and is, by implication, cheeky.

Inasmuch as the incident occurs while Seta was carrying out Vao's orders, gathering rubbish, the issue between them is hierarchical respect. Seta, however, dates the episode to her thirteenth year, that is, to the beginning of puberty, intimating that puberty and, hence, sexuality may also be at issue. This intimation is confirmed by the questionable nature of Seta's dating: she was possessed by her deceased grandmother, but her grandmother's death occurred when Seta was seventeen. Further, Sanele recollects Seta being possessed, and he is eleven years her junior. He believes Seta's possession occurred a year after the grandmother's death, which would have made her eighteen.

Seta expands upon this sexual subtext by telling us that Vao cut her daughters' hair because Seta could not find the ribbons used to bind their plaits. Here plaiting hair is analogous to binding hair in a bun or shaving heads or cutting off the girl's hair when she is caught in a sexual indiscretion. All are symbolic methods of exercising control over the girl's erotic potential. The ribbons used to bind the plaits signify control; losing them signifies a loosening. Again, a lack of hierarchical respect (not producing the hair ribbons when told to do so) seems to be the issue; however, the symbolic character of Seta's punishment suggests that her crime really had to do with keeping her erotic side in bounds, that is, with sexual respect. In scene 2, as Seta muses on why "my mom was always harsh on me," this subtextual scenario takes on more depth.

■ ■ ■

Act 1, Scene 2: Father Ifi

Seta: It must have been because my father . . . was always drunk. . . . He was out of the family for a couple of days. . . . Maybe because I was the elder of the girls . . . when they . . . quarreled . . . it was only me and my dad, he just had to grab [me] and we go and stay somewhere else for a week or two weeks. . . . Twice I remember . . . we left, only my dad and myself, and went and stayed with my dad's family at Vaiala. . . . We left Vao and all the other kids. . . . I always get . . . the *sasa* [hit] during those times. . . . Must of been she was tied up with all of this. . . .³

I remember, when we were young . . . we were all treated equally by my dad. . . . When . . . on Saturday he . . . posted a list, and you just have to look at the list. [Chores were assigned equitably every day to each child old enough to work.] In those times the family . . . we have been working together and . . . we never quarrel . . . we are all cooperating in our work, but then . . . I was going to high school and . . . some of them [Seta's siblings] . . . were transferred here to American Samoa and . . . Fe'e was picked by my mom and I was really the one who was tied down on all our family affairs. . . .⁴

Telling you the truth . . . before my dad died . . . all my life was dedicated onto my dad and . . . when he died that really put me back and that's what I been telling most of the people . . . I always say to them, I really don't love my mom. . . . Then I tried to ease it out . . . it was only three or four years . . . that I was getting along with my mom until she died. . . .

Telling the truth . . . when my dad was alive, I always don't think twice of my mom . . . .[After his death] we have to spend times together . . . and I have to tell her. . . . My mom seems to have ideas that today she would say you're good, tomorrow that you are bad. Or today, she would say the other one is good, next time or in fifteen or twenty minutes . . . she been turning all around. I don't have that in me. . . . I always have to face straight and say straight to what she was saying and maybe that is why . . . she doesn't like what I been telling her . . . but it seems she really turned to what I have been telling her. . . . That's why she has been spending most of her time before she died with me in Western Samoa.

Commentary

Seta, the little girl whose hair is pulled and cut and who is made to pick up rubbish while others play, is a Cinderella.[5] Seta paints Vao as the familiar figure of the wicked stepmother. In his analysis of Cinderella, Bettelheim explicates wicked stepmothers through Melanie Klein's idea that the girl splits the image of her mother in two (1976:236–76). The "good" mother is a memory of the preoedipal mother and a projection of the love the child experienced toward her. The "bad" mother, who appears like a wicked stepmother and who places restrictions and demands upon the child, is a projected form of the daughter's oedipal jealousy and of her resentment at losing the indulgences of infancy. Cinderella's name, tasks, and habit of sleeping by the hearth (in the cinders) associates her with dirt, a metaphor for "dirty" oedipal feelings.

Seta's story begins with picking up rubbish and the strength of Seta's attachment to Ifi is oedipal: Seta reflects that Ifi's drinking tied her to him and excluded Vao and says, "all my life was dedicated onto my dad." We saw in chapter 9 that an increasing cloistering within the family over the course of this century because of Samoan-Christian values channeled girls' emotion into nuclear family relations, making girls more oedipal in orientation.

Seta begins by reiterating the binary terms of the Samoan moral lexicon—which in its childhood version opposes cheekiness to respect—but uses the Cinderella motif to annul its personal significance. All along Seta makes a narrative claim that the negative term of this moral set does not apply to her. Vao is made the guilty party in regard to hierarchical respect; she has failed to respect Seta's grandmother. Ifi is made the guilty party in regard to sexual respect; he has favored Seta inappropriately. These relations cast doubt on the justice of the Samoan moral lexicon and raise a larger question about the meaning of respect, the regent moral idea of the Samoan cultural universe. The rest of Seta's narrative will pursue this question, a pursuit Seta begins through the figure of Ifi.

In "Grandmother Possession" a spirit attested to Seta's innocence; however, Seta's innocence was merely negative: her spirit grandmother's actions implied that Seta was *not* cheeky and that Vao's action were, therefore, unjustified. In "Father Ifi" Ifi assumes the role of the spirit grandmother in the previous scene by taking her place in contrast to Vao. Seta was identified with her grandmother through possession; she identifies with Ifi by being *saʻo*, "straight." Ifi tells the truth and is fair, as is evident in his distribution of tasks to children; Seta "always has to face straight." Ifi is also *saʻo* by virtue of his role as a catechist, what Seta studies to become. In contrast, Vao is portrayed as "turning all around." Thus, in the figure of Ifi Seta's innocence, a moral negative, becomes positive.

Remember, the high chief is said to be *saʻo*. The orator serves the high chief primarily by speaking for him. In this office he is famous for his clever arguments, which are often circuitous; one might call them "turning all around"; Samoans call them *kuluku*, "crooked," a term that refers to something circuitous but that is also morally shady. By calling Ifi *saʻo* and saying that Vao is turning all around, Seta evokes the high chief/orator set and uses it to characterize the Ifi/Vao relationship.[6] She thereby offers a new lexicon to replace respect/cheekiness: it is as if she were saying that what respect really means is *saʻo*—being straight or true—and that the real opposite of respect is not cheekiness but *kuluku*. Here Seta is evoking Christian probity in the figure of her catechist father to rewrite Samoan moral discourse, as will become obvious in the next scene, in which Seta tells the story of a second Ifi, the son of her brother Kapilieli, named after her father.

■ ■ ■

Act 1, Scene 3: Burning Ifi

Seta: Kapilieli and Nofo [his wife] was up at the [catechism] college. . . . She [Vao] was angry with Kapilieli and Nofo . . . before . . . young Ifi got his hand burnt. . . . She [Vao] called me and said Kapilieli is not calling her "mother" anymore and so I said to her "Why?" . . . I said to her to talk that over. . . . She thought no, Kapilieli is not to be called her son anymore. . . . But it's only two weeks that Kapilieli and Nofo come back to Western Samoa, Ifi had a burnt hand. . . . She said she knew Ifi was going to have something wrong with him and so we talk it over . . . that was the day we solve all the problems.

Jeannette: What happened to young Ifi?

Seta: The electric kettle was being left on the back of the house [stoop]. . . . The kettle lid was open . . . so Ifi just crawled there. . . . It must have been the silver of the kettle . . . he just put his hand happily to it . . . he was burned all down his body. . . . It must have been a punishment to Kapilieli because of what he was saying to Vao.

Jeannette: Would it have been all right if Vao had forgiven Kapilieli?

Seta: That's what I was thinking because when I talked to her . . . she knew there would be something happening to Ifi. . . . It seems Ifi at that time was the only boy [Kapilieli's only son] . . . or else maybe . . . because Ifi looks like

Kapilieli. . . . I could easily tell out that if only she would let it go, her anger . . . there wouldn't have been anything happening to Ifi.

Jeannette: Was the accident like a curse?

Seta: That what I was thinking of . . . it's good he [young Ifi] was still alive because if it's a curse, then he would die of it. . . . I never answered back, when she talks to me . . . when she hits me, or whatever she does to me. . . . I never say a word back to her. [Seta says that several of her siblings incurred spirit injuries for answering their parents back. Kapilieli's son, however, sustains the only lasting injury. Seta then speaks of her father's service to his own family and Vao's family. She paints Ifi to me as the soul of respect, I suspect, to absolve him of these spirit associations. I draw her back to Vao and suggest to Seta that, although she never actually talked back to her mother, her persona (the gentle, dutiful Samoan daughter) was like a reproach. It was as if she were telling Vao the sort of women—straight, as Seta says of herself, rather than turning all around—Vao should have been].

Seta: I think so . . . to me [it] was really hard to say "Mom you're wrong." . . .That was what I was doing a few weeks before she died.

Commentary

If *saʻo* is Christian by implication, turning all around is heathen; appropriately, we now discover Vao has heathen powers. Although I have changed the names of Seta's father and nephew, in reality they share the same name. Inasmuch as this boy shares his name with Seta's father, and inasmuch as the boy is injured because of Vao's anger at a father, there is a textual identification between the two Ifi. This identification suggests that Ifi Junior is a stand-in for Ifi Senior. Seta has already identified with Ifi Senior; therefore, by standing in for Ifi Senior, Ifi Junior stands in for Seta as well.

As Vao originally punished Seta, now she punishes Ifi. As Seta was innocent, so is Ifi Junior. This punitive relationship, however, has undergone reversal: in the Seta/Vao dyad a grandmother spirit protected Seta; here the spirits appear to have taken the other side, carrying out Vao's curse. Curses are efficacious because of the cursor's *mana; mana* works through the agency of spirits. A similar reversal has taken place even with the props through which the events are played out. Both Seta and Sanele remember that boiling water was splashed on Seta as a cure when she was possessed by her grandmother. Pouring boiling water on the graves is a traditional method of getting disturbing ghosts to rest. In "Burning Ifi" boiling water becomes the medium of the curse.

Samoans typically ascribe *mana,* "spirit power," to the high chief and *pule,* "civic authority," to the orator (Shore 1977, 1982). In Seta's portrait of Ifi and Vao the husband is high chief–like and the wife is orator–like, yet Seta does not attribute spirit power to the husband and civic authority to the wife. Rather, she attributes different kinds of "spiritual" power to each: Ifi models Christian spirituality; Vao has *mana.*[7]

As Seta is the protagonist of her tale, she represents its moral problematic: How can a Samoan-Christian girl personify both respect and assertion/achievement? In "Grandmother Possession" we learn that, prior to the first scene, Vao accused Seta of enacting the antinomy of respect, that is, of being cheeky. Because of this retrospective tarnish, respect was represented for Seta by surrogates who stood in for her in opposition to Vao. In "Grandmother Possession" the spirit grandmother stands in for Seta, defending her innocence. In "Father Ifi," Ifi Senior stands in for Seta, defining this innocence as *sa'o*. Now Ifi Junior embodies Seta's innocence, but here innocence appears to be a lack of awareness, happily putting one's hand in a kettle of boiling water. The replacement of Ifi Senior by the figure of a victimized child also hints that innocence can be affiliated with powerlessness, a hint more loudly insinuated in the next scene, "The Healer."

■ ■ ■

Act 1, Scene 4: The Healer

Seta goes on to recount a recent illness. She had come over to American Samoa to consult a Western physician. Her mother took her to a *fofō*, a Samoan healer working in message and herbal treatment. Despite the fact Seta felt the *fofō* was making her worse, when her mother asked Seta how she was feeling, Seta replied *"Feololo,"* "All right." I remark that, whatever Vao's liabilities, she was good at standing up for herself, and I tell Seta that Sanele and I worry she will not stand up for herself and will not, therefore, get respect.

Seta turns to the subject of Vao's recent funeral. Her brothers planned the funeral without consulting her, which Seta attributes to three factors.

First, she was with Vao during Vao's last hours. Seta's implication here is that she was privy to Vao's *māvaega*. A *māvaega* is the will of a parent expressed during his or her last days, or at any time, that concerns the disposal of the person's body, titles, or property. In a society that relies upon oral traditions a final will is tantamount to the last wishes expressed by the dying person. Being present at the bedside of a dying relative, therefore, has legal implications. Seta believes that Vao's last wishes were at odds with those of Seta's brothers. Seta says Vao did not want to be buried in American Samoa with her husbands' family, where she is currently buried, but back in Western Samoa with Vao's own family.

Second, Seta believes she was left out because she is going to catechist school and, therefore, has no money. Seta says what is important spiritually is not wealth but doing what Vao wants.

Third, Seta thinks her siblings avoided discussing the funeral with both her and Sanele because she and he are honest and forthright, *sa'o:* "when we put something up we just have to straighten up, cause we never go around the bush. We just have to go straight."

Commentary

In "Burning Ifi," contemplating Ifi Junior's injury, Seta says she "never answered back." In "The Healer" this passive innocence is replaced by active deference. In her attempt to respect Vao, Seta is deference itself, accepting treatment from a Samoan healer (*fofō*) when she wants to go to a Western physician and telling Vao she is "*Feololo*" (Okay), because she thinks this is what Vao wants to hear. Seta is effectively silent: she cannot tell Vao how she really feels. We saw in previous chapters that, historically, orators made a composite of respect and indirection, thereby effectively manipulating high chiefs. By virtue of a strategic approach to the high chief, orators were reputed to "speak out plainly to those above them . . . saying very unpalatable things" (Stair 1897:70). In contrast, Seta's combination of respect and indirection equals the lack of a voice of her own.

By her misleading reticence, Seta reverses the moral opposition she formerly constructed between Vao and Ifi Senior and the moral equation she made between respect and probity. Previously, Seta painted Ifi as straight and as respectful; in contrast, Vao was portrayed as turning all around. Now it appears that for Seta to give respect to Vao requires a degree of prevarication. Although Seta is still identified with the Ifi pole of the Ifi/Vao opposition, she has begun to borrow meanings from the other pole to portray herself; in turn, Vao's pole has begun to change.

Fofō actually means "to massage" but has become a synonym for traditional Samoan medicine. Sometimes a *fofō* will specialize in Spirit Sickness; however, even *fofō* who specialize in physical ailments are often thought to be friends to spirits. Once I sought the help of a *fofō* who specialized in liver ailments. One day Sanele and I arrived at her house, and she was not there, but another client was, a woman who said that she was afraid of the *fofō* and insinuated that the *fofō* had commerce with spirits. In fact, this was Vao's personal *fofō* and probably the healer to whom she had referred Seta.

The figure of the *fofō* symbolizes Vao's spirit power. In "Father Ifi" Vao's *kuluku* tendencies—contrasted to Ifi's Christian probity and fairness—signified her heathenness. In "Burning Ifi" heathenness takes on a more positive, or at least more powerful, form as *mana*. In "The Healer" Vao's *mana*, as personified by the *fofō*, suffers "spiritualization." While this power begins in "Burning Ifi" as a power to curse, in the person of the *fofō* it is, potentially, a power to heal. The ancient Polynesian concept of *mana* was manifest in fertility, in the ability to command spirits, and in healing. Healing is one of the few situations in which the word *mana* is still used. What Seta finds in the *fofō*, or in Vao-as-*fofō*, however, is only the specter of healing power, for Seta grows worse. Thus, in "The Healer" both Vao and Seta are characterized by different forms of powerlessness and—in their ineffectuality—resemble each other. In drawing this implicit narrative comparison between herself and Vao, Seta begins to deconstruct the poles of the moral opposition she originally paints between cheekiness and respect and, secondarily, between turning all around and *saʻo* (straightforwardness, fairness, probity). In "The Healer" Vao's pole becomes less negative and Seta's pole less positive.

"The Healer" articulates yet another cultural opposition—this one between Samoan medicine and Western medicine—representing a larger opposition between local and foreign custom. Seta identifies with the Western side (she wants Western treatment) and identifies Vao with the Samoan side (who offers a *fofō*). Through this identification Seta symbolically sheds her former lack of awareness, embodied by Ifi Junior: Seta's preference for Western medicine associates her with foreign knowledge, an association she will expand as her tale progresses.

In Seta's monologue there is an implied parallelism between the full sequence of opposition we have so far encountered—*saʻo:kuluku*::Christian:heathen::Western:local. As Ifi and Seta are *saʻo*, Vao is *kuluku*; as Ifi and Seta have Christian power, Vao has spirit power; and, last, while Seta prefers Western physicians, Vao prefers Samoan *fofō*. This series presents a rather surprising ensemble of correlations that can be summarized as follows. As *saʻo* (read respect) is to Christianity and to foreign custom generally, so *kuluku* (read an inversion of respect) is to the heathen and to Samoan custom generally. The last in this series of oppositions (local/foreign), however, portends a collapse of the entire series. While a Samoan girl brought up under circumstances of missionization might identify with probity and Christianity and reject the dissimulative and the heathen, no Samoan could but be ambivalent about rejecting Samoan custom in preference for the foreign, even if, as I have argued throughout, Samoan girls carry a symbolic weight of foreign ideas.

Building on Thomas's work, I suggested earlier that in Samoa "the heathen" is a sign for ineffaceably local elements in cultural identity. The Samoan medicine/foreign medicine dyad might be seen as a rephrased and softened version of the heathen/Christian dichotomy, through which Seta has characterized her relation to Vao in earlier scenes. Here Vao-as-ancestress still represents a highly problematical "tradition" but one with good maternal intentions, unlike the intentions underlying Vao's heathen powers in "Burning Ifi."

In the process of missionization girls' lost voices were linked with heathen practices, most particularly bawdy joking at Joking Nights. If girls lost their voices because of an association of these voices with heathenness, then, in order to redeem her voice, Seta must redeem the heathen. "The Healer" represents a recognition of this need in an idiom of healing. In Samoan medicine it is said that the gift of healing is a kind of *mana* that the daughter receives from her mother (Macpherson and Macpherson 1990:108). Thus, inasmuch as the *fofō* stands in for Vao, "The Healer" presages a passage of Vao's *mana* to her daughter, Seta, and with it a deconstruction of the moral dichotomy between the Christian and the heathen. This passage is again intimated in Vao's final words, the *māvaega*.

The word *māvaega* refers to a person's last will but also to the last ordinances of a chief or other authority figure, which include appointing a successor (Krämer [1902] 1942, vol. 2: 118; Hjarnø 1979–80:93). Vao's choice of Seta for her final words confers moral authority on Seta. But, as the *fofō* had only the specter of *mana* (she failed to heal), now Seta has only a specter of authority, for Seta's brothers ignore her in the matter of Vao's funeral. Thus, the powerlessness Seta implicitly shared with Vao-as-*fofō* becomes explicit in the form of voicelessness: the decision reached by the brothers about Vao's burial is opposed to Vao's and Seta's wishes, but neither has a voice in the matter. Remember, however, that violating a mother's wishes, just as those of sisters, is reputed to have supernatural consequences for sons and brothers. The spirits of old Samoa, the vehicles of *mana*, are said to visit degenerative illness and death on impious males and their descendants. Thus, there is a subtextual suggestion that the *māvaega* (Vao's final words) is both a form of Christian moral authority and of spirit power, again portending a collapse of the dichotomy between Christian morality and heathenness.

Seta's story began with a moral dichotomy between respect and cheekiness, and Seta's problem vis-à-vis her brothers is still one of respect. Respect, however, has metamorphosed: it now seems to be wedded to questions of authority, voice, and achievement; it is no longer solely moral in nature. Seta says her brothers ignore her, at least in part because she has no money or position. Seta apparently allows herself to be ignored. Although she obviously resents the brothers' decision, she reports no argument between herself and them about where Vao shall rest, either before or after the burial. Seta seems trapped in the cultural expectation that she act like a Samoan-Christian sister, manifesting those qualities she has displayed throughout her story—piety, dignity, and restraint—which Samoans associate with formal contexts and which, since the advent of Samoan Christianity, they tend to attribute to sisters. She inhibits her own need to be assertive or competitive, qualities associated with informal contexts and attributed to brothers. The logical solution is to rewrite contextual discourses, which Seta does in the next scene.

■ ■ ■

Act 1, Scene 5: The Grandfather Spirit

Seta now begins telling me about an incident when she was a child in Fagaloa. Fagaloa is a vast, recessed, mountain-ringed bay, around the shore of which are many villages. In ancient Samoa long-distance transportation was most often by sea. The bay of Fagaloa is, therefore, charged with legends of grand precontact historical dramas, but now, being far from Apia and accessible only by poor roads, it has become remote.

During the schoolyear Vao's children lived in Apia, but during the holidays they would go to Fagaloa, to the small village where Vao's family lived. There her brother held an important family title; let us call it the Tutu 'Āiga title. Sanele has glorious memories of these days, of floating coconuts harvested in their plantation down the rim of the bay to their home by the beach in the lingering afternoons, of lantern light dotting the distant margins of the bay in the falling darkness, and of falling asleep to his waggish grandmother's sometimes intentionally disgusting, always funny, bedtime stories. Seta's memories are not so glorious.

Over the May holidays most Fagaloa children went to a school session on Samoan culture given by the local Protestant ministers. Vao and her brother Tutu forbade the family children to attend because they were Catholic. At the end of the school session children sat for an exam, followed by a day of celebration, with awards and prizes for the winners. Sanele says Seta was a very smart girl, who always did extraordinarily well at exams. It ran in the family. Ifi Senior's brother, a priest, had studied at Harvard, sponsored by the church.

The family boys were sent to gather wood in the direction of the celebration and would pass by on their way. Seta was sent to weed her grandfather's grave, which she did crying, because she would not see who won the prizes. Later she was sent up into the mountains to get pure drinking water for the cooking, two large buckets hung on a pole across her shoulders. Not far from the house she had to climb a stone fence. After getting the water, she noticed an old man behind her, calling to her.

> "Hey, where are you taking that water."
> "To Tutu's house to make food," Seta replies.
> "I could help you."

The old man takes the freighted pole and walks behind Seta. I think this circumstance odd because, in Samoa, children serve older people and walk behind them, not vice versa. Evidently, Seta is too carried away by her disappointment to notice the unconventional nature of the situation.

> Seta asks "Where are you going?"
> "To the prize giving," he says.
> "Do you have any sons or daughters attending the prize giving?" she asks.
> "Two" he answers.
> "My mom said no one of us should go. I really want to go to see whose getting the prizes."

Seta tells the old man that Tutu 'Āiga (calling her uncle by his title) will not let her go and "is very bad." She says Tutu and Vao "make bad rules for children."

Seta and the old man arrive at the stone fence. He tells her to walk around to a break in the fence instead of trying to climb over. Seta turns around to take back the water buckets and to thank the man. It occurs to her that, although her village is composed of only two extended families, "you look at his face and couldn't tell who that person is," but his voice is familiar.[8] Later she describes the old man to her brothers, and none of them have ever seen such a person in the village. One brother tells me that, at the time, Seta told him the old man had disappeared after helping her. After Seta describes the man, Vao says he is Seta's deceased grandfather, Tutu, the previous holder of the Tutu 'Āiga title, whose grave Seta had been weeding.

Seta then tells me that, when she attended school at Momoa, she was the most "talented student in the whole school," although she says she never studied. Seta received a scholarship to go to nursing school in New Zealand. Sanele says she had one of the top scores on the scholarship exam. According to Seta, her father stopped her from going. She got stomach aches and would faint at the sight of blood. Seta says the scholarship committee interviewed her father, and he told them that, because of Seta's reaction to blood, going to nursing school was not a good idea. Seta says she told Ifi she might get used to the sight of blood, but really Ifi did not want her to go so far away. In Sanele's recollection Vao was angry because Seta got married instead of going for her scholarship, and Ifi grumbled about it.

Commentary

From contact until well into the twentieth century Samoan schools were mission schools, usually set up either in the local church or in the home of the preacher (Huebner 1986:399). Eventually, government schools were instituted, separating schooling and religion somewhat, although various churches also opened primary and secondary schools and, in the villages, continued to teach children the Bible and religion generally.

Today the holiday White Sunday helps to carry on the custom of biblical education for children. Samoans compare it to Christmas because White Sunday is children's day: most children get new white clothes, and, while Samoan children normally serve their elders food, on White Sunday parents serve their children. The family goes to church and youngsters, rather than sitting quietly as usual, give memorized speeches out of the Bible while their elders listen. These speeches may be elaborated into little plays.

White Sunday is an early archetype for schooling in the experience of children. Like White Sunday performances, school tends to be conceived of as a project in memorization, imitatively duplicating a text either in oral or in written form.[9] As parents and other relatives attend White Sunday performances, so also they attend school award ceremonies as well as graduations and like events, to applaud their child's accomplishments. In this regard, as unlikely as it seems, White Sunday performances resemble traditional entertainments. In describing nighttime dancing in the 1920s, Mead says:

> In the case of small children . . . [audience participation] consists of an endless stream of good-natured comments. . . . In the dancing of the more expert boys and girls the group takes part by a steady murmur of "Thank

you, thank you, for your dancing!" "Beautiful!" "Engaging!" "Charming!" "Bravo!" which gives very much the effect of the irregular stream of "Amens" at an evangelistic revival. ([1928] 1961:112)

Formerly at Joking Nights, now on White Sunday and at school award ceremonies, Samoans suspend strictures against exhibitionism normally applied to young people; youngsters are lauded for their performances and gain social recognition.[10] In Samoan categories, therefore, school is an informal context in which competitiveness and assertiveness are apposite.[11] This is why Seta's description of school resembles an entertainment for which, Seta says, she does not need to "work." In contrast, *feau,* those tasks normally assigned to youngsters in the Samoan household, are not associated with recognition. Parents believe that to praise the performance of these tasks is to spoil children (Sutter 1980). Further, for Seta to be denied the opportunity to go to school is tantamount to restriction to formal contexts—necessitating dutifulness and deferentially all the time—even when brothers are allowed greater freedom.

If Seta's memories picture delimiting circumstances, they also reveal another of Seta's selves that counterpoints the Seta one meets in "The Healer." Rather than deferentially disguising her feelings, this Seta is straightforward in her emotions and has a voice of her own. Seta meets an old man, who Vao later says is the most august of Seta's known ancestors, the deceased and titled grandfather Tutu. Seta tells him exactly what she thinks: her living and titled uncle Tutu "is very bad" and that he and Vao "make bad rules for children." This old man counterpoints her living guardians: while they burden Seta with chores, he helps Seta with her burdens. While they order, he listens and is gently concerned about Seta's well-being. Further, he is a parent who lets his children sit for exams and who gives them his support by attending the awards ceremony. The episode itself serves as a substitute for the missed awards ceremony.

For the first time Seta actively enters into a relationship with a spirit, not only in the sense that she befriends the old man but also by crying on his grave before he appears. Praying on graves is a pre-Christian technique for evoking the aid of spirits (Turner [1884] 1984:151). By her wordless but moving invocation at Tutu's graveside, Seta claims her own *mana,* the *mana* implicitly conveyed by Vao's *māvaega.* Thus, the poles of the former dichotomy between Christian and heathen continue their collapse. Remember that heathenness was a sign of Samoan difference in the context of missionization. Here missionaries' intellectual descendants, Protestant ministers, are teaching Samoan culture classes, and Samoans' spiritual ancestors, the spirits (*aitu*), have converted to Christianity: the grandfather spirit is sending his children to a church school and encourages their scholastic endeavors. This venerable grandfather spirit also portends a collapse of the dichotomy between local and foreign: he seems to be a stranger—foreign to the village—but he is really an important relative. Through this interchange Seta identifies a context in which she can be assertive and achieve, school, and poses a contextual contrast: Vao plus the living Tutu represent the context of home, while Seta plus the spirit Tutu represent the context of school.

Seta's further report about her scholastic success in school makes it clear that not only does she eventually sits for exams but also wins the prize, a scholarship to New Zealand. Indeed, Seta is that girl missionaries trained to be a native pastor's wife, although in fact it is her husband who has followed her in that vocation. If the historical package one might label "Christianity plus Western education" was in many respects limiting, Seta, like her pre-Christian counterparts, seems to adopt it at least in part because she has an eye for opportunity.

There is some question about whether Ifi objects to Seta's taking the nursing scholarship because of her reaction to blood, or if he objects to Seta's husband-to-be.[12] The theme of blood has a symbolic resonance in this regard. While it seems to relate to Seta's career, in Samoan semiotics the shedding of blood is connected to defloration and, therefore, to marriage (Shore 1989). This ambiguity about the nature of Ifi's objections places winning prizes at school, on the one hand, and marriage and sexuality, on the other, in an analogous relationship; they both stand opposed to deference to one's parents and substitute for each other in variant explanations of the tale. Rather than meekly deferring to Ifi's objections, Seta argues that maturation will cure her blood revulsion. Here Seta casts Ifi into the delimiting role taken by Vao plus the living Tutu but with a difference. Throughout, Ifi, like the spirit Tutu, is partial to Seta and restrains her because of this partiality.[13]

The replacement of Vao plus the living Tutu by Ifi represents a softening of the family side of the family/school antinomy and is answered by a softening of Seta's school side. Seta discovers she can compete and win a scholarship and still be deferential by not taking it in response to Ifi's feelings. This mutual softening of a previously antagonistic boundary completes Seta's rewriting of contextual discourse. She learns to become deferential and competitive by turns, which is, after all, what one does in contextual discourse: sometimes one behaves formerly, sometimes informally. Nonetheless, Seta still has a problem. She cannot afford her brothers the same intermittent deference she accords to Ifi. Seta clearly feels that the lingering dispute around Vao's recent death calls for a more sustained assertiveness.

■ ■ ■

Act 2, Scene 1: The Family Meeting

The day after this interview, July 22, 1990, I learn there is a family meeting about Vao's estate. The meeting is to decide who shall be Vao's trustee. Because Vao's will is oral, the trusteeship is a powerful position. Vao has left: two pieces of land (a one-acre piece and a half-acre piece in Western Samoa), two houses (one in

Pago Pago, American Samoa, and another in the environs of Apia, Western Samoa), a pickup, much in the way of personal possessions, and 40,000 *tala* (Western Samoan dollars, at that time around $20,000 U.S. dollars). To all of us this seems a great deal. Sanele's understanding—both of Vao's intent and of his sibling's view of her intent—is that the two houses have been left to the youngest sister, Sina, the pickup will go to Vao's church in Western Samoa, and the money will be used to pay off the lease on Seta's house in Apia (actually a house held jointly by the siblings) as well as to fix up Vao's Pago Pago house.

One of the brothers, Kalo, had been living with Vao in her Pago Pago house for several years prior to her death and remains there with his wife and children. Sanele believes Vao wanted Kalo to build his own house but could not make him leave because he was her son. There has been talk that Kalo intends to build a house around the bend of the mountain from Vao's house, vacating Vao's house for Sina (the youngest of the sisters). Outside the meeting Kalo's eldest daughter tells me the house may be held in common by Vao's children, and there is still some question about whether or not Kalo will be allowed to keep the house. Presently, Sina and Meke (Sina's baby) are living in a small apartment Sanele is renting in Nu'uuli village. With them lives Fa (daughter of Sia, who is one of the middle sisters). Fa is Sina's baby helper. Semisi, Fa's brother and their bodyguard, also stays with them. Seta has told me this group should be living in Vao's house—her implication, minus Kalo and his family.

Sanele attends the meeting and afterward summarizes the events as follows. Sanele says Seta should be trustee. Most of Vao's property is in Western Samoa, and there is a lot of running around in Western Samoa for the trustee to do. Seta is the only one of Vao's children who currently stays there. Kalo disagrees, saying that in the *fa'aSāmoa* (the Samoan way) the sister should sit and the brother should run around, taking care of worldly affairs such as trusteeships. Seta cries and then becomes angry. She points at Kalo and tells him this is his own view, that she has her own view, and he should not dare to tell her what is right. After further discussion Seta gets the trusteeship, and the meeting breaks up.

Commentary

In "The Family Meeting" inheriting and appropriating are confused categories; the confusion is about which of Vao's descendants should rightfully inherit and which is using her death as a pretext to purloin what is not rightfully his or hers. This confusion anticipates a final collapse of the antinomy between *sa'o* and *kuluku* that, from the outset of the tale, has been a delimiting feature of Seta's identity. Remember that *sa'o* means "to talk straight" but also refers to probity, while *kuluku* refers to an indirect form of speech but literally means "crooked," sharing the English connotation of "nefarious."

In Seta's story she identified with *sa'o* in counterpoint to *kuluku*, but now Seta is indirect with Kalo in that he and she play an oratorical game of chess in which her moves are the more efficacious. Kalo says that sisters should sit and brothers run around, framing the trusteeship issue in terms of brother:sister::active:passive oppositions. We saw that in Samoa high status is associated with being served and thus with passivity and that in Christian Samoa the brother's status vis-à-vis the sister declined. If Kalo appears to be iterating his status inferiority, he uses his position much as does the orator who serves the high chief—to wrest power—in this case away from Seta. Seta reframes the trusteeship issue. She declares that Kalo is not qualified to instruct her on Samoan custom and that what he forwards as tradition is merely his individual viewpoint. She thereby deconstructs the former antinomy between *Western* (individualistic) and *indigenous* (traditional). Instead of being caught in cultural oppositions between respect and assertiveness, Western or local, sister or brother, Seta employs all these categories to her advantage, as they further the aim she seeks to achieve.

While Seta has become a consummate orator, she also transforms the orator category: she is playing chess, but she is not dissimulative (*kuluku*). Indeed, never has Seta been more *saʻo*—never has she spoken more directly—as her pointing directly at Kalo symbolizes. In "The Healer" Seta found that she could not talk straight in family relations; "The Family Meeting" is a straightening out of Seta's indirection. Seta may be 180 degrees from where she began (when she saw Vao as turning all around), but she is, nonetheless, in her own words, still "telling you the truth" (*saʻo*). It is just that, progressively, her style of being straight becomes more complex. Seta's *saʻo* style has come to include its opposite, the discourse of the orator. Remember, in the series of binary sets that Seta iterates over the course of her tale, the orator represents the pre-Christian side of a Christian/heathen opposition; by implication, Seta's *saʻo* style has come to include the spirits who were culturally exorcised by Christianity. These implications are realized in the final scene.

■ ■ ■

Act 2, Scene 2: The Curse

The meeting has taken place in Vao's Pago Pago house and several people, Seta among them, remain there with Kalo. Kalo is angry. Seta's adopted son, Tamaʻi, had been living with him, awaiting his immigration papers, so he can go and live with another of Seta's sisters in Canada. Kalo says the boy should get out of "his" house and that Mose and Eleni [other brothers living adjacently] do not want him either.

Seta's retort is to remind Kalo that Tamaʻi is actually Ifi and Vao's youngest biological son, who she adopted, and thus Kalo's youngest brother. Referring to the house as "our" house, Seta asks, what right he has to call it his, and says that as the eldest daughter all the things in the house belong to her.

Kalo tells Seta to get out. She stands up and says Kalo and his children are now *mālaia*, "cursed," that she will go and cry on Vao's grave, and that no good shall ever come to Kalo and his children. She leaves. Another of the sisters, Sia, who has supported Kalo, comes to him and reminds him that his wife is pregnant and councils him to run after Seta and beg her forgiveness. He does, but another brother, Eleni, is already driving Seta away in his car.[14]

Commentary

Here the Kalo/Tamaʻi relation parallels the former relations between Vao/Seta and Vao/Ifi Junior, in which an innocent junior was beleaguered by an abusive senior. As Seta's adopted son, Tamaʻi is a stand-in for her: Kalo tells Tamaʻi to get out when he would really like to tell Seta to do so. Unlike in former scenes, however, Seta fights back, expanding on her newfound oratorical powers. By responding that Tamaʻi is Vao and Ifi's biological son, Seta evokes a contemporary American Samoan legal precedent. In American Samoan civil actions about inheritance, property is judged to be held jointly by the spouse and the children of the deceased when there is no will. In the case of sale the money is to be divided equally among these parties. In the present case the spouse (Ifi) is deceased, and so, legally, Vao's property would be held jointly by her children. Inasmuch as Tamaʻi is Vao's biological son, the house belongs to him too.

Seta then follows this legalistic argument by her own invocation of tradition. She says she is the oldest daughter and that, as such, the contents of the house belong to her. She is using a gender-tinged version of an older sibling/younger sibling opposition. In colonial Samoa—probably borrowing a Victorian missionary division of male and female spheres—work in domestic interiors was a female responsibility; males had responsibility for exterior work. Like most divisions graphed from one culture onto another, this gendered dichotomy between interior and exterior was far from exact, as females might work on inland plantations and had responsibility for reef fishing. But house and garden, those territories that fit a Victorian socioscape, were neatly divided. Cutting the grass around the house to make a lawn was male, sweeping the floor was a female, so much so that in Sanele's youth boys might signify their desire to become transvestites by sweeping up.

As the eldest sibling—and, furthermore, one with gender associations to the household—Seta asserts that the contents of the house belong to her. Seta then curses Kalo and his descendants. By doing so, she explicitly evokes the brother's ancient duty to propitiate his sister in all things and the legendary consequences of his failure to do so: sterility and degenerative illness visited upon him and his descendants. The still lethal nature of cursing was evident in "Burning Ifi": Seta says that, if Vao had actually cursed Ifi Junior, the child would have died. This significance is not lost on Seta's siblings, for her sister Sia councils Kalo to beg Seta to remove the curse to protect his unborn child.

In summary, Seta casts her son's right to reside in Vao's house in terms of American Samoan legal precedents; she casts her own right to Vao's property in terms of a colonial gender schema, compounded with a precontact age-grade schema. She ends it all by invoking an empowering aspect of the pre-Christian brother/sister schema.

In earlier chapters I suggested that Samoan girls' voices were displaced onto the ubiquitous spirit girls of possession stories. For Seta to reclaim her voice, therefore, she must reappropriate it from the spirit realm. She does so by an evolving identification with spirits: in the first scene Seta is possessed by her spirit grandmother, who replaces Seta's conscious identity; second, Seta meets with her spirit grandfather, who is empathetic, identifying with her and taking up her burdens; now Seta evokes the aid of her recently deceased spirit mother by threatening to cry on Vao's grave when Kalo opposes her, thereby identifying with Vao. Through these three identifications Seta's relation to the spirit world progresses from passive to active. This progression involves three variables: belief, consciousness or intentionality, and problem solving.

In "Grandmother Possession" Seta imputes a belief that the incident was possession to her siblings, feigning skepticism; she says "I didn't think it was *Ma'i Aitu* [spirit possession]." Seta also alleges innocence of any consciousness (and therefore any intentionality) in relation to the experience, telling us, "I don't think I know much about it." Seta is passive when it comes to problem solving: she does not resolve her problem with Vao; her spirit grandmother does it for her.

In "The Spirit Grandfather" Seta ascribes a belief that the man was a spirit to Vao but does not cast doubt upon it herself. Her lack of intentionality in "Grandmother Possession" changes to what one might call inadvertence: she inadvertently invokes her grandfather's aid by crying on his grave. Seta is also less passive in problem solving. The old man performs the task that rightly belongs to Seta. Symbolically, by taking up Seta's freighted pole, he takes up Seta's problems and plays a role that is structurally parallel to that of Seta's spirit grandmother. Seta, however, intentionally gives this tutelary spirit her burdens, getting the pole off her shoulders and her feelings off her chest.

In "Grandmother Possession" the siblings served as an audience that authenticated Seta's relations to spirits. In "The Grandfather Spirit" it is Vao who did so. In "The Funeral" the audience was Seta's brothers, who ignored and thereby cast doubt upon her relation to the dying Vao: Seta's brothers behaved as if Seta had no special bond to Vao nor was privy to Vao's wishes. It was Seta who asserted the legitimacy of her link to spirits by telling me it was to her that the deceased Vao conveyed her *māvaega* (final words). In "The Curse" Seta ceases to disbelieve her spirit experience, and her relation to spirits becomes fully intentional: she threatens to enlist Vao's aid by crying on her grave. Seta becomes active, even commanding, in relations to the spirit world, expecting Vao to carry out her behests. Through this identification with spirit power Seta compounds elements of self that she formerly separated—initially, through a moral discourse that opposed straight to crooked and Christian to heathen and, secondarily, through a contextual discourse that assigned one set of behaviors to home and another to school. Now Seta identifies herself as having those heathen spirit powers that she ascribed to Vao. Seta thereby publicly claims the *māvaega*, becoming Vao's successor. If Seta begins as an avatar of the Christian catechist, she ends by inheriting Vao's pre-Christian *mana*. And yet Seta gives up nothing; she remains in school studying to become a catechist and has since become one. Thus, Seta bends Samoan semiotics to her own purposes and rewrites her role as a sister.[15] Sisters in Samoa are conceived of as *teine*, girls, while wives are conceived of as women (*fafine*). Seta, rewriting her role as a sister, is also redefining that of the girl, giving, perhaps, a happier ending to this historical tale in which the figure of the *teine* has been our protagonist.

■ ■ ■

Self Theory

In culture history it is possible only to speak of a moment in an ongoing reconfiguration of a person, a woman, a family, and a society—for culture consists in just this reconfiguring process. In the few years since I have visited Samoa, and even as I write, Samoan girls with their hair up or down, the spirit girls who possess them, Samoan transvestites and their jokes, Seta and her family, are all changing yet again. What I hope I have saved from this ceaseless flux is a theory that sheds some cross-cultural light on the self.

For lack of a better term, anxious about the temerity of the title, I call the theory presented in these pages "self theory." If it seems a pretentious title, let me attempt to justify it by saying that I only mean to delineate a territory. About its theoretical contents, no doubt many will disagree. But, if *Theorizing Self* is successful, it will have marked a territory that psychological anthropologists must survey inasmuch as they would chart the self. Differently put, I offer the title *self theory* by virtue of the breadth of work this theory attempts, readily admitting it is at best a beginning.

Self theory seeks to provide a basis for a comparative study of cultural psychology without doing violence to the cultural specificity of personhood. It offers a language with which to trace a relationship among discourses on self within a culture and a progression among discourse types. It suggests that enculturation is a discursive process—one residing equally in the domain of sociality and in the cultural crafting of interiorities—and focuses on the relation between the two. In this relational focus self theory represents an alternative to analyses that heretofore have focused too one-sidedly on the construction of interior character, be it national or moral or cognitive.

Since anthropologists discovered that cultures were not islands, even those that are islands, but, rather, crossroads—chimerical concatenations of local and foreign customs—we have wondered how to disentangle the confluence of discourses that characterizes contact. By offering categories through which a related series of cultural discourses can be identified and then contrasted with the discourse series of an intruding culture, self theory can serve as a tool in an analytical process of disentanglement.

Self theory also offers perspectives on a relatively unexplored territory—cultural definitions of selves in relation to gender and to power. It explores why humans—these admittedly cultural animals—are so insistent upon subverting the imprints of culture with humor, deception, intrigue, negotiation, art, and so on. Why is it that we seem ever tempted to thwart the very cultures that defines us and that we inevitably and continually impose upon one another? Bringing these whys to bear upon enculturation, self theory illumines the recursive nature of the process and demonstrates that resistance is as pivotal to it as compliance. Self theory also reflects upon how restrictions imposed on us in the form of gender identities—restrictions implicit in our discursive habits and which infiltrate our most personal fantasies and experiences of embodiment—threaten to limit our development as persons. Self theory explores the homegrown strategies people use to circumvent these limits as well as the reasons why people borrow the discourses of other cultures in a project of resistance. Here self theory provides an alternative to idioms of victimization that may view colonized cultures as merely passive or reactive and the experience of colonization in overly simplistic terms.

As anthropologists, we have wondered about the inevitable dialectic between historical change and the inmost experience of cultural subjects, and here self theory provides a perspective through which to grasp the ways in which history is forever leaving its fingerprints upon human lives. As in Seta's case, self theory shows that, while elaborating an identity is always an existential problem, it is one situated in historically mutating cultural discourses, inevitably linking personal problems with social problems and life history with cultural history. Self theory also reflects upon the nature of personal change in culture: change is a rewriting process through which people in general—and women just as much as men—improvise with inherited discursive forms and author culture, bridging the distance between structure and agency. Self theory also expands our understanding of human community by showing that, as much as selves differ from one culture to another, we share a predilection for greater scope in the exercise of our humanity.

Notes

Preface

1. My major missionary sources are as follows. Rev. John Williams was a minister of the London Missionary Society (LMS) and is generally credited with christianizing Samoa. He arrived in Samoa in 1830. I draw from his 1830 and 1832 journals. Rev. John B. Stair, also of the London Mission, resided in Samoa from 1838 to 1845. Rev. George Turner, a representative of the London mission, was initially in Samoa from 1841 to 1859, and his ethnographic work derives from this period (Turner [1861] 1984, O'Reilly 1957:226).

2. The major late-nineteenth-century and early-twentieth-century reports I employ on Samoa were made by the following individuals. William Pritchard arrived in Samoa in the company of John Williams in 1839. Originally a representative of the London Missionary Society, Pritchard had become British consul in Tahiti. He returned to reside in Samoa in 1845 (Gilson 1970:150–51, 167–69). William B. Churchward was British consul to Samoa from 1881 to 1884. O. Stuebel was German consul to Samoa from 1889 to 1891. Stabsartz Augustin Krämer was a German naval medical officer, stationed at the German Naval Hospital at Apia, who resided in Samoa from 1893 to 1895 and from 1897 to 1899 (Gray 1980:118). Dr. Erich Schultz became chairman of the German Lands and Titles Commission at its inception in 1903 and was acting governor of German Samoa from 1910 to 1912 (Davidson 1967:81, 88).

3. My major anthropological sources are as follows. Margaret Mead resided in Samoa between 1925 and 1926. Felix Keesing visited Samoa intermittently from the 1930s through the mid-1950s. I also include one travelogue from the 1930s by Donald Sloan because Sloan stayed in Manuʻa for close to a year, lived with a Samoan family, and learned Samoan. Derek Freeman first visited Samoa from 1940 to 1943, returning again between 1965 and 1967 and again in 1981 (Freeman 1983:xiii–xvi). Lowell Holmes came to Samoa originally in 1954. Moyle did fieldwork in Samoa from 1966 to 1969 and Richard Goodman from July 1968 until July 1969. Penelope Schoeffel first visited Samoa in 1973; her dissertation research was conducted between 1976 and 1977. Bradd Shore went to Samoa as a Peace Corps volunteer in 1968, returning in 1971 as a Ph.D. student. I resided in Samoa from 1981 to 1989, visiting again during the summers of 1990 and 1991.

4. In *Out of Time* Thomas debunks the anthropological prejudice against older, particularly missionary, sources as inevitably unprofessional and biased, noting that these authors were often motivated by ethnographic curiosity, that their work with local languages necessitated the use of informants, specific inquiry and often systematic data collection (1996b:69–73).

5. Thomas notes that missionaries in many Pacific locales had a tendency to believe in indigenous magic and sorcery (1996b:73).

6. For a 1920s missionary account that shows a similar susceptibility, see Brewer 1975:65–67, 181–89.

7. There have been too many contributors to the Mead/Freeman controversy to make complete citation practical. For examples, see the *American Anthropologist* 85:908–47, and Caton 1990.

8. I thank Obeyesekere for this term (pers. comm.).

9. On socialization in Polynesia, see, for example, Howard 1970, Levy 1973, Ritchie and Ritchie 1979, and Morton 1996.

10. It is nonetheless true, however, that American and Western Samoans participate in a politics of place, often identifying with their own Samoa and behaving competitively toward people of the other Samoa. Further, the differing governments and economies of the two Samoas give residents of the two places differing life issues. While Western Samoa is more influenced by New Zealand, American Samoa is more influenced by the United States. This study, however, addresses aspects of self that are shared between the two Samoas.

11. Karen Wheat's photographs are from the collection of her great uncle, J. L. Dwyer, who resided in Samoa from 1908 to 1913. Several of the photographs were probably taken by him. Others were probably souvenir prints or picture postcards, which became popular around 1880 and were an international fashion by 1900 (Nordström 1995:20).

Chapter 1

1. Here is the full text and translation of the song. (Translation by Sanele Mageo.)

Le Aganu'u Sāmoa
Pe 'ana mafai ona ou liliu le lalolagi,
Pe ua tu Sāmoa i lana māsani?
O mea uma lava e ai i le felagolagoma'i,
Loto alofa ma talia so'o se tasi.

Tu laia i le tu fa'aSāmoa moni,
E mafai ai mea uma i le fa'amaoni.
Sau laia sau ia tia 'oe i pagātia
Si ou fulitua i si au aganu'u mānaia.

Le aganu'u sili o Sāmoa i atunu'u uma,
O le fiafia ma le fa'aaloalo i tagata.
Ae fai mai o le fa'aSāmoa e leaga,
Ae galo ia 'oe ua si'itia ai lou tūlaga.

Samoan custom
If it is possible to turn the world,
Will Samoa stand on its habit?
Everything is made from mutual support,
Love with your inner self and accept everyone.

Stand now on your real Samoan custom,
When everything is possible in truthfulness.
Come now, come here dear before you suffer
For turning your back on your beautiful Samoan custom.

Samoan custom is the best of all countries,
Happiness and respect to people.
But it is said the Samoan custom is bad,
But you are forgetting that it puts you in a high position [makes you renown].

2. For examples of ethnographers who have radically different views of the self in the same culture, see: (1) the contrary views of the Zuni presented by Li An-Che 1937 versus Stevenson 1904, Kroeber 1917, Bunzel 1932, Benedict 1934; (2) or Redfield 1960 versus O. Lewis 1951 on Tepoztlan; (3) more recently see the contrary versions of the Yanamamo presented by Chagnon 1968, and Good 1991; (4) or the controversy about the "Group Model" of Japanese society (Nakane 1970, Lebra 1976, Dale 1986, Befu 1980, Fujita 1991).

3. For examples of those who distinguish between sociocentric and egocentric cultures, sometimes in different but analogous terminology, see Mauss [1938] 1985, Read 1955, Dumont 1966, Fogelson 1982, Levy 1983, Rosaldo 1984, Shweder and Bourne 1984, White and Kirkpatrick 1985, Sampson 1988, Harris 1989, Kondo 1990, Markus and Kitayama 1991, and Murray 1993.

4. I admit, however, that sometimes Samoans may act revengefully when their personal feelings are not involved. In *Pouliuli,* for example, the protagonist Faleasa must revenge an insult to his mother to maintain family honor, although he has no personal anger toward his victim; he feels personal anger, but this emotion is directed toward his dead mother, who he believes acted unreasonably.

5. Hollan (1992) is also interested in the discrepancy between cultural conceptions of self and experience, although he sometimes calls this experience "subjective"; I am interested in social experiences as well as subjective, indeed all experience not encompassed by cultural ways of talking about the self.

6. Markus and Wurf use the term *self system* for an assortment of self-regulatory schemata (1987).

7. Kondo (1990) would further argue that nobody anywhere has a self that is distinguishable from the public discursive order. I argue that there are dimensions of self that elude this order.

8. On this overgeneralization, see further Markus and Kitayama 1991:225, and Battaglia 1995. Even then the proverbial shoe fits, one of these terms may best apply to a dominant cultural group and the other term to nondominant groups, on whom forms of cultural "otherness" may be projected.

9. Markus and Kitayama (1991) report that, in sociocentric societies, sociocentric

premises, modes of thought, emotions, and so forth are perceived to be natural and egocentric correlatives as unnatural, while the reverse is true of egocentric societies.

10. Ontological premises about persons are probably related to degrees of integration in a group posited in grid/group theory (Douglas 1982a, 1982b; Thompson, Ellis, Wildavsky 1990). Grid/group theory places social systems on the basis of two indices: group integration and degree of social control. Social relations that are "high group" correlate to sociocentric premises about the self, whereas "low group" relations suggest egocentric premises. Grid indices are not evident, however, until one considers moral discourse. On the range of possible moral assumptions about human nature, see Thompson, Ellis, and Wildavsky 1990:33–37.

11. Similarly, the Quiché Maya believe that everyone is born with one of twenty possible faces, which in dreams or death may leave the body as a "free soul" (Tedlock 1992:110, 115). Once again there is confusion because English lacks a term for a noncorporal being that is not a disembodied subjectivity

12. For other examples, see Wikan 1990:29, 35–37, 95, 137–39, 248, on the Balinese; or Tedlock 1992:109, 112, on the Zuni and Quiché Maya.

13. Aborigines provide another example, making marvelously subtle kinship distinctions with an elaborate kinship terminology (Spiro 1990:50).

14. For a similar view, see Douglas 1973.

15. More recently Hollan's and Wellenkemp's American informants tell them that one should have "spine" (backbone?) and "stand on one's own": "you just have to say that I don't need any of these ties at all" (Hollan 1992:288).

16. On this group sensitivity, see further Su'apa'ia 1962:57.

17. For an interesting discussion of these obligations, see O'Meara 1990:111, 203–6, 210. Shore also discusses the Samoan concept of social obligations as entangling (1982:169–70; 1989).

18. On *malaga*, see further Keesing and Keesing 1956:80–82, and Holmes 1969:343.

19. Presumably, Stevenson used one of the early editions of Pratt's *Grammar and Dictionary of the Samoan Language*.

20. The g in Samoan is pronounced as *ng*. In many older texts, therefore, it is spelled as *ng*. Today ʻaisiga, "formal begging parties," make *malaga* to raise funds. O'Meara says villagers "sometimes flee their houses to avoid contributing" (1990:199). For a proverb on visitors who overstay, see Schultz [1949–50] 1985:80.

21. Shore bases his ethnography of Samoa on an explication of contexts (1977, 1978, 1982). He distinguishes between complementary and symmetrical contexts, which correspond to what I call hierarchical and peer contexts respectively. The significant distinction between our perspectives is that his primary focus is on social structure and mine is on discourse. Contextual discourses are, in my view, rhetorical. I will show that there is no one-to-one correspondence between actual social structure and discourse. In formal discourse, for example, people speak as if there is a hierarchical status difference between interlocutors whether or not there is. That is why, again in Stevenson's words, children "my-lord" one another when they play marbles. For a lengthier discussion of the relation between his work on Samoan contexts and my own, see Mageo 1995:292.

22. Like Shweder et al. (1990), I dispute Turiel's social interactionalist theory of moral development in which moral systems turn on a distinction between the moral and the conventional (1983). I suspect that *conventional* is simply a pejorative term for what I call *contextual*, that is, for performative versions of cultural virtue and vice. Egocentric cultures may be suspicious about contextual discourses—as indicated by the negative connotations of terms like *conventional*—because contextual discourses are performative, accenting the social.

23. On dependent characters being perceived as "weak or troubled" personalities in egocentric cultures, see Markus and Kitayama 1991:240.

24. Holland (1992a) applies Dreyfus's model to understanding motivation to use cognitive schemata.

25. Strauss (1990) discusses three responses to heteroglossia, by which she means multiple voices within the person: vertical containment, integration, and horizontal containment. In vertical containment one schema is salient in awareness, and another is less so; in integration there is only a single schema, or a closely related set of schemata; in horizontal containment there are two schemata, both salient in awareness but compartmentalized.

26. See, for example, Lutz 1988, and Abu-Lughod and Lutz 1990.

27. See, for example, Battaglia 1995.

28. For a parallel in India, see Kurtz 1992, and Trawick 1990b.

29. In her work on gender identity Chodorow (1974) argues that the structure of early interpersonal relations is the most formative element in the child's life; however, in sociocentric societies interpersonal relations are downplayed. What is most formative is not "early interpersonal relations" but "early relations."

30. American middle-class child-rearing practices ranked average on the amount of autonomy the child is actually expected to exercise in Whiting and Child's cross-cultural study (1953:94–98).

31. In a recent conference paper, Capps and Ochs argue that conventional narratives "involve a quest for moral clarity and legitimacy" (1996:12).

32. For examples, see my analysis of courting in Bali and Tahiti (Mageo 1991b).

33. For a useful discussion of essentialism, see Bocock 1986:112–17.

34. On this view of need in critical theory, see, for example, Marcuse 1966.

35. The timing of intellectual development and its stage-by-stage nature is currently in dispute. Piaget (1952) argues an ability to distinguish between symbols and things develops in Concrete Operations and that an understanding of the principles underlying thought forms develops only in Formal Operations. For a recent study that challenges this argument, see Gelman and Baillargeon 1983. See further White 1978:7–12, on Piaget's stages as related to four phases of discourse, or consciousness.

36. For an American antebellum example, see Fitzhugh 1854, and Harper et al. 1852. In the antebellum South, blacks were thought of as moral savages and cognitive children. Slavery was seen as the means of their development; however, as with Chatterjee's British colonists in India (1993), the point at which slaves might reach moral and cognitive adulthood was more or less infinitely deferred.

37. In societies marked by an age-grade division, those in the lowest age group are assigned ontological premises and are expected simply to obey their superiors. Inasmuch as age is a relative factor, however, from early on youngsters may have a dominant position vis-à-vis someone yet younger, and, in this position, some level of achievement will be expected. Conversely, for most adults there are older, higher-status individuals they must simply obey unquestioningly. Samoa is an example of an age-grade society.

38. One reason why women cross-culturally have a reputation for gossip is because gossip is a form of moral discourse.

39. This view of women as specialists in moral discourse also characterized English society of the period. See, for example, Millar 1806, Wheeler and Thompson 1825, Wollstonecraft [1787] 1993, Ellis 1842, and Davidoff and Hall 1987, chap. 3.

40. See Bocock 1986, on hegemony as beliefs that are widely shared despite the unequal power relations they legitimate.

41. See, for example, Kohlberg and Kramer 1969. Here again, whether or not women actually conform to attributions is another matter. See, for example, Tavris 1992. Thus Lutz (1990) finds that American women are attributed tendencies toward emotionalism and believe their behavior to be consonant with these attributions, although when studied they are no more emotional than men. Since Gilligan (1982), Kohlberg, Levine, and Hewer have reformulated Kohlberg's position, stating "there may be other principles" besides a justice of individual rights that can serve as the basis for the highest stage of moral reasoning such as "responsible love" or "a morality of particularistic relationships" (1983:63). My intent is not to criticize Kohlberg for past errors but to illustrate a form of reasoning about development evident in Kohlberg's earlier work.

42. Lamphere is right to question whether or not all cultures make a public/private gender distinction (1993; see also Rosaldo 1980), and I am not suggesting that they do—quite the contrary.

43. On Byron's popularity, see Davidoff and Hall 1987:159.

44. On the rise of the incidence of possession in twentieth-century Samoa, see Mageo 1994, 1996a, and 1996b.

45. The Frankfurt school, Marcuse in particular (1966), began to build a bridge between work on the self and relations of power, but little systematic work has been done to bridge these territories in anthropology. For a recent exception, see Battaglia 1995; however, the accounts of self in Battgalia's volume, while historically situated, are not particularly concerned with cultural history.

Chapter 2

1. See further Haraway 1989.
2. In Samoan the characteristic sentence is "'O aga na a ai?"
3. In Samoan the characteristic sentence is "Se vā'ai 'i aga a . . . !"
4. The Tongan word *agatala* means "to imitate" or "to copy." Although the word *agatala* does not exist in Samoan, the fact that Tongans think of imitation as an activity proper to *aga* implies an *aga* is a manner one can pick up from others in Tongan as well.
5. Thus Ochs (1988:167) notes that Samoan children are taught to perform before they can speak.
6. While Samoans do not see inner experience as definitive of personhood, they agree that it is unitary. The term *āmio* refers to behavior that stems from within the person and that is personally motivated, rather than role derived. One can also say "Behave nicely!" using the term *āmio*, but one uses the singular form (Faifa'alelei lau āmio!); here one might gloss the admonition as "Make your personal behavior nice!" The terms *aga* and *āmio* have been the subject of debate in the ethnographic literature. For a summary of this debate and my position in it, see Mageo 1989a.
7. See, for example, Fogelson 1982, and Harris 1989.
8. Jung saw the persona as a self-image, as this image is reflected back to the person through social roles. I take the persona to originate in the eyes of others during what Lacan calls the mirror phase (1977). Persona also corresponds to what G. H. Mead (1934) called the "me." For Mead the me is that phase of self originating in others who are mimicked by the individual and thereby interiorized.
9. In Holland and Quinn's terminology (1987:24–32) one might say the persona

reflects an "image schema" of the self, while ontological premises that emphasize inner experience tend to be propositional.

10. Psychoanalytic anthropology typically investigates repressed parts of the self, but the reasons for repression are not lack of fit with egocentric or sociocentric constructions of personhood.

11. Levy (1973) uses the term *hypocognized* for culturally undercoded emotions.

12. On the *loto* and private thoughts, see also Gerber 1975:187–89, 1985:135–36. On words having to do with thought processes and the *loto*, see Mageo 1989a:192. Milner's gloss for emotion is *lagona loloto*, literally "deep feeling." As inner events are played down in Samoa, the term *lagona*, like the term *loto*, is somewhat undifferentiated, referring both to sensations and to emotions. Gerber points out, however, that Samoans distinguish emotions from sensations on the basis of their source: emotions grow up in the *loto* (1975:187).

13. See further Markus and Kitayama, on the limitations of attachment theory and the culturally bounded nature of the "strange situation" through which it is tested (1991:237). Recent psychological studies tend to view separation as the most important early trauma (Kramer 1993).

14. In marriage ceremonies *tōga* goes from the female side to the male side, so the brother/sister exchange of children reverses this arrangement.

15. For a summary of Samoan law concerning "adoption," see Schultz [1911] n.d.:30–31, and Krämer [1902] 1995:63–65.

16. On adoption in Polynesia, see Levy 1969, 1973:473–84; Carrol 1970; Brady 1976; Howard and Kirkpatrick 1989; and particularly Borofsky 1987:153, who also views adoption as promoting identification within a kin group.

17. See particularly Schoeffel 1979a:101–2. For more detailed considerations of birth and early infancy, see Mead [1928] 1961, Gardner 1965, Schoeffel 1979a, Sutter 1980, and Mageo 1988, 1989b, 1991a, 1991b.

18. On physical contact in the early life of the Samoan child, see Gardner 1965:146–47, Schoeffel 1979a:101–2, and Sutter 1980.

19. On the family as one body, see Schultz [1911] n.d.:26, and Hjarnø 1979–80:88–89.

20. On porous conceptions of the body in other sociocentric cultures, see further Marriott 1976, Strathern 1990, Comaroff and Comaroff 1992:76, and Scheper-Hughes and Lock 1992.

21. Derrida (1994), commenting on Mauss's *The Gift*, argues that the right to beg suggests rights in property.

22. On parental attitudes toward siblings' property, see Sutter 1980:39–40.

23. These distancing practices are paralleled throughout Polynesia. See Beaglehole and Beaglehole 1938, 1946; Ritchie and Ritchie 1979, 1989; James Ritchie 1956; Gardner 1965; Levy 1973, 1978; Gallimore, Boggs and Jordan 1974; Howard 1974; Sutter 1980; Martini and Kirkpatrick 1981; and Morton 1996.

24. See Mead [1928] 1961:22; Mead [1930] 1969:90; Schoeffel 1979a:102, 126; Sutter 1980:31.

25. See Gardner 1965:145–46, 153; Gerber 1975:51, 53.

26. Gerber also notes that Samoan parents "deliberately conceal loving feelings from their children" (1975:161).

27. See Bindon and Zansky 1986:236; Marples 1950:327–29.

28. See Gardner 1965:153–54. For a parallel in Tonga see Morton 1996:156–57.

29. See Gardner 1965:153–54. On the discouragement of early verbal assertiveness in Samoa see further Mead [1928] 1961:24, Gardner 1965:145–46, 149, 153–54, Gerber 1975:45, Sutter 1980:31–41 and Ochs 1988:128–44.

30. For a parallel in Tonga see Morton 1996:157. Ochs argues that lower status persons in Samoa, which includes infants and children, are taught to "decenter," adjusting to the perspective of higher status seniors (1982:95).

31. On Samoan parent/child communication in Samoa see further Sutter 1980:37–38.

Chapter 3

1. For further explanation and examples of these dispositions, see Gerber 1975.

2. *Fua* is the more precise word for "jealousy," although, as shown in the text, *lotoleaga* may also refer to a coveted person.

3. This appears to be true of scaring practices across Polynesia. See, for example, Levy 1973:448–49.

4. After the child cries, parents will often relent saying, "Oh my poor, dear child, my poor, dear child" (Ōi si au tama, si au tama). Thus scaring may involve a sequence: first stimulating emotionality; then communicating that affective display is likely to provoke ridicule; finally rewarding display with demonstrations of affection. This sequence makes it even more likely that scaring will produce contradictory tendencies in character. On scaring children as an amusement, see Mead on the Balinese 1942:31; on scaring practices as an amusement see Levy on Tahitians 1973:448–49.

5. On Samoan ogres, see Moyle 1981, and Freeman 1983:211.

6. The Samoan phrase for being taken alive is 'ave ola. The first stanza of the Afono song is as follows.

Auē musu'e fa'alogo o le tala pa mai ia Afono.
Le 'alaga 'ua so'o
'Ua so'o foi ole ala sopo
'Ua so'o foi le vao loloto
Salote ma le Malie pele 'ua goto.

Alas, I don't want to hear the story from Afono.
They are calling out all around,
All over the village
All over the path
All over the forest.
Probably Salote and Malie have drowned.

The song does not directly refer to spirits taking the children, but villagers told the tale as an example of a spirit abduction when my Samoan-Pacific Studies class was doing interviews on spirits in Afono village.

7. Moyle also notes the presence of this kind of humor in Samoa (1988:101, 115, 127).

8. See further Gerber 1975:60, and Schoeffel 1979a:104–5, on Samoan children being called insulting or obscene names by elders.

9. For another example of nonverbal *musu*, see Krämer [1902] 1995:61.

10. Aptly, Goodman says punishments begin at about six months of age, that is, in the initial period of parental withdrawal (1983:19).

11. Like orders, punishment may exhibit the idea that children are a collective unit. Gerber describes the children of a household being arranged in a row along a wall "all crying, but only one having any idea of what he did to deserve it" (1975:61).

12. Ochs points out that in Samoa threats are more common than blows (1988:151–53); however, Shore remarks, "What makes Samoa distinctive is the frequency with which threats are matched by physical abuse" (qtd. in Mageo 1991b:33).

13. See further Kirkpatrick and White 1985:5–6. Shore calls Samoa a "shame culture" (1982:158–67).

Chapter 4

1. Shore's ethnography of Sala'ilua begins with a murder that vents an old rivalry between its two highest-ranking families (1982:14).

2. It is probably because of this moral ambiguity that gossips manipulate their audience into becoming coproducers (Besnier 1989, 1990).

3. According to Lacan, speech is the primary metaphor for the subjective self, because language is its original instrument (Coward and Ellis 1977:105–21). Lacan says that infants feel an undifferentiated and total need for the mother. As they learn to talk, they attempt to satisfy this need by verbal demands for specific things. This translation of need into concrete demands is part of children's first attempt to exert their personal will upon the environment. Evidently, because speech is the first version of language for all of us, free expression is a fundamental metaphor for personal freedom. In the U.S. Bill of Rights (which seeks, at least in theory, to provide maximum freedom for the individual subject) freedom of speech is the first tenet. Because Samoan culture promotes a communal self and curtails the subject, unruly speech becomes a symbol of antisocial behavior.

4. On the association of exhibitionism and *tautalaitiiti*, see further Mageo 1989b:394–97, 1991c.

5. For other examples of *tautoga*, see Turner [1861] 1986:24, [1884] 1984:19, 39–40; Churchward 1887:186–89; Stuebel 1976:156; and Wendt 1977:21–28.

6. Scaring can also produce independence as a counterreaction (Mageo 1991b). Te'e stands alone before the village. The nineteenth-century missionary Turner remarks, "A Samoan is very independent: he prefers liberty to money; any attempt to force him to do more than he feels inclined, would only cause him to turn on his heels and say, 'Good-buy, I'm going'" ([1861] 1986:22).

7. A fantasized replacement of successful sinners with more "worthy" persons, with whom the listener identifies, may characterize other forms of moral discourse, sermons for example.

Chapter 5

1. This phrase has received much ethnographic discussion. See Shore 1977:161, 1982:136; Tuiteleleapaga 1980:32; and Duranti 1981:29–30.

2. In popular entertainments, however, the rhetoric of informal contexts may be regent. Thus, in American soap operas life is about the personal involvements of the

characters, and these relationships take precedence over every other sort of social reality. Here the frame entertainment itself supplies the as-if quotation marks.

3. Baudrillard associates simulacra with late capitalism (1988). I am suggesting that simulacra are intrinsic to contextual discourses and, therefore, to all cultures.

4. On renderings to family and village chiefs, see Schultz [1949–50] 1985:55, and Stuebel 1976:110–13.

5. Title conferring ceremonies (*sofaʻi*), however, which are largely conducted within groups rather than between them, convey real authority.

6. The philologist of the Hudson expedition refers to the dancing at the Joking Night as "*ula*" (Hale 1846:377, qtd. in Moyle 1988:206). Krämer describes *ula* as a specific dance in which a group of males and females alternate and which resembles the first part of Joking Nights ([1902] 1995:367–68). Krämer, however, also uses the term *ula* in general reference to Joking Nights and notes day dances were called *aoula*, literally "daytime *ula*" ([1902] 1995:367–68). Similar constructions are noted elsewhere. For example, the ethnomusicologist Moyle tells us that *aosoa* was a "day song" (1988:23).

7. On respect relations and the brother-sister relationship, see Shore 1977, 1978, 1982; and Schoeffel 1979a.

8. On the competitive nature of Joking Nights, see also Moyle 1988:207, 231, 234.

9. The idea is that inhibitions can result in compulsive performances reminiscent of those associated with obsessive-compulsive neurosis. On these neurotic performances, see Sarason 1976:269–73. On denial as a defense mechanism, see A. Freud 1937, Haan 1977, and Vaillant 1986.

10. Freeman makes a similar point (1983:208–9).

11. On the prerogatives of older children to command and punish younger children, see further Gerber 1975:36, 61; Schoeffel 1979a:125; and Freeman 1983:208–9.

12. On the role of the adolescent girl, see further Mead [1928] 1961; Gerber 1975:36, 41, 65; and Schoeffel 1979a:138.

13. On the ʻaumāga in old Samoa, see Mead [1930] 1969:17, and Keesing and Keesing 1956:48.

14. These beatings are now illegal in American Samoa; examples of them can be found in the criminal records of the High Court of American Samoa. In the district court case *American Samoa Government versus Moananu* a runner was jogging along the main road through a village during the *Sā*. He was chased, caught, and forced to sit at the feet of the chief, just as the punished child is forced to sit at the feet of its parents in demonstrating submission to their authority (no. 55–89, 4/5/89). For further examples of the policing activities of the ʻaumāga, see Stair 1897:90, and Tuiteleleapaga 1980:56–57.

15. For other examples of this type of joking, see Moyle 1988:101, 114, 130.

16. On the symbolic interchangeability of beating up another and competitive games in Samoa, see the legend of Filo and Mea in Schultz [1949–50] 1985:117. On these games see also Nightingale 1835 (cited in Freeman 1983:143–44); Turner [1884] 1984:29, 126; Moyle 1988:96; and Holmes 1969:343.

17. For another example of sports as a form of joking, see Hoffman and Trudeau 1976:37.

18. On formal marriage arrangements in old Samoa, see further Stair 1897:124, Stuebel 1976:114, and Moyle 1988:185–87. On the *āvaga*, see further Pritchard 1866:134–35, Schultz [1911] n.d.:22–25, Stuebel 1976:126–30, and Mead [1928] 1961:103–4.

19. On defloration, see also Turner [1861] 1986:93; Schoeffel 1978:75.

20. Shore discusses the significance of the flowing of blood in Samoa (1981:198). He suggests controlled flow, as in formal nuptial blood, is honorable, while uncontrolled flowing, as in menstrual blood, is defiling. I argue that in Samoa blood is intrinsically defiling. Although it appeared to elevate parties in formal nuptials, this resignification of blood was camouflage for another, more problematic significance.

21. On women's role in Joking Nights, see Williams [1830–32] 1984:247–48; Wilkes [1839] 1845 2:130, 134, 140; and Colvocoresses 1852:87.

Chapter 6

1. Dreyfus's own term is *reference situation* (1984).

2. See further Thomas, on dual figures in Polynesian art 1995. In a recent article Thomas (1996a) objects to the use of hybridization as marking an evolutionist postmodern stage of sociohistorical development. In consonance with this argument I am suggesting that such a stage is characteristic of all self systems.

3. In old Samoa a village's organization of untitled men might kidnap the *tāupōu* of another village and marry her to one of their highborn young men. Such a coup was considered a significant accomplishment in the status rivalry between villages. See further Mead [1928] 1961:102, [1930] 1969:227; Schoeffel 1979a:188; and Freeman 1983:244–45. Girls sometimes "crawl" at night, but they are called *totolo*.

4. On the relative status of sisters and brothers, and husbands and wives, in Samoa, see Shore 1977, 1981, 1982; and Schoeffel 1978, 1979a.

5. On girls marrying for this reason, see Schoeffel 1979a:184, and Freeman 1983:230–31.

6. Should the boy clearly outrank the girl—for example, if he were the son of a chief and she were of undistinguished lineage—she would not consider his advances cheeky; however, on the whole higher-status boys are trained to behave demurely.

7. For examples of this parental ambition, see Tuiteleleapaga 1980:44–46.

8. Actually, when a chief desired to marry a lower-ranking girl informally, he would send a *soa* directly to her (Pritchard 1866:134–35). On the *soa* of the common boy, see further Turner [1884] 1984:92; Mead [1928] 1961:91, 96; Sloan 1941:92; Stuebel 1976:126–30; and Tuiteleleapaga 1980:64–65.

9. Schultz records a Samoan proverb that says: "The fauna of Samoa is poor. For the chase offers only feathered game" ([1949–50] 1985:30), explaining that "the people hunted mostly with the help of decoy birds." On pigeon catching as chiefly sport in old Samoa, see Pritchard 1866:161–62; Turner [1884] 1984:127–28, [1861] 1986:119–20; Churchward 1887:139–41; and Herdrich 1991.

10. On these mounds, referred to in the literature as "star mounds," see further Davidson 1974:225–44, and Herdrich 1991.

11. For an example of these comparisons, see Schultz 1965:32–33 (qtd. in Herdrich 1991:406–7).

12. On these expectation, see further Goodman 1983.

13. Nineteenth-century missionaries complain about this meretriciousness. Stair remarks that children are "encouraged to follow deception as a virtue" and that in this virtue they prove themselves "too apt scholars" (1897:178). This plaint could also be heard from early secular visitors such as Commodore Wilkes, who says that Samoans were "adepts" in "giving a false impression" of "their feelings and designs . . . particu-

larly when . . . their personal interest may be promoted by dissimulation" (1845 vol. 23:66, qtd. in Freeman 1983:217). Perhaps it is because of the importance of duplicity in Samoan culture that in Samoan cosmology suspicion is generated at the same time as humankind, evolving along with heart, will (*loto*), and spirit. These four qualities are further said to be the source of human intelligence (Mead [1930] 1969:156–61).

14. The raised grave mounds of high chiefs and the star mounds on which archaeologists surmise pigeon catching took place were called by the same term, *tia*. On *tia*, see Pritchard 1866:161, Davidson 1974:225–44, and Herdrich 1991:393.

15. On their mythology, see Luomala [1955] 1986:101–2.

16. For a fuller version of this story, see Muse and Muse 1982:12–13 (qtd. in Herdrich 1991:410).

17. For a Samoan parallel, see Sio 1984:24–28.

18. The Samoan sentence is "'Ua gālue fa'asoa le tulāfale mō lona ali'i." On orators as arranging chiefly marriages, see also Schultz 1911:49.

19. On oratory as a net, see Matā'afa Tu'i 1987:66, 71, 80–81, 84. On delivering a speech as catching a pigeon, see Schultz [1949–50] 1985:32.

20. On these marital arrangements, see Krämer [1923] 1949, Su'apa'ia 1962:55, Hjarnø 1979–80:96–98, and Tuiteleleapaga 1980:71.

21. In Samoan the saying is "O mea a ali'i e pala 'i le tulāfale."

22. By *taani'o* the Keesings probably mean *ta'ali'o*, "to circle," or "to proceed in a circular fashion." Even the linguistics of *fono* speeches are equivocal, exploiting ambiguous pronouns and the unoriented nature of Samoan transitive verbs (Duranti 1981:133–35).

23. On *fono* speeches and their construction, see Duranti 1981, 1983, 1984b, 1994. In the nineteenth century joking was used at *fono* by representatives of lower-status families to get participants to attend to their orations (Stair 1897:187–88). On the more recent use of joking in *fono* speeches, see also Tuiteleleapaga 1980:65, Holmes 1969:349, Shore 1982:10, and Freeman 1983:276–77.

24. The Samoan sentence is "O le ala i le pule 'o le tautua."

25. See sec. 6.0107 of the America Samoa Code. The code is summarized and explained in the *American Samoa Digest* (1982:91–124).

26. For example, in one dispute about the Mauga title of Pago Pago the winning claimant was preferred by the court, at least in part because of his superior knowledge of the village *fa'alupega* (*American Samoa Report* 1978:650).

27. For other examples that qualify the stereotype of Polynesian hierarchy, see Thomas 1990, 1996. On the Samoan version, see further Hjarnø 1979–80.

28. My inspiration for this particular depiction of self systems is Dreyfus's five-stage theory on the development of expertise (1984).

Chapter 7

1. For examples of females fighting females for their *'āiga*, see Tuiteleleapaga 1980:58, Wendt 1979:110–11, and Mageo 1988:55–56.

2. Students of Freud will realize that I am invoking his theory of dreams here as a trash can of day residues ([1900] 1953, [1917] 1966).

3. The bracketed Samoan words are Moyle's; the other brackets are mine. The emphasis is also mine. Krämer ([1902] 1995:374) gives an example of girls flaunting their charms.

4. On male and female hairdos, see also Stair 1897:120, and Churchward 1887:400.

5. For further depictions of the *tutagita* style, see Stair 1897:121, Turner [1884] 1984:122, Willis 1889:17, and Schoeffel 1979a:433.

6. On this bleaching, see Turner [1884] 1984:122, Stair 1897:132, and Freeman 1983:229.

7. On the head as *mana*, see Handy [1927] 1978, Goldman 1970, and Valeri 1985. Keesing (1984) points out that *mana* is often used as a stative verb or an adjective, rather than a noun. As Valeri (1985) notes, however, the word is also used in a substantive sense. On the usages of the term in Polynesia, see also Shore 1989.

8. See Sahlins 1985:15–17, Pukui 1972, vol. 1:183, and Ralston 1989, on the genital glorification of Hawaiian royalty. The parallel between penises and hair is recurrent in the cross-cultural semiotics of the body. Obeyesekere's Sri Lankan informants, for example, see the long, matted locks of Sinhalese female ascetics as penis-like "buds of flesh" and "tender fleshy growths," which Obeyesekere concludes are symbolical penises "stuck on the head," or "sublated" penises (1981:35). Leach (1958) argues that this correlation is universal, Hallpike (1969) that it is not. I have discussed this debate in detail elsewhere (Mageo 1994).

9. On chiefly sexual appetites, see, for example, Stuebel 1976:78–81. On seductions by spirits, see Krämer [1923] 1949:16–17, Mead 1929:269, Stuebel 1976:94–95, Shore 1977:342–50, and Mageo 1991a:361, 1992b.

10. On *mana* and fecundity, see Handy [1927] 1978, Firth 1949, Koskinen 1967, Goldman 1970, and Shore 1989.

11. On the *tuiga*, see Stair 1897:121, Turner [1884] 1984:122, Angas 1866:275, Willis 1889:17, Freeman 1983:124, and Shore 1989:157.

12. See, for example, Stuebel 1976:94. Accounts of female spirits' hair color vary, but light-reddish hair is the color typically ascribed to them. See Schoeffel 1979a:406–8, and Mageo 1991c.

13. On mats and red feathers, see Wilkes 1845:141, Stair 1897:117, Krämer [1902] 1995:334, Stuebel 1976:126, and Hjarnø 1979–80:103–5. On the sacred character of fine mats, see Hutton 1874:150–51, and Krämer [1923] 1949:63.

14. In the 1890s Krämer reports adult men and women cut their hair short but that girls' hair was left to grow long prior to puberty ([1902] 1995:329). The photographic record on feminine hairstyles for the period is mixed (Blanton 1995), some adolescent girls having long and some short hair, suggesting that it was a transitional period from short to long hair for women.

15. There was also a council of chiefs and a council of chief's wives. For a further discussion of village social structure, see Shore 1982.

16. On the role of the *aualuma*, see further Moyle 1975:239, Schoeffel 1979a:436, Shore 1981:203, Meleiseā 1987b:7, and Mageo 1996a.

17. The English translation is based upon Moyle's but amended by Sanele and myself. The Samoan version is as follows.

'Ava. 'O 'ava. Tamāloa e fai polo 'afa
'Ae lē tū tonu lona 'ausasa. 'Ave loa atu, tū i le 'auaga.
'A masa'a, masa'a. 'Ua tumu i luga o le fala.
'Ā ō 'ese 'ua etoeto maile. 'Ua tafai laga aua 'ua mataga.
'Ua taufete'ia i laua ina 'ua maua.

Le masisi tui, le masisi tui. Faʻatafatafa ʻese.
Seʻi alu atu ʻo laʻu malaga. ʻUa fia alu e tū iʻinā i le mataʻaga.
ʻUa alu atu, ʻua lē alu ʻuma. ʻA ʻua tūtū i luga.
ʻAe i lalo ʻua faʻaofi ina pula.
ʻAe teʻi ane ʻua fula, ʻae mulimuli ane puta.

In our translation we have made substantive amendments only in the last two lines of the song.
Moyle's translation:

I fit in at the base, where it is soft.
Suddenly I swell; and at last I am fat. (1975:239)

Mageo translation:

I squeeze in underneath until ripe.
And later the girl's belly is swollen, and lastly it is fat.

In the original Samoan the pronoun is left unspecified in several lines of this song. Sometimes Moyle renders these unspecified pronouns as *it,* and sometimes he assumes that there is a more definite implied pronoun. The lack of a definite pronoun allows the subject of succeeding lines to drift from one object to another. This drifting occurs early in the song and is evident in Moyle's translation. Thus, the subject in the second line of the song is the man's penis, but in the third and the fourth lines the subject is his ejaculate. While Sanele and I concur with Moyle's rendering of these earlier lines, we disagree with his rendering of the last two lines of the song. In the second to last line Moyle translates the word *pula* as "soft," referring to the softness of the girl's vagina; however, the word *pula* actually means "ripe" and in this case refers to a ripening toward orgasm. Moyle believes that the term *swell* and the term *fat* in the last line refer to the man's penis. We believe they refer to a woman and her pregnant condition, which results from the orgasm mentioned in the preceding line. One cannot deduce the proper subject of the last line from the text itself but only through common usage. The term *fula* is often used to denote the beginnings of a pregnancy and *puta* to denote its full development. I have supplied the song with a title for ease of reference.

18. On these entertainments, see further Moyle 1975, 1988. On women's dancing, see also Williams [1830–32] 1984:247–48, Colvocoresses 1852:87, Stair 1897:134, and Shore 1977:314. Hjarnø's view of female sexuality in old Samoa differs from mine (1979–80:109), but his position is not supported by the breadth of data I present.

19. If village sex roles and associated discourses were dimorphic in old Samoa, they were also flexible. There were notable exceptions to the rule that war was a male occupation: the most famous legendary warrior was Nafanua, a female spirit (Stuebel 1976:38–44). A village princess (*tāupōu*) made the requisite kava for chiefly ceremonies and was treated as a titled dignitary. In entertaining, sometimes a party of girls and women would visit another village, and then the organization of untitled boys and men (*ʻaumāga*) hosted them.

20. Ortner, discussing the Polynesian family (1981), and Sahlins, Hawaiians (1985:1–31), argue for a similar attitude toward female sexuality.

21. On ranking marriage and political ascent in old Samoa, see Krämer [1902] 1994, 1995, [1923] 1949; Hjarnø 1979–80:96–102; and Henry 1980.

22. For examples of short-term *āvaga*, see Kessing 1937:8; Tuiteleleapaga 1980:50, 63, 69, 70, 90. For a general discussion of *āvaga*, see Freeman 1983:240–41.

23. Sometimes, Turner notes, even the marriages of common folk included a defloration, and this "had some influence in cultivating chastity" ([1884] 1984:95–96). He adds, however, this influence applied with force only among young women of rank.

24. For legendary material that implies an equation between marriage and intercourse, see Turner [1884] 1984:103.

25. There are mixed reports on how frequently parents resorted to blows in the nineteenth century. Krämer says physical punishment was infrequent ([1902] 1995:61). Stair, however, says children were "severely beaten for the most trivial offense" (qtd. in Freeman 1983:205). Willis reports that young people are beaten (1889:62–63). See Mageo 1988:48–54, on a possible resolution to this seeming contradiction.

26. The rule that men, rather than women, held titles was not absolute; a very exalted blood line could trump gender and could entitle a woman to high office.

27. On the sister's cures, see Stuebel 1976:114; Mead [1928] 1961:82; Kessing 1934:376; Gilson 1970:36; Cain 1971:176; and Shore 1981:200, 1982:237.

28. On the boy's role in contemporary Samoa see Shore 1977, 1981, 1982, and Schoeffel 1978 and 1979a.

Chapter 8

1. Sometimes governmental intrusions by foreign powers were sufficiently distressing that Samoans generally became involved in resistance and in defining themselves against outsiders, the 1920s resistance movement in Western Samoa against the New Zealand government being the most prominent instance (Field 1984).

2. For another example, see Turner [1861] 1986:23. The patronage of chiefs did help to stimulate rapid conversion (Gilson 1970:75).

3. On these missions to Samoa, see further Gilson 1970:65–94, and Garrett 1982.

4. On missionaries' enthusiasm for instructing their converts in literacy, see also Turner [1861] 1986:18–19, 27, 61–78; Holmes 1974:61; and Huebner 1986:399.

5. On this proliferation of schools, see also Willis 1889:52, Gilson 1970:102, and Garrett 1982:125.

6. Even missionaries sometimes realized their translations were enigmatically inexact (Gunson 1978:261–62).

7. In his later work Foucault also sees Christian self-abnegation as a strategy for developing the self (1990).

8. Sanele and I were taking a walk when he gave me this example, and this passage, therefore, mixes paraphrase with direct quotation.

9. The term *āmio* has been much debated in the literature. Shore, listening to moral usage, says that *āmio* refers to the impulsive side of the person (1983, 1984, 1985). Freeman (1984, 1985), looking at the word's exact definition and Christian usage, echoes Pratt ([1862/1911] 1977), and Love (1983). See further Mageo 1989a. I believe these disparities stems from historical layering.

10. On Samoans expecting orators to be familiar with Christian usage, see, for example, Drummond 1845.

11. On these two styles, see Milner 1966:xiv–xv, Shore 1982:267–76, and Ochs 1988:54–58.

12. On sleeping in the *aualuma* and *'aumāga,* see Brewer 1975:38–40, Stuebel 1976:126–31, Schoeffel 1979a:433, and Meleiseā 1987b:7.

13. Thus, Vaiao Ala'ilima says that "respectable young Samoan ladies at a critical age usually lived with the village pastor for safekeeping" (qtd. in Freeman 1983:350; see also Gunson 1978:135).

14. On defloration, see further Turner [1861] 1986:93, Schoeffel 1978:75, and Freeman 1983:230–31.

15. On the *lagi* as the preserve of high gods and defied chiefs, see Stair 1897:184, 211–12.

16. Similarly, Marcus also suggests that today "the chiefly ideal of proper behavior has become synonymous with a populist one; it is a way of talking about exemplary personhood that anyone can approximate" (1989:191).

17. The Samoan sentence is "O ai a ete te'e iai?"

18. A similar expression is used of boys, *O le fa'ateteine ia,* which glosses as "He is uneasy around girls" but actually means he does not want to do his chores when girls are near, so as to appear to be high status.

19. On purchasing wives, see Williams [1830–32] 1984:77. On slavery as a missionary cause célèbre, see Comaroff and Comaroff 1991:118–22.

20. Mead misspells the Samoan word *tāupōu.*

21. Keesing (1937) also suggests that with the establishment of stable colonial governments in Western and American Samoa the political purpose of *tāupōu* marriages was nullified. He sees this purpose as uniting municipalities. Sloan estimates that during this period in Tau village, Manu'a, where he resided for close to a year, one-third of the babies were born out of wedlock, one-third were of uncertain parentage, and one-third were legitimate (1941:100).

22. For earlier work on Samoan sexual history see Mageo 1992a, 1994, 1996a, and Shankman 1996.

23. Economics were probably also an important factor in culture change during the war. From 1941–45 savings deposits, many of the accounts being those of native Samoans, rose nearly 320 percent (Stanner 1953:327; see also Gray 1960:245).

24. The song was recorded from memory by Sanele Mageo and Loia Fiaui. I translated the song based on translations made by Sanele Mageo and Loia Fiaui. Here is the Samoan version.

> Outou teine ole atunu'u
> Sa ou fa'apea e lē valea lou ulu
> Tama mai Meleke 'ua taunu'u
> 'Ae tavali ai fua lava ou laugutu,
> Su'e mai se'evae ma fa'amaulu
> Ete lē māsani talu ona e tupu
> Ete i'u lava i le togā'ulu,
>
> E su'e mai ni 'ulu e fai se umu.
> Sosola uma o seila i Meleke
> Tia'i 'oe ile alatele.

Nofonofo solo i le aualatele
Ma si ou foga 'ua tau malepe.
'Ua uma fo'i aso ole fa'afetefete
I talane ole tama mai Meleke.
'Ua uma ona 'ou faiatu 'aua ete mateletele
Ete i'u lava i le tusameme.

Ti'ai lou 'āiga a'e sola,
Sola nofo i Satapuala,
E nofo ai fa'alatalata
I le faitoto'a ole agasala.
Nofonofo solo ile ala,
Pei ose teine mai le tāulaga,
A 'ua e iloaina lava
E mamao lou nu'u ma lou alalafaga.

25. Here again I supply the song with a title.

26. Sahlins argues that the penchant for sequestering foreign status through sexual liaisons was a salient practice throughout Polynesian history (1981, 1985).

27. My portrayal of village symbolic topography is coincident in many respects with Shore's (1982:48–51), but he does not suggest this topography is historically layered.

Chapter 9

1. For Freud primary process thought is intrinsically unconscious, is tropic, and operates on the pleasure principle, rather than the reality principle ([1900] 1953:592, 595; [1933] 1964:17; [1940] 1964:164, all qtd. in Spiro 1992:168–69). Spiro rejects tropes as characteristic of primary processes because their place in normal discourse indicates they are not intrinsically unconscious. He further distinguishes between tropes and defenses, which he believes enlist the same modes of thought, but, while tropes aim at revealing thoughts, defenses aim at concealing them. Concealment is achieved by splitting the literal and figurative meanings of tropes, where the literal becomes camouflage for the figurative meaning. The narrative tropes explored in this chapter also involve this splitting, but here "defensiveness" is protection, not for unconsciousness per se but for a progressive if disguised form of thinking. For another example of this type of thinking in stories, see Bettelheim 1976.

2. For examples of possession as predominately performative, see Mead 1942. For examples of possession as narrative, see Lambek 1981, and Landerman 1991. For examples of both, see Mageo and Howard 1996.

3. For several Pacific examples, see Mageo and Howard 1996. Modernity, however, sometimes destroys institutions of possession, thereby canceling the stimulating effect of moral cacophony.

4. On Mead and psychology, see Mageo 1988:28–37.

5. Freeman mentions girls who commit suicide because of illicit sexual liaisons (1983:221), but girls are not the particular victims of suicide in Samoa (Macpherson and Macpherson 1985, 1987). What is interesting about suicide versus possession is that suicide often occurs after the fact of illicit sex (Freeman 1983:221), while possession may be

a symptom of an unconscious and, therefore, more radically dissociated desire (Mageo 1991c:367–75).

6. On illness as spirit induced in old Samoa, see further Turner [1861] 1986:130; Macpherson and Macpherson 1985:1–16, 1990:38–41, 61, 151.

7. On *taulāitu*, see further Williams 1832 (qtd. in Freeman 1983:176–77, 339), Stair 1897:220–25, Shore 1977:308, Freeman 1983:177–78, and Meleiseā 1987a:36–37.

8. There are additional names for these healers that emphasize their doctorly qualities: they may be called *faivai*, "medicine maker," or they may be called *fofō*, "masseur," a featured practice in traditional Samoan healing that has become a synecdoche for the indigenous medicine.

9. On female spirit seductions, see Mead 1929:269, Krämer [1923] 1949:16a, 16–17; and Schoeffel 1979a:401–11; Mead 1929:269; Goodman 1971:470–71; Holmes 1974:63; and Stuebel 1976:94–95.

10. On the frequency of possession among young women, see further Goodman 1971:471; Schoeffel 1979a:394–95, 412; and Mageo 1991c, 1996a, 1996b.

11. For a beautiful example of the Matā'afa as an icon of chiefliness in the colonial encounter, see J. Matā'afa Amaile, Upolu, August 16, 1899, qtd. in Meleiseā 1987a:102–5.

12. On possession and colonialism, see further Mageo and Howard 1996, and Boddy 1989.

13. On fair-haired girls and possession, see further Goodman 1971:470–71; and Schoeffel 1979a:399, 402.

14. On Telesā and Sauma'iafe as *tāupōu*, see further Goodman 1971:469–71; Clement 1974:83; and Schoeffel 1979a:404–5, 421.

15. On possession and girls wearing their hair down, see also Schoeffel 1979a:402, 411.

16. The most important of these early spirit reports is Stair's, written from fieldnotes collected during a seven-year residence in the 1830s and 1840s (1897:12–13).

17. On these travels, see further Schoeffel 1979a:406–7; Mageo 1991b:361, 1996a, and 1996b.

18. The Samoan sentence is "O le aitu mo'i, le teinetiti lale."

19. The Samoan sentence is "E filo lava i mea e iai tama, pei se aitu."

20. The Samoan sentences are "Pei se aitu" and "'Ai se aitu."

21. On *aitu* taking animal form, see, for example, Stair 1897:216, Holmes 1974:64, Shore 1977:308, Meleiseā 1987a:36–37, and Schoeffel 1979a:407.

22. See Shore 1977:342–50, for a case of possession, where being "entered" is explicitly sexual.

23. On TuiFiti, see further Turner [1884] 1984:62–63; Stuebel 1976:14–20, 54; Cain 1979:204–5, 209; Shore 1977:350–65; Meleiseā 1987a:42.

24. On this symbolism, see further Leach 1958.

25. For two examples, see Goodman 1971:470, and Mageo 1991c:361.

26. See Kurtz 1992, and Obeyesekere 1990, on cultural variations of the Oedipus complex.

27. Sometimes the girl gives evidence of having been "entered" prior to treatment by speaking in a voice not their own. See further Shore 1977:335–36, 1978:177. On remedies for Spirit Sickness, see further Macpherson and Macpherson 1990:118, 199–201.

28. For other possession stories that entail haircutting, see Goodman 1971:469; Schoeffel 1979a:399, and Mageo 1991b:365–66, 369–71.

29. The Samoan term is *gutupi'o*, literally "bent mouth."

30. For examples, see Boddy 1989, Mageo and Howard 1996.

Chapter 10

1. On missionary efforts to suppress erotic entertainments, see further Gilson 1970:96, Moyle 1988:205–6.

2. On this rapid conversion, see Daws 1961; Tiffany 1978; Schoeffel 1979a:446–47, 1979b:3, 1983.

3. For a period there was also a colonial female-only entertainment (*koneseti*). There is insufficient data on this theater to include a discussion of it in this chapter. Sanele, however, watched these plays as a boy and has described typical plots to me; they featured village princess figures, thus girls were the preoccupation of this theater as well. *Koneseti* was dramatic, mythological and biblical, rather than comic (Shore 1977:319). Sanele believes it evolved into church plays called Tala that included both boys and girls. In these plays girl were often given the Christ role (Schoeffel 1979a:212).

4. This split may have begun before contact and then been consolidated in the colonial period (see Kneubuhl 1987). It is unlikely, however, that precontact Samoans made rigid distinctions between dancing and theater. Even today Samoan dance, like hula, may include mimetic figures. On this relation between song and dance in Tonga see Kaeppler 1978. For an example of comic dancing turning into a theatrical skit see Sinavaiana 1992a:213.

5. On old woman and joking, see Churchward 1887:230, and Schoeffel 1979a:215–21.

6. During the period that I associate with a high incidence of possession among Samoan girls, there was a suicide epidemic among Samoan boys (Bowles 1985; Macpherson and Macpherson 1985, 1987). Boys' suicide also represented a moral crisis and was the male analogue of possession for girls. But the moral problem centered on the boy's service relation to elders, which expanded in colonial times and will be explored later in the chapter. The gender patterns of these moral problems varied: girls were teased for sexual feelings when young, felt shame at these feelings in adolescence, and then coded these feelings liminally in possession. Boys resisted elders' authority, were shamed by elders on the spot via reproaches, and shortly thereafter committed suicide. Girls also committed suicide but much less frequently, just as boys also get possessed but less frequently. While boys' suicides are predominately related to issues of hierarchical respect, girls' have to do with illicit passion (Freeman 1983:221).

7. My other sources on the Joking Night are as follows: Williams [1830–32] 1984:247–48; Pritchard 1866:78; Stair 1897:133–34; Turner [1884] 1984:132; Sloan 1940:100–107; Kneubuhl 1987; Moyle 1988:209, 213–19.

8. Alternatively, Moyle suggests Joking Night had a tripartite structure (1988:205–20); Shore breaks the Joking Night into five stages (1977:315–16). These views, including my own, are interpretive.

9. These occasions included investitures, marriages of rank, births of ranking children, first birthdays of ranking children, deaths of ranking persons, and pigeon hunting expeditions (Stair 1897:235; Turner [1884] 1984:90; Churchward 1887:141; Tuiteleleapaga 1980:70, 102).

10. For examples of audience members being the brunt of this kind of humor, see Sloan (1941:68), who finds himself caricatured at an evening festivity, and Sinavaiana (1992a:214), who describes a pastor laughing so hard when caricatured that he falls off a chair.

11. On sex, elopement, and Joking Nights, see also Williams [1830–32] 1984:247–48, and Krämer 1995:377.

12. On these sports, see Wilkes 1845:137; Stair 1897:137–38, 236–38; Turner [1884] 1984:29, 126; Moyle 1971, 1988:96; and Holmes 1969:343. While ceremonies were as-if pledges of fealty, these games were as-if wars. Today, sports competitions from cricket to longboat races betray their resemblance to intervillage wars by occasionally devolving into actual skirmishes.

13. The same fractal quality appears in Samoan ceremonies. In ceremonial presentations in the nineteenth century, for example, accompanying songs might contain the insulting and provocative language typically used prior to battle; still today, important ceremonies include ritualized prestations called *taʻalolo*, in which lead presenters perform choreographic war gestures and brandish the "death clubs" of ancient battles (Moyle 1988:180). On the fractal nature of cultural reality, see Strathern 1991.

14. When I call these entertainments "colonial," I do not mean to suggest they are no longer performed. I refer only to the entertainment's period of inception.

15. Readers may complain that I said in moral discourse tropes were used naively, whereas in contextual discourse tropes were used with awareness. In the present example, however, Samoans seem unaware of what the comic dancer's movements signified. Remember, these actions do not literally signify disrespect but only flagrant joking, and Samoans know that the *ʻaiʻaiuli* dancer is joking: they get the point of this type of joking very well. Further, in *siva*, this joking is tropically subordinated to the girl's dancing. So there is a measure of truth to the typical explanation. It must be added, however, that naïveté/awareness in regards to tropes is always a matter of degree.

16. On girls' bodies speaking a more unblushing language than those of boys, see Churchward 1887:230; Williams [1830–32] 1984:247; Wilkes [1839] 1845, vol. 2:130, 134, 140; and Colvocoresses 1852:87.

17. There is still a tendency to select high-status girls to dance a *taualuga*, and democratization is limited by the money economy. It is customary to throw money at the *taualuga* dancer or insert it in her clothes. Often *taualuga* are danced to raise money; then selection of a dancer is likely to be based on the wealth of a potential dancer's relatives and connections, who will attend and elevate her status—and theirs by extension—by giving as much as they can. On the other hand, if a girl is asked to be her school's village princess—that is, to dance the *taualuga* in an entertainment presentation—and her family is poor, family members will often persuade her to tell the school officials she does not want to dance to save themselves financial embarrassment.

18. On transvestism as a favorite theatrical device, see Shore 1977:318–33, 1978:178; and Sinavaiana 1992a, 1992b.

19. On Samoan sisters and wives and on the terms *teine* and *fafine*, see further Schoeffel 1979a:178, 180; and Shore 1981:199, 204.

20. Schoeffel makes this same point in relation to the *komiti*, which grew out of church auxiliary groups in Western Samoa during the 1920s and 1930s and which took a leading role in village governance and national politics (1979a:459, 1979b, 1983). Missionization is often thought to compromise the status of women (Gailey 1987, Etienne and Leacock 1993). We will see, however, that its effects in Samoa are complex.

21. Sinavaiana recorded this skit, and to the best of her recollection the word *Mama* was in English (pers. comm.), as its English colloquial quality and its capitalization imply. I have seen other Spirit House "wives," when criticized for infidelity, respond by discarding the plastic doll that represented the husband's baby.

22. I have supplied the title here.

23. In the following characterization of Samoan transvestites I refer to a social role rather than the variety of actual individuals. Not all Samoan transvestites seek the role of the stand-up comic. Not all are promiscuous. Nonetheless, these attributes do characterize the role as it is popularly understood.

24. For missionaries who documented Samoan sexual behaviors of which they disapproved, see, for example, Williams [1830–32] 1984:117, 196, 246–48, 232–33; Stair 1897:130–34; and Turner ([1884] 1984:125. For early secular reports that include data on sexuality and marriage but that do not mention transvestism in nineteenth-century Samoa, see, for example, Pritchard 1866, Churchward 1886, Krämer [1902] 1995, Stuebel 1976, and Schultz [1911] n.d. For examples in other Polynesian locales of early comments on both unchristian heterosexuality and upon transvestism, see Levy 1971:12–13; 1973:130–32; Williams 1986:255–56; Watts 1992; Robertson 1989; Morris 1992; and Besnier 1994.

25. The habitation of village buildings illustrates this point, as I have demonstrated elsewhere (Mageo 1996c:595–96).

26. The only song I have heard transvestites perform without explicit sexual reference is "My Way," a song that valorizes individual choice. By their very identity, however, these singers associate individual choice with sex and gender—just as did the missionary encounter—albeit with a rather different set of choices than chastity before marriage and spiritual compatibility in marriage that missionaries recommended to Samoan girls. This song also adds yet another a layer of meaning to the Samoan term for transvestite, as persons of the feminine "way" (fa'a).

Chapter 11

1. See further Mageo 1992b. Obviously, I build on Lévi-Strauss 1970.

2. These pseudonyms and nicknames are typical.

3. Seta refers to the state of being *saisaitia*, "tied up emotionally." Entanglement is an important trope for Samoan psychological and social experience.

4. In Sanele's memory their mother did not favor Fe'e, and he felt sad that Ifi never gave Seta as much attention as she deserved.

5. "Cinderella" is a cross-culturally recurrent tale. The first known version is from China, dating to the eighth century B.C. (Bettelheim 1976:236). We saw in chapter 1 that there is also a Cinderella story in the corpus of Samoan legendary tales (Moyle 1981).

6. In the Samoan mythological view the husband and wife are portrayed as two halves of a larger whole, rather than as vehicles of oppositional meanings. See Holmes 1974:8.

7. *Mana* is one of those pre-Christian terms that has been rewritten by Christianity. Originally, the word signified spiritual power in its light and dark aspects: it was the power of bounty and the power to curse. Today, *mana* is little used and then mainly in church for God, where it signifies the lighter aspects of power. The spirits of old Samoa are now treated as if they have *mana* only in its darker aspects.

8. In small villages people generally know everyone. Absence of familiarity in a visage is one mark of a spirit. Voice is key in Samoan states of possession: the possessed individual is said to speak in a voice not her own, and the identity of the spirit is often determined by its voice, as in "The Girl Scout."

9. On this conception, see also Ochs 1988:23–26.

10. This is not to say that children are supported for doing homework. When Samoan children come home from school they are often expected to do chores for their household and may be hard-pressed to find time to study.

11. Sutter (1980) sees formal schooling as a nontraditional context leading Samoan children away from the indigenous communal values of Samoan society. Formal schooling does introduce a Western set of values, as I have shown. In Samoa, however, competition is as salient a practice as cooperation. Sutter is led astray by the fact that he uses children working at home as his example of children in a traditional setting and children at school as his example of children in a nontraditional setting. In fact, Samoans construe the home setting as communal. In school Samoan youngsters mix with the children of other families. It is, therefore, a legitimate arena for competition. Sutter's comparison should have been between school and a traditionally competitive situation.

12. Sanele's version revives oedipal themes: Seta does not defer to Ifi but marries Vae, a husband to whom Ifi objects; Vae—through the vocation Seta chooses for him—comes to resemble Ifi.

13. Sanele says Ifi was protective of Seta. Early in her marriage Seta's husband, Vae, tried to beat her. Husbands outrank wives, and superiors may beat their juniors. Seta returned home. Several days later Vae came to get her. There was a meeting between Ifi, Vao, Seta, and Vae in which Ifi calmly explained that it was not acceptable to beat Seta. Vae apologized and never attempted to beat her again.

14. A few days later Eleni's wife remarked of Kalo, "Pancakes [*panikeke*] in the morning, pancakes in the afternoon, pancakes in the evening." She meant: he's getting so poor that he is going to be on the Samoan facsimile of a bread and water diet. Sia added that he was running out of money but was not aware of what was happening to him.

15. Samoans conceive of the brother/sister as a complementary relationship (Shore 1977, 1982). Shore argues that the sister tends to be dominant and the brother subordinate, particularly when—as in the present case—the sister is older (1982:233–36). This is true in cultural ideology, but Seta and her brothers are actually engaged in a symmetrical struggle for dominance in which culture history is differentially empowering.

Glossary

This glossary includes only terms that are used repeatedly in the text and that are not redefined with every use.

ʻāiga	extended family
aga	persona
aitu	spirit
aliʻi	high chief
ʻaleʻaleaitu	spirit frenzy, concluding dance at Joking Nights
ʻaumāga	organization of untitled men
aualuma	organization of village sisters and daughters
āvaga	elope
faʻaaloalo	respect
faʻaaluma	conductor clown
faʻafafine	male transvestite
faʻalata	dissimulative
FaʻaSāmoa	the Samoan way of life
Faleaitu	Spirit House
fofō	traditional healer
kuluku	crooked, roguish, but also circuitous, manipulative
loto	inner self
Maʻi Aitu	Spirit Sickness
malae	oval open area at the village center
māvaega	final words, wishes, ordinances, often appointing a successor
mā	shy
pōula	Joking Night
sāʻē	a bawdy dance at Joking Nights
saʻo	straightforward, fair, honest
soa	go-between
tāupōu	village princess

taualuga	dignified dance, putatively danced by the highest-status person present
tautalaitiiti	cheeky
tulāfale	orator
ula	to joke

References

Some of my references are from the London Missionary Archives, which are now called the Council of World Missions Archives, and which I abbreviate CWM Archives. These archival materials are held at the main library in the School for Oriental and African Studies at the University of London. The numbers at the end of these references indicate the box, folder, and jacket in which each letter can be found, in that order.

Ainsworth, M. D. S. 1973. The Development of Infant-Mother Attachment. In *Review of Child Development Research*, vol. 3, ed. B. M. Caldwell and H. N. Ricciuti. Chicago: University of Chicago Press.

Althusser, L. 1971. *Lenin and Philosophy and Other Essays*. Trans. B. Brewster. New York: Monthly Review Press.

American Samoa Digest. 1982. Digest of the headnotes by D. S. Kaufman of the first four volumes of the *American Samoa Report*. Orford, N.H.: Equity.

American Samoa Report. 1978. Vol. 4: 1961–75, ed. W. O'Connor and D. S. Kaufman. Orford, N.H.: Equity.

Anderson, B. 1965. *Mythology and the Tolerance of the Javanese*. Ithaca: Cornell University Press.

Angas, G. F. 1866. *Polynesia: A Popular Description of Islands of the Pacific*. London: Society for the Promotion of Christian Knowledge.

Aronson, E. 1984. *The Social Animal*. New York: W. H. Freeman and Co.

Barthes, R. 1977. The Death of the Author. *Image-Music-Text*. Trans. S. Heath. New York: Hill and Wang.

Bateson, G. 1958. *Naven*. Stanford: Stanford University Press.

Berne, E. 1968. *A Layman's Guide to Psychiatry and Psychoanalysis*. New York: Simon and Schuster.

———. 1972. *Steps to an Ecology of Mind: Collected Essays in Anthropology, Psychiatry, Evolution, and Epistemology*. San Francisco: Chandler.

Battaglia, D., ed. 1995. *Rhetorics of Self-Making*. Berkeley: University of California Press.

Baudrillard, J. 1988. *Jean Baudrillard: Selected Writings*, ed. M. Poster. Stanford: Stanford University Press.

Befu, H. 1980. A Critique of the Group Model of Japanese Society. *Social Analysis* 5(6): 29–43.

Beaglehole, E. and P. Beaglehole. 1938. *Ethnology of Pukapuka*. B. P. Bishop Museum Bulletin 150. Honolulu: Bishop Museum Press.

———. 1946. *Some Modern Maoris*. Wellington: New Zealand Council of Educational Research.

Benedict, Ruth. 1934. *Patterns of Culture*. Boston: Houghton Mifflin.

Besnier, N. 1989. Information Withholding as a Manipulative and Collusive Strategy in Nukulaelae Gossip. *Language in Society* 18:315–41.

———. 1990. Conflict Management, Gossip, and Affective Meaning on Nukulaelae. In *Distentangling: Conflict Discourse in Pacific Societies*, ed. K. A. Watson-Gegeo and G. White. Stanford: Stanford University Press.

———. 1994. Polynesian Gender Liminality through Time and Space. In *Third Sex/Third Gender: Beyond Sexual Dimorphism in Culture and History*, ed. G. Herdt. New York: Zone Books.

———. 1996. Heteroglossic Discourses on Nukulaelae Spirits. In *Spirits in Culture, History, and Mind*, ed. J. Mageo and A. Howard. New York: Routledge.

Bettelheim, B. 1976. *The Uses of Enchantment: The Meaning and Importance of Fairy Tales*. New York: Alfred A. Knopf.

Bindon, J. R., and S. Zansky. 1986. Growth and Body Composition. In *The Changing Samoans: Behavior and Health in Transition*, ed. P. T. Baker, J. M. Hanna, and T. S. Baker. New York: Oxford University Press.

Blanton, C. 1995. *Picturing Paradise: Colonial Photography of Samoa, 1875 to 1925*. Daytona Beach, Fla., and Cologne, Ger.: Southeast Museum of Photography and Rautenstrauch-Joest-Museum of Ethnology.

Bocock, R. 1986. *Hegemony*. London: Tavistock Publications.

Boddy, J. 1989. *Wombs and Alien Spirits: Women, Men, and Zar Cult in Northern Sudan*. Madison: University of Wisconsin Press.

Borofsky, R. 1987. *Making History: Pukapukan and Anthropological Constructions of Knowledge*. Cambridge: Cambridge University Press.

Bowlby, J. 1969. Attachment. *Attachment and Loss*, vol. 1. London: Hogarth.

———. 1980. Loss: Sadness and Depression. *Attachment and Loss*, vol. 3. London: Hogarth.

Bowles, J. R. 1985. Suicide and Attempted Suicide in Contemporary Western Samoa. In *Culture, Youth and Suicide in the Pacific: Papers from an East-West Center Conference*, ed. F. X. Hezel, D. H. Rubinstein, and G. M. White. Honolulu: Center for Asian and Pacific Studies, University of Hawaii.

Brady, I. 1976. *Transactions in Kinship: Adoption and Fosterage in Oceania*. Honolulu: University of Hawaii Press.

Brewer, K. W. 1975. *Armed with the Spirit: Missionary Experiences in Samoa*. Provo, Utah: Brigham Young Press.

Brontë, E. [1847] 1976. *Wuthering Heights*. Oxford: Clarendon.

Bullen, T. 1847. June 12 letter to London Missionary Society Headquarters from Leone, CMW Archives [20/5/C], School of Oriental and African Studies, University of London.

Bunzel, R. L. 1932. Introduction to Zuni Ceremonialism; Zuni Origin Myths; Zuni Ritual Poetry; Auni Katcinas. *Annual Report of the Bureau of American Ethnology to the Secretary of the Smithsonian Institution* 47:467–1086.

Cain, H. 1971. The Sacred Child and the Origins of Spirits in Samoa. *Anthropos* 66:173–81.
———. 1979. *Aitu.* Wiesbaden: Franz Steiner Verlag GMBH.
Canaan, J. E. 1990. Passing Notes and Telling Jokes. In *Uncertain Terms,* ed. F. Ginsburg and A. L. Tsing. Boston: Beacon.
Capps, L. and E. Ochs. 1997. Narrative as Prayer. Paper delivered at the biennial meetings of the Society for Psychological Anthropology.
Carrol, V. 1970. *Adoption in Eastern Oceania.* Honolulu: University of Hawaii Press.
Caton, H., ed. 1990. *The Samoan Reader: Anthropologists Take Stock.* Lanham, Md.: University Press of America.
Chagnon, N. 1968. *Yanomamö, the Fierce People.* New York: Holt, Rinehart and Winston.
Chatterjee, P. 1993. *The Nation and Its Fragments: Colonial and Postcolonial Histories.* Princeton: Princeton University Press.
Chodorow, N. 1974. Family Structure and Feminine Personality. In *Women, Culture and Society,* ed. M. A. Rosaldo and L. Lamphere. Stanford: Stanford University Press.
Churchward, W. B. 1887. *My Consulate in Samoa.* London: Richard Bentley and Son.
Clement [Holland], D. 1974. Samoan Concepts of Mental Illness and Treatment. Ph.D. diss., University of California at Irvine, University Microfilms # DCJ74–27849, Ann Arbor, Mich.
Clifford, J. 1992. Traveling Cultures. In *Cultural Studies,* ed. L. Grossberg, C. Nelson, and P. A. Treichler. New York: Routledge.
Colvocoresses, G. M. 1852. *Four Years in a Government Exploring Expedition.* New York: Cornish and Lampost.
Comaroff, J. 1975. Talking Politics. In *Political Language and Oratory in Traditional Society,* ed. M. Block. London: Academic Press.
Comaroff, J., and J. Comaroff. 1991. *Of Revelation and Revolution: Christianity, Colonialism and Consciousness in South Africa,* vol. 1. Chicago: University of Chicago Press.
———. 1992. *Ethnography and the Historical Imagination.* Boulder: Westview Press.
Coward, R., and J. Ellis. 1977. On the Subject of Lacan. In *Language and Materialism: Developments in Semiology and the Theory of the Subject.* Boston: Routledge and Kegan Paul.
Dale, P. 1986. *The Myth of Japanese Uniqueness.* London: Croom Helm.
Davidoff, L., and C. Hall. 1987. *Family Fortunes: Men and Women of the English Middle Class, 1780–1850.* Chicago: University of Chicago Press.
Davidson, J. M. 1974. Samoan Structural Remains and Settlement Patterns. *Archaeology in Western Samoa,* vol. 2:225–44. Auckland: Auckland Institute and Museum.
Davidson, J. W. 1967. *Samoa mo Samoa: The Emergence of the Independent State of Western Samoa.* Melbourne: Oxford University Press.
Davies, H. 1961. *Worship and Theology in England from Watts and Wesley to Maurice, 1690–1850.* Princeton: Princeton University Press.
Daws, A. G. 1961. The Great Samoan Awakening of 1839. *Journal of the Polynesian Society* 70:326–37.
Day, W. 1839. November 4 letter to London Missionary Society Headquarters from 'Upolu, CWM Archives (12/6/F), School of Oriental and African Studies, University of London.
Derrida, J. 1978. *Writing and Difference.* Trans. A. Bass. Chicago: University of Chicago Press.

---. 1994. *Given Time: I. Counterfeit Money.* Trans. P. Kamuf. Chicago: University of Chicago Press.
Douglas, M. 1973. The Two Bodies. *Natural Symbols.* New York: Vintage.
---. 1982a. *In the Active Voice.* London: Routledge and Kegan Paul.
---. 1982b. *Essays in the Sociology of Perception.* London: Routledge and Kegan Paul.
Dreyfus, H. L. 1984. What Expert Systems Can't Do. *Raritan* 3(4): 22–36.
Drummond, G. 1845. August 23 letter to London Missionary Society Headquarters from Sapapalii, CWM Archives (18/7/B), School of Oriental and African Studies, University of London.
Dumont, L. 1966. *Homo Hierarchicus.* Trans. M. Sainsbury. Chicago: University of Chicago Press.
Duranti, A. 1981. *The Samoan Fono: A Sociolinguistic Study.* Canberra: Research School of Pacific Studies, Australian National University.
---. 1983. Samoan Speechmaking across Social Events: One Genre In and Out of Fono. *Language and Society* 12:1–22.
---. 1984a. *Intentions, Self, and Local Theories of Meaning: Words and Social Action in a Samoan Context.* La Jolla: Center for Human Information Processing.
---. 1984b. *Lauga* and *Talanoaga:* Structure and Variation in the Language of a Samoan Speech Event. In *Dangerous Words: Language and Politics in the Pacific,* ed. D. Brenneis and F. Meyers. New York: New York University Press.
---. 1994. *From Grammar to Politics.* Berkeley: University of California Press.
Ellis, S. 1842. *Daughters of England: Their Position in Society, Character and Responsibilities.* London: Fisher.
Emerson, R. W. 1882. *Essays and Representative Men.* London: Collins Clear-Type.
Erikson, E. 1963. *Childhood and Society.* New York: Norton.
Etiene, M., and E. Leacock, eds. 1993. *Women and Colonization.* New York: Praeger.
Ewing, K. P. 1990. The Illusion of Wholeness. *Ethos* 18(3): 251–78.
Festinger, L. 1957. *A Theory of Cognitive Dissonance.* Stanford: Stanford University Press.
Field, J. M. 1984. *Mau: Samoa's Struggle for Freedom.* Auckland: Polynesian Press.
Firth, R. W. 1949. The Analysis of Mana. *Journal of the Polynesian Society* 49:483–510.
Fitzhugh, G. 1854. *Sociology for the South, or the Failure of Free Society.* Richmond: A. Morris.
Fogelson, R. D. 1982. Person, Self, and Identity: Some Anthropological Retrospects, Circumspects, and Prospects. In *Psychosocial Theories of the Self,* ed. B. Lee. New York: Plenum Press.
Foucault, M. 1977. *Discipline and Punish.* Trans. A. Sheridan. New York: Pantheon.
---. 1980. *Power/Knowledge: Selected Interviews and Other Writings, 1972–1977.* Trans. C. Gordon. New York: Pantheon Books.
---. 1986. *The History of Sexuality,* vol. 2: *The Use of Pleasure;* vol. 3: *The Care of the Self.* Trans. R. Hurley. New York: Pantheon.
---. 1988. Technologies of the Self. In *Technologies of the Self,* ed. L. H. Martin, H. Gutman, and P. H. Hutton. Amherst: University of Massachusetts Press.
---. 1990. *The History of Sexuality,* vol. 1: *An Introduction.* Trans. R. Hurley. New York: Random House.
Franco, R. W. 1989. Samoan Representations of World War II and Military Work: The Emergence of International Movement Networks. In *The Pacific Theater: Island Representations of World War II,* ed. G. M. White and L. Lindstrom. Honolulu: University of Hawaii Press.

Freeman, D. 1983. *Margaret Mead and Samoa: The Making and Unmaking of an Anthropological Myth.* Cambridge: Harvard University Press.

———. 1984. The Burthen of a Mystery. *Oceania* 54(3): 247–54.

———. 1985. Reply to Shore. *Oceania* 55(3): 247–54.

Freud, A. 1937. *The Ego and the Mechanisms of Defense.* London: Hogarth Press and the Institute of Psycho-Analysis.

———. 1966. *The Ego and the Mechanisms of Defense.* New York: International Universities Press.

Freud, S. [1900] 1953. Interpretation of Dreams. *The Standard Edition of the Complete Psychological Works of Sigmund Freud,* vol. 10. Trans. J. Strachey. London: Hogarth Press.

———. [1917] 1966. Introductory Lectures on Psychoanalysis. *The Standard Edition of the Complete Psychological Works of Sigmund Freud,* vol. 15. Trans. J. Strachey. New York: Norton.

———. 1923. The Ego and the Id. *The Standard Edition of the Complete Psychological Works of Sigmund Freud,* vol. 19. Trans. J. Strachey. New York: Norton.

———. [1933] 1964. New Introdutory Lectures on Psycho-Analysis. *The Standard Edition of the Complete Psychological Works of Sigmund Freud,* vol. 22. Trans. J. Strachey. London: Hogarth Press.

———. [1940] 1964. An Outline of Psycho-Analysis. *The Standard Edition of the Complete Psychological Works of Sigmund Freud,* vol. 22. Trans. J. Strachey. London: Hogarth Press.

———. 1961. *Civilization and Its Discontents.* Trans. J. Strachey. New York: Norton.

Fujita, M. 1991. The Diversity of Concepts of Selves and Its Implications for Conducting Cross-Cultural Research. *Anthropological and Humanism Quarterly* 16(1): 20–21.

Gailey, C. W. 1987. *Kinship to Kingship: Gender Hierarchy and State Formation in the Tongan Islands.* Austin: University of Texas Press.

———. 1993. Putting Down Sisters and Wives: Tongan Women and Colonization. In *Women and Colonization,* ed. M. Etiene and E. Leacock. New York: Praeger.

Gallimore, R., J. W. Boggs, and C. Jordan. 1974. *Culture, Behavior and Education: A Study of Hawaiian Americans.* Beverly Hills: Sage.

Gardner, L. C. 1965. Gautavai: *A Study of Samoan Values.* Master's thesis, University of Hawaii.

Garrett, J. 1982. *To Live among the Stars: Christian Origins in Oceania.* Geneva: World Council of Churches, in association with the Institute of Pacific Studies.

Geertz, C. 1973. Person, Time and Conduct in Bali. In *Interpretations of Culture.* New York: Basic Books.

———. [1974] 1984. "From the Natives' Point of View": On the Nature of Anthropological Understanding. In *Culture Theory,* ed. R. A. Shweder and R. A. LeVine. Cambridge: Cambridge University Press.

———. 1980. *Negara: The Theater State in Nineteenth-Century Bali.* Princeton: Princeton University Press.

Gelman, R., and R. Baillargeon. 1983. A Review of Some Piagetian Concepts. In *Manual of Child Psychology,* vol. 3: *Cognitive Development,* ed. J. H. Flavell and E. M. Markman. New York: John Wiley.

Gerber, E. R. 1975. The Cultural Patterning of Emotions in Samoa. Ph.D. diss., University of California at San Diego.

———. 1985. Rage and Obligation: Samoan Emotion in Conflict. In *Person, Self and Experience: Exploring Pacific Ethnopsychologies*, ed. G. M. White and J. Kirkpatrick. Berkeley: University of California Press.
Gilligan, C. 1982. *In a Different Voice*. Cambridge: Harvard University Press.
Gilson, R. P. 1970. *Samoa: 1830 to 1900*. Melbourne: Oxford University Press.
Goldman, I. 1970. *Ancient Polynesian Society*. Chicago: University of Chicago Press.
Good, K. 1991. *Into the Heart: One Man's Pursuit of Love and Knowledge among the Yanomama*. New York: Simon and Schuster.
Goodman, R. A. 1971. Some Aitu Beliefs of Modern Samoans. *Journal of the Polynesian Society* 80:463–79.
———. 1983. *Mead's Coming of Age in Samoa: A Dissenting View*. Oakland: Piperine Press.
Gray, J. A. C. 1960. *Amerika Samoa: A History of American Samoa and Its United States Naval Administration*. New York: Arno Press.
———. 1980. *Amerika Samoa*. Annapolis: U.S. Naval Institute.
Grimshaw, B. E. 1907. *In the Strange South Seas*. London: Hutchinson.
Gunson, Niel. 1978. *Messengers of Grace: Evangelical Missionaries in the South Seas, 1797–1860*. New York: Oxford University Press.
Haan, N. 1977. *Coping and Defending: Processes of Self-Environment Organization*. New York: Academic Press.
Hallpike, C. R. 1969. Social Hair. *Man* n.s. 4:254–64.
Handy, E. S. C. [1927] 1978. Polynesian Religion. In *Bernice P. Bishop Museum [Honolulu] Bulletin 34*. Millwood: Kraus.
Hanson, A. 1989. The Making of the Maori: Cultural Invention and Its Logic. *American Anthropologist* 91:890–902.
Haraway, D. 1989. *Primate Visions: Gender, Race, and Nature in the World of Modern Science*. New York: Routledge.
Harbutt, W. 1841. April 21 letter to London Missionary Society Headquarters from 'Upolu, CWM Archives (14/5/C), School of Oriental and African Studies, University of London.
Hardie, C. 1839. November 3 letter to London Missionary Society Headquarters from Savai'i, CWM Archives (12/6/E), School of Oriental and African Studies, University of London.
———. 1842. February 9 letter to London Missionary Society Headquarters from Savai'i, CWM Archives (15/5/A), School of Oriental and African Studies, University of London.
Harper, C., Governor Hammond, Dr. Simms, and Professor Dew. 1852. *The Pro-Slavery Argument*. Charleston: Walker, Richards and Co.
Harris, G. G. 1989. Concepts of Individual, Self, and Person in Description and Analysis. *American Anthropologist* 91(3): 599–612.
Hebdige, D. 1988. *Hiding in the Light: On Images and Things*. London: Routledge.
Henry, Brother Fred. [1979] 1983. *History of Samoa*. Apia: Commercial Printers Ltd.
———. 1980. *Samoa: An Early History*. Revised by N. I. T. P., Tuiteleleapaga. Tutuila: American Samoa Department of Education.
Herdrich, D. J. 1991. Towards an Understanding of Samoan Pigeon Mounds. *Journal of the Polynesian Society* 100: 381–435.
Hjarnø, J. 1979–80. Social Reproduction: Towards an Understanding of Aboriginal Samoa. *Folk* 21–22:72–123.

Hobsbawm, E., and T. Ranger. 1983. *The Invention of Tradition.* Cambridge: Cambridge University Press.

Hoffman, N. von, and G. B. Trudeau. 1976. *Tales from Margaret Mead's Taproom.* Kansas City: Sheed and Ward.

Hollan, D. 1992. Cross-Cultural Differences in Self. *Journal of Anthropological Research* 48:283–300.

Holland, D. 1992a. How Cultural Systems Become Desire. In *Human Motives and Cultural Models,* ed. R. G. D'Andrade and C. Strauss. Cambridge: Cambridge University Press.

———. 1992b. Review of Thinking through Culture. *American Anthropologist* 94:747–48.

Holland, D., and N. Quinn. 1987. *Cultural Models in Language and in Thought.* Cambridge: Cambridge University Press.

Holmes, L. D. 1957. The Restudy of Manu'an Culture. Ph.D. diss., Northwestern University.

———. 1958. *Ta'u: Stability and Change in a Samoan Village.* Wellington: Polynesian Society.

———. 1967. The Function of Kava in Modern Samoan Culture. In *Ethnopharmacologic Search for Psychoactive Drugs,* ed. D. H. Erform. Washington, D.C.: Department of Health, Education and Welfare.

———. 1969. Samoan Oratory. *Journal of American Folklore* 82:342–45.

———. 1974. *Samoan Village.* Palo Alto: Stanford University Press.

———. 1987. *Quest for the Real Samoa.* South Hadley, Mass.: Bergin and Garvey.

Howard, A. 1970. *Learning to Be Rotuman.* New York: Teachers College Press.

———. 1974. *Ain't No Big Thing: Coping Strategies in a Hawaiian-American Community.* Honolulu: University of Hawaii Press.

Howard, A., and J. Kirkpatrick. 1989. Social Organization. In *Developments in Polynesian Ethnology,* ed. A. Howard and R. Borofsky. Honolulu: University of Hawaii Press.

Howard, A., and J. Mageo. 1996. Introduction. In *Spirits in Culture, History, and Mind,* ed. J. Mageo and A. Howard. New York: Routledge.

Hsu, F. L. K. 1961. American Core Value and National Character. In *Psychological Anthropology: Approaches to Culture and Personality,* ed. F. L. K. Hsu. Homewood, Ill.: Dorsey.

———. 1981. *Americans and Chinese: Passage to Differences.* Honolulu: University of Hawaii Press.

Huebner, T. 1986. Vernacular Literacy: English as a Language of Wider Communication and Language Shift in American Samoa. *Journal of Multi-Lingual and Multi-Cultural Development* 7(5): 393–411.

Hutton, J. 1874. *Missionary Life in the Southern Seas.* London: Henry S. King.

Inkeles, A., E. Hanfmann, and H. Beier. 1961. Modal Personality and Adjustment to the Soviet Socio-Political System. In *Studying Personality Cross-Culturally,* ed. B. Kaplan. New York: Harper and Row.

Institutions and Customs of the Samoans: Ofu ma Amioga Taua FaaSamoa mo Aoga i Samoa i Sisifo. MS. [1944] 1954. Trans. Brother Herman [Seringer]. Le'ala.

James, K. 1994. Effeminate Males and Changes in the Construction of Gender in Tonga. *Pacific Studies* 17:39–69.

Jolly, M. 1992. Specter of Inauthenticity. *Contemporary Pacific* 4:49–72.

Jung, C. G. 1956. On the Psychology of the Trickster Figure. In *The Trickster: A Study in American Indian Mythology, with Commentaries by K. Kerenyi and C. G. Jung*, ed. P. Radin. London: Routledge and Kegan Paul.

———. 1962–73. *The Collected Works*. Trans. R.F.C. Hull. Bollingen Series no. 20. Princeton: Princeton University Press.

———. 1963. Aion: Researches into the Phenomenology of the Self. *The Collected Works*, vol. 9:2. Trans. R. F. C. Hull. Bollingen Series no. 20. Princeton: Princeton University Press.

———. 1966. Two Essays on Analytical Psychology. *The Collected Works*, vol. 7. Trans. R. F. C. Hull. Bollingen Series no. 20. Princeton: Princeton University Press.

———. 1970. Civilization in Transition. *The Collected Works*, vol. 10. Trans. R. F. C. Hull. Bollingen Series no. 20. Princeton: Princeton University Press.

———. 1971. Psychological Types. *The Collected Works*, vol. 6. Trans. R. F. C. Hull. Bollingen Series no. 20. Princeton: Princeton University Press.

Kaeppler, A. L. 1978. Melody, Drone, and Decoration: Underlying Structures and Surface Manifestations in Tongan Art and Society. In *Art in Society: Studies in Styles, Culture and Aesthetics*, ed. M. Greenhalgh and V. Megaw. Washington, D.C.: National Gallery of Art.

———. 1839. January 15 letter to London Missionary Society Headquarters from Tutuila. Council of World Mission Archives (12/6/A). School of Oriental and African Studies. London: University of London.

———. 1839. June 10 letter to London Missionary Society Headquarters from Tutuila. Council of World Mission Archives (12/6/D). School of Oriental and African Studies. London: University of London.

———. 1840. March 20 letter to London Missionary Society Headquarters from Tutuila. Council of World Mission Archives (13/5/A). School of Oriental and African Studies. London: University of London.

Karp, I. 1989. Power and Capacity in Rituals of Possession. In *Creativity of Power*, ed. W. Arens and I. Karp. Washington, D.C.: Smithsonian Institution Press.

Keesing, F. M. 1934. *Modern Samoa: Its Government and Changing Life*. London: Allen and Unwin.

———. 1937. The Taupo System of Samoa: A Study of Institutional Change. *Oceania* 8:1–14.

Keesing, F. M., and M. M. Keesing. 1956. *Elite Communication in Samoa*. New York: Farrar, Straus and Giroux.

Keesing, R. 1984. Rethinking Mana. *Journal of Anthropological Research* 40(1): 137–56.

———. 1990. Creating the Past: Custom and Identity in the Contemporary Pacific. *Contemporary Pacific* 1(1): 19–42.

Kelly, J. 1984. *Women, History, and Theory: The Essays of Joan Kelly*. Chicago: University of Chicago Press.

———. 1991. *The Politics of Virtue: Hinduism, Sexuality, and Countercolonial Discourse in Fiji*. Chicago: University of Chicago Press.

Kikuchi, W. K. 1964. Petroglyphs in American Samoa. *Journal of the Polynesian Society* 73:163–66.

Kirch, P. V. 1984. *The Evolution of the Polynesian Chiefdoms*. Cambridge: Cambridge University Press.

Kneubuhl, V. 1987. Traditional Performances in Samoan Culture: Two Forms. *Asian Theater Journal* 4(2): 166–76.

Kohlberg, L. 1973. Continuities and Discontinuities in Childhood and Adult Moral Development Revisited. In *Collected Papers on Moral Development and Moral Education,* essay no. 3. Cambridge, Mass: Moral Education Research Foundation, Harvard University. (This collection has no editor and no pagination.)

Kohlberg, L., and R. Kramer 1969. Continuities and Discontinuities in Childhood and Adult Moral Development. *Human Development* 12:93–120.

Kohlberg, L., C. Levine, and A. Hewer. 1983. *Moral Stages: A Current Formulation and a Response to Critics.* Basel: Karger.

Kondo, D. K. 1990. *Crafting Selves: Power, Gender, and Discourses of Identity in a Japanese Workplace.* Chicago: University of Chicago Press.

Koskinen, A. A. 1967. *Linking of Symbols: Polynesian Patterns 2.* Helsinki: Finnish Society for Missionary Research.

Krämer, A. [1902] 1994. *The Samoan Islands: The Outline of a Monograph Giving Special Consideration to German Samoa,* vol. 1. Trans. T. Verhaaren. Honolulu: University of Hawai'i Press.

———. [1902] 1995. *The Samoan Islands: The Outline of a Monograph Giving Special Consideration to German Samoa,* vol. 2. Trans. T. Verhaaren. Honolulu: University of Hawai'i Press.

———. [1902] 1942. The Samoan Islands. Unpublished translations of *Die Samoa Inseln,* vols. 2. Trans. D. H. and M. Debeer. Apia, W. Samoa: Department of Native Affairs.

———. [1923] 1949. *Salamasina: Scenes from Ancient Samoan Culture and History.* MS. Trans. unknown. American Samoa Community College Pacific Collection.

Kramer, P. D. 1993. *Listening to Prozac.* New York: Penguin.

Kirkpatrick, J., and G. M. White. 1985. Exploring Ethnopsychologies. In *Person, Self and Experience,* ed. G. White and J. Kirkpatrick. Berkeley: University of California Press.

Kristeva, J. 1980. *Desire in Language: A Semiotic Approach to Literature and Art,* ed. L. S. Roudiez. Trans. T. Gora, A. Jardine and L. S. Roudiez. New York: Columbia University Press.

Kroeber, A. L. 1917. Zuni Kin and Clan. In *Anthropological Papers,* vol. 18, pt. 2. New York: American Museum of Natural History.

Kurtz, S. 1992. *All the Mothers Are One.* New York: Colombia University Press.

Lacan, J. 1968. The Mirror Phase. *New Left Review* 51:70–79.

———. 1977. *Écrits: A Selection.* Trans. A. Sheridan. New York: W. W. Norton.

Lamb, M. E. 1987. Predictive Implications of Individual Differences in Attachment. *Journal of Counseling and Clinical Psychology* 55:817–24.

Lambek, Michael. 1981. *Human Spirits: A Cultural Account of Trance in Mayotte.* Cambridge Studies in Cultural Systems, 6. Cambridge: Cambridge University Press.

Lamphere, L. 1993. The Domestic Sphere of Women and the Public World of Men: The Strengths and Limitations of an Anthropological Dichotomy. In *Gender in Cross-Cultural Perspective,* ed. C. B. Brettell and C. F. Sargent. Englewood Cliffs, N.J.: Prentice-Hall.

Landerman, Carol. 1991. *Taming the Wind of Desire: Psychology, Medicine, and Aesthetics in Malay Shamanistic Performance.* Berkeley: University of California Press.

Leach, E. R. 1958. Magical Hair. *Journal of the Royal Anthropological Institute* 88:147–64.

Leacock, E. 1972. Introduction to Engel's *Origins of the Family, Private Property and the State.* New York: International Publishers.

Lebra, T. S. 1976. *Japanese Patterns of Behavior*. Honolulu: University of Hawaii Press.

Lévi-Strauss, C. 1956. The Family. In *Man, Culture and Society*, ed. H. L. Shapiro. London: Oxford University Press.

———. 1966. *The Savage Mind*. Trans. G. Weidenfeld. Chicago: University of Chicago Press.

———. 1970. *The Raw and the Cooked*. Trans. J. and D. Weightnor. New York: Harper and Row.

LeVine, R. A., and P. M. Miller. 1990. Commentary. *Human Development* 33:78–80.

Levy, R. I. 1969. Tahitian Adoption as a Psychological Message. In *Adoption in Eastern Oceania*, ed. V. Carroll. Honolulu: University of Hawaii Press.

———. 1971. The Community Function of Tahitian Male Transvestism: A Hypothesis. *Anthropological Quarterly* 44(1): 12–21.

———. 1973. *Tahitians: Mind and Experience in the Society Islands*. Chicago: University of Chicago Press.

———. 1974. Tahiti, Sin, and the Question of Integration between Personality and Sociocultural Systems. In *Culture and Personality*, ed. R. A. LeVine. New York: Aldine.

———. 1978. Tahitian Gentleness and Redundant Controls. In *Learning Non-Aggression: The Experience of Non-Literate Societies*, ed. A. Montagu. New York: Oxford University Press.

———. 1983. Introduction: Self and Emotion. *Ethos* 11(3): 128–34.

Levy, R, J. M. Mageo, and A. Howard. 1996. Gods, Spirits and History. In *Spirits in Culture, History, and Mind*, ed. J. M. Mageo and A. Howard. New York: Routledge.

Lewis, O. 1951. *Life in a Mexican Village: Tepoztlan Restudied*. Urbana: University of Illinois Press.

Love, J. W. 1983. Review of Sala'ilua: A Samoan Mystery by Bradd Shore. *Pacific Studies* 7(1):122–45.

Li An-Che. 1937. Zuni: Some Observations and Queries. *American Anthropologist* 39:62–76.

Linnekin, J. 1991a. Structural History and Political Economy: The Contact Encounter in Hawaii and Samoa. *History and Anthropology* 5:203–32.

———. 1991b. Fine Mats and Money: Contending Exchange Paradigms in Colonial Samoa. *Anthropological Quarterly* 64(1): 1–13.

———. 1991c. Cultural Invention and the Dilemma of Authenticity. *American Anthropologist* 93(2): 446–49.

Luhrmann, T. M. 1994. The Good Parsi: The Postcolonial "Feminization" of a Colonial Elite. *Man* 29(2): 333–58.

Luomala, K. [1955] 1986. *Voices on the Wind*. Honolulu: Bishop Museum Press.

Lutz, C. 1988. *Unnatural Emotions: Everyday Sentiments on a Micronesian Atoll and their Challenge to Western Theory*. Chicago: University of Chicago Press.

———. 1990. Engendered Emotions. In *Language and the Politics of Emotion*, ed. C. Lutz and L. Abu-Lughod. Cambridge: Cambridge University Press.

Lutz, C., and L. Abu-Lughod, eds. 1990. *Language and the Politics of Emotion*. Cambridge: Cambridge University Press.

Macdonald, A. 1842. May 27 letter to London Missionary Society Headquarters from Savai'i. Council of World Missions Archives (15/5/C). School of Oriental and African Studies, University of London.

Macpherson, C. 1991. Samoan Kinship in New Zealand. Talk presented for the Pacific

Islands Studies Occasional Seminar Series (Feb. 15). University of Hawai'i at Manoa.

Macpherson, C., and L. Macpherson. 1985. Suicide in Western Samoa: A Sociological Perspective. In *Culture, Youth and Suicide in the Pacific: Papers from an East-West Center Conference*, ed. F. K. Hezel, D. H. Rubinstein, and G. M. White. Honolulu: Center for Asian and Pacific Studies, University of Hawaii at Manoa.

———. 1987. Towards an Explanation of Recent Trends in Suicide in Western Samoa. *Man* n.s. 22:305–30.

———. 1990. *Samoan Medical Belief and Practice*. Auckland: Auckland University Press.

Mageo, J. M. [Danaan]. 1979. The Image and the Soul. Ph.D. diss., University of California at Santa Cruz.

———. 1988. *Mālosi:* A Psychological Exploration of Mead's and Freeman's Work and of Samoan Aggression. *Pacific Studies* 11(2): 25–65.

———. 1989a. *Āmio/Aga* and *Loto:* Perspectives on the Structure of the Self in Samoa. *Oceania* 59:181–99.

———. 1989b. Ferocious Is the Centipede: A Study of the Significance of Eating and Speaking in Samoa. *Ethos* 17:387–427.

———. 1991a. Moral Discourse and the *Loto*. *American Anthropologist* 93:405–20.

———. 1991b. Inhibitions and Compensations: A Study of the Effects of Negative Sanctions in Three Pacific Cultures. *Pacific Studies* 14(3): 1–40.

———. 1991c. *Ma'i Aitu:* The Cultural Logic of Possession in Samoa. *Ethos* 19:352–83.

———. 1992a. Male Transvestism and Culture Change in Samoa. *American Ethnologist* 19(3): 443–59.

———. 1992b. Submerged Forms: Properties of Plot in Narrative Discourse. *Semiotica* 92(1–2): 49–73.

———. 1994. Hairdos and Don'ts: Hair Symbolism and Sexual History in Samoa. *Man* 29:407–32.

———. 1995. The Reconfiguring Self. *American Anthropologist* 97(2): 282–96.

———. 1996a. Spirit Girls and Marines: Historicizing Possession and Historicized Ethnopsychiatry in Samoa. *American Ethnologist* 23:61–82.

———. 1996b. Continuity and Shape Shifting: Samoan Spirits in Culture History. In *Spirits in Culture, History, and Mind*, ed. J. Mageo and A. Howard. New York: Routledge.

———. 1996c. Samoa, on the Wilde Side: Male Transvestism, Oscar Wilde, and Liminality in Making Gender. *Ethos* 24(4): 588–627.

———. n.d. *On Writing Semiotic Histories: Joking Nights, or a Genealogy of Samoan Entertainments*. MS.

Mageo, J., and A. Howard. 1996. *Spirits in Culture, History, and Mind*. New York: Routledge.

Marcus, G. C. 1989. Chieftainship. In *Developments in Polynesian Ethnology*, ed. A. Howard and R. Borofsky. Honolulu: University of Hawaii Press.

Marcus, S. 1966. *The Other Victorians: A Study of Sexuality and Pornography in Mid-Nineteenth-Century England*. New York: Basic Books.

Marcuse, H. 1966. *Eros and Civilization*. Boston: Beacon.

Markus, H. R., and S. Kitayama. 1991. Culture and the Self: Implications for Cognition, Emotion and Motivation. *Psychological Review* 98:224–53.

Markus, H. R., and E. Wurf. 1987. The Dynamic Self-Concept: A Social Psychological Perspective. *Annual Review of Psychology* 38:299–337.

Marples, M. J. 1950. The Incidence of Certain Skin Diseases in Western Samoa: A Preliminary Survey. *Transactions of the Royal Society of Tropical Medicine and Hygiene* 44(3): 327–32.

Marriott, M. 1976. Hindu Transactions: Diversity without Dualism. In *Transactions and Meaning*, ed. B. Kapferer. Philadelphia: Institute for the Study of Human Issues.

Marsack, C. C. 1961. *A Samoan Medely*. London: Robert Hale.

Matāʻafa Tuʻi, T. F. 1987. *Lāuga: Samoan Oratory*. Suva: University of the South Pacific (USP) and the National University of Western Samoa.

Martini, M., and J. Kirkpatrick. 1981. Early Interactions in the Marquesas Islands. In *Culture and Early Interactions*, ed. T. M. Field, A. M. Sostek, P. Vietze, and P. H. Leiderman. Hillsdale, N.J.: Erlbaum.

Mauss, M. [1938] 1985. A Category of the Human Mind: The Notion of Person; the Notion of Self. Trans. W. D. Halls. In *The Category of the Person*, ed. S. Collins and S. Lukes. Cambridge: Cambridge University Press.

———. 1990. *The Gift: The Form and Reason for Exchange in Archaic Society*. Trans. W. D. Halls. London: Routledge.

Maynard, J. 1993. *Victorian Discourses on Sexuality and Religion*. New York: Cambridge University Press.

Mead, G. H. 1934. *Mind, Self and Society*, pt. 3, ed. C. W. Norris. Chicago: University of Chicago Press.

Mead, M. [1928] 1961. *Coming of Age in Samoa*. New York: Morrow Quill.

———. 1929. Americanization in Samoa. *American Mercury*, no. 63 (March): 264–70.

———.[1930] 1969. *The Social Organization of Manuʻa*. Honolulu: Bishop Museum Press.

———. 1935. *Sex and Temperament in Three Primitive Societies*. New York: William Morrow.

———. 1937. The Samoans. *Cooperation and Competition among Primitive Peoples*. New York: McGraw-Hill.

———. 1942. Balinese Character. In *Balinese Character*, by G. Bateson and M. Mead. New York: New York Academy of Sciences.

———. 1968. The Samoans. In *Peoples and Cultures of the Pacific*, ed. A. Vayada. New York: Natural History Press.

Meleiseā, M. 1987a. *Lagāga: A Short History of Western Samoa*. Suva: Institute of Pacific Studies, USP.

———. 1987b. *The Making of Modern Samoa*. Suva: Institute of Pacific Studies, USP.

Millar, J. 1806. *Origins of the Distinction of Ranks*. Edinburgh: William Blackwood.

Miller, P. J., H. Fung, and J. Mintz. 1996. Self-Construction through Narrative Practices. *Ethos* 24(2): 237–80.

Mills, W. 1844. March 19, letter to London Missionary Society Headquarters from ʻUpolu. Council of World Missions (17/6/B). School of Oriental and African Studies, University of London.

Milner, G. B. 1966. *Samoan Dictionary*. Pago Pago: American Samoa Government. Reprinted 1979.

Morris, R. J. 1992. Same-Sex Friendships in Hawaiian Lore: Constructing the Canon. In *Oceanic Homosexualities*, ed. S. O. Murry. New York: Garland.

Morton, H. 1996. *Becoming Tongan: An Ethnography of Childhood*. Honolulu: Unversity of Hawai'i Press.
Moyle, R. 1971. Samoan Traditional Music. Ph.D. diss., University of Auckland.
———. 1975. Sexuality in Samoan Art Forms. *Archives of Sexual Behavior* 4(3): 227–47.
———. 1981. *Fāgogo: Fables from Samoa in Samoan and English*. Oxford: Oxford University Press, for Auckland University Press.
———. 1988. *Traditional Samoan Music*. Auckland: Auckland University Press, in association with the Institute for Polynesian Studies.
Murray, A. 1838. August 29 letter to London Missionary Society Headquarters from Tutuila. Council of World Mission Archives (11/8/B). School of Oriental and African Studies. London: University of London.
———. 1839. January 15 letter to London Missionary Society Headquarters from Tutuila. Council of World Missions Archives (12/6/A). School of Oriental and African Studies, University of London.
———. 1840. March 20 letter to London Missionary Society Headquarters from Tutuila. Council of World Missions Archives (13/5/A). School of Oriental and African Studies, University of London.
Murray, D. W. 1993. What Is the Western Concept of Self? On Fogetting David Hume. *Ethos* 23:3–23.
Muse, C., and S. Muse. 1982. *The Birds and Birdlore of Samoa*. Walla Walla, Wash.: Pioneer Press.
Nakane, C. 1970. *Japanese Society*. Berkeley: University of California Press.
Neuman. K. S. 1988. *Falling from Grace: The Experience of Downward Mobility in the American Middle Class*. New York: Free Press.
Nordström, A. D. 1995. Photography of Samoa: Production, Dissemination, and Use. In *Picturing Paradise: Colonial Photography of Samoa, 1875 to 1925*, ed. C. Blanton. Daytona Beach, Florida: Southeast Museum of Photography in collaboration with the Rautenstrauch-Joset-Museum of Ethnology.
Obeyesekere, G. 1981. *Medusa's Hair*. Chicago: University of Chicago Press.
———. 1990. *The Work of Culture: Symbolic Transformations in Psychoanalysis and Anthropology*. Chicago: University of Chicago Press.
———. 1992. *The Apotheosis of Captain Cook*. Princeton: Princeton University Press.
Ochs, E. 1982. Talking to Children in Western Samoa. *Language in Society* 11:77–104.
———. 1988. *Culture and Language Development: Language Acquisition and Language Socialization in a Samoan Village*. New York: Cambridge University Press.
Oliver, D. 1974. *Ancient Tahitian Society*, vol. 3. Honolulu: University of Hawaii Press.
O'Meara, T. 1990. *Samoan Planters*. Forth Worth: Holt, Rinehart and Winston.
O'Reilly, P. 1957. *Hebridais: Répertoire Bio-Bibliographique des Nouvelles-Hebrides*. Paris: Société des Oceanistes.
Ortner, S. B. 1981. Gender and Sexuality in Hierarchical Societies. In *Sexual Meanings*, ed. S. B. Ortner and H. Whitehead. New York: Cambridge University Press.
———. 1991. Reading America: Preliminary Notes on Class Cultures. In *Recapturing Anthropology: Working in the Present*, ed. R. G. Fox. Santa Fe: School of American Research Press.
Perry, A. F. 1974. The American Board of Commissioners for Foreign Missions and the London Missionary Society in the Nineteenth Century: A Study of Ideas. Ph.D. diss. (History), Washington University.

Piaget, J. 1952. *The Origins of Intelligence in Children.* Trans. M. Cook. New York: International University Press.

Piers, G., and M. B. Singer. 1953. *Shame and Guilt: A Psychoanalytic and a Cultural Study.* Springfield, Ill.: Thomas.

Powell, T. A. 1845. November 3 letter to London Missionary Society Headquarters from 'Upolu. Council of World Missions Archives (18/8/B). School of Oriental and African Studies, University of London.

Pratt, G. 1840. April 1 letter to London Missionary Society Headquarters from Savai'i. Council of World Missions Archives (13/5/B). School of Oriental and African Studies, University of London.

———. [1862/1911] 1977. *Pratt's Grammar and Dictionary of the Samoan Language.* Apia: Malua.

Pritchard, W. T. 1866. *Polynesian Reminiscences; or, Life in the South Pacific Islands.* London: Chapman and Hall.

Pukui, M. K. 1972. *Nama i ke Kumu (Look to the Source),* vol. 1. Honolulu: Hui Hanai.

Quinn, N. 1987. Convergent Evidence for a Cultural Model of American Marriage. In *Cultural Models in Language and Thought,* ed. D. Holland and N. Quinn. London: Cambridge University Press.

———. 1992. The Motivational Force of Self-Understanding: Evidence from Wives' Inner Conflicts. In *Human Motives and Cultural Models,* ed. R. D'Andrade and C. Strauss. Cambridge: Cambridge University Press.

Ralsoton, C. 1989. Changes in the Lives of Ordinary Women in Early Postcontact Hawaii. In *Family and Gender in the Pacific: Domestic Contradiciton and the Colonial Impact,* ed. M. Jolly and M. Macintyre. Cambridge: Cambridge University Press.

Read, K. E. 1955. Morality and the Concept of the Person among the Gahuku-Gama. *Oceania* 25:233–82.

Redfield, R. 1960. *The Little Community.* Chicago: University of Chicago Press.

Richardson, S. [1748] 1985. *Clarissa, or, The History of a Young Lady.* Harmondsworth, Eng.: Penguin.

Ritchie, J. 1956. Basic Personality in Rakau. In *Publications in Psychology,* no. 8. Wellington, N.Z.: Victoria University Press.

Ritchie, J., and J. Ritchie. 1979. *Growing Up in Polynesia.* Sydney: George Allen and Unwin.

———. 1989. Socialization and Character Development. *In Developments in Polynesian Ethnology,* ed. A. Howard and R. Borofsky. Honolulu: University of Hawaii Press.

Robertson, C. E. 1989. Art Essay: The Māhū of Hawai'i. *Feminist Studies* 15(2): 313–26.

Rosaldo, M. Z. 1980. The Use and Abuse of Anthropology: Reflections of Femininism and Cross-Cultural Understanding. *Signs* 5(3): 389–417.

———. 1984. Towards an Anthropology of Self and Feeling. In *Culture Theory,* ed. R. A. Shweder and R. S. Levine. Cambridge: Cambridge University Press.

Ryan, M. 1975. *Womanhood in America.* New York: Franklin Watts.

Sahlins, M. 1981. *Historical Metaphors and Mythical Realities.* Ann Arbor: University of Michigan Press.

———. 1985. *Islands of History.* Chicago: University of Chicago Press.

———. 1993. Goodbye to Triste Tropes: Ethnography in the Context of Modern World History. *Journal of Modern History.* 65:1–25.

Sampson, E. E. 1988. The Debate on Individualism: Indigenous Psychologies of Self and Their Role in Personal Societal Functioning. *American Psychologist* 43(1): 15–22.

Sarason, I. G. 1976. *Abnormal Psychology: The Problem of Maladaptive Behavior.* New York: Appleton, Century, Crofts.

Scheper-Hughes, N. 1992a. Hungry Bodies, Medicine, and the State. In *New Directions in Psychological Anthropology,* ed. T. Schwartz, G. M. White, and C. Lutz. Cambridge: Cambridge University Press.

———. 1992b. *Death without Weeping.* Berkeley: University of California Press.

Scheper-Hughes, N., and M. Lock. 1992. The Mindful Body. *Medical Anthropology Quarterly,* n.s. 1(1): 6–41.

Schoeffel, P. 1978. Gender, Status and Power in Western Samoa. *Canberra Anthropology* 1:69–81.

———. 1979a. Daughters of Sina. Ph.D. diss., Australian National University.

———. 1979b. The Ladies Row of Thatch: Women and Rural Development in Western Samoa. *Pacific Perspective* 8(2): 1–11.

———. 1983. Women's Associations and Rural Development in Western Samoa and East New Britain. *Pacific Perspective* 11(2): 56–61.

———. 1987. Rank, Gender, and Politics in Ancient Samoa: The Genealogy of Salamasina O Le Tafa'ifa. *Journal of Pacific History* 22(4): 174–94.

Schultz, Dr. E. 1911. The Most Important Principles of Samoan Family Law. *Journal of the Polynesian Society* 20:43–53.

———. [1911] n.d. *Samoan Laws Concerning the Family, Real Estate and Succession.* Trans. Rev. E. Bellward and R. C. Hisaioa. Housed in the University of Hawai'i Pacific Collection.

———. 1965. *Proverbial Expressions of Samoans.* Wellington: Polynesian Society.

———. [1949–50] 1985. *Samoan Proverbial Expressions.* Trans. Brother Herman. Suva: Polynesian Press and the Institute for Pacific Studies. Rpt. from *Journal of the Polynesian Society.*

Searle, J. R. (1969). *Speech Acts.* Cambridge: Cambridge University Press.

Shankman, P. 1996. The History of Samoan Sexual Conduct and the Mead-Freman Controversy. *American Anthropologist* 98:555–67.

Shore, B. 1977. *A Samoan Theory of Action.* Ph.D diss., University of Chicago.

———. 1978. Ghosts and Government. *Man* 13:175–99.

———. 1981. Sexuality and Gender in Samoa. In *Sexual Meanings,* ed. S. B. Ortner and H. Whitehead. New York: Cambridge University Press.

———. 1982. *Sala'ilua: A Samoan Mystery.* New York: Columbia University Press.

———. 1983. A Response to the "Book Review Forum." *Pacific Studies* 7(1): 145–56.

———. 1984. Reply to Derek Freeman's Review of Sala'ilua: A Samoan Mystery. *Oceania* 54(1): 254–60.

———. 1985. Response to Freeman. *Oceania* 55(3): 218–23.

———. 1989. Mana and Tapu. *Developments in Polynesian Ethnology,* ed. A. Howard and R. Borofsky. Honolulu: University of Hawaii Press.

Shweder, R. A., and E. J. Bourne. 1984. Does the Concept of the Person Vary Cross-Culturally? In *Cultural Conceptions of Mental Health and Therapy,* ed. A. J. Marsella and G. M. White. Dordrecht, Neth.: D. Reidel.

Shweder, R. A., M. Mahapatra, and J. G. Miller. 1990. Culture and Moral Development. In *Cultural Psychology: Essays on Comparative Human Development,* ed. J. W. Stigler, R. A. Shweder, and G. Herdt. New York: Cambridge University Press.

Sinavaiana, C. 1992a. Traditional Comic Theater in Samoa: A Holographic View. Ph.D. diss. (American Studies), University of Hawai'i at Manoa.

———. 1992b. Where the Spirits Laugh Last: Comic Theater in Samoa. In *Clowning as Critical Practice*, ed. W. E. Mitchell. Pittsburgh: University of Pittsburgh Press.

Sixteenth Census of the United States (1940). 1942. Jesse H. Jones, secretary. Published by the U.S. Department of Commerce. Washington D.C.: U.S. Goverment Printing Office.

Sio, G. P. S. 1984. *Tapasā O Folauga I Aso Afā: Compass of Sailing in Storm*. Apia: Samoa Printing and Publishing.

Sloan, D. 1940. *The Shadow Catcher*. New York: Book League of America.

———. 1941. *Polynesian Paradise: An Elaborated Travel Journal Based on Ethnological Facts*. London: Robert Hale.

Spiro, M. E. 1982. *Oedipus in the Trobriands*. Chicago: University of Chicago Press.

———. 1987. *Cultural and Human Nature: Theoretical Papers of Melford E. Spiro*, ed. B. Kilborne and L. L. Langness. Chicago: University of Chicago Press.

———. 1990. On the Strange and the Familiar in Recent Anthropological Thought. In *Cultural Psychology: Essays on Comparative Human Development*, ed. J. Stigler, R. Shweder, and G. Herdt. New York: Cambridge University Press.

———. 1992. Tropes, Defenses, and Unconscious Mental Representations: Some Critical Reflections on the "Primary Process." In *Psychoanalytic Anthropology after Freud: Essays Marking the Fifty Anniversary of Freud's Death*, ed. D. Spain. New York: Psyche Press.

———. 1993. Is the Western Conception of Self "Peculiar" within the Context of World Cultures? *Ethos* 21(2): 107–53.

Stair, Rev. J. B. 1897. *Old Samoa: Flotsam and Jetsam from the Pacific Ocean*. London: Religious Tract Society.

Stanner, W. E. H. 1953. *The South Seas in Transition: A Study of Post-War Rehabilitation and Reconstruction in Three British Pacific Dependencies*. Sydney: Australian Publishing Co.

Stevenson, C. M. 1904. The Zuni Indians: Their Mythology, Esoteric Fraternities and Ceremonies. *Annual Report of the Bureau of American Ethnology to the Secretary of the Smithsonian Institution* 23:3–608.

Stevenson, R. L. 1892. *A Footnote to History: Eight Years of Trouble in Samoa*. London: Cassell.

Stone, L.. 1997. *Kinship and Gender*. Boulder: Westview Press.

Strathern, M. 1990. *The Gender of the Gift*. Berkelely: University of California Press.

———. 1991. *Partial Connections*. Savage, Md.: Rowman and Littlefield.

Strauss, C. 1990. Who Gets Ahead? Cognitive Responses to Heteroglossia in American Political Culture. *American Ethnologist* 17(2): 312–28.

Stuebel, C. 1976. *Myths and Legends of Samoa: Tala O le Vavau*. Wellington and Apia: A. H. and A. W. Reed and Wesley Productions.

Su'apa'ia, K. 1962. *Samoa: The Polynesian Paradise*. New York: Exposition Press.

Sutter, F. K. 1980. Communal versus Individual Socialization at Home and in School in Rural and Urban Samoa. Ph.D diss., University of Hawai'i.

Tannen, D. 1990. *You Just Don't Understand*. New York: Ballantine.

Tavris, C. 1992. *The Mismeasure of Women*. New York: Simon and Schuster.

Tedlock, B. 1992. *Dreaming: Anthropological and Psychological Interpretations*. Santa Fe,

N.M.: School of American Research, Advanced Seminar Series (distributed by University of Washington Press).
Thomas, N. 1990. *Marquesan Societies.* New York: Oxford University Press.
———. 1992. The Inversion of Tradition. *American Ethnologist* 19:213–32.
———. 1995. *Oceanic Art.* London: Thames and Hudson.
———. 1996a. Cold Fusion. *American Anthropologist* 96(1): 9–25.
———. 1996b. *Out of Time: History and Evolution in Anthropological Discourse.* 2d ed. Ann Arbor: University of Michigan Press.
Thompson, M., R. Ellis, and A. Wildavsky. 1990. *Cultural Theory.* Boulder: Westview Press.
Tiffany, S. W. 1978. The Politics of Denominational Organization in Samoa. In *Mission, Church, and Sect in Oceania,* ed. J. Boutillier, D. R. Hughes, and S. W. Tiffany. Lanham, Md.: University Press of America.
Trawick, Margaret. 1990a. Untouchability and the Fear of Death in a Tamil Song. In *Language and the Politics of Emotion,* ed. C. Lutz and L. Abu-Lughod. Cambridge: Cambridge University Press.
———. 1990b. *Notes on Love in a Tamil Family.* Berkeley: University of California Press.
Tuiteleleapaga, N. A. 1980. *Samoa Yesterday, Today and Tomorrow.* New York: Todd and Honeywell.
Turiel, E. 1983. *The Development of School Knowledge: Morality and Convention.* New York: Cambridge University Press.
Turner, G. 1842. February 10 letter to London Missionary Society Headquarters from 'Upolu. Council of World Missions Archives (15/5/A). School of Oriental and African Studies, University of London.
———. [1861] 1986. *Selections from Nineteen Years in Polynesia: Missionary Life, Travel and Researches.* Apia: Western Samoa Historical and Cultural Trust.
———. [1861] 1984a. *Nineteen Years In Polynesia.* Papkura, N.Z.: Macmillan.
———. [1884] 1984b. *Samoa: A Hundred Years Ago and Long Before.* London: Macmillan.
Turner, V. 1977. *The Ritual Process: Structure and Anti-Structure.* Chicago: Aldine.
Vaillant, G. 1986. *Empirical Studies of Ego Mechanism of Defense.* Washington, D.C.: American Psychiatric Press.
Valeri, V. 1985. *Kingship and Sacrifice: Ritual and Society in Ancient Hawaii.* Chicago: University of Chicago Press.
Vygotsky, L. S . 1981. The Genesis of the Higher Mental Functions. In *The Concept of Activity in Soviet Psychology,* ed. James V. Wertsch. Armonk, N.Y.: M. E. Sharpe.
Wagner, R. 1991. The Fractal Person. In *Big Men and Great Men: Personifications of Power in Melanesia,* ed. M. Godelier and M. Strathern. Cambridge: Cambridge University Press.
Watts, R. 1992. The Polynesian Mahu. In *Oceanic Homosexualities,* ed. S. O. Murry. New York: Garland.
Welter, B. 1966. The Cult of True Womanhood: 1820–1860. *American Quarterly* 18:151–74.
Wendt, A. 1977. *Pouliuli.* Auckland: Longman Paul.
———. 1979. *Leaves of the Banyan Tree.* Auckland: Longman Paul.
Wheeler, A., and W. Thompson. 1825. *An Appeal of One-Half the Human Race, Women, Against the Pretension's of the Other Half, Men, to Retain Them in Political and*

Thence in Civil and Domestic Slavery. London: Longman, Hurst, Rees, Orme, Brown, and Green, R. Taylor.

White, G. M. 1991. *Identity through History: Living Stories in a Solomon Islands Society.* Cambridge: Cambridge University Press.

White, G. M., and J. Kirkpatrick, eds. 1985. *Person, Self and Experience.* Berkeley: University of California Press.

White, H. 1978. *Tropics of Discourse: Essays in Cultural Criticism.* Baltimore: Johns Hopkins University Press.

Whiting, J. W. M. 1961. Socialization Process and Personality. In *Psychological Anthropology: Approaches to Culture and Personality,* ed. F. L. K. Hsu. Homewood, Ill.: Dorsey.

Whiting, J. W. M. and I. L. Child. 1953. *Child Training and Personality: A Cross-Cultural Study.* New Haven: Yale University Press.

Wikan, U. 1977. Man Becomes Women: Transsexualism in Oman as a Key to Gender Roles. *Man* n.s. 12:304–19.

———. 1987. Public Grace and Private Fears: Gaiety, Offense, and Sorcery in Northern Bali. *Ethos* 15(4):337–65.

———. 1990. *Managing Turbulent Hearts: A Balinese Formula for Living.* Chicago: University of Chicago Press.

Wilkes, C. 1845. *Narrative of the United States Exploring Expedition during the Years 1838, 1839, 1840, 1841, 1842.* Philadelphia: Lea and Blanchard.

Williams, J. [1830–32] 1984. *The Samoan Journals of John Williams,* ed. R. M. Moyle. Canberra: Australian National University Press.

Williams, W. L. 1986. *The Spirit and the Flesh: Sexual Diversity in American Indian Culture.* Boston: Beacon.

Willis, L. 1889. *The Story of Laulii: A Daughter of Samoa,* ed. W. H. Barnes. San Francisco: Jos. Winterburn.

Wilson, J. 1799. *A Missionary Voyage to the South Pacific Ocean in 1796, 1797, 1798.* London: T. Chapman.

Wollstonecraft, M. [1787] 1993. *Vindication of the Rights of Women.* London: Dutton.

Index

References to illustrations are in italics.

Agency, 22, 24–25, 57, 76, 79, 109, 112, 115, 120, 145–46, 168–69, 226, 240
   antiagency, 186, 192
'Āiga (extended family), xv, 70–71
   children, 41, *44–45*
   girls, 133–37, 148
   fighting, 252n. 2
   rivalry, 69
   titles, 112–13, 120
Ainsworth, Mary D. Salter, 40–41, 46
America
   ancestry, 173
   antebellum, 245n.36
   children, 41, 48
   contexts, 14–15, 81–83, 249n. 2, 249–50n. 3
   democracy, 114
   egocentric, 9–11, 37, 40
   fantasy, 11
   homosexuality and transvestism, 209, 212, 214
   influence, 242
   jurisprudence, 27
   kinship, 10
   metaphor, 14
   morality, 12, 27, 28, 40, 81–83, 244n. 15, 246n. 41
   movies (film), 15, 53, 79, 82
   servicemen, 30–31, 141, 151–53, 157–59, 166, 169, 179
   army, 78, 177, 181
   marine, 151, 158–59, 166, 173, 176, 181, 193
   social context(s), 14, 23
   socialization, 20, 23–24, 48, 59, 245n. 28
   United States (U.S.), 21, 151, 214
   See also Romance
Attention, 17, 195, 198
   enculturation, role in, 20, 47–50, 58, 63–64
   girls' need for, 93, 121, 137, 147, 176–77, 261n. 4
Aualuma (organization of village sisters and daughters), xv, 131–32, 147, 153, 156, 160, 191, 202, 204
'*Aumāga* (organization of untitled men), 93, 131, 156, 160, 250n. 14
Āvaga (elope), 97, 133, 136, 138, 148, 155–56, 158, 178, 250n. 19, 255n. 22

Balinese, 5–7, 9, 10
   socialization, 59–60, 74
   trance, 193
Bateson, Gregory, 82
Battaglia, Debbora, 243, 246
Beauty contests, 77, 127, 129, 149, 180, 187, 201, 207–8, 211–13, 219
Bettelheim, Bruno, 181, 208, 224
Bodies, 10–11, 20, 43–46, 48, 51, 101, 119, 121, 123–24, 126, 131–32, 136–37, 154, 171, 188, 193, 196, 211, 227, 247n. 20

283

Bodies (*continued*)
  language of, 67, 86, 200–202, 208, 214–16, 260n. 12
  semiotics of, 253n. 8
  See also Nudity
Brother, 103, 137, 138, 159, 170, 233
  See also Sister

Caucasian (*palagi*), 63, 67, 157
Ceremonies
  events, 13, 15–16, 42, 56, 75, 89–90, 94, 100, 107, 122, 127, 132, 164, 191, 195, 232–33, 247n. 14, 250n. 5, 260n. 12
  greeting, 3, 85, 148
  ifoga, 12, 146
  obligations, 94
  prestations, 15, 83–85, 90, 94, 97, 100, 194, 260n. 12
  See also Discourse; Tropes
Chatterjee, Partha, 245
Cheeky (*tautalaitiiti*), 3, 21, 72, 74–75, 91, 99–100, 103, 157, 179, 222, 249n. 4
  asserting dominance, 103–4
Chiefs
  high chief (*aliʻi*), 49, 52, 71, 107–8, 110–11, 114–15, 133, 181–82, 194–96, 200, 225–26, 228, 252n. 14
  orator/talking chief (*tulāfale*), 4, 15–16, 97, 101, 110–15, 120, 142, 148, 195, 200, 225–26, 228, 236, 252n. 18
Children, 44–45
  adoption, 42, 71, 185, 220, 247n. 15, 16
  belonging, 41–42
  illegitimate (*ʻo le pepe o le po, tama pōuliuli*), 71, 152, 155
  tamaʻāiga, 29, 137, 148
Chodorow, Nancy, 245
Christianity
  influence on
    culture change, 31–33, 121–22, 127, 129, 139–40, 141–63, 164, 168, 169, 191–92, 198, 201, 212
    discourse, 30–32, 168, 182, 206
    girls, 168, 170–72, 180, 202, 205, 209, 219, 227
    self, 255

spirit possession, 168, 170–71, 173, 179, 202
Samoan Christianity, 31–32, 87, 140, 164, 168, 169, 173, 177, 178, 180, 184, 187–90, 203, 204, 206, 207, 211, 216, 219, 224, 225, 227–34, 236, 238–39
See also Romance
Clown (*faʻaaluma*), 191, 194, 196
  clowning, 54, 208
Cognitive dissonance, 70
Colonialism, xii, 171, 192, 204, 209
Comaroff, John, 8
Comedy, 32, 159, 192, 207, 209
  See also Theater
Conscience, 52, 67–68, 145, 150, 192, 202, 219
  Ego ideal, 67–68
Contact, 40–47, 58–61
Contexts, 14–15, 23, 82–83, 89–91, 155–56, 230–34
Counterreactions, 21–23, 74–80, 91–92, 94, 97, 100–101, 105, 111, 136, 137, 209, 216, 249n. 4
  See also Inhibition; Negative sanctions; Shame
Cultural projects, 91–94, 97, 101, 103, 105, 119, 123, 133, 139, 155
Curses, 137, 226, 228, 261
  cursing, 70
  mālaia, 236
  sister's (and mother's), 137, 231, 236–38

Dance, 174
  ʻaiʻaiuli, 198–201, 260n. 14
  ʻaleʻaleaitu, 160, 163, 196–97
  choreography, 88–89
  colonial, 197–202
  democratizing, 201
  gendered, 200
  individualism, 201–2
  night dances (*see* Joking Nights)
  sāʻē, 194, 196, 197, 198
  siva, 197–202, 212, 214, 260n. 14
  taualuga, 194–96, 198–201, 206, 211, 260n. 16
  See also Joking
Defenses, 111, 250
Derrida, Jacques, 56, 209–10, 248n. 21

Dignity (*mamalu*), 54, 88–89, 103
   joking about, 96, 87–88, 195, 196, 211
   See also Girls
Discourse, 17–18, 25–26
   contextual, 14–15, 23, 153–54, 156–62, 191–217, 260n. 14
   gendering of, 27–29, 31–32, 118, 131–34
   moral, 13–14, 21–22, 146–47, 150–52, 164–90, 230, 260n. 14
   positioning, 120–23
   strategic, 15–17, 23–24, 102–16, 141–43, 235–36
Distancing, 19–21, 41, 47–50, 59–66, 68, 73, 91
Dominance, 74, 137, 196
   dominance/submission motif, 66–67, 85–90
   need for, 100–101, 216
   seeking, 15, 93–95, 97–99, 107, 110–11, 136, 177
   See also Cheeky
Doubles (*soa*), 24, 104–9, 110, 114, 118, 213
Dreyfus, Hubert L., 16, 102, 112, 118, 251n. 1, 252n. 28

Egocentrism, 5, 7, 9–11, 14, 20–22, 28, 37–38, 46, 50, 52, 53, 114, 243n. 3, 244n. 8, 247n. 10
   ego, 19, 79
   individualism, 15
   See also Identity; Lexicons; *Loto;* Soul
Elision, 17, 28, 38–40
Elopement (*āvaga*), 106, 108, 138, 259n. 10
   as affected by
      Christianity, 149
      World War II, 155
   common marriage tantamount to, 97
   Joking Nights as venue of, 98–99, 103, 161, 196
   kinds of, 136
   relation of intercourse to, 7
   rights associated with, 133
   spirits used to disguise, 161–62, 178
   tāupōu, 151
Emotion, 5, 60, 67
   affect, 48–49, 61–63
   solicitude, 184–85
   See also Distancing; Morality

England, 29, 123, 144, 148, 153
   English society, 29–30, 31, 122, 142, 145, 150, 204, 245n. 39
   See also Missionaries
Entertainment
   colonial, 197–205
   postcolonial, 205–7, 211–13
   pre-Christian, 193–97
   See also Comedy; Dance; Theater
Erasure, 162–63
Erikson, Erik, 25, 40, 91
Essentialism, 5, 8–10, 25, 37–38, 89, 118, 245n. 33
Evangelicalism. *See* England; Missionaries
Ewing, Katherine, 9

Faʻa Sāmoa (Samoan way of life), 3, 30, 210, 235, 242n. 1
Festinger, Leon, 70
Flaunting (*faʻalialia*), 129–31, 136–37, 155–57, 160–63, 166, 168, 170, 172, 177, 180–83, 187–89, 203, 252n. 3
   flowers, 163, 180–81
   lipstick, 37, 156, 204
   showing off, 6, 63–64, 74, 76–79, 92, 111, 132, 137, 157, 219
   See also Hair, red or fair
Foucault, Michel, 7, 25, 36, 111, 123, 144, 155, 169, 255n. 7
Freeman, Derek
   and Mead/Freeman controversy, xiii, 242n. 7
   observations on
      children, 61, 73, 250n. 11
      nature, 37, 255n. 9
      sexuality, 103, 216, 257n. 5
      spirit possession, 166
      titles, 112, 149
Freud, Sigmund, 11, 20, 25, 38, 40, 79, 165, 252n. 2, 257n. 1
Freudian diction, 23
   See also Psychoanalysis

Geertz, Clifford, 5, 6, 10
Genealogy, 110, 113–14, 120, 131, 148, 198, 201

German
  ancestry, 171, 173
  colonists, 173
  language, 156
Gilligan, Carol, 29
Girls, Samoan, *126*, *136*, 156–57, 158, 177, 187
  dignity of, 99, 104, 140, 164, 208, 219
  pre-Christian, 123–25, 134–37
  role as sisters (*teine*), 178, 203
  See also Spirits; Transvestites
Goldman, Irving, 72, 148
Guilt
  relation to moral discourse, 79–80
  role in cultures, 68
  role in possession, 187–88
  See Psychoanalysis, superego

Hair, 124–31
  comb, 129
  cut, 124
  disheveled, 156
  long, 125, 127, *128*, 129, *130*
  red or fair, 127, 129, *174*
  shaved, 127–29
  tuft/tail, 125–27
  tuiga, *126*, 127
  tutagita, 129
  worn down, 125, 129, *130*
  worn up, *128*, 129, *130*
Half-caste (*'afakasi*), 173, 179
  blue eyes of, 173
  fair hair of, 173
Hawai'i, 149, 179, 188, 253n. 8, 254n. 20
Healers (traditional), 167, 183, 184
  ethnoanalyst, 169, 186, 193
  faivai, 259n. 9
  fofō, 227–30
Hitting. *See* Negative sanctions
Husbands, 42
  luring of, 104, 163
  relationship with wives, 6, 55, 62, 84, 103, 142, 185–86, 192, 203, 204–5, 226, 251n. 4, 260nn. 6, 20, 262n. 13
Hsu, Francis, 10

Identity, 17
  adult, 8, 110–11, 240
  choreographic, 200
  cognitive dissonance, role in, 70
  colonialism, influence on, 142, 144
  corporate, 43–46, 247n. 16
  cultural identity, 4–5, 7–11, 13–16, 158–59, 165–66, 169–71, 172–73, 187–88, 190
    authenticity, 185–86
    early, 40, 41–43, 50–51
    gender, 32, 105, 240, 245n. 30
    identification, process of, 21–22, 76–77, 78–79, 176–77, 179, 220, 225, 226–27, 228–29, 232–34, 235, 238–39, 249n. 7
  personal, 189, 240, 261n. 26
  pride, role in, 58
  romanticism, influence on, 29
  Samoan, 37–38, 138, 208, 242n. 10
    male, 103
    female, 123–31, 134–40, 219
  sexual, 31–32, 178
  spirits, relation to, 175, 179, 187, 226, 238–39
  transvestite, 209–12
  See also Egocentrism; Sociocentric
Inhibition, 20, 59–60, 61, 62, 63, 64, 66, 67–68, 74, 79, 91, 98, 100, 176, 230
  performative inhibition, 78, 92–93, 250n. 9
  See also Counterreactions; Negative sanctions
Intertexts, 76, 165, 168, 171–88, 190
  See also Narratives; Tropes
Irony
  presence in
    colonial dance, 197–202
    Joking Nights, 194–97
    Spirit House, 202–5
  role in
    contextual discourse, 90
    strategic discourse, 104
  transvestites, relation to, 207–8, 210–13, 214–17
  See also Joking

Joking
  bawdy, 89–90, 97, 147, 156, 229
  choreographic (dance), 31, 96

"Exchanging Farts," 214–16
faipona (lampooning), 64, 67, 86–88, 95, 137, 195–96
poka, 214
scatological, 96, 196
teasing, 15, 60, 63–64, 74, 87, 104, 111, 136–37, 164, 177
ula, 86–89, 96–97, 100, 132, 164, 196, 198, 205–8, 211, 213, 250n. 6
See also Irony; Mimesis, mimicry; Transvestites
Joking Nights (*pōula*), 191–97
See also Dance; Entertainment
Jung, Carl G., 18, 38, 160–61, 246n. 8

Kohlberg, Lawrence, 28, 246n. 41
Kristeva, Julia, 76

Lacan, Jacques, 25, 246n. 8, 249n. 3
Lamphere, Louise, 246n. 42
Lexicons, 16–18
 moral, 11–13, 19–22, 24–26, 52–68, 69–72, 83, 89, 118, 145–46, 222–23, 224–25
 ontological, 9–11, 19, 37–51, 143–45
Liminality, 183–84
Loto (inner self), 10–11, 39–40, 83, 219, 247n. 12
 presence in
  contextual discourse, 84, 86
  moral discourse, 69–72, 77–79
  moral lexicons, 14, 53–58, 63, 64, 66
  strategic discourse, 107
 relation to
  elopement, 136
  missionaries, 145
  spirit possession, 137, 161, 177
 saʻoloto (freedom), 139, 163
 See also Egocentrism; Morality; Soul
Lutz, Catherine, 246n. 41

Malae (village center), 81
 relation to
  culture change, 160–61
  spirits, 183–84
Mana, 125, 127–29, 137, 170, 227–30, 233, 239, 254n. 7, 261n. 7
Marriage (weddings), 96–99

āvaga (elopement), 97, 133, 136, 138, 148, 155–56, 158, 178, 250n. 19, 255n. 22
 bridesmaids, 71–73, 77–78, 80, 92, 111, 137
 changing, 148, 155–56
 faʻaipoipoga, 97, 149, 155
 faʻapōuliuli, 155
 See also Girls; Husbands; Sex; Wives
Mauss, Marcel, 38, 210
Mead, George H., 18, 246n. 8, 257n. 4
Mead, Margaret
 and Mead/Freeman controversy, xiii, 242n. 7
 observations on
  Bali, 59–60
  dancing, 201, 232
  emotion, 5, 62
  family relations, 185
  musu, 65
  punishment, 129
  rank, 112
  sex roles, 131, 139, 156, 201
  siblings, 93
  spirit possession, 166, 168
  wooing, 104, 106, 108, 213
Mimesis, 168, 202
 mimicry, 87–88, 159, 195, 204, 213
 See also Joking; Joking Nights; Sports
Missionaries, xi–xii, 141, 241n. 1, 242nn. 4, 5
 aitu, 214, 232, 242n. 6
 evangelicalism, 29, 31, 143–45, 150, 153, 246n. 43
 influence on
  lexicons and discourse of self, 141–51, 153–55, 158, 169
  transvestism, 206, 207, 214, 237
  wives, 204–5
 influence on and observations of
  entertainment, 191–92, 197–98, 200, 202, 259n. 1
  girls, 121–22, 123–25, 129, 136, 138–39, 147, 166–67, 178, 180, 187, 192, 212, 234
  sexuality, 29–31, 122, 151, 153–54, 164, 197–98, 262n. 24
 London Missionary Society, 29

Missionaries (*continued*)
  missionization, 229, 232, 260n. 19
  observations of
    children/childrearing, 42, 251n. 13
    emotion, 54, 90, 184
    joking, 86–87, 99, 196
    politics, 111, 142
    purchasing wives, 151, 256n. 19
    Samoan preferences, 249n. 6
  schooling, 138–39, 142–43, 147, 205, 232, 234, 256n. 5
  schools, 142–43, 147, 255n. 4
  sex roles, 238
  translations, 10, 88, 143–45, 146, 150, 155, 170, 181, 191, 255n. 6
  See also Girls; School; Wives
Morality, 52–53, 70
  vices
    egotistical pride (*lotofa'amaualuga*), 56–57
    emotionalism (*lotovaivai*), 54
    envy (*lotoleaga*), 14, 55–56, 72, 77, 78, 79, 137, 176–77, 248n. 2
  virtues
    compassion (*alofa*), 55
    noble conduct (*fa'atamāli'i*)
    personal abasement (*lotofa'amaualalo*), 57
    personal effacingness (*lotomamā*), 56, 79
    personal restraint (*lototele*), 55
    respect (*fa'aaloalo*), 56
  See also Cheeky; Dignity; *Musu*; Respect
Musu (refuse), 65–66, 100, 249n. 9

Narratives, 219
  fāgogo, 77
  historical, 33
  legends, 62
  mythology
    American, 10, 53
    Biblical, 259n. 3
    Polynesian, 108, 252n. 15
    Samoan, 85–86, 106, 181, 259n. 3, 261n. 6
    Western, 160
  narrative tropes, 171–90, 257n. 1

narrators, 168
  relation to
    contextual discourse, 73, 90–91, 193
    moral discourse, 21–23, 26, 72–73, 76–77, 80, 83, 90, 110, 115, 165–67, 193, 219–20, 224–25, 226–27, 228–30, 232–34
    moral lexicons, 222–23, 224–25
    spirit possession, 168–69, 193, 257n. 2
  Seta's life history narrative, 221–22, 223–24, 225–26, 227, 230–32
  stories, 21–22, 62, 76–77, 83
    "Beauty Contest," 212–13
    "Dead Mother," 185–86
    "Exchanging Farts," 214–16
    "Haircut," 187–88
    "Kicking a Toad," 180, 181, 182, 183
    "Miss Blue Eyes," 171–72, 173, 175, 179
    "Satan the Anus," 205–7, 216
    "Wearing Perfume," 182–83, 184
    "What's In a Name?" 175–77, 179–80, 182
  See also Intertexts; Tropes
Negative sanctions, 66–67
  punishing, 31, 60–61, 65–67, 73–76
  scaring, 60–65, 67, 74, 76
  teasing, 20, 60, 63–64, 67, 74, 98, 136–37
  See also Counterreactions; Inhibition; Shyness
Nudity, 69, 75, 88, 98, 99, 121, 123, 137, 139, 154, 171–72

Obeyesekere, Gananath, 25, 253n. 8
Ochs, Elinor, 26, 50, 79, 245n. 28, 246n. 5, 249n. 12
O'Meara, Tim, 47, 244n. 20
Oratory, 85–86, 90
  effects of Christianity on, 145–46
  relation to
    contextual discourses and cultural projects, 94–95, 97, 101
    strategic discourse, 111–15, 252n. 19

Persona (*aga*), 5, 10, 37–38, 40, 138, 143–44, 187, 188, 209, 218, 246n. 8
  See also Identity; Lexicons; Sociocentric

Piaget, Jean, 245n. 35
Piers, Gerhart, 67
Polynesia, xiv
   child development, 42, 242n. 9, 247n. 16, 247n. 23, 248n. 3
   colonialization, 141
   dual figures, 252n. 2
   genealogy, 10, 148
   mana, 125, 228, 253n. 7
   mythology, 108
   politics, 114, 148, 253n. 27
   sex roles, 252n. 27
   sexuality, 254n. 20, 257n. 26, 261n. 24
   spirits, 125, 228
   transvestism, 207
   value systems, 189–90
Politics, 120
   aualuma, role in, 260n. 19
   local, 242n. 10
   marriage, relation to
      English, 150
      Samoan, 97, 110, 138, 148, 255, 257n. 21
   Samoan, 110–14, 118
      colonialism, use in, 142
      Western interference in, 141
   self, relation to, 26–29
      Samoan self, relation to, 29–33, 218
Postcolonial
   entertainments, 205–8, 211–13, 260n. 21
   transvestites, 33, 207, 217
   virginity cult, 216
Pre-Christian Samoa
   dress, 123–24
   gender roles, 132, 137, 156, 161–62, 177
   hairdos, 124, 125–31, 157, 180
   sex roles, 178
   sexuality, 136–37, 140, 180
   See also Girls
Prestations
   'oloa, 84, 194
   tōga, 42, 75, 84, 194, 247n. 14
Psychoanalysis
   dreams, 79, 165, 168, 169, 175, 244n. 10, 252n. 2
   Freudians, 67
   Oedipus complex, 185, 224, 262n. 12
   overdetermination, 175
   reaction formation, 250n. 10
   sublimation, 23, 91, 101
   superego, 67–68
Punishing. *See* Counterreactions; Negative sanctions

Respect (*fa'aaloalo*), 3, 15, 52, 56, 222
Romance, 24, 213
   American, 31–32, 153
   Christianity, relation to, 180
   romantic ideal, 180
   romantic movement, 29
   romanticism, 29

Sanele, ix–x
   childhood, 230
   experiences with, 205–6, 212, 228
   family role, 235
   fantasies, 173
   observations on
      cheekiness, 75
      children, 149
      emotion, 55
      family obligations, 78
      lotofuatiaifo, 145
      love, 153
      marriage, 138
      narration, 77
      rivalry, 69, 205–6
      Seta, 222, 224, 226, 232, 261n. 4, 262n. 12
      sex roles, 238
      sexuality, 139, 152, 153, 159
      sibling relations, 47
      theater, 203, 259n. 3
   spirit possession, accounts of, 180, 181–82, 183
   translations, 204–5, 243n. 1, 253–54n. 17, 255n. 8, 256–57n. 24
Savai'i, xiv, 49, 64, 172–73
Scaring. *See* Counterreactions; Negative sanctions
Scheper-Hughes, Nancy, 36, 46
School, 211, 230–34, 261n. 16, 262n. 10
   Sunday school, 179
   See also Missionaries
Searle, John. R., 83

Service (*tautua*), 55–56, 78, 84–85, 105, 252n. 24
Sex
  control of, 129, 136, 187, 257n. 5, 259n. 5
  joking, 82, 96–97, 196–97, 198, 202, 204–5, 206
  pre-Christian, 29, 178, 253n. 9, 254n. 18, 257n. 26
  rape, 103, 106–7
  relation to
    Christian moral discourse, 30, 150–51
    contextual discourse, 96–98
    culture change, 31–32, 62, 137–40, 152–55, 157–63, 166–69, 177, 180
    language, 15, 24, 90, 96, 203, 219, 223, 234, 257n. 22
    missionaries, 121, 125, 147, 191–92, 207, 261n. 24
  status, relation to, 103
  strategic discourse, relation to, 109
  subjectivity, 145
  transvestites, 210–13, 215–16
  virtue, 73, 184–85
  vocabulary
    eva, evaga, 139
    pipi, 64
    taʻa, taʻapō, 139, 178
  wooing, 103–6
  See also *Āvaga*; Beauty contests; Flaunting; Hair; Joking; Joking Nights; Romance; Spirits; Wandering; World War II
Shore, Bradd, 244n. 3
  observations on
    blood, 251n. 21
    comedy, 159, 204
    pōula, 163, 259n. 7
    punishment, 249n. 12
    Samoan contexts, 26, 244n. 21
    Samoan semiotics, 257n. 27
    sex roles, 139, 262n. 15
    shame, 249n. 1, 251n. 20
    social obligation, 244n. 17
    spirit possession, 258n. 22
  translation of
    alofa, 153
    āmio, 145, 245n. 9
    loto, 39
Shyness, 59–60
  mā, 64, 67, 98
  See also Counterreactions; Inhibition
Siblings, 43–46, 47, 63
  See also Sister (brother/sister relationship)
Singer, Milton B., 67
Sister
  brother/sister relationship, 42, 90, 120, 140, 167, 170, 178, 206–8, 235–36
  status of, 103–4, 157, 204
  village princess, relation to, 164
  violence of, 5, 55–56
  See also *Aualuma*; Curses; Girls; Transvestites
Sociocentric, 5–14, 17, 20, 21, 28, 38, 52, 68, 107, 108, 114, 121, 143, 188, 189, 218, 243–45
  See also Identity; Persona
Songs
  Afono song, 62, 248n. 6
  individualistic, 261n. 26
  love, 153, 212–13
  marriage, 97
  relation to
    Joking Nights, 89, 121, 154, 160, 196
    prestations, 260n. 12
  siva, 197–98
  "Girl's Belly," 132, 139, 183, 253–54n. 17
  "Girls of Samoa," 156–58, 162, 177, 181, 187, 256n. 24
  "Pass the Fire," 205–6
  "Samoan Custom," 4, 13, 242–43n. 1
  "*Savalivali*," 158–59
  "Wriggle, Wriggle, Wriggle," 39
Soul, 11, 143–45, 150, 153, 170, 244n. 10
  See also Missionaries
Speeches, 15, 94, 106, 112, 146, 164, 215, 232, 252n. 23
  ceremonial, 15, 94, 106, 112, 164, 215
  fono, 112, 252n. 23
Spirit House (*Faleaitu*), 192, 202–5, 207, 208, 211, 213, 217, 260n. 20
  See also Theater; Transvestite
Spirit possession (*Maʻi aitu*)
  Hitting Sickness, 167–68

reconfiguration of, 167–68
remedies, 186–89
Samoan Sickness, 170, 173
Spirits
  agāga, 10, 144, 170
  aitu, 127, 160–61, 167, 170, 176, 196, 214, 238, 258n. 14
    devils, 69–70, 170, 206
    ghosts, 144, 176
    LeTelesā, 170–72, 175–76, 196, 214, 238, 258n. 21
    Moso, 181
    Nifoloa, 181–83
    Sauma'iafe, 178, 187, 258n. 14
    spirit girls, 158 202
    TuiAtua, 180–81
  sexuality, relation to, 179, 181–82, 258n. 22
Spiro, Melford E. 38, 165, 244n. 12, 257n. 1
Sports, 95–97, 100, 196, 197, 250n. 17, 260n. 11
Status
  American, 10, 82
  brokering of, 17, 31, 99, 103, 104, 109, 120, 132–33, 141, 148, 192, 196–97, 218, 252n. 3, 257n. 26
  challenging, 21, 212
  relation to
    children, 48–49, 65, 94–95
    Christianity, 142, 147, 149–50, 155, 198–202, 204–5
    gender, 29, 118, 208–9, 236, 252n. 4, 252n. 6, 256n. 18
    girls, 132–33, 134, 147, 149–51, 155, 157–58, 161, 164, 177, 179, 220, 260n. 16
    missionaries, 122, 164, 260n. 19
    Samoan contextual discourses, 86–87, 90–91, 194, 196–97, 252n. 23
    Samoan moral discourse, 4, 52, 54, 56–57, 66–67, 72, 74–78
    Samoan strategic discourse, 110
  status hierarchy, 20, 22, 185, 245n. 37
  tropes for, 14, 107, 113
  See also Cheeky; Dignity; Dominance; Joking; Respect

Stevenson, Robert Louis, 3, 13, 47, 105, 111, 197, 243n. 2, 244n. 19
Strathern, Marilyn, 17, 38
Straus, Claudia, 8, 245n. 25

Tahiti, 47, 74, 124, 183, 207
Tausala, 71, 77, 149, 150, 154, 179, 180, 192, 211
  See also Girls; Virginity
Teasing. *See* Negative Sanctions
Theater, 31, 32, 159, 192–94, 197, 202–4, 207, 259n. 3
  comedy, 31, 32, 159, 192, 197
  Spirit House (*Faleaitu*), 192, 202–5, 207, 208, 211, 213, 217, 260n. 20
Thomas, Nicholas, 158, 169, 229, 242n. 4, 251n. 2, 252n. 27
Titles
  fa'alupega, 16, 107, 113, 252n. 26
  rank, 3
  relation to
    beauty contests, 150, 201, 212–13
    ceremonies, 85, 90, 110, 250n. 5, 254n. 19
    children, 134–37, 148
    Christianity, 142
    dominance-seeking, 74, 112–14, 177, 206
    gender, 209, 255n. 26
    marriage, 90, 132–33, 138
    respect, concept of, 72, 195
    spirits, 170, 178, 181–82
  See also Dominance; Girls
Tonga, xiv, 151, 246n. 4, 260n. 13
Transvestites (*fa'afafine*), 32, 96, 157, 203, 204, 207–17, 237, 239, 260n. 17, 261n. 24
  beauty contests, 211–13
  culture change, 32, 96, 157, 207–8
  joking, 209–10, 214–16
  names, 210–11
  relation to
    girls, 209, 213, 217
    sisters, 208, 209
    theater, presence in, 202–4
  See also Sex; Theater

Tropes, 46, 48, 257
   height, 14
   pigeon, 39, 47, 106–10, 113–14, 132, 134, 137, 139, 158, 208, 213, 251n. 9, 252n. 14, 259n. 8
   relation to
      ceremonies, 83–86
      contextual discourse, 26, 83–86, 98, 99, 101, 102, 196, 261n. 3
      narrative, 165–66
      spirit possession, 163, 169, 171–90, 193, 202
      strategic discourse, 108, 110
   saisaitia, 261n. 3
   See also Intertexts; Narratives
Turiel, E., 100, 244n. 22
Turner, Victor, 100
Tutuila, xvi, 12, 151, 181

'Upolu, xiv, 31, 146, 172, 173

Village Princesses (*tāupōu*), 12, 126, 127, *130*, 131, *135*, *174*, *199*
   relation to
      Christianity, 180
      culture change, 151, 179, 192, 200–201, 261n. 16
      Spirit House, 203–4
      spirits, 178
      transvestites 211, 213, 215–16
   role, 12, 133, 164, 191, 194–96, 254n. 19
Virginity, 138, 148
   culture change, 151, 162, 179, 200–202
   defloration, 97
   and high-status girls, 29
   lack of, 87
   pre-contact, 125, 150, 156
   relation to
      Christianity, 147, 149, 153–54, 155, 192
      spirits, 178
      transvestism, 203, 207, 209–11, 213–16
Vygotsky, Leont'ev, 25

Wagner, Roy, 17, 38
Wandering, 179, 211
   eva, 139, 172, 176–78, 181
   roaming, 139, 172, 177, 181
   ta'a, ta'apō, 139, 178
Wendt, Albert, 4, 5, 69, 71, 81
White, Geoffrey M., 7
White Sundays, 232–33
Wikan, Unni, 6, 244n. 11
Willis, Laulii, 42, 127, 129, 151, 255n. 25
Wives
   behavior of, 5–6, 42, 138
   relation to
      Christianity, 143, 147, 204, 256n. 19
      intercourse, 103, 133, 214
      Spirit House, 205
   social role, 55–56, 62, 178, 203, 253n. 15, 260n. 18
   status of, 104, 110, 185, 251n. 4, 262n. 13
   See also Elopement
World War II, xiv
   relation to
      discourse, 177
      morality, 30–31, 151–53, 156–58
      spirit possession, 162, 166, 167, 173, 179, 181, 187, 188, 189
      transvestites, 213